JOHN FORD

JOHN FORD

(Five Plays)

Edited, with an Introduction and Notes

by

HAVELOCK ELLIS

A MERMAID DRAMABOOK

 HILL AND WANG · NEW YORK

FIRST DRAMABOOK PRINTING JANUARY 1957

ISBN 0-8090-0704-5

Library of Congress Catalog Card Number: 57-5839

Copyright © 1957 by Hill and Wang, Inc.
Published by special arrangement with Ernest Benn, Ltd.

7 8 9 10 11 12

CONTENTS

I DO not know where to find in any play a catastrophe so grand, so solemn, and so surprising as this [of *The Broken Heart*]. This is indeed, according to Milton, to "describe high passions and high actions." The fortitude of the Spartan boy who let a beast gnaw out his bowels till he died without expressing a groan, is a faint bodily image of this dilaceration of the spirit and exenteration of the inmost mind, which Calantha with a holy violence against her nature keeps closely covered, till the last duties of a wife and a queen are fulfilled. Stories of martyrdom are but of chains and the stake; a little bodily suffering; these torments

> On the purest spirits prey
> As on entrail, joints, and limbs,
> With answerable pains, but more intense.

What a noble thing is the soul in its strength and in its weaknesses! Who would be less weak than Calantha? Who can be so strong? The expression of this transcendent scene almost bears me in imagination to Calvary and the Cross; and I seem to perceive some analogy between the scenical sufferings which I am here contemplating, and the real agonies of that final completion to which I dare no more than hint a reference.

Ford was of the first order of poets. He sought for sublimity, not by parcels in metaphors or visible images, but directly where she has her full residence in the heart of man; in the actions and sufferings of the greatest minds. There is a grandeur of the soul above mountains, seas, and the elements. Even in the poor perverted reason of Giovanni and Annabella we discover traces of that fiery particle, which in the irregular starting from out of the road of beaten action, discovers something of a right line even in obliquity, and shows hints of an improvable greatness in the lowest descents and degradations of our nature.

CHARLES LAMB

THE BANKSIDE AND ITS THEATRES

THE BANKSIDE in Southwark was from an early date, even before the days of Henry VIII., one of the favourite resorts of Londoners. It was a semi-rural spot, very easy of access, either by walking over Old London Bridge or by means of the river, at that time a delightful and much frequented highway. Swans floated beneath London Bridge; magnificent barges were frequently to be seen; and in the reign of James I. (according to Taylor, "the Water Poet") "the number of watermen, and those that live and are maintained by them, and by the only labour of the oar and scull, betwixt the bridge of Windsor and Gravesend, cannot be fewer than forty thousand; the cause of the greater half of which multitude hath been the players playing on the Bankside."

Various amusements—sports, shows, fencings—took place on the Bankside long before any theatres arose there. Chief among these amusements were bull-baitings and bear-baitings at Paris Garden, and when the theatres began to grow up here—as at a later day they grew up along the opposite Strand—the baitings and plays were to some extent combined, the stage being movable. The Rose, close to the Bear and Paris Garden, was the first theatre built on the Bankside. Its origin and exact date are not known; it may have existed even before 1584, when it was called the Little Rose. The Swan Theatre was at the western end of the Bankside. Both the Rose and the Swan Theatres were named after existing tenements mentioned in Edward the Sixth's charter, granting the manor of Southwark to the City of London. The Hope Theatre, which was both a bear-garden and a theatre, was erected prior to the year 1600, and it was here that Ben Jonson's *Bartholomew Fair* was first acted in 1614. The building was demolished in 1656 and houses were built upon its site. About a year previously seven of the bears belonging to the Bear Garden had been shot by order of Pride, then Sheriff of Surrey, by a company of soldiers. Paris Garden itself became a theatre in 1613. In Dekker's *Untrussing of the Humorous Poet* we find it thus alluded to:

vii

> *Tucca.* Thou hast been in Paris Garden, hast not?
> *Horace.* Yes, captain, I ha' played Zulziman there.

The most famous of all the Bankside theatres was the Globe, built on the site occupied by Barclay's Brewery in Park Street.

Many persons connected with the theatres lived on the Bankside—Beaumont and Fletcher, Henslowe, Alleyn, Kempe, Lowin. The Falcon Inn was the favourite resort of dramatists and players; and St. Saviour's, close by, is the burial-place of Gower, Fletcher, Massinger, Sir Edward Dyer, the poet, Shakespeare's younger brother, Edmund, and Henslowe, the manager.

JOHN FORD CHRONOLOGY

1586. John Ford was baptised at Ilsington, in Devonshire, on April 17th.

1602. He was admitted to the Middle Temple.

1606. He published *Fame's Memorial,* an elegiac poem on the death of the Earl of Devonshire, and dedicated it to the Countess. Also, a pamphlet called *Honor Triumphant,* "in honour of all faire ladies and in defence of these foure positions following—1, Knights in Ladies service have no free-will. 2, Beauty is the mainteiner of valour. 3, Faire Lady was never false. 4, Perfect lovers are onely wise."

1612. The Prince of Wales died.

1613. Ford's comedy, *An ill Beginning has a good End,* was acted at the Cockpit. This was one of the plays destroyed by Warburton's cook.

1615. Ford's *Sir Thomas Overbury's Life and untimely Death* (an event which had taken place two years previously), probably an elegy or a pamphlet, was entered in the Stationers' books.

1616. Shakespeare died.

1618. Sir Walter Raleigh executed.

1620. Ford published *The Line of Life,* a prose pamphlet.

1622. *The Witch of Edmonton,* a tragedy by Rowley, Dekker, Ford, &c., was probably acted about this time.

1624. *The Sun's Darling,* a masque by Ford and Dekker, was acted at the Cockpit.

1625. Fletcher died.

1628. *The Lover's Melancholy* was acted at the Blackfriars and Globe theatres.

1631. Dryden born.

1632. Prynne published his *Histrio-Mastix.*

1633. *'Tis Pity She's a Whore, The Broken Heart,* and *Love's Sacrifice* were all printed in this year.

1634. *Perkin Warbeck* printed.

1635. Ben Jonson died.

ix

1637. Hampden refused to pay ship-money.

1638. Ford's comedy, *The Fancies Chaste and Noble,* was
      printed; and his tragi-comedy, *The Lady's Trial,* acted
      at the Cockpit.[1]

1639. Massinger died. It is probable that at about this period
      Ford left London to live at his native place, Ilsington.

1640. Election of the Long Parliament.

1641. Actors lament their "sad and solitary conditions." "Pro-
      jectors are downe, the High Commission Court is downe,
      the Starre-Chambre is down, and (some think) Bishops
      will down, and why should we then that are farre in-
      ferior to any of these justly feare, least we should be
      downe too." (*The Stage-Players-Complaint.*)

1642. The Civil War began, the Register of the Master of the
      Revels was closed, and on the 2nd of September was
      published the Ordinance of the Lords and Commons
      commanding "that while these sad causes and set-times
      of humiliation do continue, public stage plays shall
      cease and be forborne."

---

[1] Other plays of Ford's, of which now only the names are known, were two
comedies, *The London Merchant* and *The Royal Combat,* a tragedy called *Beauty
in a Trance, The Bristowe Merchant* and *The Fairy Knight,* both written in conjunction with Dekker, and *A late Murther of the Sonne upon the Mother* in conjunction with Webster. The three first-named plays were immolated by Warburton's
cook.

INTRODUCTION

Deep in a dump John Forde was alone got,
With folded arms and melancholy hat.

THAT vivid touch of portraiture is the one record that has
come down to us concerning Ford. His shy and reserved
temperament corresponds to his artistic position: he stands
alone. Of himself he has nothing to tell us beyond one early
and perhaps not over-serious allusion, in the youthful *Fame's
Memorial,* to an unkind mistress—

The goddess whom in heart I serve
Though never mine, bright Lycia the cruel,
The cruel-subtle.

Little, also, is recorded of him; of that little nothing that is
not to his honour; while the tone of his dedications is
manly, independent, and, towards his personal friends, affec-
tionate. That he was not afraid to take a losing side is shown
by his *Fame's Memorial,* an elegy which, called forth as it
evidently was by the strange story of the lady, Penelope,
Countess of Devonshire, to whom it was dedicated, is the
earliest witness to Ford's interest in the problems of romantic passion.

Born in the north-west of Devonshire, and issuing from
an old-established nest of Fords, while on the mother's side
he was the grandson of the Lord Chief Justice Popham,
John Ford came up to London at an early age to be trained
to the law, becoming eventually, it is probable, a trusted
agent for several noblemen, and he refers to his business with
that ostentation not uncommon in people who know that
their true calling is elsewhere. During the years of his London life he wrote many plays, some of which have perished;
they were received with a remarkable share of applause, and
gained for their author a general esteem among the decreas-

ing minority who cared for plays. After nearly forty years
spent in London he seems to have retired, just before the
outbreak of the Civil War, to his native place. According
to a faint tradition he married and had children, ending his
days as peacefully as he might; for Ilsington was in the
centre of a Royalist district, and is known to have suffered
heavily at the hands of the Parliamentary forces.

Ford was more than forty years old when the earliest sur-
viving play written by himself alone was first acted. *The
Lover's Melancholy,* although as a whole it is rather dreary,
reveals his peculiar style already at its highest point of de-
velopment. This style, with its slow, subtle melody, its sudden pauses on the suspension of a long breath, its words that
are gestures, has nothing of the half delirious freedom of
Marlowe or Beaumont, those strong-winged poets of an earlier and more robust age. This artist wrought, laboriously,
cool, lucid lines that are sometimes absolutely frozen. In his
second extant play, *'Tis Pity She's a Whore,* Ford touched
the highest point that he ever reached. He never after suc-
ceeded in presenting an image so simple, passionate, and
complete, so free comparatively from mixture of weak or
base elements, as that of the boy and girl lovers who were
brother and sister. The tragic story is unrolled from first to
last with fine truth and clear perceptions. At one point only
is it possible to detect any failure in Ford's grasp of the situation. When at the climax of their histories Giovanni stabs
Annabella, her feeble exclamation, "Brother *unkind!*" fails
to carry the impress of truth, and falls short of the tragic
height of passion to which we are uplifted. Such a failure
of insight is rare with Ford, much rarer than touches of
extravagant physical horror like the introduction of Annabella's heart on a dagger. It is profitable to compare *'Tis Pity
She's a Whore* with a rather similar play by Beaumont and
Fletcher, *A King and no King.* Dryden thought that this
play was the finest that Beaumont and Fletcher ever wrote;
it is certainly full of splendid rhetoric, tragic or tender, always broad, various and facile in style; but for the qualities
of insight and sincerity, for fineness of moral perception, for
the sure and deliberate grasp of the central situation, Ford's
play is as far above Beaumont and Fletcher's, with its shifty
conclusion, as it is below it in all the qualities which make

a play effective on the stage. *The Broken Heart* is a monument of sorrows, a Niobe group of frozen griefs. There is little movement, no definite plot or story; only this row of heart-broken figures—Orgilus, Panthea, Ithocles, Calantha, with many forms of minor melancholy:

> And 'twere a comely music when in parts
> One sung another's knell.

The unity of the play lies in the cumulative touches by which these figures are realised for us, and by which we are lifted naturally to the heroic self-restraint of Calantha. Into *Love's Sacrifice,* the history of the ardent and reckless Bianca, Ford has put his subtlest work, marred though it is by the feeble and foolish sentiment of the conclusion. The story of the youth who falls in love with his friend's wife, and when he has aroused in her stronger nature a passion far deeper than his own, shrinks back realising his falsehood, is true to nature and wrought with Ford's finest art and insight. But we can only smile when we hear these lovers—

> Hid in a rock of fire,
> Guarded by ministers of flaming hell—

celebrated as miracles of chastity and truth. In so complete a moral collapse as this (unless we choose to regard it as intentional irony), as well as in the occasional touches of forced material horror with which he startles us, Ford shows that he was the child of a society tainted by the affectation of purity, and a court that had ceased to be national and robust—both soon to vanish like a fantastic dream. In *Perkin Warbeck* he laid aside his characteristic defects, and also his characteristic merits, to achieve a distinct dramatic success. It is the least interesting of his plays for those who care for the peculiar qualities which mark Ford's genius, but it certainly ranks among our best historical dramas. Ford's interest in psychological problems may be detected in his impartial, even sympathetic, treatment of Warbeck; but for the most part this play is an exception to every generalisation that may be arrived at concerning his work. It is of a masculine temperature, with few flaws, and of fine characterisation throughout. These five plays embody whatever is best in Ford's work.

Of his remaining plays, *The Lady's Trial* contains most that is beautiful in language and character; *The Fancies Chaste and Noble* has a little that is characteristic, set in a weak and absurd story; *The Sun's Darling,* a "moral masque," of which Dekker wrote the larger and happier part, exhibits Ford's most level and frigid manner. *The Witch of Edmonton,* a noble and more human work of art than any of these, was written in conjunction with Dekker and Rowley.[1] It contains a few touches that are unmistakably Ford's, together with much that, without being very characteristic, has been plausibly assigned to him; on the whole, it is one of those plays, not uncommon at that time, in which two or more writers united to produce something that was unlike their individual work, and often superior to anything they produced singly. Ford's early work in prose and verse may be neglected.

The burden of a passionate and heavy-laden heart—that is the centre of every picture that Ford presents to us; on the painting of it he lavishes all his care. The rest of the canvas is filled in with a rapid and careless hand. His superior persons are generally uninteresting. As to his comic figures, it is for once impossible to go beyond the dictum of Gifford: they are "a despicable set of buffoons." He is reckless of consistency in action or time, indifferent generally to dramatic effect, but when the mysteries of the heart are in question he elaborates his art to the highest point. The conflict between the world's opinion and the heart's desire he paints and repaints, not as a moralist browbeating the cynical or conventional world, but as an artist, presenting problems which he does not undertake to solve save by the rough methods of the tragic stage. It is the grief deeper than language that he strives to express. He seeks in his own words to

> Sigh out a lamentable tale of things
> Done long ago, and ill done; and when sighs
> Are wearied, piece up what remains behind
> With weeping eyes, and hearts that bleed to death.

He is a master of the brief mysterious words, so calm in seeming, which well up from the depths of despair. He con-

[1] *The Witch of Edmonton* is included with Dekker's plays in the Mermaid Series.

centrates the revelation of a soul's agony into a sob or a sigh. The surface seems calm; we scarcely suspect that there is anything beneath; one gasp bubbles up from the drowning heart below, and all is silence. He is rich in those words and lines of sweet and subtle music—

> Parthenophil is lost, and I would see him;
> For he is like to something I remember,
> A great while since, a long, long time ago.

When we think of Ford we think of Giovanni and Annabella, passionate children who had given the world for love; of the childish sophistry with which they justified themselves, and of their last marvellous dialogue through which pierced a vague sense of guilt—a lurid shadow cast from the world they had contemned. We think of that Bianca (she that "owned the poor style of Duchess") who had thrown such scorn on her lover that he vowed never to speak to her again of unlawful love, and who comes to him in his sleep the night after, unclad and alone, in the last abandonment of passion. We think of Flavia in *The Fancies Chaste and Noble,* coldly dismissing her first husband with the one sign of tenderness as she turns at length to her new husband:—

> Beshrew 't, the brim of your hat
> Struck in mine eye.

We think of Calantha, still gracious and calm in the festive dance, as the leaden messages of awful death are shot at slow intervals in her ear,—her father, her friend, her lover —still gracious and calm until her duties are ended.

> When one news straight came huddling on another,
> Of death! and death! and death! still I danced forward;
> But it struck home, and here, and in an instant.

> They are the silent griefs which cut the heart-strings;
> Let me die smiling.

Ford is the most modern of the tribe to whom he belonged. When Shelley in his last days began a new drama, of which only fragments remain, he reproduced with added sweetness the tones and cadences of Ford's verse; and the writers to-day who seek, and in vain, to revive our ancient drama on its old lines, instinctively ally themselves with Ford. When we enumerate his great qualities we are enumerating the qualities which make him an ineffectual dramatist. Notwithstanding the ungrudging admiration of his relatives, legal friends, and fellow dramatists, and the "generally well received" report of the outside public, he could at no time have been a really popular playwright; and with the exception of *Perkin Warbeck* his plays have probably never been represented in more recent times. He was a sensitive observer who had meditated deeply on the springs of human action, especially in women. Of none of his fellows, even the greatest of them, can we say this. They have left us pictures of women which are incomparably more tender, or picturesque, or tragic than the searching, deliberate art of Ford could compass. But they looked nearly all from the outside, and were satisfied with the gracious or gorgeous stage-pictures which they knew so well how to present. This man writes of women not as a dramatist nor as a lover, but as one who had searched intimately and felt with instinctive sympathy the fibres of their hearts. He was an analyst; he strained the limits of his art to the utmost; he foreboded new ways of expression. Thus he is less nearly related to the men who wrote *Othello,* and *A Woman killed with Kindness,* and *Valentinian,* than to those poets and artists of the naked human soul, the writer of *Le Rouge et le Noir,* and the yet greater writer of *Madame Bovary.*

HAVELOCK ELLIS

THE LOVER'S MELANCHOLY

SIR HENRY HERBERT licensed this play for the stage in 1628, and it was acted by the King's Servants at the Blackfriars and Globe Theatres. It was published in the following year, and was the first play that Ford printed, perhaps on account of its success on the stage. In one of the commendatory poems prefixed to the quarto we read:—

> Nor seek I fame for thee, when thine own pen
> Hath forced a praise long since from knowing men.

And although this appears to be Ford's earliest extant play, we know that plays of his had been acted during the previous fifteen years. For the material of the masque and the passage leading up to it, Ford was indebted to Burton's *Anatomy of Melancholy,* published a year or two previously. The play was revived at Drury Lane in 1748 by Macklin, for his wife's benefit; apparently without success.

To his worthy Friend the Author
MASTER JOHN FORD

I write not to thy play: I'll not begin
To throw a censure upon what hath been
By the best approved: it can nor fear nor want
The rage or liking of the ignorant.
Nor seek I fame for thee, when thine own pen
Hath forced a praise long since from knowing men.
I speak my thoughts, and wish unto the stage
A glory from thy studies; that the age
May be indebted to thee for reprieve
Of purer language, and that spite may grieve
To see itself outdone. When thou art read,
The theatre may hope arts are not dead,
Though long concealed; that poet-apes may fear
To vent their weakness, mend, or quite forbear.
This I dare promise; and keep this in store,
As thou hast done enough, thou canst do more.

WILLIAM SINGLETON[1]

[1] In a copy of verses prefixed to Massinger's *Emperor of the East*, Singleton calls himself "the friend and kinsman" of that poet.

To my Worthily Respected Friends,
NATHANIEL FINCH, JOHN FORD, Esquires,
Master HENRY BLUNT, Master ROBERT ELLICE,
and all the rest of the
NOBLE SOCIETY OF GRAY'S INN

My Honoured Friends,

The account of some leisurable hours is here summed up, and offered to examination. Importunity of others, or opinion of mine own, hath not urged on any confidence of running the hazard of a censure. A plurality hath reference to a multitude, so I care not to please many; but where there is a parity of condition, there the freedom of construction makes the best music. This concord hath equally held between you the patrons and me the presenter. I am cleared of all scruple of disrespect on your parts; as I am of too slack a merit in myself. My presumption of coming in print in this kind [1] hath hitherto been unreprovable, this piece being the first that ever courted reader; and it is very possible that the like compliment with me may soon grow out of fashion. A practice of which that I may avoid now, I commend to the continuance of your loves the memory of his, who, without the protestation of a service, is readily your friend.

John Ford

---

[1] He had previously printed "Fame's Memorial," and, probably, other poems, now lost.

PROLOGUE

To tell ye, gentlemen, in what true sense
The writer, actors, or the audience
Should mould their judgments for a play, might draw
Truth into rules; but we have no such law.
Our writer, for himself, would have ye know
That in his following scenes he doth not owe
To others' fancies, nor hath lain in wait
For any stolen invention, from whose height
He might commend his own, more than the right
A scholar claims,[1] may warrant for delight.
It is art's scorn, that some of late have made
The noble use of poetry a trade.
For your parts, gentlemen, to quit his pains,
Yet you will please, that as you meet with strains
Of lighter mixture, but to cast your eye
Rather upon the *main* than on the *bye,*
His hopes stand firm, and we shall find it true,
The Lover's Melancholy cured by you.

[1] An allusion to his debt to Burton, and to the version of the story of "the Nightingale's death," taken from Strada's *Prolusiones Academicæ* (i. 1).

DRAMATIS PERSONÆ

PALADOR, Prince of Cyprus
AMETHUS, Cousin to the Prince
MELEANDER, an old Lord
SOPHRONOS, Brother of MELEANDER
MENAPHON, Son of SOPHRONOS
ARETUS, Tutor to the Prince
CORAX, a Physician
PELIAS, ⎱ two foolish Courtiers
CUCULUS, ⎰
RHETIAS (a reduced Courtier), Servant to EROCLEA
TROLLIO, Servant to MELEANDER
GRILLA, a Page of CUCULUS, in woman's dress
Officers, Attendants, &c.

THAMASTA, Sister of AMETHUS, and Cousin to the Prince
EROCLEA (as PARTHENOPHIL), ⎱ Daughters of MELEANDER
CLEOPHILA ⎰
KALA, Waiting-maid to THAMASTA

SCENE—FAMAGOSTA in CYPRUS

THE LOVER'S MELANCHOLY

ACT THE FIRST

SCENE I—*A Room in the Palace*

Enter MENAPHON *and* PELIAS.

MENAPHON. Dangers! how mean you dangers? that so
    courtly
You gratulate my safe return from dangers?
  Pelias. From travels, noble sir.
  Menaphon.   These are delights;
If my experience hath not, truant-like,
Misspent the time, which I have strove to use
For bettering my mind with observation.
  Pelias. As I am modest, I protest 'tis strange.
But is it possible?
  Menaphon.   What?
  Pelias.   To bestride
The frothy foams of Neptune's surging waves,
When blustering Boreas tosseth up the deep
And thumps a thunder-bounce?
  Menaphon.   Sweet sir, 'tis nothing:
Straight comes a dolphin, playing near your ship,
Heaving his crookèd back up, and presents
A feather-bed to waft ye to the shore
As easily as if you slept i' the court.
  Pelias. Indeed! is't true, I pray?
  Menaphon.   I will not stretch
Your faith upon the tenters.—Prithee, Pelias,
Where didst thou learn this language?
  Pelias.   I this language!
Alas, sir, we that study words and forms
Of compliment must fashion all discourse
According to the nature of the subject.

But I am silent:—now appears a sun,
Whose shadow I adore.

Enter AMETHUS, SOPHRONOS, *and* Attendants.

Menaphon.   My honoured father!
Sophronos. From mine eyes, son of my care, my love,
The joys that bid thee welcome do too much
Speak me a child.
Menaphon.   O princely sir, your hand.
Amethus. Perform your duties where you owe them first;
I dare not be so sudden in the pleasures
Thy presence hath brought home.
Sophronos.   Here thou still find'st
A friend as noble, Menaphon, as when
Thou left'st at thy departure.
Menaphon.   Yes, I know it,
To him I owe more service—
Amethus.   Pray give leave:
He shall attend your entertainments soon,
Next day, and next day: for an hour or two
I would engross him only.
Sophronos.   Noble lord!
Amethus. Ye're both dismissed.
Pelias.   Your creature and your servant.
        [*Exeunt all but* AMETHUS *and* MENAPHON.
Amethus. Give me thy hand. I will not say, "Thou'rt
    welcome;"
That is the common road of common friends.
I'm glad I have thee here—O, I want words
To let thee know my heart!
Menaphon.   'Tis pieced to mine.
Amethus. Yes, 'tis; as firmly as that holy thing
Called friendship can unite it. Menaphon,
My Menaphon, now all the goodly blessings
That can create a Heaven on earth dwell with thee!
Twelve months we have been sundered; but henceforth
We never more will part, till that sad hour
In which death leaves the one of us behind,
To see the other's funerals performed.

Let's now awhile be free.—How have thy travels
Disburthened thee abroad of discontents?

Menaphon. Such cure as sick men find in changing beds
I found in change of airs: the fancy flattered
My hopes with ease, as theirs do: but the grief
Is still the same.

Amethus.   Such is my case at home.
Cleophila, thy kinswoman, that maid
Of sweetness and humility, more pities
Her father's poor afflictions than the tide
Of my complaints.

Menaphon.   Thamasta, my great mistress,
Your princely sister, hath, I hope, ere this
Confirmed affection on some worthy choice.

Amethus. Not any, Menaphon. Her bosom yet
Is intermured with ice; though, by the truth
Of love, no day hath ever passed wherein
I have not mentioned thy deserts, thy constancy,
Thy—Come, in troth, I dare not tell thee what,
Lest thou mightst think I fawned upon[1]—a sin
Friendship was never guilty of; for flattery
Is monstrous in a true friend.

Menaphon.   Does the court
Wear the old looks too?

Amethus.   If thou mean'st the prince,
It does. He's the same melancholy man
He was at's father's death; sometimes speaks sense,
But seldom mirth; will smile, but seldom laugh;
Will lend an ear to business, deal in none;
Gaze upon revels, antic fopperies,
But is not moved; will sparingly discourse,
Hear music; but what most he takes delight in
Are handsome pictures. One so young and goodly,
So sweet in his own nature, any story
Hath seldom mentioned.

Menaphon.   Why should such as I am
Groan under the light burthen of small sorrows,
Whenas a prince so potent cannot shun

---

[1] So the old edition; probably equivalent to "fawned."

Motions of passion? [2] To be man, my lord,
Is to be but the exercise of cares
In several shapes: as miseries do grow,
They alter as men's forms; but how none know.

Amethus. This little isle of Cyprus sure abounds
In greater wonders both for change and fortune
Than any you have seen abroad.

Menaphon.   Than any
I have observed abroad: all countries else
To a free eye and mind yield something rare;
And I, for my part, have brought home one jewel
Of admirable value.

Amethus.   Jewel, Menaphon!

Menaphon. A jewel, my Amethus, a fair youth;
A youth, whom, if I were but superstitious,
I should repute an excellence more high
Than mere creations are: to add delight,
I'll tell ye how I found him.

Amethus.   Prithee do.

Menaphon. Passing from Italy to Greece, the tales
Which poets of an elder time have feigned
To glorify their Tempe, bred in me
Desire of visiting that paradise.
To Thessaly I came; and living private,
Without acquaintance of more sweet companions
Than the old inmates to my love, my thoughts,
I day by day frequented silent groves
And solitary walks. One morning early
This accident encountered me: I heard
The sweetest and most ravishing contention
That art and nature ever were at strife in. [3]

Amethus. I cannot yet conceive what you infer
By art and nature.

Menaphon.   I shall soon resolve ye.
A sound of music touched mine ears, or rather
Indeed entranced my soul. As I stole nearer,
Invited by the melody, I saw

---

[2] Sorrow.
[3] *Vide* (Ford says) *Fami. Stradam*, lib. ii. Prolus. 6. Acad. 2. *Imitat. Claudian.*
This story has been paraphrased by Crashaw, Ambrose Philips, and others.

This youth, this fair-faced youth, upon his lute,
With strains of strange variety and harmony,
Proclaiming, as it seemed, so bold a challenge
To the clear quiristers of the woods, the birds,
That, as they flocked about him, all stood silent,
Wondering at what they heard. I wondered too.

    Amethus. And so do I; good, on!

    Menaphon.   A nightingale,
Nature's best skilled musician, undertakes
The challenge, and for every several strain
The well-shaped youth could touch, she sung her own;
He could not run division with more art
Upon his quaking instrument than she,
The nightingale, did with her various notes
Reply to: for a voice and for a sound,
Amethus, 'tis much easier to believe
That such they were than hope to hear again.

    Amethus. How did the rivals part?

    Menaphon.   You term them rightly;
For they were rivals, and their mistress, harmony.
Some time thus spent, the young man grew at last
Into a pretty anger, that a bird,
Whom art had never taught cliffs, moods, or notes,
Should vie with him for mastery, whose study
Had busied many hours to perfect practice:
To end the controversy, in a rapture
Upon his instrument he plays so swiftly.
So many voluntaries and so quick,
That there was curiosity and cunning,
Concord in discord, lines of differing method
Meeting in one full centre of delight.

    Amethus. Now for the bird.

    Menaphon.   The bird, ordained to be
Music's first martyr, strove to imitate
These several sounds; which when her warbling throat
Failed in, for grief down dropped she on his lute,
And brake her heart. It was the quaintest sadness,
To see the conqueror upon her hearse
To weep a funeral elegy of tears;
That, trust me, my Amethus, I could chide

Mine own unmanly weakness, that made me
A fellow-mourner with him.

    Amethus.   I believe thee.

    Menaphon. He looked upon the trophies of his art,
Then sighed, then wiped his eyes, then sighed and cried,
"Alas, poor creature! I will soon revenge
This cruelty upon the author of it;
Henceforth this lute, guilty of innocent blood,
Shall never more betray a harmless peace
To an untimely end:" and in that sorrow,
As he was pashing[4] it against a tree,
I suddenly stept in.

    Amethus.   Thou hast discoursed
A truth of mirth and pity.

    Menaphon.   I reprieved
The intended execution with entreaties
And interruption.—But, my princely friend,
It was not strange the music of his hand
Did overmatch birds, when his voice and beauty,
Youth, carriage, and discretion must, from men
Endued with reason, ravish admiration:
From me they did.

    Amethus.   But is this miracle
Not to be seen?

    Menaphon.   I won him by degrees
To choose me his companion. Whence he is,
Or who, as I durst modestly inquire,
So gently he would woo not to make known;
Only—for reasons to himself reserved—
He told me, that some remnant of his life
Was to be spent in travel: for his fortunes,
They were nor mean nor riotous; his friends
Not published to the world, though not obscure;
His country Athens, and his name Parthenophil.

    Amethus. Came he with you to Cyprus?

    Menaphon.   Willingly.
The fame of our young melancholy prince,
Meleander's rare distractions, the obedience
Of young Cleophila, Thamasta's glory,

[4] Dashing.

Your matchless friendship, and my desperate love,
Prevailed with him; and I have lodged him privately
In Famagosta.

Amethus.   Now thou'rt doubly welcome:
I will not lose the sight of such a rarity
For one part of my hopes. When d'ye intend
To visit my great-spirited sister?

Menaphon.   May I
Without offence?

Amethus.   Without offence.—Parthenophil
Shall find a worthy entertainment too.
Thou art not still a coward?

Menaphon.   She's too excellent,
And I too low in merit.

Amethus.   I'll prepare
A noble welcome; and, friend, ere we part,
Unload to thee an overchargèd heart.   [*Exeunt.*

SCENE II—*Another Room in the Palace*

Enter RHETIAS, *carelessly attired.*

Rhetias. I will not court the madness of the times;
Nor fawn upon the riots that embalm
Our wanton gentry, to preserve the dust
Of their affected vanities in coffins
Of memorable shame. When commonwealths
Totter and reel from that nobility
And ancient virtue which renowns the great,
Who steer the helm of government, while mushrooms
Grow up, and make new laws to license folly;
Why should not I, a May-game, scorn the weight
Of my sunk fortunes? snarl [5] at the vices
Which rot the land, and, without fear or wit [6]
Be mine own antic? [7] 'Tis a sport to live

---

[5] "Snarl" as well as "girl," is commonly made a dissyllable by our poet: he passed his youth in the neighbourhood of Dartmoor, and probably adopted the practice of that wild district.—*Gifford.*

[6] *i.e.* Carelessly.

[7] Buffoon.

When life is irksome, if we will not hug
Prosperity in others, and contemn
Affliction in ourselves. This rule is certain,
"He that pursues his safety from the school
Of state must learn to be madman or fool."
Ambition, wealth, ease, I renounce—the devil
That damns ye here on earth. Or I will be
Mine own mirth, or mine own tormentor.—So!
Here comes intelligence; a buzz o' the court.

Enter PELIAS.

Pelias. Rhetias, I sought thee out to tell thee news,
New, excellent new news. Cuculus, sirrah,
That gull, that young old gull, is coming this way.

 Rhetias. And thou art his forerunner?

 Pelias.   Prithee, hear me.
Instead of a fine guarded [8] page we've got him
A boy, tricked up in neat and handsome fashion;
Persuaded him that 'tis indeed a wench,
And he has entertained him: he does follow him,
Carries his sword and buckler, waits on's trencher,
Fills him his wine, tobacco; whets his knife,
Lackeys his letters, does what service else
He would employ his man in. Being asked
Why he is so irregular in courtship,[9]
His answer is, that since great ladies use
Gentleman ushers to go bare before them,
He knows no reason but he may reduce
The courtiers to have women wait on them;
And he begins the fashion: he is laughed at
Most complimentally. Thou'lt burst to see him.

 Rhetias. Agelastus, so surnamed for his gravity,[10] was a
very wise fellow, kept his countenance all days of his life as
demurely as a judge that pronounceth sentence of death on
a poor rogue for stealing as much bacon as would serve at a
meal with a calf's head. Yet he smiled once, and never but
once:—thou art no scholar?

---

[8] *i.e.* With a livery richly laced or turned up.

[9] Court etiquette.

[10] The story is in Pliny, who tells it of Crassus, the grandfather of the unfortunate Crassus who fell the victim of his rapacity in Parthia.—*Gifford.*

Pelias. I have read pamphlets dedicated to me.—
Dost call him Agelastus? Why did he laugh?

Rhetias. To see an ass eat thistles. Puppy, go study to be
a singular coxcomb. Cuculus is an ordinary ape; but thou
art an ape of an ape.

Pelias. Thou hast a patent to abuse thy friends.—
Look, look, he comes! observe him seriously.

Enter CUCULUS *followed by* GRILLA, *both fantastically
dressed.*

Cuculus. Reach me my sword and buckler.

Grilla. They are here, forsooth.

Cuculus. How now, minx, how now! where is your duty,
your distance? Let me have service methodically tendered;
you are now one of us. Your curtsy. [GRILLA *curtsies.*]
Good! remember that you are to practise courtship. Was thy
father a piper, sayest thou?

Grilla. A sounder of some such wind-instrument, forsooth.[11]

Cuculus. Was he so?—Hold up thy head. Be thou musical
to me, and I will marry thee to a dancer; one that shall ride
on his footcloth,[12] and maintain thee in thy muff and hood.

Grilla. That will be fine indeed.

Cuculus. Thou art yet but simple.

Grilla. D'ye think so?

Cuculus. I have a brain, I have a head-piece: o' my conscience, if I take pains with thee, I should raise thy understanding, girl, to the height of a nurse, or a court-midwife
at least: I will make thee big in time, wench.

Grilla. E'en do your pleasure with me, sir.

Pelias. [*Coming forward*] Noble, accomplished Cuculus!

Rhetias. [*Coming forward*] Give me thy fist, innocent.

Cuculus. Would 'twere in thy belly! there 'tis.

Pelias. That's well; he's an honest blade, though he be
blunt.

---

[11] Grilla's answer is meant to intimate that her father was a sow-gelder. Sow-
gelders, it appears, used formerly to blow a horn. So in Fletcher's *Beggar's Bush*,
act iii. sc. i:

> "*Enter* Higgen *disguised as a sow-gelder, singing as follows,*
>
> Have ye any work for the sow-gelder, oh?
> My horn goes to high, to low, to high, to low."—*Dyce.*

[12] *i.e.* A horse's cloth housings.

Cuculus. Who cares? We can be as blunt as he, for's life.

Rhetias. Cuculus, there is, within a mile or two, a sow-pig hath sucked a brach,[13] and now hunts the deer, the hare, nay, most unnaturally, the wild-boar, as well as any hound in Cyprus.

Cuculus. Monstrous sow-pig! is't true?

Pelias. I'll be at charge of a banquet on thee for a sight of her.

Rhetias. Every thing takes after the dam that gave it suck. Where hadst thou thy milk?

Cuculus. I? Why, my nurse's husband was a most excellent maker of shittlecocks.

Pelias. My nurse was a woman-surgeon.[14]

Rhetias. And who gave thee pap, mouse?

Grilla. I never sucked, that I remember.

Rhetias. La now, a shittlecock maker! all thy brains are stuck with cork and feather, Cuculus. This learned courtier takes after the nurse too; a she-surgeon; which is, in effect, a mere matcher of colours. Go learn to paint and daub compliments, 'tis the next step to run into a new suit. My Lady Periwinkle here never sucked: suck thy master, and bring forth moon-calves, fop, do! This is good philosophy, sirs; make use on't.

Grilla. Bless us, what a strange creature this is!

Cuculus. A gull, an arrant gull by proclamation.

Enter CORAX, *passing over the stage.*

Pelias. Corax, the prince's chief physician!
What business speeds his haste?—Are all things well, sir?

Corax. Yes, yes, yes.

Rhetias. Phew! you may wheel about, man; we know you're proud of your slovenry and practice; 'tis your virtue. The prince's melancholy fit, I presume, holds still.

Corax. So do thy knavery and desperate beggary.

Cuculus. Aha! here's one will tickle the ban-dog.[15]

---

[13] The kennel term for a bitch-hound. This anecdote is taken from Burton, who took it from *Giraldus Cambrensis*. The late Sir Harry Mildmay had a sow-pig that would apparently do all that Cuculus thinks so monstrous, without having sucked a brach for the matter.—*Gifford.*

[14] *i.e.* A dealer in paints and cosmetics for ladies.

[15] A dog kept fastened up on account of its fierceness. The term was also applied to dogs employed in bull and bear baiting.

Rhetias. You must not go yet.

Corax. I'll stay in spite of thy teeth. There lies my gravity. [*Throws off his gown.*] Do what thou darest; I stand thee.

Rhetias. Mountebanks, empirics, quack-salvers, mineralists, wizards, alchemists, cast-apothecaries, old wives and barbers, are all suppositors to the right worshipful doctor, as I take it. Some of ye are the head of your art, and the horns too—but they come by nature. Thou livest single for no other end but that thou fearest to be a cuckold.

Corax. Have at thee! Thou affectest railing only for thy health; thy miseries are so thick and so lasting, that thou hast not one poor denier to bestow on opening a vein: wherefore, to avoid a pleurisy, thou'lt be sure to prate thyself once a month into a whipping, and bleed in the breech instead of the arm.

Rhetias. Have at thee again!

Corax. Come!

Cuculus. There, there, there! O brave doctor!

Pelias. Let 'em alone.

Rhetias. Thou art in thy religion an atheist, in thy condition[16] a cur, in thy diet an epicure, in thy lust a goat, in thy sleep a hog; thou takest upon thee the habit of a grave physician, but art indeed an impostorous empiric. Physicians are the cobblers, rather the botchers, of men's bodies; as the one patches our tattered clothes, so the other solders our diseased flesh. Come on.

Cuculus. To't, to't! hold him to't! hold him to't! to't, to't, to't!

Corax. The best worth in thee is the corruption of thy mind, for that only entitles thee to the dignity of a louse, a thing bred out of the filth and superfluity of ill humours. Thou bitest anywhere, and any man who defends not himself with the clean linen of secure honesty; him thou darest not come near. Thou art fortune's idiot, virtue's bankrupt, time's dunghill, manhood's scandal, and thine own scourge. Thou wouldst hang thyself, so wretchedly miserable thou art, but that no man will trust thee with as much money as will buy a halter; and all thy stock to be sold is not worth half as much as may procure it.

16 Disposition.

Rhetias. Ha, ha, ha! this is flattery, gross flattery.

Corax. I have employment for thee, and for ye all. Tut, these are but good-morrows between us.

Rhetias. Are thy bottles full?

Corax. Of rich wine; let's all suck together.

Rhetias. Like so many swine in a trough.

Corax. I'll shape ye all for a device before the prince: we'll try how that can move him.

Rhetias. He shall fret or laugh.

Cuculus. Must I make one?

Corax. Yes, and your feminine page too.

Grilla. Thanks, most egregiously.

Pelias. I will not slack my part.

Cuculus. Wench, take my buckler.

Corax. Come all unto my chamber: the project is cast: the time only we must attend.

Rhetias. The melody must agree well and yield sport,
When such as these are, knaves and fools, consort.

[*Exeunt.*

SCENE III—*An Apartment in the House of*
THAMASTA

Enter AMETHUS, THAMASTA *and* KALA.

Amethus. Does this show well?

Thamasta.   What would you have me do?

Amethus. Not like a lady of the trim, new crept
Out of the shell of sluttish sweat and labour
Into the glittering pomp of ease and wantonness,
Embroideries, and all these antic fashions
That shape a woman monstrous; to transform
Your education and a noble birth
Into contempt and laughter. Sister, sister,
She who derives her blood from princes ought
To glorify her greatness by humility.

Thamasta. Then you conclude me proud?

Amethus.   Young Menaphon,
My worthy friend, has loved you long and truly:
To witness his obedience to your scorn,

Twelve months, wronged gentleman, he undertook
A voluntary exile. Wherefore, sister,
In this time of his absence have you not
Disposed of your affections on some monarch?
Or sent ambassadors to some neighbouring king
With fawning protestations of your graces,
Your rare perfections, admirable beauty?
This had been a new piece of modesty
Would have deserved a chronicle!

   Thamasta.   You're bitter;
And, brother, by your leave, not kindly[17] wise.
My freedom is my birth's; I am not bound
To fancy your approvements, but my own.
Indeed, you are an humble youth! I hear of
Your visits and your loving commendation
To your heart's saint, Cleophila, a virgin
Of a rare excellence. What though she want
A portion to maintain a portly greatness?
Yet 'tis your gracious sweetness to descend
So low; the meekness of your pity leads ye!
She is your dear friend's sister! a good soul!
An innocent!—

   Amethus.   Thamasta!

   Thamasta.   I have given
Your Menaphon a welcome home, as fits me;
For his sake entertained Parthenophil,
The handsome stranger, more familiarly
Than, I may fear, becomes me; yet, for his part,
I not repent my courtesies: but you—

   Amethus. No more, no more! be affable to both;
Time may reclaim your cruelty.

   Thamasta.   I pity
The youth; and, trust me, brother, love his sadness:
He talks the prettiest stories: he delivers
His tales so gracefully, that I could sit
And listen, nay, forget my meals and sleep,
To hear his neat discourses. Menaphon
Was well advised in choosing such a friend
For pleading his true love.

<hr>

[17] *i.e.* According to kin.

Amethus. Now I commend thee;
Thou'lt change at last, I hope.

Thamasta. I fear I shall. [*Aside.*

Enter MENAPHON *and* PARTHENOPHIL.

Amethus. Have ye surveyed the garden?

Menaphon. 'Tis a curious,
A pleasantly contrived delight.

Thamasta. Your eye, sir,
Hath in your travels often met contents
Of more variety?

Parthenophil. Not any, lady.

Menaphon. It were impossible, since your fair presence
Makes every place, where it vouchsafes to shine,
More lovely than all other helps of art
Can equal.

Thamasta. What you mean by "helps of art,"
You know yourself best: be they as they are;
You need none, I am sure, to set me forth.

Menaphon. 'Twould argue want of manners, more than
skill,
Not to praise praise itself.

Thamasta. For your reward,
Henceforth I'll call you servant.[18]

Amethus. Excellent sister!

Menaphon. 'Tis my first step to honour. May I fall
Lower than shame, when I neglect all service
That may confirm this favour!

Thamasta. Are you well, sir?

Parthenophil. Great princess, I am well. To see a league
Between an humble love, such as my friend's is,
And a commanding virtue, such as yours is,
Are sure restoratives.

Thamasta. You speak ingeniously.—[19]
Brother, be pleased to show the gallery
To this young stranger. Use the time a while,
And we will all together to the court:
I will present ye, sir, unto the prince.

18 *i.e.* Acknowledge you as a lover.
19 *i.e.* Wittily.

Parthenophil. You're all composed of fairness and true
bounty.

Amethus. Come, come.—We'll wait thee, sister. This beginning
Doth relish happy process.

Menaphon.   You have blessed me.

[*Exeunt* MENAPHON, AMETHUS, *and* PARTHENOPHIL.

Thamasta. Kala, O Kala!

Kala.   Lady?

Thamasta.   We are private;
Thou art my closet.

Kala.   Lock your secrets close, then;
I am not to be forced.

Thamasta.   Never till now
Could I be sensible of being traitor
To honour and to shame.

Kala.   You are in love.

Thamasta. I am grown base.—Parthenophil—

Kala.   He's handsome.
Richly endowed; he hath a lovely face,
A winning tongue.

Thamasta.   If ever I must fall,
In him my greatness sinks: Love is a tyrant,
Resisted. Whisper in his ear, how gladly
I would steal time to talk with him one hour:
But do it honourably; prithee, Kala,
Do not betray me.

Kala.   Madam, I will make it
Mine own case; he shall think I am in love with him.

Thamasta. I hope thou art not, Kala.

Kala.   'Tis for your sake:
I'll tell him so; but, 'faith, I am not, lady.

Thamasta. Pray, use me kindly; let me not too soon
Be lost in my new follies. 'Tis a fate
That overrules our wisdoms; whilst we strive
To live most free, we're caught in our own toils.
Diamonds cut diamonds; they who will prove
To thrive in cunning must cure love with love.   [*Exeunt.*

ACT THE SECOND

SCENE I—*An Apartment in the Palace*

Enter SOPHRONOS *and* ARETUS.

SOPHRONOS. Our commonwealth is sick: 'tis more than time
That we should wake the head thereof, who sleeps
In the dull lethargy of lost security.
The commons murmur, and the nobles grieve;
The court is now turned antic, and grows wild,
Whiles all the neighbouring nations stand at gaze,
And watch fit opportunity to wreak
Their just-conceivèd fury on such injuries
As the late prince, our living master's father,
Committed against laws of truth or honour.
Intelligence comes flying in on all sides;
Whilst the unsteady multitude presume
How that you, Aretus, and I engross,
Out of particular ambition,
The affairs of government; which I, for my part,
Groan under and am weary of.

    Aretus.   Sophronos,
I am as zealous too of shaking off
My gay state-fetters, that I have bethought
Of speedy remedy; and to that end,
As I have told ye, have concluded with
Corax, the prince's chief physician.

    Sophronos. You should have done this sooner, Aretus;
You were his tutor, and could best discern
His dispositions, to inform them rightly.

    Aretus. Passions of violent nature, by degrees
Are easiliest reclaimed. There's something hid
Of his distemper, which we'll now find out.

      Enter CORAX, RHETIAS, PELIAS, CUCULUS, *and*
                  GRILLA.

You come on just appointment. Welcome, gentlemen!
Have you won Rhetias, Corax?

Corax.   Most sincerely.

Cuculus. Save ye, nobilities! Do your lordships take notice
of my page? 'Tis a fashion of the newest edition, spick and
span new, without example.—Do your honour, housewife.

Grilla. There's a curtsey for you,—and a curtsey for you.

Sophronos. 'Tis excellent: we must all follow fashion,
And entertain she-waiters.

Aretus.   'Twill be courtly.

Cuculus. I think so; I hope the chronicles will rear me one
day for a headpiece—

Rhetias. Of woodcock,[20] without brains in't! Barbers shall
wear thee on their citterns,[21] and hucksters set thee out in
gingerbread.

Cuculus. Devil take thee! I say nothing to thee now; can'st
let me be quiet?

Grilla. You're too perstreperous, saucebox.

Cuculus. Good girl!—If we begin to puff once—

Pelias. Prithee, hold thy tongue; the lords are in the
presence.

Rhetias. Mum, butterfly!

Pelias.   The prince! stand and keep silence.

Cuculus. O, the prince!—Wench, thou shalt see the prince
now.   [*Soft music.*

Enter PALADOR *with a book.*

Sophronos. Sir!

Aretus.   Gracious sir!

Palador.   Why all this company?

Corax. A book! is this the early exercise
I did prescribe? instead of following health,
Which all men covet, you pursue disease.
Where's your great horse, your hounds, your set at tennis,

---

20 Simpleton.

21 It appears from innumerable passages in our old writers, that barbers' shops
were furnished with some musical instrument (commonly a cittern or guitar), for
the amusement of such customers as chose to strum upon it while waiting for
their turn to be shaved, &c.—*Gifford*. "Citterns," Dyce adds, "were usually
ornamented with grotesque heads carved at the extremity of the neck and finger-
board."

Your balloon-ball,[22] the practice of your dancing,
Your casting of the sledge, or learning how
To toss a pike? all changed into a sonnet!
Pray, sir, grant me free liberty to leave
The court; it does infect me with the sloth
Of sleep and surfeit: in the university
I have employments, which to my profession
Add profit and report; here I am lost,
And in your wilful dulness held a man
Of neither art nor honesty. You may
Command my head:—pray, take it, do! 'twere better
For me to lose it than to lose my wits,
And live in Bedlam; you will force me to't;
I'm almost mad already.

    Palador.   I believe it.

    Sophronos. Letters are come from Crete, which do require
A speedy restitution of such ships
As by your father were long since detained;
If not, defiance threatened.

    Aretus.   These near parts
Of Syria that adjoin muster their friends;
And by intelligence we learn for certain
The Syrian will pretend an ancient interest
Of tribute intermitted.

    Sophronos.   Through your land
Your subjects mutter strangely, and imagine
More than they dare speak publicly.

    Corax.   And yet
They talk but oddly of you.

    Cuculus.   Hang 'em, mongrels.

    Palador. Of me! my subjects talk of me!

    Corax.   Yes, scurvily,
And think worse, prince.

    Palador.   I'll borrow patience
A little time to listen to these wrongs;
And from the few of you which are here present
Conceive the general voice.

    Corax.   So! now he's nettled.   [*Aside.*

    Palador. By all your loves I charge ye, without fear

[22] A large inflated ball of leather used in a game called balloon.

Or flattery, to let me know your thoughts,
And how I am interpreted: speak boldly.

Sophronos. For my part, sir, I will be plain and brief.
I think you are of nature mild and easy,
Not willingly provoked, but withal headstrong
In any passion that misleads your judgment:
I think you too indulgent to such motions
As spring out of your own affections;
Too old to be reformed, and yet too young
To take fit counsel from yourself of what
Is most amiss.

Palador.   So!—Tutor, your conceit?

Aretus. I think you dote—with pardon let me speak it—
Too much upon your pleasures; and these pleasures
Are so wrapt up in self-love, that you covet
No other change of fortune; would be still
What your birth makes you; but are loth to toil
In such affairs of state as break your sleeps.

Corax. I think you would be by the world reputed
A man in every point complete; but are
In manners and effect [23] indeed a child,
A boy, a very boy.

Pelias.   May't please your grace,
I think you do contain within yourself
The great elixir, soul, and quintessence
Of all divine perfections; are the glory
Of mankind, and the only strict example
For earthly monarchs to square out their lives by;
Time's miracle, Fame's pride; in knowledge, wit,
Sweetness, discourse, arms, arts—

Palador.   You are a courtier.

Cuculus. But not of the ancient fashion, an't like your
highness. 'Tis I; I that am the credit of the court, noble
prince; and if thou wouldst, by proclamation or patent,
create me overseer of all the tailors in thy dominions, then,
then the golden days should appear again; bread should be
cheaper, fools should have more wit, knaves more honesty,
and beggars more money.

---

[23] Qy. "Affect."—*Dyce.*

Grilla. I think now—

Cuculus. Peace, you squall!

Palador. [*to* RHETIAS] You have not spoken yet.

Cuculus. Hang him! he'll nothing but rail.

Grilla. Most abominable;—out upon him!

Corax. Away, Cuculus; follow the lords.

Cuculus. Close, page, close.

> [*They all silently withdraw except* PALADOR *and*
> RHETIAS.

Palador. You are somewhat long a' thinking.

Rhetias. I do not think at all.

Palador. Am I not worthy of your thought?

Rhetias. My pity you are, but not my reprehension.

Palador. Pity!

Rhetias. Yes, for I pity such to whom I owe service, who exchange their happiness for a misery.

Palador. Is it a misery to be a prince?

Rhetias. Princes who forget their sovereignty, and yield to affected passion, are weary of command.—You had a father, sir.

Palador. Your sovereign, whiles he lived: but what of him?

Rhetias. Nothing. I only dared to name him; that's all.

Palador. I charge thee, by the duty that thou ow'st us, Be plain in what thou mean'st to speak: there's something That we must know: be free; our ears are open.

Rhetias. O, sir, I had rather hold a wolf by the ears than stroke a lion: the greatest danger is the last.

Palador. This is mere trifling.—Ha! are all stol'n hence? We are alone: thou hast an honest look; Thou hast a tongue, I hope, that is not oiled With flattery: be open. Though 'tis true That in my younger days I oft have heard Agenor's name, my father, more traduced Than I could then observe; yet I protest I never had a friend, a certain friend, That would inform me throughly of such errors As oftentimes are incident to princes.

Rhetias. All this may be. I have seen a man so curious in feeling of the edge of a keen knife, that he has cut his fingers. My flesh is not of proof against the metal I am to handle; the one is tenderer than the other.

Palador. I see, then, I must court thee. Take the word
Of a just prince; for anything thou speakest
I have more than a pardon,—thanks and love.

Rhetias. I will remember you of an old tale that something concerns you. Meleander, the great but unfortunate statesman, was by your father treated with for a match between you and his eldest daughter, the Lady Eroclea: you were both near of an age. I presume you remember a contract, and cannot forget her.

Palador. She was a lovely beauty. Prithee, forward!

Rhetias. To court was Eroclea brought; was courted by your father, not for Prince Palador, as it followed, but to be made a prey to some less noble design. With your favour, I have forgot the rest.

Palador. Good, call it back again into thy memory;
Else, losing the remainder, I am lost too.

Rhetias. You charm[24] me. In brief, a rape by some bad agents was attempted; by the Lord Meleander her father rescued, she conveyed away; Meleander accused of treason, his land seized, he himself distracted and confined to the castle, where he yet lives. What had ensued was doubtful; but your father shortly after died.

Palador. But what became of fair Eroclea?

Rhetias. She never since was heard of.

Palador. No hope lives, then,
Of ever, ever seeing her again?

Rhetias. Sir, I feared I should anger thee. There was, as I said, an old tale:—I have now a new one, which may perhaps season the first with a more delightful relish.

Palador. I am prepared to hear; say what you please.

Rhetias. My Lord Meleander failing,—on whose favour my fortunes relied,—I furnished myself for travel, and bent my course to Athens; where a pretty accident, after a while, came to my knowledge,

Palador. My ear is open to thee.

Rhetias. A young lady contracted to a noble gentleman, as the lady we last mentioned and your highness were, being

[24] Persuade.

hindered by their jarring parents, stole from her home, and
was conveyed like a ship-boy in a merchant[25] from the
country where she lived, into Corinth first, afterwards to
Athens; where in much solitariness she lived, like a youth,
almost two years, courted by all for acquaintance, but friend
to none by familiarity.

Palador. In habit of a man?

Rhetias. A handsome young man—till, within these three
months or less,—her sweetheart's father dying some year
before or more,—she had notice of it, and with much joy
returned home, and, as report voiced it at Athens, enjoyed
her happiness she was long an exile for. Now, noble sir, if
you did love the Lady Eroclea, why may not such safety and
fate direct her as directed the other? 'tis not impossible.

Palador. If I *did* love her, Rhetias! Yes, I did.
Give me thy hand: as thou didst serve Meleander,
And art still true to these, henceforth serve me.

Rhetias. My duty and my obedience are my surety;
But I have been too bold.

Palador. Forget the sadder story of my father,
And only, Rhetias, learn to read [26] me well;
For I must ever thank thee: thou'st unlocked
A tongue was vowed to silence; for requital,
Open my bosom, Rhetias.

Rhetias.   What's your meaning?

Palador. To tie thee to an oath of secrecy.
Unloose the buttons, man: thou dost it faintly.
What find'st thou there?

Rhetias.   A picture in a tablet.

Palador. Look well upon't.

Rhetias.   I do—yes—let me observe it—
'Tis hers, the lady's.

Palador.   Whose?

Rhetias.   Eroclea's.

Palador. Hers that was once Eroclea. For her sake
Have I advanced Sophronos to the helm
Of government; for her sake will restore
Meleander's honours to him; will, for her sake,

[25] *i.e.* A merchant ship.
[26] Comprehend.

Beg friendship from thee, Rhetias. O, be faithful,
And let no politic lord work from thy bosom
My griefs: I know thou wert put on to sift me;
But be not too secure.

Rhetias.   I am your creature.

Palador. Continue still thy discontented fashion,
Humour the lords, as they would humour me;
I'll not live in thy debt.—We are discovered.

Enter AMETHUS, MENAPHON, THAMASTA, KALA, *and*
PARTHENOPHIL.

Amethus. Honour and health still wait upon the prince!
Sir, I am bold with favour to present
Unto your highness Menaphon my friend,
Returned from travel.

Menaphon.   Humbly on my knees
I kiss your gracious hand.

Palador.   It is our duty
To love the virtuous.

Menaphon.   If my prayers or service
Hold any value, they are vowed yours ever.

Rhetias. I have a fist for thee too, stripling; thou'rt started
up prettily since I saw thee. Hast learned any wit abroad?
Canst tell news and swear lies with a grace, like a true trav-
eller?—what new ouzel's this?

Thamasta. Your highness shall do right to your own
            judgment
In taking more than common notice of
This stranger, an Athenian, named Parthenophil;
One who, if mine opinion do not soothe me
Too grossly, for the fashion of his mind
Deserves a dear respect.

Palador.   Your commendations,
Sweet cousin, speak him nobly.

Parthenophil.   All the powers
That sentinel just thrones double their guards
About your sacred excellence!

Palador.   What fortune
Led him to Cyprus?

Menaphon.   My persuasions won him.

Amethus. And if your highness please to hear the entrance
Into their first acquaintance, you will say—

Thamasta. It was the newest, sweetest, prettiest accident
That e'er delighted your attention:
I can discourse it, sir.

Palador.   Some other time.
How is he called?

Thamasta.   Parthenophil.

Palador.   Parthenophil!
We shall sort time to take more notice of him.   [*Exit.*

Menaphon. His wonted melancholy still pursues him.

Amethus. I told you so.

Thamasta.   You must not wonder at it.

Parthenophil. I do not, lady.

Amethus.   Shall we to the castle?

Menaphon. We will attend ye both.

Rhetias. All three,—I'll go too. Hark in thine ear, gallant,
I'll keep the old madman in chat, whilst thou gabblest to
the girl: my thumb's upon my lips; not a word.

Amethus. I need not fear thee, Rhetias. Sister, soon
Expect us: this day we will range the city.

Thamasta. Well, soon I shall expect ye.—Kala!
                              [*Aside to* KALA.

Kala.   Trust me.

Rhetias. Troop on!—Love, love, what a wonder thou art!
          [*Exeunt all but* PARTHENOPHIL *and* KALA.

Kala. May I not be offensive, sir?

Parthenophil.   Your pleasure?
Yet, pray, be brief.

Kala.   Then, briefly; good, resolve me;
Have you a mistress or a wife?

Parthenophil.   I've neither.

Kala. Nor did you ever love in earnest any
Fair lady, whom you wished to make your own?

Parthenophil. Not any, truly.

Kala.   What your friends or means are
I will not be inquisitive to know,
Nor do I care to hope for. But admit
A dowry were thrown down before your choice,
Of beauty, noble birth, sincere affection,

How gladly would you entertain it! Young man,
I do not tempt you idly.
   Parthenophil.   I shall thank you,
When my unsettled thoughts can make me sensible
Of what 'tis to be happy; for the present
I am your debtor; and, fair gentlewoman,
Pray give me leave as yet to study ignorance,
For my weak brains conceive not what concerns me.
Another time—   [*Going.*

Re-enter THAMASTA.

   Thamasta.   Do I break off your parley,
That you are parting? Sure, my woman loves you:
Can she speak well, Parthenophil?
   Parthenophil.   Yes, madam,
Discreetly chaste she can; she hath much won
On my belief, and in few words, but pithy,
Much moved my thankfulness. You are her lady;
Your goodness aims, I know, at her preferment;
Therefore I may be bold to make confession
Of truth: if ever I desire to thrive
In woman's favour, Kala is the first
Whom my ambition shall bend to.
   Thamasta.   Indeed!
But say a nobler love should interpose.
   Parthenophil. Where real worth and constancy first settle
A hearty truth, there greatness cannot shake it;
Nor shall it mine: yet I am but an infant
In that construction, which must give clear light
To Kala's merit; riper hours hereafter
Must learn me how to grow rich in deserts.
Madam, my duty waits on you.   [*Exit.*
   Thamasta.   Come hither:—
"If ever henceforth I desire to thrive
In woman's favour, Kala is the first
Whom my ambition shall bend to." 'Twas so!
   Kala. These very words he spake.
   Thamasta.   These very words
Curse thee, unfaithful creature, to thy grave.
Thou woo'dst him for thyself?

Kala.   You said I should.

Thamasta. My name was never mentioned?

Kala.   Madam, no;
We were not come to that.

Thamasta.   Not come to that!
Art thou a rival fit to cross my fate?
Now poverty and a dishonest fame,
The waiting-woman's wages, be thy payment,
False, faithless, wanton beast! I'll spoil your marriage.[27]
There's not a page, a groom, nay, not a citizen
That shall be cast away upon ye, Kala;
I'll keep thee in my service all thy lifetime,
Without hope of a husband or a suitor.

    Kala. I have not verily deserved this cruelty.

    Thamasta. Parthenophil shall know, if he respect
My birth, the danger of a fond [28] neglect.   [*Exit.*

    Kala. Are you so quick? Well, I may chance to cross
Your peevishness. Now, though I never meant
The young man for myself, yet, if he love me,
I'll have him, or I'll run away with him;
And let her do her worst then! What! we're all
But flesh and blood; the same thing that will do
My lady good will please her woman too.   [*Exit.*

SCENE II—*An Apartment in the Castle*

Enter CLEOPHILA *and* TROLLIO.

Cleophila. Tread softly, Trollio; my father sleeps still.

Trollio. Ay, forsooth; but he sleeps like a hare, with his
eyes open, and that's no good sign.

Cleophila. Sure, thou art weary of this sullen living:
But I am not; for I take more content
In my obedience here than all delights
The time presents elsewhere.

Meleander. [*Within*] O!

Cleophila.   Dost hear that groan?

---

[27] "Carriage" in the old eds.
[28] Foolish.

Trollio. Hear it! I shudder: it was a strong blast, young mistress, able to root up heart, liver, lungs, and all.

Cleophila. My much-wronged father! let me view his face.

> [*Draws the arras:*[29] MELEANDER *discovered in a chair, sleeping.*

Trollio. Lady mistress, shall I fetch a barber to steal away his rough beard whiles he sleeps? In's naps he never looks in a glass—and 'tis high time, on conscience, for him to be trimmed; 'has not been under the shaver's hand almost these four years.

Cleophila. Peace, fool!

Trollio. [*Aside*] I could clip the old ruffian; there's hair enough to stuff all the great codpieces in Switzerland. 'A begins to stir; 'a stirs. Bless us, how his eyes roll!—A good year keep your lordship in your right wits, I beseech ye!

Meleander. Cleophila!

Cleophila. Sir, I am here; how d'ye, sir?

Trollio. Sir, is your stomach up yet? get some warm porridge in your belly; 'tis a very good settle-brain.

Meleander. The raven croaked, and hollow shrieks of owls
Sung dirges at her funeral; I laughed
The whiles, for 'twas no boot to weep. The girl
Was fresh and full of youth: but, O, the cunning
Of tyrants, that look big! their very frowns
Doom poor souls guilty ere their cause be heard.—
Good, what art thou?—and thou?

Cleophila.   I am Cleophila,
Your woeful daughter.

Trollio.   I am Trollio,
Your honest implement.

Meleander. I know ye both, 'Las, why d'ye use me thus?
Thy sister, my Eroclea, was so gentle,
That turtles in their down do feed more gall
Than her spleen mixed with: yet, when winds and storm
Drive dirt and dust on banks of spotless snow,
The purest whiteness is no such defence

---

[29] Arras was used precisely as a curtain: it hung (on tenters or lines) from the rafters, or from some temporary stay, and was opened, held up, or drawn aside, as occasion required.—*Gifford.*

Against the sullying foulness of that fury.
So raved Agenor, that great man, mischief
Against the girl: 'twas a politic trick!
We were too old in honour. I am lean,
And fall'n away extremely; most assuredly
I have not dined these three days.

 Cleophila.   Will you now, sir?

 Trollio. I beseech ye heartily, sir: I feel a horrible puking
myself.

 Meleander. Am I stark mad?

 Trollio. [*Aside*] No, no, you are but a little staring; there's
difference between staring and stark mad. You are but
whimsied yet; crotcheted, conumdrumed, or so.

 Meleander. Here's all my care; and I do often sigh
For thee, Cleophila; we are secluded
From all good people. But take heed; Amethus
Was son to Doryla, Agenor's sister;
There's some ill blood about him, if the surgeon
Have not been very skilful to let all out.

 Cleophila. I am, alas, too grieved to think of love;
That must concern me least.

 Meleander. Sirrah, be wise! be wise!

 Trollio. Who, I? I will be monstrous and wise immedi-
ately.

  Enter AMETHUS, MENAPHON, PARTHENOPHIL, *and*
       RHETIAS.

Welcome, gentlemen; the more the merrier. I'll lay the cloth,
and set the stools in a readiness, for I see here is some hope
of dinner now.   [*Exit.*

 Amethus. My Lord Meleander, Menaphon, your kinsman,
Newly returned from travel, comes to tender
His duty t'ye;—to you his love, fair mistress.

 Menaphon. I would I could as easily remove
Sadness from your remembrance, sir, as study
To do you faithful service.—My dear cousin,
All best of comforts bless your sweet obedience!

 Cleophila. One chief of 'em, my worthy cousin, lives
In you and your well-doing.

Menaphon.   This young stranger
Will well deserve your knowledge.
  Amethus.   For my friend's sake,
Lady, pray give him welcome.
  Cleophila.   He has met it,
If sorrows can look kindly.
  Parthenophil.   You much honour me.
  Rhetias. [*Aside*] How he eyes the company! sure my
passion will betray my weakness.—O my master, my noble
master, do not forget me; I am still the humblest and the
most faithful in heart of those that serve you.
  Meleander. Ha, ha, ha!
  Rhetias. [*Aside*] There's wormwood in that laughter; 'tis
the usher to a violent extremity.
  Meleander. I am a weak old man. All these are come
To jeer my ripe calamities.
  Menaphon.   Good uncle!
  Meleander. But I'll outstare ye all: fools, desperate fools!
You're cheated, grossly cheated; range, range on,
And roll about the world to gather moss,
The moss of honour, gay reports, gay clothes,
Gay wives, huge empty buildings, whose proud roofs
Shall with their pinnacles even reach the stars.
Ye work and work like moles, blind in the paths
That are bored through the crannies of the earth,
To charge your hungry souls with such full surfeits
As being gorged once, make ye lean with plenty;
And when ye've skimmed the vomit of your riots,
Ye're fat in no felicity but folly:
Then your last sleeps seize on ye; then the troops
Of worms crawl round and feast; good cheer, rich fare,
Dainty, delicious!—Here's Cleophila;
All the poor stock of my remaining thrift:
You, you, the prince's cousin, how d'ye like her?
Amethus, how d'ye like her?
  Amethus.   My intents
Are just and honourable.
  Menaphon.   Sir, believe him.
  Meleander. Take her.—We two must part; go to him do.

Parthenophil. This sight is full of horror.

Rhetias.   There is sense yet
In this distraction.

Meleander. In this jewel I have given away
All what I can call mine. When I am dead,
Save charge; let me buried in a nook:
No guns, no pompous whining; these are fooleries.
If, whiles we live, we stalk about the streets
Jostled by carmen, footposts, and fine apes
In silken coats, unminded and scarce thought on
It is not comely to be haled to the earth,
Like high-fed jades upon a tilting-day,
In antic trappings. Scorn to useless tears!
Eroclea was not coffined so; she perished,
And no eye dropped save mine—and I am childish:
I talk like one that dotes: laugh at me, Rhetias,
Or rail at me. They will not give me meat,
They've starved me; but I'll henceforth be mine own cook.
Good morrow! 'tis too early for my cares
To revel; I will break my heart a little,
And tell ye more hereafter. Pray be merry.   [*Exit.*

Rhetias. I'll follow him.—My Lord Amethus, use your
time respectively: few words to purpose soonest prevail:
study no long orations; be plain and short.—I'll follow him.
                                                      [*Exit.*

Amethus. Cleophila, although these blacker clouds
Of sadness thicken and make dark the sky
Of thy fair eyes, yet give me leave to follow
The stream of my affections: they are pure,
Without all mixture of unnoble thoughts.
Can you be ever mine?

Cleophila.   I am so low
In mine own fortunes and my father's woes,
That I want words to tell ye you deserve
A worthier choice.

Amethus.   But give me leave to hope.

Menaphon. My friend is serious.

Cleophila. Sir, this for answer. If I ever thrive
In any earthly happiness, the next
To my good father's wished recovery

Must be my thankfulness to your great merit,
Which I dare promise: for the present time
You cannot urge more from me.

 Meleander. [*Within*]   Ho, Cleophila!

 Cleophila. This gentleman is moved.

 Amethus.   Your eyes, Parthenophil,
Are guilty of some passion.[30]

 Menaphon.   Friend, what ails thee?

 Parthenophil. All is not well within me, sir.

 Meleander. [*Within*]   Cleophila!

 Amethus. Sweet maid, forget me not; we now must part.

 Cleophila. Still you shall have my prayer.

 Amethus.   Still you my truth.

               [*Exeunt.*

ACT THE THIRD

SCENE I—*A Room in the Palace*

Enter CUCULUS *and* GRILLA; *the former in a black velvet
cap and a white feather, with a paper in his hand.*

CUCULUS. Do not I look freshly, and like a youth of the
trim?

 Grilla. As rare an old youth as ever walked cross-gartered.

 Cuculus. Here are my mistresses mustered in white and
black. [*Reads*] "Kala, the waiting-woman"—I will first begin at the foot: stand thou for Kala.

 Grilla. I stand for Kala; do your best and your worst.

 Cuculus. I must look big, and care little or nothing for
her, because she is a creature that stands at livery. Thus I
talk wisely, and to no purpose:—Wench, as it is not fit that
thou shouldst be either fair or honest, so, considering thy
service, thou art as thou art, and so are thy betters, let them
be what they can be. Thus, in despite and defiance of all
thy good parts, if I cannot endure thy baseness, 'tis more out
of thy courtesy than my deserving; and so I expect thy
answer.

[30] Grief.

Grilla. I must confess—

Cuculus.   Well said.

Grilla.   You are—

Cuculus.   That's true too.

Grilla. To speak you right, a very scurvy fellow.

Cuculus, Away, away!—dost think so?

Grilla. A very foul-mouthed and misshapen coxcomb.

Cuculus. I'll never believe it, by this hand.

Grilla. A maggot, most unworthy to creep in
To the least wrinkle of a gentlewoman's—
What d'ye call—good conceit, or so, or what
You will else,—were you not refined by courtship
And education, which in my blear eyes
Makes you appear as sweet as any nosegay,
Or savoury cod of musk new fall'n from the cat.

Cuculus. This shall serve well enough for the waiting-woman. My next mistress is Cleophila, the old madman's daughter. I must come to her in whining tune; sigh, wipe mine eyes, fold my arms, and blubber out my speech as thus:—Even as a kennel of hounds, sweet lady, cannot catch a hare when they are full-paunched on the carrion of a dead horse; so, even so, the gorge of my affections being full-crammed with the garboils[31] of your condolements doth tickle me with the prick, as it were, about me, and fellow-feeling of howling outright.

Grilla. This will do't, if we will hear.

Cuculus. Thou seest I am crying ripe, I am such another tender-hearted fool.

Grilla. Even as the snuff of a candle that is burnt in the socket goes out, and leaves a strong perfume behind it; or as a piece of toasted cheese next the heart in a morning is a restorative for a sweet breath; so, even so, the odoriferous savour of your love doth perfume my heart—heigh-ho!—with the pure scent of an intolerable content, and not to be endured.

Cuculus. By this hand, 'tis excellent! Have at thee, last of all, for the Princess Thamasta, she that is my mistress indeed. She is abominably proud, a lady of a damnable high, turbulent, and generous spirit: but I have a loud-mouthed

[31] Tumult.

cannon of mine own to batter her, and a penned speech of
purpose: observe it.

Grilla. Thus I walk by, hear, and mind you not.

Cuculus. [*Reads*] "Though haughty as the devil or his
dam

Thou dost appear, great mistress, yet I am
Like to an ugly firework, and can mount
Above the region of thy sweet ac—count.
Wert thou the moon herself, yet having seen thee,
Behold the man ordained to move within thee."

Look to yourself, housewife! answer me in strong lines,
you're best.

Grilla. Keep off, poor fool, my beams will strike thee
blind;

Else, if thou touch me, touch me but behind.
In palaces, such as pass in before
Must be great princes; for at the back-door
Tatterdemalions wait, who know not how
To get admittance; such a one—art thou.

Cuculus. 'Sfoot, this is downright roaring.[32]

Grilla. I know how to present a big lady in her own cue.
But, pray, in earnest, are you in love with all these?

Cuculus. Pish! I have not a rag of love about me; 'tis
only a foolish humour I am possessed with, to be surnamed
the conqueror. I will court anything; be in love with nothing, nor no—thing.

Grilla. A rare man you are, I protest.

Cuculus. Yes, I know I am a rare man, and I ever held
myself so.

Enter PELIAS *and* CORAX.

Pelias. In amorous contemplation, on my life;
Courting his page, by Helicon!

Cuculus.   'Tis false.

Grilla. A gross untruth; I'll justify it, sir,
At any time, place, weapon.

Cuculus.   Marry, shall she.

Corax. No quarrels, Goody Whisk! lay-by your trum-
peries, and fall-to your practice. Instructions are ready for

[32] The quarrelsome language of the bullies of the day.

you all. Pelias is your leader; follow him: get credit now or
never. Vanish, doodles, vanish!

   Cuculus. For the device?

   Corax. The same; get ye gone, and make no bawling.

                          [*Exeunt all but* CORAX.

To waste my time thus, drone-like, in the court,
And lose so many hours as my studies
Have hoarded up, is to be like a man
That creeps both on his hands and knees to climb
A mountain's top; where, when he is ascended,
One careless slip down-tumbles him again
Into the bottom, whence he first began.
I need no prince's favour; princes need
My art: then, Corax, be no more a gull;
The best of 'em cannot fool thee, nay, they shall not.

Enter SOPHRONOS *and* ARETUS.

   Sophronos. We find him timely now; let's learn the cause.

   Aretus. 'Tis fit we should.—Sir, we approve you learned.
And, since your skill can best discern the humours
That are predominant in bodies subject
To alteration, tell us, pray, what devil
This Melancholy is, which can transform
Men into monsters.

   Corax.   You're yourself a scholar,
And quick of apprehension. Melancholy
Is not, as you conceive, indisposition
Of body, but the mind's disease. So Ecstasy,
Fantastic Dotage, Madness, Frenzy, Rapture
Of mere imagination, differ partly
From Melancholy;[33] which is briefly this,
A mere commotion of the mind, o'ercharged
With fear and sorrow; first begot i' the brain,
The seat of reason, and from thence derived
As suddenly into the heart, the seat
Of our affection.

   Aretus.   There are sundry kinds
Of this disturbance?

---

[33] *Vide* (Ford says) Democritus Junior. He is alluding to Burton's *Anatomy of
Melancholy.*

Corax.   Infinite: it were
More easy to conjecture every hour
We have to live than reckon up the kinds
Or causes of this anguish of the mind.

Sophronos. Thus you conclude that, as the cause is doubt-
     ful,
The cure must be impossible; and then
Our prince, poor gentleman, is lost for ever
As well unto himself as to his subjects.

Corax. My lord, you are too quick: thus much I dare
Promise and do; ere many minutes pass
I will discover whence his sadness is,
Or undergo the censure of my ignorance.

Aretus. You are a noble scholar.

Sophronos.   For reward
You shall make your own demand.

Corax.   May I be sure?

Aretus. We both will pledge our truth.

Corax.   'Tis soon performed:
That I may be discharged from my attendance
At court, and never more be sent for after;
Or—if I be, may rats gnaw all my books,
If I get home once, and come here again!
Though my neck stretch a halter for't, I care not.

Sophronos. Come, come, you shall not fear it.

Corax.   I'll acquaint ye
With what is to be done; and you shall fashion it.

                                        [*Exeunt.*

SCENE II—*A Room in* THAMASTA'S *House*

Enter KALA *and* PARTHENOPHIL.

Kala. My lady does expect ye, thinks all time
Too slow till you come to her: wherefore, young man,
If you intend to love me, and me only,
Before we part, without more circumstance,
Let us betroth ourselves.

Parthenophil.   I dare not wrong ye;—
You are too violent.

Kala.   Wrong me no more
Than I wrong you; be mine, and I am yours:
I cannot stand on points.
    Parthenophil.   Then, to resolve
All further hopes, you never can be mine,
Must not, and—pardon though I say—you shall not.
    Kala. [*Aside*] The thing is sure a gelding.—Shall not!
      Well,
You're best to prate unto my lady now,
What proffer I have made.
    Parthenophil.   Never, I vow.
    Kala. Do, do! 'tis but a kind heart of mine own,
And ill luck can undo me.—Be refused!
O scurvy!—Pray walk on, I'll overtake ye.
                    [*Exit* PARTHENOPHIL.
What a green-sinkness-livered boy is this!
My maidenhead will shortly grow so stale
That 'twill be mouldy:—but I'll mar her market.

Enter MENAPHON.

    Menaphon. Parthenophil passed this way: prithee, Kala,
Direct me to him.
    Kala.   Yes, I can direct ye;
But you, sir, must forbear.
    Menaphon.   Forbear!
    Kala.   I said so.
Your bounty has engaged my truth: receive
A secret, that will, as you are a man,
Startle your reason; 'tis but mere respect
Of what I owe to thankfulness. Dear sir,
The stranger whom your courtesy received
For friend is made your rival.
    Menaphon.   Rival, Kala!
Take heed; thou art too credulous.
    Kala.   My lady
Dotes on him. I will place you in a room
Where, though you cannot hear, yet you shall see
Such passages as will confirm the truth
Of my intelligence.

Menaphon.   'Twill make me mad.

Kala. Yes, yes.
It makes me mad too, that a gentleman
So excellently sweet, so liberal,
So kind, so proper, should be so betrayed
By a young smooth-chinned straggler: but for love's
          sake,
Bear all with manly courage. Not a word;
I am undone then.

Menaphon.   That were too much pity:
Honest, most honest Kala, 'tis thy care,
Thy serviceable care.

Kala.   You have even spoken
All can be said or thought.

Menaphon.   I will reward thee:
But as for him, ungentle boy, I'll whip
His falsehood with a vengeance.

Kala.   O, speak little.
Walk up these stairs; and take this key: it opens
A chamber-door, where, at that window yonder,
You may see all their courtship.

Menaphon.   I am silent.

Kala. As little noise as may be, I beseech ye:
There is a back-stair to convey ye forth
Unseen or unsuspected.   [*Exit* MENAPHON.
          He that cheats
A waiting-woman of a free good turn
She longs for must expect a shrewd revenge.
Sheep-spirited boy! although he had not married me,
He might have proffered kindness in a corner,
And ne'er have been the worse for't.—They are come:
On goes my set of faces most demurely.

Enter THAMASTA *and* PARTHENOPHIL.

Thamasta. Forbear the room.

Kala.   Yes, madam.

Thamasta.   Whosoever
Requires access to me, deny him entrance
Till I call thee; and wait without.

Kala.   I shall.—
Sweet Venus, turn his courage to a snow-ball;
I heartily beseech it!   [*Aside, and exit.*
    Thamasta.   I expose
The honour of my birth, my fame, my youth,
To hazard of much hard construction,
In seeking an adventure of a parley,
So private, with a stranger: if your thoughts
Censure me not with mercy, you may soon
Conceive I have laid by that modesty
Which should preserve a virtuous name unstained.
    Parthenophil. Lady,—to shorten long excuses,—time
And safe experience have so throughly armed
My apprehension with a real taste
Of your most noble nature, that to question
The least part of your bounties, or that freedom
Which heaven hath with a plenty made you rich in,
Would argue me uncivil;[34] which is more,
Base-bred; and, which is most of all, unthankful.
    Thamasta. The constant loadstone and the steel are found
In several mines; yet is there such a league
Between these minerals as if one vein
Of earth had nourished both. The gentle myrtle
Is not engraft upon an olive's stock,
Yet nature hath between them locked a secret
Of sympathy, that, being planted near,
They will, both in their branches and their roots,
Embrace each other: twines of ivy round
The well-grown oak; the vine doth court the elm;
Yet these are different plants. Parthenophil,
Consider this aright; then these slight creatures
Will fortify the reasons I should frame
For that ungrounded—as thou think'st—affection
Which is submitted to a stranger's pity.
True love may blush, when shame repents too late
But in all actions nature yields to fate.
    Parthenophil. Great lady, 'twere a dulness must exceed
The grossest and most sottish kind of ignorance
Not to be sensible of your intents;

---

[34] Ignorant of the language and manners of good society.

I clearly understand them. Yet so much
The difference between that height and lowness
Which doth distinguish our unequal fortunes
Dissuades me from ambition, that I am
Humbler in my desires than love's own power
Can any way raise up.

    Thamasta.   I am a princess,
And know no law of slavery; to sue,
Yet be denied!

    Parthenophil. I am so much a subject
To every law of noble honesty,
That to transgress the vows of perfect friendship
I hold a sacrilege as foul and cursed
As if some holy temple had been robbed,
And I the thief.

    Thamasta.   Thou art unwise, young man,
T' enrage a lioness.

    Parthenophil.   It were unjust
To falsify a faith, and ever after,
Disrobed of that fair ornament, live naked,
A scorn to time and truth.

    Thamasta.   Remember well
Who I am, and what thou art.

    Parthenophil.   That remembrance
Prompts me to worthy duty. O, great lady,
If some few days have tempted your free heart
To cast away affection on a stranger;
If that affection have so overswayed
Your judgment, that it, in a manner, hath
Declined your sovereignty of birth and spirit;
How can ye turn your eyes off from that glass
Wherein you may new-trim and settle right
A memorable name?

    Thamasta.   The youth is idle.[35]

    Parthenophil. Days, months, and years are passed since
         Menaphon
Hath loved and served you truly; Menaphon,
A man of no large distance in his blood
From yours; in qualities desertful, graced

[35] *i.e.* Talks idly.

With youth, experience, every happy gift
That can by nature or by education
Improve a gentleman: for him, great lady,
Let me prevail, that you will yet at last
Unlock the bounty which your love and care
Have wisely treasured up, t'enrich his life.

 Thamasta. Thou hast a moving eloquence, Partheno-
   phil!—
Parthenophil, in vain we strive to cross
The destiny that guides us. My great heart
Is stooped so much beneath that wonted pride
That first disguised it, that I now prefer
A miserable life with thee before
All other earthly comforts.

 Parthenophil.   Menaphon,
By me, repeats the self-same words to you:
You are too cruel, if you can distrust
His truth or my report.

 Thamasta.   Go where thou wilt,
I'll be an exile with thee; I will learn
To bear all change of fortunes.

 Parthenophil.   For my friend
I plead with grounds of reason.

 Thamasta.   For thy love,
Hard-hearted youth, I here renounce all thoughts
Of other hopes, of other entertainments,—

 Parthenophil. Stay, as you honour virtue.

 Thamasta.   When the proffers
Of other greatness,—

 Parthenophil. Lady!

 Thamasta.   When entreats
Of friends,—

 Parthenophil. I'll ease your grief.

 Thamasta.   Respect of kindred,—

 Parthenophil. Pray, give me hearing.

 Thamasta.   Loss of fame,—

 Parthenophil.   I crave
But some few minutes.

 Thamasta.   Shall infringe my vows,
Let heaven,—

Parthenophil. My love speaks t'ye: hear, then go on.

Thamasta. Thy love! why, 'tis a charm to stop a vow
In its most violent course.

Parthenophil.   Cupid has broke
His arrows here; and, like a child unarmed,
Comes to make sport between us with no weapon
But feathers stolen from his mother's doves.

Thamasta. This is mere trifling.

Parthenophil.   Lady, take a secret.
I am as you are—in a lower rank,
Else of the self-same sex—a maid, a virgin.
And now, to use your own words, "if your thoughts
Censure me not with mercy, you may soon
Conceive I have laid by that modesty
Which should preserve a virtuous name unstained."

Thamasta. Are you not mankind, then?

Parthenophil.   When you shall read
The story of my sorrows, with the change
Of my misfortunes, in a letter printed [36]
From my unforged relation, I believe
You will not think the shedding of one tear
A prodigality that misbecomes
Your pity and my fortune.

Thamasta.   Pray, conceal
The errors of my passion.

Parthenophil.   Would I had
Much more of honour—as for life, I value't not—
To venture on your secrecy!

Thamasta.   It will be
A hard task for my reason to relinquish
The affection which was once devoted thine
I shall awhile repute thee still the youth
I loved so dearly.

Parthenophil. You shall find me ever
Your ready faithful servant.

Thamasta.   O, the powers
Who do direct our hearts laugh at our follies!
We must not part yet.

---

[36] "Printed" was used in the sense merely of "recorded."

Parthenophil.   Let not my unworthiness
Alter your good opinion.
    Thamasta.   I shall henceforth
Be jealous of thy company with any:
My fears are strong and many.

Re-enter KALA.

Kala.   Did your ladyship
Call me?
    Thamasta. For what?
    Kala.   Your servant Menaphon
Desires admittance.

Enter MENAPHON.

Menaphon.   With your leave, great mistress,
I come,—So private! is this well, Parthenophil?
    Parthenophil. Sir, noble sir,—
    Menaphon.   You are unkind and treacherous;
This 'tis to trust a straggler!
    Thamasta.   Prithee, servant,—
    Menaphon. I dare not question you; you are my mistress,
My prince's nearest kinswoman: but he—
    Thamasta. Come, you are angry.
    Menaphon.   Henceforth I will bury
Unmanly passion in perpetual silence:
I'll court mine own distraction, dote on folly,
Creep to the mirth and madness of the age,
Rather than be so slaved again to woman,
Which in her best of constancy is steadiest
In change and scorn.
    Thamasta.   How dare ye talk to me thus?
    Menaphon. Dare! Were you not own sister to my friend,
Sister to my Amethus, I would hurl ye
As far off from mine eyes as from my heart;
For I would never more look on ye. Take
Your jewel t'ye!—And, youth, keep under wing,
Or—boy!—boy!—
    Thamasta.   If commands be of no force,
Let me entreat thee, Menaphon.
    Menaphon.   'Tis naught.

Fie, fie, Parthenophil! have I deserved
To be thus used?

Parthenophil.   I do protest—

Menaphon.   You shall not:
Henceforth I will be free, and hate my bondage.

Enter AMETHUS.

Amethus. Away, away to court! The prince is pleased
To see a masque to-night; we must attend him:
'Tis near upon the time.—How thrives your suit?

Menaphon. The judge, your sister, will decide it shortly.

Thamasta. Parthenophil, I will not trust you from me.

[*Exeunt.*

SCENE III—*A Room in the Palace*

Enter PALADOR, SOPHRONOS, ARETUS, *and* CORAX;
Servants *with torches.*

Corax. Lights and attendance!—I will show your high-
ness
A trifle of mine own brain. If you can,
Imagine you were now in the university,
You'll take it well enough; a scholar's fancy,
A quab—'tis nothing else—a very quab.[37]

Palador. We will observe it.

Sophronos.   Yes, and grace it too, sir,
For Corax else is humorous and testy.

Aretus. By any means; men singular in art
Have always some odd whimsey more than usual.

Palador. The name of this conceit?

Corax.   Sir, it is called
The Masque of Melancholy.[38]

---

[37] An unfledged bird, a nestling: metaphorically, anything in an imperfect, unfinished state. In the first sense the word is still used in that part of Devonshire
where Ford was born, and perhaps in many other places.—It is undoubtedly
(among other things) a small fish of some kind; but I have given it a meaning
more familiar to me, as I am persuaded it was to Ford.—*Gifford.*

[38] Ford has here introduced one of those interludes in which the old stage so
much delighted. The various characters of these "apish frenzies," as he calls them,
he has taken from Burton's *Anatomy of Melancholy,* the book to which he
refers in a former scene. He cannot be said to have improved what he has borrowed, which, on the contrary, reads better in Burton's pages than his own.—
Gifford.

Aretus.   We must look for
Nothing but sadness here, then.
    Corax.   Madness rather
In several changes. Melancholy is
The root as well of every apish frenzy,
Laughter, and mirth, as dulness. Pray, my lord,
Hold, and observe the plot [*Gives* PALADOR *a paper*]: 'tis
        there expressed
In kind, what shall be now expressed in action.

Enter AMETHUS, MENAPHON, THAMASTA, *and* PAR-
                        THENOPHIL.

No interruption; take your places quickly;
Nay, nay, leave ceremony.—Sound to the entrance!
                                            [*Flourish.*

Enter RHETIAS, *his face whited, with black shag hair and
        long nails, and with a piece of raw meat.*

Rhetias. Bow, bow! wow, wow! the moon's eclipsed; I'll
to the churchyard and sup. Since I turned wolf, I bark, and
howl, and dig up graves: I will never have the sun shine
again: 'tis midnight, deep dark midnight,—get a prey, and
fall to—I have catched thee now—Arre!—
    Corax. This kind is called Lycanthropia, sir; when men
conceive themselves wolves.[39]
    Palador. Here I find it.   [*Looking at the paper.*

Enter PELIAS, *with a crown of feathers and anticly rich.*

Pelias. I will hang 'em all, and burn my wife. Was I not
an emperor? my hand was kissed, and ladies lay down before me; in triumph did I ride with my nobles about me till
the mad dog bit me: I fell, and I fell, and I fell. It shall be
treason by statute for any man to name water, or wash his
hands, throughout all my dominions. Break all the looking-
glasses; I will not see my horns: my wife cuckolds me; she is
a whore, a whore, a whore, a whore!

---

[39] "Lycanthropia, which Avicenna calls *Cucubuth*, others *Lupinam insaniam* or
Wolf-madness, when men run howling about graves and fields in the night,
and will not be perswaded but that they are Wolves, or some such beasts," &c.—
Anat. of Mel.

Palador. Hydrophobia[40] term you this?

Corax. And men possessed so shun all sight of water:
Sometimes, if mixed with jealousy, it renders them
Incurable, and oftentimes brings death.

Enter a Philosopher *in black rags, with a copper chain,
an old gown half off, and a book.*

Philosopher. Philosophers dwell in the moon. Speculation
and theory girdle the world about like a wall. Ignorance, like
an atheist, must be damned in the pit. I am very, very poor,
and poverty is the physic for the soul: my opinions are pure
and perfect. Envy is a monster, and I defy the beast.

Corax. Delirium this is called, which is mere dotage,[41]
Sprung from ambition first and singularity,
Self-love, and blind opinion of true merit.

Palador. I not dislike the course.

Enter GRILLA, *in a rich gown, a great farthingale, a great
ruff, a muff, a fan, and a coxcomb*[42] *on her head.*

Grilla. Yes forsooth, and no forsooth; is not this fine? I
pray your blessing, gaffer. Here, here, here—did he give me a
shough,[43] and cut off's tail! Buss, buss, nuncle, and there's a
pum for daddy.

Corax. You find this noted there phrenitis.[44]

---

[40] Hydrophobia is a kind of madness, well known in every village, which comes
by the biting of a mad dog, or scratching, saith Aurelianus; touching, or smelling
alone sometimes, as Sckenkius proves. . . . so called, because the parties affected
cannot endure the sight of water, or any liquor, supposing still they see a mad
dog in it. And which is more wonderful, though they be very dry (as in this
malady they are), they will rather dye than drink."—*Anat. of Mel.*

[41] "*Dotage*, Fatuity, or Folly, is a common name to all the following species, as
some will have it. Laurentius and Altomarus comprehended Madness, Melancholy,
and the rest under this name, and call it the *summum genus* of them all. If it
be distinguished from them, it is *natural* or *ingenite*, which comes by some
defect of the organs, and over-much brain, as we see in our common fools; and
is for the most part intended or remitted in particular men, and thereupon some
are wiser than other; or else it is acquisite, an appendix or symptome of some
other disease, which comes or goes; or if it continue, a sign of Melancholy itself."
—*Anat. of Mel.*

[42] A fool's cap.

[43] A shock-dog, a water spaniel.

[44] "Phrenitis, which the Greeks derive from the word φϱὴν, is a disease of the
mind, with a continual madness or dotage, which hath an acute fever annexed, or
else an inflammation of the brain, or the membranes or kells of it, with an
acute feaver, which causeth madness and dotage. It differs from Melancholy and
Madness, because their dotage is without an ague: this continual, with waking, or
memory decayed, &c. Melancholy is most part silent, this clamorous; and many
such like differences are assigned by physitians."—*Anat. of Mel.*

Palador.   True.

Corax. Pride is the ground on't; it reigns most in women.

Enter CUCULUS *like a* Bedlam, *singing.*

Cuculus. They that will learn to drink a health in hell
           Must learn on earth to take tobacco well,
           To take tobacco well, to take tobacco well;
           For in hell they drink nor wine nor ale nor beer,
           But fire and smoke and stench, as we do here.

Rhetias. I'll swoop thee up.

Pelias.   Thou'st straight to execution.

Grilla. Fool, fool, fool! catch me an thou canst.

Philosopher. Expel him the house; 'tis a dunce.

Cuculus. [*Sings*]
                        Hark! did ye not hear a rumbling?
                        The goblins are now a tumbling:
                        I'll tear 'em, I'll sear 'em,
                        I'll roar 'em, I'll gore 'em!
                        Now, now, now! my brains are a
                                jumbling,—
Bounce! the gun's off.

Palador. You name this here hypochondriacal? [45]

Corax. Which is a windy flatuous humour, stuffing
The head, and thence derived to the animal parts.
To be too over-curious, loss of goods
Or friends, excess of fear, or sorrows cause it.

Enter a Sea-Nymph *big-bellied, singing and dancing.*

Nymph. Good your honours,
          Pray your worships,
          Dear your beauties,—

Cuculus. Hang thee!
           To lash your sides,
           To tame your hides,
           To scourge your prides;
           And bang thee.

Nymph. We're pretty and dainty, and I will begin:

---

[45] "The third [species of melancholy] ariseth from the bowels, liver, spleen, or membrane called mesenterium, named Hypochondriacal or windy Melancholy," &c. —*Anat. of Mel.*

    See, how they do jeer me, deride me, and grin!
    Come sport me, come court me, your topsail
        advance,
      And let us conclude our delights in a dance!
  All. A dance, a dance, a dance!
  Corax. This is the Wanton Melancholy. Women
With child, possessed with this strange fury, often
Have danced three days together without ceasing.[46]
  Palador. 'Tis very strange: but Heaven is full of miracles.

    [*A Dance, after which the* Masquers *run out in couples.*

We are thy debtor, Corax, for the gift
Of this invention; but the plot deceives us:
What means this empty space?   [*Pointing to the paper.*
  Corax.   One kind of Melancholy
Is only left untouched: 'twas not in art
To personate the shadow of that fancy;
'Tis named Love-Melancholy. As, for instance,
Admit this stranger here,—young man, stand forth—
                        [*To* PARTHENOPHIL.
Entangled by the beauty of this lady,
The great Thamasta, cherished in his heart
The weight of hopes and fears; it were impossible
To limn his passions in such lively colours
As his own proper sufferance could express.
  Parthenophil. You are not modest, sir.
  Thamasta.   Am I your mirth?
  Corax. Love is the tyrant of the heart; it darkens
Reason, confounds discretion; deaf to counsel,
It runs a headlong course to desperate madness.
O, were your highness but touched home and throughly
With this—what shall I call it—devil—
  Palador.   Hold!

---

[46] "*Chorus Sancti Viti,* or S. Vitus' dance; the lascivious dance Paracelsus calls it, because they that are taken with it can do nothing but dance till they be dead or cured. It is so called, for that the parties so troubled were wont to go to S. Vitus for help, and after they had danced there a while, they were certainly freed. 'Tis strange to hear how long they will dance, and in what manner, over stools, forms, tables; even great-bellied women sometimes (and yet never hurt their children) will dance so long that they can stir neither hand nor foot, but seem to be quite dead."—*Anat. of Mel.*

Let no man henceforth name the word again.—

Wait you my pleasure, youth.—'Tis late; to rest! [*Exit.*

   Corax. My lords,—

   Sophronos.   Enough; thou art a perfect arts-man.

   Corax. Panthers may hide their heads, not change the skin;

And love pent ne'er so close, yet will be seen. [*Exeunt.*

ACT THE FOURTH

SCENE I—*A Room in* THAMASTA'S *House*

Enter AMETHUS *and* MENAPHON.

AMETHUS. Dote on a stranger?

   Menaphon.   Court him; plead, and sue to him.

   Amethus. Affectionately?

   Menaphon.   Servilely; and pardon me

If I say basely.

   Amethus.   Women, in their passions,

Like false fires, flash, to fright our trembling senses,

Yet in themselves contain nor light nor heat.

My sister do this! she, whose pride did scorn

All thoughts that were not busied on a crown,

To fall so far beneath her fortunes now!—

You are my friend.

   Menaphon.   What I confirm is truth.

   Amethus. Truth, Menaphon?

   Menaphon.   If I conceived you were

Jealous of my sincerity and plainness,

Then, sir,—

   Amethus. What then, sir?

   Menaphon.   I would then resolve

You were as changeable in vows of friendship

As is Thamasta in her choice of love:

That sin is double, running in a blood,

Which justifies another being worse.

   Amethus. My Menaphon, excuse me; I grow wild,

And would not willingly believe the truth

Of my dishonour: she shall know how much
I am a debtor to thy noble goodness
By checking the contempt her poor desires
Have sunk her fame in. Prithee tell me, friend,
How did the youth receive her?

Menaphon.   With a coldness
As modest and as hopeless as the trust
I did repose in him could wish or merit.

Amethus. I will esteem him dearly.

Enter THAMASTA *and* KALA.

Menaphon.   Sir, your sister.

Thamasta. Servant, I have employment for ye.

Amethus.   Hark ye!
The mask of your ambition is fall'n off;
Your pride hath stooped to such an abject lowness,
That you have now discovered to report
Your nakedness in virtue, honours, shame,—

Thamasta. You are turned satire.[47]

Amethus.   All the flatteries
Of greatness have exposed ye to contempt.

Thamasta. This is mere railing.

Amethus.   You have sold your birth
For lust.

Thamasta. Lust!

Amethus.   Yes; and at a dear expense
Purchased the only glories of a wanton.

Thamasta. A wanton!

Amethus.   Let repentance stop your mouth;
Learn to redeem your fault.

Kala. [*Aside to* MENAPHON.] I hope your tongue
Has not betrayed my honesty.

Menaphon. [*Aside to* KALA.] Fear nothing.

Thamasta. If, Menaphon, I hitherto have strove
To keep a wary guard about my fame;
If I have used a woman's skill to sift
The constancy of your protested love;
You cannot, in the justice of your judgment,
Impute that to a coyness or neglect,

---

[47] Satirist.

Which my discretion and your service aimed
For noble purposes.

   Menaphon.   Great mistress, no.
I rather quarrel with mine own ambition,
That durst to soar so high as to feed hope
Of any least desert that might entitle
My duty to a pension from your favours.

   Amethus. And therefore, lady,—pray, observe him well,—
He henceforth covets plain equality;
Endeavouring to rank his fortunes low,
With some fit partner, whom, without presumption,
Without offence or danger, he may cherish,
Yes, and command too, as a wife,—a wife,
A wife, my most great lady!

   Kala. [*Aside*]   All will out.

   Thamasta. Now I perceive the league of amity,
Which you have long between ye vowed and kept,
Is sacred and inviolable; secrets
Of every nature are in common to you.
I have trespassed, and I have been faulty;
Let not too rude a censure deem me guilty,
Or judge my error wilful without pardon.

   Menaphon. Gracious and virtuous mistress!

   Amethus.   'Tis a trick;
There is no trust in female cunning, friend.
Let her first purge her follies past, and clear
The wrong done to her honour, by some sure
Apparent testimony of her constancy;
Or we will not believe these childish plots:
As you respect my friendship, lend no ear
To a reply.—Think on't!

   Menaphon.   Pray, love your fame.

                    [*Exeunt* MENAPHON *and* AMETHUS.

   Thamasta. Gone! I am sure awaked. Kala, I find
You have not been so trusty as the duty
You owed required.

   Kala.   Not I? I do protest
I have been, madam.

   Thamasta.   Be—no matter what,
I'm paid in my own coin; something I must,

And speedily.—So!—Seek out Cuculus;
Bid him attend me instantly.
    Kala.   That antic!
The trim old youth shall wait ye.
    Thamasta. Wounds may be mortal, which are wounds
        indeed;
But no wound's deadly till our honours bleed.   [*Exeunt.*

SCENE II—*A Room in the Castle*

Enter RHETIAS *and* CORAX.

    Rhetias. Thou'rt an excellent fellow. Diabolo! O these
lousy close-stool empirics, that will undertake all cures, yet
know not the causes of any disease! Dog-leeches! [48] By the
four elements, I honour thee; could find in my heart to turn
knave, and be thy flatterer.

    Corax. Sirrah, 'tis pity thou'st not been a scholar;
Thou'rt honest, blunt, and rude enough, o' conscience.
But for thy lord now, I have put him to't.

    Rhetias. He chafes hugely, fumes like a stew-pot: is he
not monstrously overgone in frenzy?

    Corax. Rhetias, 'tis not a madness, but his sorrows—
Close-griping grief and anguish of the soul—
That torture him; he carries hell on earth
Within his bosom: 'twas a prince's tyranny
Caused his distraction; and a prince's sweetness
Must qualify that tempest of his mind.

    Rhetias. Corax, to praise thy art were to assure
The misbelieving world that the sun shines
When 'tis i' the full meridian of his beauty:
No cloud of black detraction can eclipse
The light of thy rare knowledge. Henceforth, casting
All poor disguises off, that play in rudeness,
Call me your servant; only for the present,
I wish a happy blessing to your labours.
Heaven crown your undertakings! and believe me,
Ere many hours can pass, at our next meeting,
The bonds my duty owes shall be full cancelled.

---

[48] Dog-doctors.

Corax. Farewell　　　　　　　　　　　　　　[*Exit* RHETIAS.
　　　　　　　　A shrewd-brained whoreson; there is pith
In his untoward plainness.

　　　　　Enter TROLLIO, *with a morion*[49] *on.*

　　　　　　　　　Now, the news?

Trollio. Worshipful Master Doctor, I have a great deal of I
cannot tell what to say t'ye. My lord thunders; every word
that comes out of his mouth roars like a cannon; the house
shook once:—my young lady dares not be seen.

Corax. We will roar with him, Trollio, if he roar.

Trollio. He has got a great poleaxe in his hand, and fences
it up and down the house, as if he were to make room for
the pageants. I have provided me a morion for fear of a
clap on the coxcomb.

Corax. No matter for the morion; here's my cap:
Thus I will pull it down, and thus outstare him.
　　　　　　　[*He produces a frightful mask and headpiece.*

Trollio. [*Aside*] The physician is got as mad as my lord.
—O brave! a man of worship.

Corax. Let him come, Trollio. I will firk his trangdido,
and bounce and bounce in metal, honest Trollio.

Trollio. [*Aside*] He vapours like a tinker, and struts like
a juggler.

Meleander. [*Within*] So ho, so ho!

Trollio. There, there, there! look to your right worshipful,
look to yourself.

　　　　　Enter MELEANDER *with a poleaxe.*

Meleander. Show me the dog whose triple-throated noise
Hath roused a lion from his uncouth den
To tear the cur in pieces.

Corax. [*Putting on his mask, and turning to* MELEANDER.
　　　　　　　　　Stay thy paws,
Courageous beast; else, lo, the Gorgon's skull,
That shall transform thee to that restless stone
Which Sisyphus rolls up against the hill,
Whence, tumbling down again, it with his weight
Shall crush thy bones and puff thee into air.

49 A helmet.

Meleander. Hold, hold thy conquering breath; 'tis stronger
    far
Than gunpowder and garlic. If the fates
Have spun my thread, and my spent clue of life
Be now untwisted, let us part like friends.—
Lay up my weapon, Trollio, and be gone.
    Trollio. Yes, sir, with all my heart.
    Meleander.   This friend and I
Will walk, and gabble wisely.

                        [*Exit* TROLLIO *with the poleaxe.*
    Corax.   I allow
The motion; on!   [*Takes off his mask.*
    Meleander.   So politicians thrive,
That, with their crabbèd faces and sly tricks,
Legerdemain, ducks, cringes, formal beards,
Crisped hairs, and punctual cheats, do wriggle in
Their heads first, like a fox, to rooms of state,
Then the whole body follows.
    Corax.   Then they fill
Lordships; steal women's hearts; with them and theirs
The world runs round; yet these are square[50] men still.
    Meleander. There are none poor but such as engross offices.
    Corax. None wise but unthrifts, bankrupts, beggars, ras-
        cals.
    Meleander. The hangman is a rare physician.
    Corax. [*Aside*] That's not so good.—It shall be granted.
    Meleander.   All
The buzz of drugs and minerals and simples,
Bloodlettings, vomits, purges, or what else
Is conjured up by men of art, to gull
Liege-people, and rear golden piles, are trash
To a strong well-wrought halter; there the gout,
The stone, yes, and the melancholy devil,
Are cured in less time than a pair of minutes:
Build me a gallows in this very plot,
And I'll dispatch your business.
    Corax.   Fix the knot
Right under the left ear.
    Meleander.   Sirrah, make ready.

⁵⁰ Honest.

Corax. Yet do not be too sudden; grant me leave
To give a farewell to a creature long
Absented from me: 'tis a daughter, sir,
Snatched from me in her youth, a handsome girl;
She comes to ask a blessing.

Meleander.   Pray, where is she?
I cannot see her yet.

Corax.   She makes more haste
In her quick prayers than her trembling steps,
Which many griefs have weakened.

Meleander.   Cruel man!
How canst thou rip a heart that's cleft already
With injuries of time?—Whilst I am frantic,
Whilst throngs of rude divisions huddle on,
And do disrank my brains from peace and sleep,
So long—I am insensible of cares.
As balls of wildfire may be safely touched,
Not violently sundered and thrown up;
So my distempered thoughts rest in their rage,
Not hurried in the air of repetition,
Or memory of my mistfortunes past:
Then are my griefs struck home, when they're reclaimed
To their own pity of themselves.—Proceed;
What of your daughter now?

Corax.   I cannot tell ye,
'Tis now out of my head again; my brains
Are crazy; I have scarce slept one sound sleep
These twelve months.

Meleander.   'Las, poor man! canst thou imagine
To prosper in the task thou tak'st in hand
By practising a cure upon my weakness,
And yet be no physician for thyself?
Go, go, turn over all thy books once more,
And learn to thrive in modesty; for impudence
Does least become a scholar. Thou'rt a fool,
A kind of learnèd fool.

Corax.   I do confess it.

Meleander. If thou canst wake with me, forget to eat,
Renounce the thought of greatness, tread on fate,
Sigh out a lamentable tale of things

Done long ago, and ill done; and, when sighs
Are wearied, piece up what remains behind
With weeping eyes, and hearts that bleed to death;
Thou shalt be a companion fit for me,
And we will sit together, like true friends,
And never be divided. With what greediness
Do I hug my afflictions! there's no mirth
Which is not truly seasoned with some madness:
As, for example,—   [*Exit hastily.*

   Corax.   What new crotchet next?
There is so much sense in this wild distraction,
That I am almost out of my wits too,
To see and hear him: some few hours more
Spent here would turn me apish, if not frantic.

Re-enter MELEANDER *with* CLEOPHILA.

   Meleander. In all the volumes thou hast turned, thou man
Of knowledge, hast thou met with any rarity,
Worthy thy contemplation, like to this?
The model of the heavens, the earth, the waters,
The harmony and sweet consent of times,
Are not of such an excellence, in form
Of their creation, as the infinite wonder
That dwells within the compass of this face:
And yet I tell thee, scholar, under this
Well-ordered sign is lodged such an obedience
As will hereafter, in another age,
Strike all comparison into a silence.
She had a sister too;—but as for her,
If I were given to talk, I could describe
A pretty piece of goodness—let that pass—
We must be wise sometimes. What would you with her?

   Corax. I with her! nothing, by your leave, sir, I;
It is not my profession.

   Meleander.   You are saucy,
And, as I take it, scurvy in your sauciness,
To use no more respect.—Good soul, be patient;
We are a pair of things the world doth laugh at:
Yet be content, Cleophila; those clouds,
Which bar the sun from shining on our miseries,

Will never be chased off till I am dead;
And then some charitable soul will take thee
Into protection: I am hasting on;
The time cannot be long.

 Cleophila.   I do beseech ye,
Sir, as you love your health, as you respect
My safety, let not passion[51] overrule you.

 Meleander. It shall not; I am friends with all the world.
Get me some wine; to witness that I will be
An absolute good fellow, I will drink with thee.

 Corax. [*Aside to* CLEOPHILA.] Have you prepared his cup?
 Cleophila. [*Aside to* CORAX.]   It is in readiness.

Enter CUCULUS *and* GRILLA.

 Cuculus. By your leave, gallants, I come to speak with a
young lady, as they say, the old Trojan's daughter of the
house.

 Meleander. Your business with my lady-daughter, toss-pot?
 Grilla. Toss-pot! O base! toss-pot!
 Cuculus. Peace! dost not see in what case he is?—I would
do my own commendations to her; that's all.

 Meleander. Do.—Come, my Genius, we will quaff in wine
Till we grow wise.

 Corax.   True nectar is divine.

           [*Exeunt* MELEANDER *and* CORAX.

 Cuculus. So! I am glad he is gone,—Page, walk aside.—
Sweet beauty, I am sent ambassador from the mistress of my
thoughts to you, the mistress of my desires.

 Cleophila. So, sir! I pray, be brief.

 Cuculus. That you may know I am not, as they say, an
animal, which is, as they say, a kind of cokes,[52] which is,
as the learned term it, an ass, a puppy, a widgeon, a dolt,
a noddy, a—

 Cleophila. As you please.

 Cuculus. Pardon me for that, it shall be as you please indeed: forsooth, I love to be courtly and in fashion.

 Cleophila. Well, to your embassy. What, and from whom?
 Cuculus. Marry, "What" is more than I know; for to

know what's what is to know what's what and for what's what:—but these are foolish figures and to little purpose.

Cleophila. From whom, then, are you sent?

Cuculus. There you come to me again. O, to be in the favour of great ladies is as much to say as to be great in ladies' favours.

Cleophila. Good time o'day t'ye! I can stay no longer.

Cuculus. By this light, but you must; for now I come to't. The most excellent, most wise, most dainty, precious, loving, kind, sweet, intolerably fair lady Thamasta commends to your little hands this letter of importance. By your leave, let me first kiss, and then deliver it in fashion to your own proper beauty. [*Delivers a letter.*

Cleophila. To me, from her? 'tis strange! I dare peruse it. [*Reads.*

Cuculus. Good.—O, that I had not resolved to live a single life! Here's temptation, able to conjure up a spirit with a witness. So, so! she has read it. [*Aside.*

Cleophila. Is't possible? Heaven, thou art great and bountiful.—

Sir, I much thank your pains; and to the princess
Let my love, duty, service, be remembered.

Cuculus. They shall mad-dam.

Cleophila. When we of hopes or helps are quite bereaven,
Our humble prayers have entrance into Heaven.

Cuculus. That's my opinion clearly and without doubt.

[*Exeunt.*

SCENE III—*A Room in the Palace*

Enter ARETUS *and* SOPHRONOS.

Aretus. The prince is throughly moved.

Sophronos.   I never saw him
So much distempered.

Aretus.   What should this young man be?
Or whither can he be conveyed?

Sophronos.   'Tis to me
A mystery; I understand it not.

Aretus.   Nor I.

Enter PALADOR, AMETHUS, *and* PELIAS.

Palador. Ye have consented all to work upon
The softness of my nature; but take heed:
Though I can sleep in silence, and look on
The mockery ye make of my dull patience,
Yet ye shall know, the best of ye, that in me
There is a masculine, a stirring spirit,
Which, once provoked, shall, like a bearded comet,
Set ye at gaze, and threaten horror.

   Pelias.   Good sir,—

   Palador. Good sir! 'tis not your active wit or language,
Nor your grave politic wisdoms, lords, shall dare
To check-mate and control my just commands.

Enter MENAPHON.

Where is the youth, your friend? is he found yet?

   Menaphon. Not to be heard of.

   Palador.   Fly, then, to the desert,
Where thou didst first encounter this fantastic,
This airy apparition; come no more
In sight! Get ye all from me: he that stays
Is not my friend.

   Amethus.   'Tis strange.

   Aretus. Sophronos.   We must obey.

                  [*Exeunt all but* PALADOR.

   Palador. Some angry power cheats with rare delusions
My credulous sense; the very soul of reason
Is troubled in me;—the physician
Presented a strange masque, the view of it
Puzzled my understanding; but the boy—

Enter RHETIAS.

Rhetias, thou art acquainted with my griefs:
Parthenophil is lost, and I would see him;
For he is like to something I remember
A great while since, a long, long time ago.

   Rhetias. I have been diligent, sir, to pry into every corner
for discovery, but cannot meet with him. There is some
trick, I am confident.

Palador. There is; there is some practice, sleight, or plot.

Rhetias. I have apprehended a fair wench in an odd private lodging in the city, as like the youth in face as can by possibility be discerned.

Palador. How, Rhetias!

Rhetias. If it be not Parthenophil in long-coats, 'tis a spirit in his likeness; answer I can get none from her: you shall see her.

Palador. The young man in disguise, upon my life,
To steal out of the land.

Rhetias.   I'll send him t'ye.

Palador. Do, do, my Rhetias.   [*Exit* RHETIAS.

                                   As there is by nature
In everything created contrariety,
So likewise is there unity and league
Between them in their kind: but man, the abstract
Of all perfection, which the workmanship
Of Heaven hath modelled, in himself contains
Passions of several qualities.

          [*Enter behind* EROCLEA (PARTHENOPHIL),
                    in female attire.

                                   The music
Of man's fair composition best accords
When 'tis in consort, not in single strains:
My heart has been untuned these many months
Wanting her presence, in whose equal love
True harmony consisted. Living here,
We are Heaven's bounty all, but Fortune's exercise.

Eroclea. Minutes are numbered by the fall of sands,
As by an hourglass; the span of time
Doth waste us to our graves, and we look on it:
An age of pleasures, revelled out, comes home
At last, and ends in sorrow; but the life,
Weary of riot, numbers every sand,
Wailing in sighs, until the last drop down;
So to conclude calamity in rest.

Palador. What echo yields a voice to my complaints?
Can I be nowhere private?

Eroclea. [*Comes forward, and kneels*] Let the substance
As suddenly be hurried from your eyes

As the vain sound can pass, sir, from your ear,
If no impression of a troth vowed yours
Retain a constant memory.

    Palador.   Stand up.   [*She rises.*
'Tis not the figure stamped upon thy cheeks,
The cozenage of thy beauty, grace or tongue,
Can draw from me a secret, that hath been
The only jewel of my speechless thoughts.

    Eroclea. I am so worn away with fears and sorrows,
So wintered with the tempests of affliction,
That the bright sun of your life-quickening presence
Hath scarce one beam of force to warm again
That spring of cheerful comfort, which youth once
Apparelled in fresh looks.

    Palador.   Cunning impostor!
Untruth hath made thee subtle in thy trade.
If any neighbouring greatness hath seduced
A free-born resolution to attempt
Some bolder act of treachery by cutting
My weary days off, wherefore, cruel-mercy,
Hast thou assumed a shape that would make treason
A piety, guilt pardonable, bloodshed
As holy as the sacrifice of peace?

    Eroclea. The incense of my love-desires are flamed
Upon an altar of more constant proof.
Sir, O, sir, turn me back into the world,
Command me to forget my name, my birth,
My father's sadness, and my death alive,
If all remembrance of my faith hath found
A burial without pity in your scorn!

    Palador. My scorn, disdainful boy, shall soon unweave
The web thy art hath twisted. Cast thy shape off,
Disrobe the mantle of a feignèd sex,
And so I may be gentle: as thou art,
There's witchcraft in thy language, in thy face,
In thy demeanours; turn, turn from me, prithee,
For my belief is armed else.—Yet, fair subtility,
Before we part,—for part we must,—be true:
Tell me, thy country.

    Eroclea.   Cyprus.

Palador.   Ha!—Thy father?

Eroclea. Meleander.

Palador.   Hast a name?

Eroclea.   A name of misery;
The unfortunate Eroclea.

Palador.   There is danger
In this seducing counterfeit. Great goodness,
Hath honesty and virtue left the time?
Are we become so impious, that to tread
The path of impudence is law and justice?—
Thou vizard of a beauty ever sacred,
Give me thy name.

Eroclea.   Whilst I was lost to memory
Parthenophil did shroud my shame in change
Of sundry rare misfortunes; but, since now
I am, before I die, returned to claim
A convoy to my grave, I must not blush
To let Prince Palador, if I offend,
Know, when he dooms me, that he dooms Eroclea:
I am that woful maid.

Palador.   Join not too fast
Thy penance with the story of my sufferings:—
So dwelt simplicity with virgin truth,
So martyrdom and holiness are twins,
As innocence and sweetness on thy tongue.
But, let me by degrees collect my senses;
I may abuse my trust. Tell me, what air
Hast thou perfumed, since tyranny first ravished
The contract of our hearts?

Eroclea.   Dear sir, in Athens
Have I been buried.

Palador.   Buried! Right; as I
In Cyprus.—Come to trial; if thou beest
Eroclea, in my bosom I can find thee.

Eroclea. As I, Prince Palador in mine: this gift
                              [*Shows him a tablet.*[53]
His bounty blessed me with, the only physic
My solitary cares have hourly took,
To keep me from despair.

---

[53] *i.e.* A miniature of the prince.

Palador.   We are but fools
To trifle in disputes, or vainly struggle
With that eternal mercy which protects us.
Come home, home to my heart, thou banished peace!
My ecstasy of joys would speak in passion,
But that I would not lose that part of man
Which is reserved to entertain content.
Eroclea, I am thine; O, let me seize thee
As my inheritance! Hymen shall now
Set all his torches burning, to give light
Throughout this land, new-settled in thy welcome.

Eroclea. You are still gracious, sir. How I have lived,
By what means been conveyed, by what preserved,
By what returned, Rhetias, my trusty servant,
Directed by the wisdom of my uncle,
The good Sophronos, can inform at large.

Palador. Enough. Instead of music, every night,
To make our sleeps delightful, thou shalt close
Our weary eyes with some part of thy story.

Eroclea. O, but my father!

Palador.   Fear not; to behold
Eroclea safe will make him young again:
It shall be our first task.—Blush, sensual follies,
Which are not guarded with thoughts chastely pure:
There is no faith in lust, but baits of arts;
'Tis virtuous love keeps clear contracted hearts.

                                          [*Exeunt.*

ACT THE FIFTH

SCENE I—*A Room in the Castle*

Enter CORAX *and* CLEOPHILA.

CORAX. 'Tis well, 'tis well; the hour is at hand,
Which must conclude the business, that no art
Could all this while make ripe for wished content.
O, lady, in the turmoils of our lives,
Men are like politic states, or troubled seas,

Tossed up and down with several storms and tempests,
Change and variety of wrecks and fortunes;
Till, labouring to the havens of our homes,
We struggle for the calm that crowns our ends.

Cleophila. A happy end Heaven bless us with!

Corax.   'Tis well said.
The old man sleeps still soundly.

Cleophila.   May soft dreams
Play in his fancy, that when he awakes,
With comfort he may, by degrees, digest
The present blessings in a moderate joy!

Corax. I drenched his cup to purpose; he ne'er stirred
At barber or at tailor. He will laugh
At his own metamorphosis, and wonder.—
We must be watchful. Does the couch stand ready?

Cleophila. All, all as you commanded.

Enter TROLLIO.

                                What's your haste for?

Trollio. A brace of big women, ushered by the young old
ape with his she-clog at his bum, are entered the castle.
Shall they come on?

Corax. By any means: the time is precious now.—Lady,
be quick and careful.—Follow, Trollio.   [*Exit.*

Trollio. I owe all sir-reverence to your right worshipful-
ness.   [*Exit.*

Cleophila. So many fears, so many joys encounter
My doubtful expectations, that I waver
Between the resolution of my hopes
And my obedience: 'tis not—O my fate!—
The apprehension of a timely blessing
In pleasures shakes my weakness; but the danger
Of a mistaken duty that confines
The limits of my reason. Let me live,
Virtue, to thee as chaste as truth to time!

Enter THAMASTA, *speaking to some one without.*

Thamasta. Attend me till I call.—My sweet Cleophila!

Cleophila. Great princess,—

Thamasta.   I bring peace, to sue a pardon

For my neglect of all those noble virtues
Thy mind and duty are apparelled with:
I have deserved ill from thee, and must say
Thou art too gentle, if thou canst forget it.

   Cleophila. Alas, you have not wronged me; for, indeed,
Acquaintance with my sorrows and my fortune
Were grown to such familiarity,
That 'twas an impudence, more than presumption,
To wish so great a lady as you are
Should lose affection on my uncle's son:
But that your brother, equal in your blood,
Should stoop to such a lowness as to love
A castaway, a poor despisèd maid,
Only for me to hope was almost sin;—
Yet, 'troth, I never tempted him.

   Thamasta.   Chide not
The grossness of my trespass, lovely sweetness,
In such an humble language; I have smarted
Already in the wounds my pride hath made
Upon your sufferings: henceforth 'tis in you
To work my happiness.

   Cleophila.   Call any service
Of mine a debt; for such it is. The letter
You lately sent me, in the blest contents
It made me privy to, hath largely quitted
Every suspicion of your grace or goodness.

   Thamasta. Let me embrace you with a sister's love,
A sister's love, Cleophila; for should
My brother henceforth study to forget
The vows that he hath made thee, I would ever
Solicit [54] thy deserts.

   Amethus. Menaphon. [*Within*] We must have entrance!

   Thamasta. Must! Who are they say *must*? you are unman-
      nerly.

Enter AMETHUS and MENAPHON.

Brother, is't you? and you too, sir?

   Amethus.   Your ladyship

---

[54] Plead.

Has had a time of scolding to your humour:
Does the storm hold still?

 Cleophila.   Never fell a shower
More seasonably gentle on the barren
Parched thirsty earth than showers of courtesy
Have from this princess been distilled on me,
To make my growth in quiet of my mind
Secure and lasting.

 Thamasta. You may both believe
That I was not uncivil.

 Amethus.   Pish! I know
Her spirit and her envy.

 Cleophila.   Now, in troth, sir,—
Pray credit me, I do not use to swear,—
The virtuous princess hath in words and carriage
Been kind, so over-kind, that I do blush
I am not rich enough in thanks sufficient
For her unequalled bounty.—My good cousin,
I have a suit to you.

 Menaphon. It shall be granted.

 Cleophila. That no time, no persuasion, no respects
Of jealousies, past, present, or hereafter
By possibility to be conceived,
Draw you from that sincerity and pureness
Of love which you have oftentimes protested
To this great worthy lady: she deserves
A duty more than what the ties of marriage
Can claim or warrant; be for ever hers,
As she is yours, and Heaven increase your comforts!

 Amethus. Cleophila hath played the churchman's part;
I'll not forbid the banns.

 Menaphon. Are you consented?

 Thamasta. I have one task in charge first, which concerns
  me.
Brother, be not more cruel than this lady;
She hath forgiven my follies, so may you.
Her youth, her beauty, innocence, discretion,
Without additions of estate or birth,
Are dower for a prince, indeed. You loved her;

For sure you swore you did: else, if you did not,
Here fix your heart; and thus resolve,[55] if now
You miss this heaven on earth, you cannot find
In any other choice aught but a hell.

   Amethus. The ladies are turned lawyers, and plead hand-
        somely
Their clients' cases: I'm an easy judge;
And so shalt thou be, Menaphon. I give thee
My sister for a wife; a good one, friend.

   Menaphon. Lady, will you confirm the gift?

   Thamasta.   The errors
Of my mistaken judgment being lost
To your remembrance, I shall ever strive
In my obedience to deserve your pity.

   Menaphon. My love, my care, my all!

   Amethus.   What rests for me?
I'm still a bachelor.—Sweet maid, resolve me,
May I yet call you mine?

   Cleophila.   My lord Amethus,
Blame not my plainness; I am young and simple,
And have not any power to dispose
Mine own will without warrant from my father;
That purchased, I am yours.

   Amethus.   It shall suffice me.

     Enter Cuculus, Pelias, *and* Trollio, *plucking in*
                    Grilla.

   Cuculus. Revenge! I must have revenge; I will have revenge, bitter and abominable revenge; I will have revenge.
This unfashionable mongrel, this linseywolsey of mortality
—by this hand, mistress, this she-rogue is drunk, and
clapper-clawed me, without any reverence to my person or
good garments.—Why d'ye not speak, gentlemen?

   Pelias. Some certain blows have passed, an't like your
        highness.

   Trollio. Some few knocks of friendship, some love-toys,
some cuffs in kindness, or so.

   Grilla. I'll turn him away; he shall be my master no
longer.

---

[55] *i.e.* Be certain.

Menaphon. Is this your she-page, Cuculus? 'tis a boy, sure.

Cuculus. A boy, an errant boy in long-coats.

Trollio. He has mumbled his nose, that 'tis as big as a great codpiece.

Cuculus. O, thou cock-vermin of iniquity!

Thamasta. Pelias, take hence the wag, and school him for't.—

For your part, servant, I'll entreat the prince
To grant you some fit place about his wardrobe.

Cuculus. Ever after a bloody nose do I dream of good luck.—I horribly thank your ladyship.—

Whilst I'm in office, the old garb shall agen
Grow in request, and tailors shall be men.—

Come, Trollio, help to wash my face, prithee.

Trollio. Yes, and to scour it too.

[*Exeunt* CUCULUS, TROLLIO, PELIAS, *and* GRILLA.

Re-enter CORAX *with* RHETIAS.

Rhetias. The prince and princess are at hand; give over
Your amorous dialogues.—Most honoured lady,
Henceforth forbear your sadness: are you ready
To practise your instructions?

Cleophila.   I have studied
My part with care, and will perform it, Rhetias,
With all the skill I can.

Corax.   I'll pass my word for her.

A flourish.—Enter PALADOR, SOPHRONOS, ARETUS, *and*
EROCLEA.

Palador. Thus princes should be circled, with a guard
Of truly noble friends and watchful subjects.
O, Rhetias, thou art just; the youth thou told'st me
That lived at Athens is returned at last
To her own fortunes and contracted love.

Rhetias. My knowledge made me sure of my report, sir.

Palador. Eroclea, clear thy fears; when the sun shines
Clouds must not dare to muster in the sky,
Nor shall they here.—

[CLEOPHILA *and* AMETHUS *kneel.*

Why do they kneel?—Stand up;

The day and place is privileged.

 Sophronos.   Your presence,
Great sir, makes every room a sanctuary.

 Palador. Wherefore does this young virgin use such circumstance
In duty to us?—Rise.

 Eroclea.   'Tis I must raise her.—[*Raises* CLEOPHILA.
Forgive me, sister, I have been too private,
In hiding from your knowledge any secret
That should have been in common 'twixt our souls;
But I was ruled by counsel.

 Cleophila.   That I show
Myself a girl, sister, and bewray
Joy in too soft a passion 'fore all these,
I hope you cannot blame me.

     [*Weeps, and falls into the arms of* EROCLEA.

 Palador.   We must part
The sudden meeting of these two fair rivulets
With the island of our arms. [*Embraces* EROCLEA]—Cle-
The custom of thy piety hath built,   [ophila,
Even to thy younger years, a monument
Of memorable fame: some great reward
Must wait on thy desert.

 Sophronos.   The prince speaks t'ye, niece.

 Corax. Chat low, I pray; let us about our business.
The good old man awakes.—My lord, withdraw.—
Rhetias, let's settle here the couch

 Palador.   Away, then! [*Exeunt.*

Soft music.—Re-enter CORAX *and* RHETIAS *with* MELEANDER
*asleep on a couch, his hair and beard trimmed, habit and
gown changed. While they are placing the couch, a* Boy
sings without.

SONG.

Fly hence, shadows, that do keep
Watchful sorrows charmed in sleep!
Though the eyes be overtaken,
Yet the heart doth ever waken
Thoughts, chained up in busy snares
Of continual woes and cares:

Love and grief are so exprest
As they rather sigh than rest.
Fly hence, shadows, that do keep
Watchful sorrows charmed in sleep!

Meleander. [*Awakes*] Where am I? ha! What sounds are
    these? 'Tis day, sure.
O. I have slept belike; 'tis but the foolery
Of some beguiling dream. So, so! I will not
Trouble the play of my delighted fancy,
But dream my dream out.
    Corax.   Morrow to your lordship!
You took a jolly nap, and slept it soundly.
    Meleander. Away, beast! let me alone.
                                [*The music ceases.*
    Corax.   O, by your leave, sir,
I must be bold to raise ye; else your physic
Will turn to further sickness.
                        [*He assists* MELEANDER *to sit up.*
    Meleander.   Physic, bear-leech? [56]
    Corax. Yes, physic; you are mad.
    Meleander. Trollio! Cleophila!
    Rhetias.   Sir, I am here.
    Meleander. I know thee, Rhetias; prithee rid the room
Of this tormenting noise. He tells me, sirrah,
I have took physic, Rhetias; physic, physic!
    Rhetias. Sir, true, you have; and this most learnèd scholar
Applied 't ye. O, you were in dangerous plight
Before he took ye in hand.
    Meleander.   These things are drunk,
Directly drunk.—Where did you get your liquor?
    Corax. I never saw a body in the wane
Of age so overspread with several sorts
Of such diseases as the strength of youth
Would groan under and sink.
    Rhetias.   The more your glory
In the miraculous cure.
    Corax.   Bring me the cordial
Prepared for him to take after his sleep;
'Twill do him good at heart.

[56] *i.e.* Bear-doctor.

Rhetias.   I hope it will, sir.   [*Exit.*

Meleander. What dost thou think I am, that thou shouldst
                                                      fiddle
So much upon my patience? Fool, the weight
Of my disease sits on my heart so heavy,
That all the hands of art cannot remove
One grain, to ease my grief. If thou couldst poison
My memory, or wrap my senses up
Into a dulness hard and cold as flints;
If thou couldst make me walk, speak, eat, and laugh
Without a sense or knowledge of my faculties,
Why, then, perhaps, at marts thou mightst make benefit
Of such an antic motion,[57] and get credit
From credulous gazers, but not profit me.
Study to gull the wise; I am too simple
To be wrought on.

Corax.   I'll burn my books, old man,
But I will do thee good, and quickly too.

Re-enter ARETUS *with a patent.*

Aretus. Most honoured Lord Meleander, our great master,
Prince Palador of Cyprus, hath by me
Sent you this patent, in which is contained
Not only confirmation of the honours
You formerly enjoyed, but the addition
Of the marshalship of Cyprus; and ere long
He means to visit you. Excuse my haste;
I must attend the prince.   [*Exit.*

Corax.   There's one pill works.

Meleander. Dost know that spirit? 'tis a grave familiar,
And talked I know not what.

Corax.   He's like, methinks,
The prince's tutor, Aretus.

Meleander.   Yes, yes;
It may be I have seen such a formality;
No matter where or when.

Re-enter AMETHUS, *with a staff.*

Amethus.   The prince hath sent ye,

[57] Puppet-show.

My lord, this staff of office, and withal
Salutes you Grand Commander of the Ports
Throughout his principalities. He shortly
Will visit you himself: I must attend him.   [*Exit.*
   Corax. D'ye feel your physic stirring yet?
   Meleander.   A devil
Is a rare juggler, and can cheat the eye,
But not corrupt the reason, in the throne
Of a pure soul.

Re-enter SOPHRONOS, with a tablet.

                Another!—I will stand thee;
Be what thou canst, I care not.
   Sophronos.   From the prince,
Dear brother, I present you this rich relic,
A jewel he hath long worn in his bosom:
Henceforth, he bade me say, he does beseech you
To call him son, for he will call you father;
It is an honour, brother, that a subject
Cannot but entertain with thankful prayers.
Be moderate in your joys: he will in person
Confirm my errand, but commands my service.   [*Exit.*
   Corax. What hope now of your cure?
   Meleander.   Stay, stay!—What earthquakes
Roll in my flesh! Here's prince, and prince, and prince;
Prince upon prince! The dotage of my sorrows
Revels in magic of ambitious scorn:
Be they enchantments deadly as the grave,
I'll look upon 'em. Patent, staff, and relic!
To the last first. [*Taking up the miniature*] Round me,
       ye guarding ministers,
And ever keep me waking, till the cliffs
That overhang my sight fall off, and leave
These hollow spaces to be crammed with dust!
   Corax. 'Tis time, I see, to fetch the cordial. Prithee,
Sit down; I'll instantly be here again.   [*Exit.*
   Meleander. Good, give me leave; I will sit down: indeed,
Here's company enough for me to prate to.
                    [*Looks at the picture.*
Eroclea!—'tis the same; the cunning arts-man

Faltered not in a line. Could he have fashioned
A little hollow space here, and blown breath
T' have made it move and whisper, 't had been excellent:—
But, faith, 'tis well, 'tis very well as 'tis,
Passing, most passing well.

Re-enter CLEOPHILA *leading* EROCLEA, *and followed
by* RHETIAS.

Cleophila.   The sovereign greatness,
Who, by commission from the powers of Heaven,
Sways both this land and us, our gracious prince,
By me presents you, sir, with this large bounty,
A gift more precious to him than his birthright.
Here let your cares take end; now set at liberty
Your long-imprisoned heart, and welcome home
The solace of your soul, too long kept from you.
   Eroclea. [*Kneeling*] Dear sir, you know me?
   Meleander.   Yes, thou art my daughter,
My eldest blessing. Know thee! why, Eroclea,
I never did forget thee in thy absence.
Poor soul, how dost?
   Eroclea.   The best of my well-being
Consists in yours.
   Meleander.   Stand up: the gods, who hitherto
                                    [EROCLEA *rises*
Have kept us both alive, preserve thee ever!—
Cleophila, I thank thee and the prince:—
I thank thee too, Eroclea, that thou wouldst,
In pity of my age, take so much pains
To live, till I might once more look upon thee,
Before I broke my heart: O, 'twas a piece
Of piety and duty unexampled!
   Rhetias. [*Aside*] The good man relisheth his comforts
                strangely;
The sight doth turn me child.
   Eroclea.   I have not words
That can express my joys.
   Cleophila.   Nor I.
   Meleander.   Nor I:

Yet let us gaze on one another freely,
And surfeit with our eyes. Let me be plain:
If I should speak as much as I should speak,
I should talk of a thousand things at once,
And all of thee; of thee, my child, of thee!
My tears, like ruffling winds locked up in caves,
Do bustle for a vent;—on t'other side,
To fly out into mirth were not so comely.
Come hither, let me kiss thee. [*To* EROCLEA] With a pride.
Strength, courage, and fresh blood, which now thy presence
Hath stored me with, I kneel before their altars,
Whose sovereignty kept guard about thy safety.
Ask, ask thy sister, prithee, she will tell thee
How I have been much mad.
   Cleophila.　　　　　　　　Much discontented,
Shunning all means that might procure him comfort.
   Eroclea. Heaven has at last been gracious.
   Meleander.　　　　　　　　So say I:
But wherefore drop thy words in such a sloth,
As if thou wert afraid to mingle truth
With thy misfortunes? Understand me throughly;
I would not have thee to report at large,
From point to point, a journal of thy absence,
'Twill take up too much time; I would securely
Engross the little remnant of my life,
That thou mightst every day be telling somewhat,
Which might convey me to my rest with comfort.
Let me bethink me: how we parted first,
Puzzles my faint remembrance—but soft—
Cleophila, thou told'st me that the prince
Sent me this present.
   Cleophila.　　　　From his own fair hands
I did receive my sister.
   Meleander.　　　　To requite him,
We will not dig his father's grave anew,
Although the mention of him much concerns
The business we inquire of:—as I said,
We parted in a hurry at the court;
I to this castle, after made my jail.
But whither thou, dear heart?

Rhetias.   Now they fall to't;
I looked for this.

Eroclea.   I, by my uncle's care,
Sophronos, my good uncle, suddenly
Was like a sailor's boy conveyed a-shipboard
That very night.

Meleander.   A policy quick and strange.

Eroclea. The ship was bound for Corinth; whither first,
Attended only with your servant Rhetias
And all fit necessaries, we arrived:
From thence, in habit of a youth, we journeyed
To Athens, where, till our return of late,
Have we lived safe.

Meleander.   O, what a thing is man,
To bandy factions of distempered passions
Against the sacred Providence above him!
Here, in the legend of thy two years' exile,
Rare pity and delight are sweetly mixed.—
And still thou wert a boy?

Eroclea.   So I obeyed
My uncle's wise command.

Meleander.   'Twas safely carried:
I humbly thank thy fate.

Eroclea.   If earthly treasures
Are poured in plenty down from Heaven on mortals,
They rain amongst those oracles that flow
In schools of sacred knowledge; such is Athens:
Yet Athens was to me but a fair prison:
The thoughts of you, my sister, country, fortunes,
And something of the prince, barred all contents,
Which else might ravish sense; for had not Rhetias
Been always comfortable to me, certainly
Things had gone worse.

Meleander.   Speak low, Eroclea.
That "something of the prince" bears danger in it:
Yet thou hast travelled, wench, for such endowments
As might create a prince a wife fit for him,
Had he the world to guide: but touch not there.
How cam'st thou home?

Rhetias.   Sir, with your noble favour,
Kissing your hand first, that point I can answer.

Meleander. Honest, right honest Rhetias!

Rhetias.   Your grave brother
Perceived with what a hopeless love his son,
Lord Menaphon, too eagerly pursued
Thamasta, cousin to our present prince;
And, to remove the violence of affection,
Sent him to Athens, where, for twelve months' space,
Your daughter, my young lady, and her cousin,
Enjoyed each other's griefs; till by his father,
The Lord Sophronos, we were all called home.

Meleander. Enough, enough: the world shall henceforth
      witness
My thankfulness to Heaven and those people
Who have been pitiful to me and mine.—
Lend me a looking-glass.—How now! how came I
So courtly, in fresh raiments?

Rhetias.   Here's the glass, sir.
                              [*Hands a glass to* MELEANDER.

Meleander. I'm in the trim too.—O Cleophila,
This was the goodness of thy care and cunning.—
                                        [*Loud music.*
Whence comes this noise? [58]

Rhetias.   The prince, my lord, in person.
                                        [*They kneel.*

Re-enter PALADOR, SOPHRONOS, ARETUS, AMETHUS,
   MENAPHON, CORAX, THAMASTA, *with* KALA.

Palador. Ye shall not kneel to us; rise all, I charge ye.—
                                        [*They rise.*
Father, you wrong your age; henceforth my arms
                              [*Embracing* MELEANDER.
And heart shall be your guard: we have o'erheard
All passages of your united loves.
Be young again, Meleander; live to number
A happy generation, and die old
In comforts as in years! The offices

[58] *i.e.* Music, in which sense the word was occasionally used.

And honours which I late on thee conferred
Are not fantastic bounties, but thy merit:
Enjoy them liberally.

   Meleander.   My tears must thank ye,
For my tongue cannot.

   Corax.   I have kept my promise,
And given you a sure cordial.

   Meleander.   O, a rare one!

   Palador. Good man, we both have shared enough of sad-
      ness,
Though thine has tasted deeper of the extreme:
Let us forget it henceforth. Where's the picture
I sent ye? Keep it; 'tis a counterfeit;
And, in exchange of that, I seize on this,

                 [*Takes* EROCLEA *by the hand.*
The real substance. With this other hand
I give away, before her father's face,
His younger joy, Cleophila, to thee,
Cousin Amethus: take her, and be to her
More than a father, a deserving husband.
Thus robbed of both thy children in a minute,
Thy cares are taken off.

   Meleander.   My brains are dulled;
I am entranced, and know not what you mean.
Great, gracious sir, alas, why do you mock me?
I am a weak old man, so poor and feeble,
That my untoward joints can scarcely creep
Unto the grave, where I must seek my rest.

   Palador. Eroclea was, you know, contracted mine;
Cleophila my cousin's, by consent
Of both their hearts; we both now claim our own:
It only rests in you to give a blessing,
For confirmation.

   Rhetias.   Sir, 'tis truth and justice.

   Meleander. The gods, that lent ye to me, bless your vows!
O, children, children, pay your prayers to Heaven,
For they have showed much mercy.—But, Sophronos,
Thou art my brother—I can say no more—
A good, good brother!

   Palador.   Leave the rest to time.—

Cousin Thamasta, I must give you too.—
She's thy wife, Menaphon.—Rhetias, for thee,
And Corax, I have more than common thanks.—
On to the temple! there all solemn rites
Performed, a general feast shall be proclaimed.
The LOVER'S MELANCHOLY hath found cure;
Sorrows are changed to bride-songs. So they thrive
Whom fate in spite of storms hath kept alive.   [*Exeunt.*

EPILOGUE

To be too confident is as unjust
In any work as too much to distrust:
Who from the laws of study have not swerved
Know begged applauses never were deserved.
We must submit to censure:[1] so doth he
Whose hours begot this issue; yet, being free,
For his part, if he have not pleased you, then
In this kind he'll not trouble you again.

[1] Judgment.

'TIS PITY SHE'S A WHORE

It is uncertain when *'Tis Pity She's a Whore* was written. It was acted at the Phœnix in Drury Lane by the Queen's Servants, and published in 1633. It was one of the plays appropriated by the Phœnix or Cockpit Theatre in 1639.

The foundation of the plot may possibly have been taken from a slight notice in Bandello. There is a story in Rosset's *Histoires Tragiques de Nostre Temps* (1615), entitled "Des Amours Incestueuses d'un Frère et d'une Sœur, et de leur fin Malheureuse et Tragique," which Ford may have read; but it has little resemblance to this play. The brother and sister are named Lyzaran and Doralice. Doralice was married to a rich old man. Subsequently, having gathered together her jewels, she is taken on to her brother's horse and the lovers flee together. After wandering in many places they take refuge in Paris, are arrested, condemned to death, and beheaded. This is said to have actually happened in France in the reign of Henry IV.

The play was very well received, and the actors earned "general commendation."

To my Friend the Author

> With admiration I beheld this Whore,
> Adorned with beauty such as might restore
> (If ever being, as thy Muse hath famed)
> Her Giovanni, in his love unblamed:
> The ready Graces lent their willing aid;
> Pallas herself now played the chambermaid,
> And helped to put her dressings on. Secure
> Rest thou that thy name herein shall endure
> To the end of age; and Annabella be
> Gloriously fair, even in her infamy.

THOMAS ELLICE[1]

[1] Probably Thomas Ellis (or Ellys), of Wyham, Lincolnshire, who was made a baronet by Charles II. He was perhaps a brother of Mr. Robert Ellice, one of "the three respected friends" to whom Ford inscribed *The Lover's Melancholy*, and also the friend of Davenant.

To the Truly Noble

JOHN, EARL OF PETERBOROUGH, LORD MORDAUNT, BARON OF TURVEY [1]

My Lord,

WHERE a truth of merit hath a general warrant, there love is but a debt, acknowledgment a justice. Greatness cannot often claim virtue by inheritance; yet, in this, yours appears most eminent, for that you are not more rightly heir to your fortunes than glory shall be to your memory. Sweetness of disposition ennobles a freedom of birth; in both your lawful interest adds honour to your own name, and mercy to my presumption. Your noble allowance of these first fruits of my leisure in the action emboldens my confidence of your as noble construction in this presentment; especially since my service must ever owe particular duty to your favours by a particular engagement. The gravity of the subject may easily excuse the lightness of the title, otherwise I had been a severe judge against mine own guilt. Princes have vouchsafed grace to trifles offered from a purity of devotion; your lordship may likewise please to admit into your good opinion, with these weak endeavours, the constancy of affection from the sincere lover of your deserts in honour,

JOHN FORD

[1] John, first Earl of Peterborough, obtained that title in the year 1627-8. He was brought up in the Roman Catholic faith, but was converted by a disputation at his own house between Bishop Usher and a Catholic, who confessed himself silenced by the just hand of God for presuming to dispute without leave from his superiors. He joined the Parliamentary army in 1642, was made General of the Ordnance and colonel of a regiment of foot, under Essex, and died in the same year.

DRAMATIS PERSONÆ

BONAVENTURA, a Friar
A CARDINAL, Nuncio to the Pope
SORANZO, a Nobleman
FLORIO, ⎱ Citizens of Parma
DONADO, ⎰
GRIMALDI, a Roman Gentleman
GIOVANNI, Son of FLORIO
BERGETTO, Nephew of DONADO
RICHARDETTO, a supposed Physician
VASQUES, Servant to SORANZO
POGGIO, Servant to BERGETTO
Banditti, Officers, Attendants, Servants, &c.

ANNABELLA, Daughter of FLORIO
HIPPOLITA, Wife of RICHARDETTO
PHILOTIS, Niece of RICHARDETTO
PUTANA, Tutoress to ANNABELLA

SCENE—PARMA

'TIS PITY SHE'S A WHORE

ACT THE FIRST

SCENE I—Friar Bonaventura's *Cell*

Enter Friar *and* Giovanni.

Friar. Dispute no more in this; for know, young man,
These are no school-points; nice philosophy
May tolerate unlikely arguments,
But Heaven admits no jest: wits that presumed
On wit too much, by striving how to prove
There was no God with foolish grounds of art,
Discovered first the nearest way to hell,
And filled the world with devilish atheism.
Such questions, youth, are fond:[1] far better 'tis
To bless the sun than reason why it shines;
Yet He thou talk'st of is above the sun.
No more! I may not hear it.
   Giovanni.   Gentle father,
To you I have unclasped my burdened soul,
Emptied the storehouse of my thoughts and heart,
Made myself poor of secrets; have not left
Another word untold, which hath not spoke
All what I ever durst or think or know;
And yet is here the comfort I shall have?
Must I not do what all men else may,—love?
   Friar. Yes, you may love, fair son.
   Giovanni.   Must I not praise
That beauty which, if framed anew, the gods
Would make a god of, if they had it there,
And kneel to it, as I do kneel to them?
   Friar. Why, foolish madman,—
   Giovanni.   Shall a peevish[2] sound,

[1] Vain.
[2] Trifling.

A customary form, from man to man,
Of brother and of sister, be a bar
'Twixt my perpetual happiness and me?
Say that we had one father; say one womb—
Curse to my joys!—gave both us life and birth;
Are we not therefore each to other bound
So much the more by nature? by the links
Of blood, of reason? nay, if you will have't,
Even of religion, to be ever one,
One soul, one flesh, one love, one heart, one all?

    Friar. Have done, unhappy youth! for thou art lost.

    Giovanni. Shall, then, for that I am her brother born,
My joys be ever banished from her bed?
No, father; in your eyes I see the change
Of pity and compassion; from your age,
As from a sacred oracle, distils
The life of counsel: tell me, holy man,
What cure shall give me ease in these extremes?

    Friar. Repentance, son, and sorrow for this sin:
For thou hast moved a Majesty above
With thy unrangèd almost blasphemy.

    Giovanni. O, do not speak of that, dear confessor!

    Friar. Art thou, my son, that miracle of wit
Who once, within these three months, wert esteemed
A wonder of thine age throughout Bononia?
How did the University applaud
Thy government, behaviour, learning, speech,
Sweetness, and all that could make up a man!
I was proud of my tutelage, and chose
Rather to leave my books than part with thee;
I did so:—but the fruits of all my hopes
Are lost in thee, as thou art in thyself.
O, Giovanni! [3] hast thou left the schools
Of knowledge to converse with lust and death?
For death waits on thy lust. Look through the world,
And thou shalt see a thousand faces shine

---

[3] Our old dramatists appear to have learned Italian entirely from books; few, if any, of them pronounced it correctly. Giovanni is here used by Ford as a quadri-syllable, as it was by Massinger and others of his contemporaries.—*Gifford.*

More glorious than this idol thou ador'st:
Leave her, and take thy choice, 'tis much less sin;
Though in such games as those they lose that win.

Giovanni. It were more ease to stop the ocean
From floats and ebbs than to dissuade my vows.

Friar. Then I have done, and in thy wilful flames
Already see thy ruin; Heaven is just.
Yet hear my counsel.

Giovanni.   As a voice of life.

Friar. Hie to thy father's house; there lock thee fast
Alone within thy chamber; then fall down
On both thy knees, and grovel on the ground;
Cry to thy heart; wash every word thou utter'st
In tears—and if't be possible—of blood:
Beg Heaven to cleanse the leprosy of lust
That rots thy soul; acknowledge what thou art,
A wretch, a worm, a nothing; weep, sigh, pray
Three times a-day and three times every night:
For seven days' space do this; then, if thou find'st
No change in thy desires, return to me:
I'll think on remedy. Pray for thyself
At home, whilst I pray for thee here.—Away!
My blessing with thee! we have need to pray.

Giovanni. All this I'll do, to free me from the rod
    Of vengeance; else I'll swear my fate's my god.

                                    [*Exeunt.*

SCENE II—*The Street before* Florio's *House*

Enter Grimaldi *and* Vasques, *with their swords drawn.*

Vasques. Come, sir, stand to your tackling; if you prove
craven, I'll make you run quickly.

Grimaldi. Thou art no equal match for me.

Vasques. Indeed, I never went to the wars to bring home
news; nor cannot play the mountebank for a meal's meat,
and swear I got my wounds in the field. See you these gray
hairs? they'll not flinch for a bloody nose. Wilt thou to this
gear?

Grimaldi. Why, slave, thinkest thou I'll balance my reputation with a cast-suit? [4] Call thy master; he shall know
that I dare—

Vasques. Scold like a cot-quean;[5]—that's your profession.
Thou poor shadow of a soldier, I will make thee know my
master keeps servants thy betters in quality and performance.
Comest thou to fight or prate?

Grimaldi. Neither, with thee. I am a Roman and a gentleman; one that have got mine honour with expense of blood.

Vasques. You are a lying coward and a fool. Fight, or by
these hilts, I'll kill thee:—brave my lord!—you'll fight?

Grimaldi. Provoke me not, for if thou dost—

Vasques.   Have at you!

[*They fight;* GRIMALDI *is worsted.*

Enter FLORIO, DONADO, *and* SORANZO, *from opposite sides.*

Florio. What mean these sudden broils so near my doors?
Have you not other places but my house
To vent the spleen of your disordered bloods?
Must I be haunted still with such unrest
As not to eat or sleep in peace at home?
Is this your love, Grimaldi? Fie! 'tis naught.

Donado. And, Vasques, I may tell thee, 'tis not well
To broach these quarrels; you are ever forward
In seconding contentions.

Enter ANNABELLA *and* PUTANA *above.*

Florio.   What's the ground?

Soranzo. That, with your patience, signiors, I'll resolve:
This gentleman, whom fame reports a soldier,—
For else I know not,—rivals me in love
To Signior Florio's daughter; to whose ears
He still prefers his suit, to my disgrace;
Thinking the way to recommend himself
Is to disparage me in his report:—
But know, Grimaldi, though, may be, thou art
My equal in thy blood, yet this bewrays
A lowness in thy mind, which, wert thou noble,

---

[4] *i.e.* Cast-off.

[5] A contemptuous term for one who concerns himself with female affairs.

Thou wouldst as much disdain as I do thee
For this unworthiness:—and on this ground
I willed my servant to correct his tongue,
Holding a man so base no match for me.

Vasques. And had not your sudden coming prevented us,
I had let my gentleman blood under the gills:—I should
have wormed you, sir, for running mad.[6]

Grimaldi. I'll be revenged, Soranzo.

Vasques. On a dish of warm broth to stay your stomach—
do, honest innocence, do! spoon-meat is a wholesomer diet
than a Spanish blade.

Grimaldi. Remember this!

Soranzo.   I fear thee not, Grimaldi.

                                        [*Exit* GRIMALDI.

Florio. My Lord Soranzo, this is strange to me,
Why you should storm, having my word engaged;
Owing[7] her heart, what need you doubt her ear?
Losers may talk by law of any game.

Vasques. Yet the villany of words, Signior Florio, may be
such as would make any unspleened dove choleric. Blame
not my lord in this.

Florio. Be you more silent:
I would not for my wealth, my daughter's love
Should cause the spilling of one drop of blood.
Vasques, put up, let's end this fray in wine.   [*Exeunt.*

Putana. How like you this, child? here's threatening, chal-
lenging, quarrelling, and fighting on every side; and all
is for your sake: you had need look to yourself, charge;
you'll be stolen away sleeping else shortly.

Annabella. But, tutoress, such a life gives no content
To me; my thoughts are fixed on other ends.
Would you would leave me!

Putana. Leave you! no marvel else; leave me no leaving,
charge; this is love outright. Indeed, I blame you not; you
have choice fit for the best lady in Italy.

Annabella. Pray do not talk so much.

Putana. Take the worst with the best, there's Grimaldi

---

[6] The allusion is to the practice of cutting what is called the worm from under
a dog's tongue, as a preventive of madness.—*Gifford.*
[7] *i.e.* Owning.

the soldier, a very well-timbered fellow. They say he is a
Roman, nephew to the Duke Montferrato; they say he did
good service in the wars against the Milanese; but, 'faith,
charge, I do not like him, an't be for nothing but for being
a soldier: not one amongst twenty of your skirmishing cap-
tains but have some privy maim or other that mars their
standing upright. I like him the worse, he crinkles so much
in the hams: though he might serve if there were no more
men, yet he's not the man I would choose.

Annabella. Fie, how thou pratest.

Putana. As I am a very woman, I like Signior Soranzo
well; he is wise, and what is more, rich; and what is more
than that, kind; and what is more than all this, a nobleman:
such a one, were I the fair Annabella myself, I would wish
and pray for. Then he is bountiful; besides, he is handsome,
and, by my troth, I think, wholesome,—and that's news in
a gallant of three-and-twenty; liberal, that I know; loving,
that you know; and a man sure, else he could never ha'
purchased such a good name with Hippolita, the lusty
widow, in her husband's lifetime: an 'twere but for that
report, sweetheart, would 'a were thine! Commend a man
for his qualities, but take a husband as he is a plain, sufficient, naked man: such a one is for your bed, and such a
one is Signior Soranzo, my life for't.

Annabella. Sure the woman took her morning's draught
too soon.

Enter BERGETTO *and* POGGIO.

Putana. But look, sweetheart, look what thing comes now!
Here's another of your ciphers to fill up the number: O,
brave old ape in a silken coat! Observe.

Bergetto. Didst thou think, Poggio, that I would spoil my
new clothes, and leave my dinner, to fight?

Poggio. No, sir, I did not take you for so arrant a baby.

Bergetto. I am wiser than so: for I hope, Poggio, thou
never heardst of an elder brother that was a coxcomb; didst,
Poggio?

Poggio. Never, indeed, sir, as long as they had either land
or money left them to inherit.

Bergetto. Is it possible, Poggio? O, monstrous! Why, I'll

undertake with a handful of silver to buy a headful of wit
at any time: but, sirrah, I have another purchase in hand; I
shall have the wench, mine uncle says. I will but wash my
face and shift socks, and then have at her, i'faith!—Mark my
pace, Poggio!

> [*Passes over the stage, and exit.*

Poggio. Sir,—I have seen an ass and a mule trot the
Spanish pavin[8] with a better grace, I know not how often.

> [*Aside, and follows him.*

Annabella. This idiot haunts me too.

Putana. Ay, ay, he needs no description. The rich mag-
nifico that is below with your father, charge, Signior
Donado his uncle, for that he means to make this, his
cousin,[9] a golden calf, thinks that you will be a right
Israelite, and fall down to him presently: but I hope I have
tutored you better. They say a fool's bauble is a lady's play-
fellow; yet you, having wealth enough, you need not cast
upon the dearth of flesh, at any rate. Hang him, innocent![10]

GIOVANNI *passes over the stage.*

Annabella. But see, Putana, see! what blessèd shape
Of some celestial creature now appears!—
What man is he, that with such sad aspéct
Walks careless of himself?

Putana.   Where?

Annabella.   Look below.

Putana. O, 'tis your brother, sweet.

Annabella.   Ha!

Putana.   'Tis your brother.

Annabella. Sure, 'tis not he; this is some woful thing
Wrapped up in grief, some shadow of a man.
Alas, he beats his breast and wipes his eyes,
Drowned all in tears: methinks I hear him sigh:
Let's down, Putana, and partake the cause.
I know my brother, in the love he bears me,

---

[8] "A grave and majestic dance; the method of performing it was anciently by
gentlemen dressed with a cap and sword; by those of the long robe, in their
gowns; by princes, in their mantles; and by ladies, in gowns with long trains,
the motion whereof in the dance resembled that of a peacock's tail."—*Hawkins.*
[9] *i.e.* Nephew.
[10] Idiot.

Will not deny me partage in his sadness.—
My soul is full of heaviness and fear.   [*Aside.*
                                        [*Exit above with* PUTANA.

SCENE III—*A Hall in* FLORIO's *House*

Enter GIOVANNI.

Giovanni. Lost! I am lost! my fates have doomed my
      death:
The more I strive, I love; the more I love,
The less I hope: I see my ruin certain.
What judgment or endeavours could apply
To my incurable and restless wounds,
I throughly have examined, but in vain.
O, that it were not in religion sin
To make our love a god, and worship it!
I have even wearied Heaven with prayers, dried up
The spring of my continual tears, even starved
My veins with daily fasts: what wit or art
Could counsel, I have practised; but, alas,
I find all these but dreams, and old men's tales,
To fright unsteady youth; I'm still the same:
Or I must speak, or burst. 'Tis not, I know,
My lust, but 'tis my fate that leads me on.
Keep fear and low faint-hearted shame with slaves!
I'll tell her that I love her, though my heart
Were rated at the price of that attempt.—
O me! she comes.

Enter ANNABELLA *and* PUTANA.

Annabella.   Brother!
Giovanni. [*Aside*]   If such a thing
As courage dwell in men, ye heavenly powers,
Now double all that virtue in my tongue!
Annabella. Why, brother,
Will you not speak to me?
Giovanni.   Yes: how d'ye, sister?
Annabella. Howe'er I am, methinks you are not well.
Putana. Bless us! Why are you so sad, sir?

Giovanni. Let me entreat you, leave us a while, Putana.—
Sister, I would be private with you.

Annabella. Withdraw, Putana.

Putana. I will.—If this were any other company for her,
I should think my absence an office of some credit: but
I will leave them together.   [*Aside, and exit.*

Giovanni. Come, sister, lend your hand: let's walk to-
      gether!
I hope you need not blush to walk with me;
Here's none but you and I.

Annabella.   How's this?

Giovanni.   I'faith,
I mean no harm.

Annabella.   Harm?

Giovanni.   No, good faith.
How is't with ye?

Annabella. [*Aside*] I trust he be not frantic.—
I am very well, brother.

Giovanni. Trust me, but I am sick; I fear so sick
'Twill cost my life.

Annabella. Mercy forbid it! 'tis not so, I hope.

Giovanni. I think you love me, sister.

Annabella.   Yes, you know
I do.

Giovanni. I know't, indeed.—You're very fair.

Annabella. Nay, then I see you have a merry sickness.

Giovanni. That's as it proves. The poets feign, I read,
That Juno for her forehead did exceed
All other goddesses; but I durst swear
Your forehead exceeds hers, as hers did theirs.

Annabella. 'Troth, this is pretty!

Giovanni.   Such a pair of stars
As are thine eyes would, like Promethean fire,
If gently glanced, give life to senseless stones.

Annabella. Fie upon ye!

Giovanni. The lily and the rose, most sweetly strange,
Upon your dimpled cheeks do strive for change:
Such lips would tempt a saint; such hands as those
Would make an anchorite lascivious.

Annabella. D'ye mock me or flatter me?

    Giovanni. If you would see a beauty more exact
Than art can counterfeit or nature frame,
Look in your glass, and there behold your own.
    Annabella. O, you are a trim youth!
    Giovanni. Here!   [*Offers his dagger to her.*
    Annabella.   What to do?
    Giovanni.   And here's my breast; strike home!
Rip up my bosom; there thou shalt behold
A heart in which is writ the truth I speak.
Why stand ye?
    Annabella.   Are you earnest?
    Giovanni.   Yes, most earnest.
You cannot love?
    Annabella.   Whom?
    Giovanni.   Me. My tortured soul
Hath felt affliction in the heat of death.
O, Annabella, I am quite undone!
The love of thee, my sister, and the view
Of thy immortal beauty have untuned
All harmony both of my rest and life.
Why d'ye not strike?
    Annabella.   Forbid it, my just fears!
If this be true, 'twere fitter I were dead.
    Giovanni. True, Annabella! 'tis no time to jest.
I have too long suppressed the hidden flames
That almost have consumed me: I have spent
Many a silent night in sighs and groans;
Ran over all my thoughts, despised my fate,
Reasoned against the reasons of my love,
Done all that smoothed-cheeked virtue could advise;
But found all bootless: 'tis my destiny
That you must either love, or I must die.
    Annabella. Comes this in sadness[11] from you?
    Giovanni.   Let some mischief
Befall me soon, if I dissemble aught.
    Annabella. You are my brother Giovanni.
    Giovanni.   You
My sister Annabella; I know this,
And could afford you instance why to love

[11] Earnest.

So much the more for this; to which intent
Wise nature first in your creation meant
To make you mine; else't had been sin and foul
To share one beauty to a double soul.
Nearness in birth and blood doth but persuade
A nearer nearness in affection.
I have asked counsel of the holy church,
Who tells me I may love you; and 'tis just
That, since I may, I should; and will, yes, will.
Must I now live or die?

    Annabella.   Live; thou hast won
The field, and never fought: what thou hast urged
My captive heart had long ago resolved.
I blush to tell thee,—but I'll tell thee now,—
For every sigh that thou hast spent for me
I have sighed ten; for every tear shed twenty:
And not so much for that I loved, as that
I durst not say I loved, nor scarcely think it.

    Giovanni. Let not this music be a dream, ye gods,
For pity's sake, I beg ye!

    Annabella.   On my knees,   [*She kneels.*
Brother, even by our mother's dust, I charge you,
Do not betray me to your mirth or hate:
Love me or kill me, brother.

    Giovanni.   On my knees,   [*He kneels.*
Sister, even by my mother's dust, I charge you,
Do not betray me to your mirth or hate:
Love me or kill me, sister.

    Annabella. You mean good sooth, then?

    Giovanni.   In good troth, I do;
And so do you, I hope: say, I'm in earnest.

    Annabella. I'll swear it, I.

    Giovanni.   And I; and by this kiss,—
                              [*Kisses her.*
Once more, yet once more: now let's rise [*They rise*],—
    by this,
I would not change this minute for Elysium.
What must we now do?

    Annabella.   What you will.

    Giovanni.   Come, then;

After so many tears as we have wept,
Let's learn to court in smiles, to kiss, and sleep.

                                                          [*Exeunt.*

SCENE IV—*A Street*

Enter FLORIO *and* DONADO.

Florio. Signior Donado, you have said enough,
I understand you; but would have you know
I will not force my daughter 'gainst her will.
You see I have but two, a son and her;
And he is so devoted to his book,
As I must tell you true, I doubt his health:
Should he miscarry, all my hopes rely
Upon my girl.[12] As for worldly fortune,
I am, I thank my stars, blessed with enough.
My care is, how to match her to her liking:
I would not have her marry wealth, but love
And if she like your nephew, let him have her.
Here's all that I can say.

Donado.   Sir, you say well,
Like a true father; and, for my part, I,
If the young folks can like,—'twixt you and me,—
Will promise to assure my nephew presently
Three thousand florins yearly during life,
And after I am dead my whole estate.

Florio. 'Tis a fair proffer, sir; meantime your nephew
Shall have free passage to commence his suit:
If he can thrive, he shall have my consent.
So for this time I'll leave you, signior.   [*Exit.*

Donado.   Well,
Here's hope yet, if my nephew would have wit;
But he is such another dunce, I fear
He'll never win the wench. When I was young,
I could have done't, i'faith; and so shall he,
If he will learn of me; and, in good time,
He comes himself.

_____

[12] "Girl" is here, and almost everywhere else in these plays, a dissyllable. The practice is not peculiar to our poet; for Fanshaw, and others of that age, have numerous examples of it.—*Gifford.*

Enter BERGETTO *and* POGGIO.

How now, Bergetto, whither away so fast?

Bergetto. O, uncle, I have heard the strangest news that ever came out of the mint!—Have I not, Poggio?

Poggio. Yes, indeed, sir.

Donado. What news, Bergetto?

Bergetto. Why, look ye, uncle, my barber told me just now that there is a fellow come to town who undertakes to make a mill go without the mortal help of any water or wind, only with sand-bags: and this fellow hath a strange horse, a most excellent beast, I'll assure you, uncle, my barber says; whose head, to the wonder of all Christian people, stands just behind where his tail is.—Is't not true, Poggio?

Poggio. So the barber swore, forsooth.

Donado. And you are running thither?

Bergetto. Ay, forsooth, uncle.

Donado. Wilt thou be a fool still? Come, sir, you shall not go: you have more mind of a puppet-play than on the business I told ye. Why, thou great baby, wilt never have wit? wilt make thyself a May-game to all the world?

Poggio. Answer for yourself, master.

Bergetto. Why, uncle, should I sit at home still, and not go abroad to see fashions like other gallants?

Donado. To see hobby-horses! What wise talk, I pray, had you with Annabella, when you were at Signior Florio's house?

Bergetto. O, the wench,—Ud's sa'me, uncle, I tickled her with a rare speech, that I made her almost burst her belly with laughing.

Donado. Nay, I think so; and what speech was't?

Bergetto. What did I say, Poggio?

Poggio. Forsooth, my master said, that he loved her almost as well as he loved parmasent;[13] and swore—I'll be sworn for him—that she wanted but such a nose as his was, to be as pretty a young woman as any was in Parma.

Donado. O, gross!

Bergetto. Nay, uncle:—then she asked me whether my

---

[13] *i.e.* Parmesan, the cheese of Parma.

father had any more children than myself; and I said "No;
'twere better he should have had his brains knocked out
first."

Donado. This is intolerable.

Bergetto. Then said she, "Will Signior Donado, your
uncle, leave you all his wealth?"

Donado. Ha! that was good; did she harp upon that
string?

Bergetto. Did she harp upon that string! ay, that she
did. I answered, "Leave me all his wealth! why, woman, he
hath no other wit; if he had, he should hear on't to his everlasting glory and confusion: I know," quoth I, "I am his
white-boy,[14] and will not be gulled:" and with that she fell
into a great smile, and went away. Nay, I did fit her.

Donado. Ah, sirrah, then I see there is no changing of
nature. Well, Bergetto, I fear thou wilt be a very ass still.

Bergetto. I should be sorry for that, uncle.

Donado. Come, come you home with me: since you are
no better a speaker, I'll have you write to her after some
courtly manner, and enclose some rich jewel in the letter.

Bergetto. Ay, marry, that will be excellent.

Donado. Peace, innocent![15]
     Once in my time I'll set my wits to school:
     If all fail, 'tis but the fortune of a fool.

Bergetto. Poggio, 'twill do, Poggio.   [*Exeunt.*

ACT THE SECOND

SCENE I—*An Apartment in* FLORIO's *House*

Enter GIOVANNI *and* ANNABELLA.

GIOVANNI. Come, Annabella,—no more sister now,
But love, a name more gracious,—do not blush,
Beauty's sweet wonder, but be proud to know

---

[14] A term of endearment. It is said that this and similar terms are still used in
some parts of Ireland. Under the ancient Irish Geilnne system of land tenure
the homestead itself, in the division of the family property, fell to the lot of the
fifth son, who was called the fair-haired or white-headed boy, *geil* meaning white.
[15] Idiot.

That yielding thou hast conquered, and inflamed
A heart whose tribute is thy brother's life.

Annabella. And mine is his. O, how these stol'n contents
Would print a modest crimson on my cheeks,
Had any but my heart's delight prevailed!

Giovanni. I marvel why the chaster of your sex
Should think this pretty toy called maidenhead
So strange a loss, when, being lost, 'tis nothing,
And you are still the same.

Annabella.   'Tis well for you;
Now you can talk.

Giovanni.   Music as well consists
In the ear as in the playing.

Annabella.   O, you're wanton!
Tell on't, you're best; do.

Giovanni.   Thou wilt chide me, then.
Kiss me:—so! Thus hung Jove on Leda's neck,
And sucked divine ambrosia from her lips.
I envy not the mightiest man alive;
But hold myself in being king of thee,
More great than were I king of all the world.
But I shall lose you, sweetheart.

Annabella.   But you shall not.

Giovanni. You must be married, mistress.

Annabella.   Yes! to whom?

Giovanni. Some one must have you.

Annabella.   You must.

Giovanni.   Nay, some other.

Annabella. Now, prithee do not speak so: without jesting
You'll make me weep in earnest.

Giovanni.   What, you will not!
But tell me, sweet, canst thou be dared to swear
That thou wilt live to me, and to no other?

Annabella. By both our loves I dare; for didst thou know,
My Giovanni, how all suitors seem
To my eyes hateful, thou wouldst trust me then.

Giovanni. Enough, I take thy word: sweet, we must part:
Remember what thou vow'st; keep well my heart.

Annabella. Will you be gone?

Giovanni. I must.

Annabella. When to return?
Giovanni.   Soon.
Annabella.   Look you do.
Giovanni.   Farewell.
Annabella. Go where thou wilt, in mind I'll keep thee
    here.
And where thou art, I know I shall be there.
                                        [*Exit* GIOVANNI.
Guardian!

Enter PUTANA.

Putana. Child, how is't, child? well, thank Heaven, ha!
Annabella. O guardian, what a paradise of joy
Have I passed over!
Putana. Nay, what a paradise of joy have you passed un-
der! Why, now I commend thee, charge. Fear nothing,
sweetheart: what though he be your brother? your brother's
a man, I hope; and I say still, if a young wench feel the fit
upon her, let her take any body, father or brother, all is one.
Annabella. I would not have it known for all the world.
Putana. Nor I, indeed; for the speech of the people: else
'twere nothing.
Florio. [*Within*] Daughter Annabella!
Annabella. O me, my father!—Here, sir!—Reach my
    work.
Florio. [*Within*] What are you doing?
Annabella.   So: let him come now.

Enter FLORIO, *followed by* RICHARDETTO *as a* Doctor of
Physic, *and* PHILOTIS *with a lute.*

Florio. So hard at work! that's well; you lose no time.
Look, I have brought you company; here's one,
A learnèd doctor lately come from Padua,
Much skilled in physic; and, for that I see
You have of late been sickly, I entreated
This reverend man to visit you some time.
Annabella. You're very welcome, sir.
Richardetto.   I thank you, mistress.
Loud fame in large report hath spoke your praise

As well for virtue as perfection:[16]
For which I have been bold to bring with me
A kinswoman of mine, a maid, for song
And music one perhaps will give content:
Please you to know her.

    Annabella.   They are parts I love.
And she for them most welcome.

    Philotis.   Thank you, lady.

    Florio. Sir, now you know my house, pray make not
        strange;
And if you find my daughter need your art,
I'll be your pay-master.

    Richardetto.   Sir, what I am
She shall command.

    Florio.   Sir, you shall bind me to you.—
Daughter, I must have conference with you
About some matters that concern us both.—
Good Master Doctor, please you but walk in,
We'll crave a little of your cousin's cunning:[17]
I think my girl hath not quite forgot
To touch an instrument; she could have done't:
We'll hear them both.

    Richardetto.   I'll wait upon you, sir.   [*Exeunt.*

SCENE II—*A Room in* SORANZO'S *House*

Enter SORANZO *with a book.*

    Soranzo. [*Reads*] "Love's measure is extreme, the comfort
        pain,
The life unrest, and the reward disdain."
What's here? look't o'er again.—'Tis so; so writes
This smooth, licentious poet in his rhymes:
But, Sannazar, thou liest; for, had thy bozom
Felt such oppression as is laid on mine,
Thou wouldst have kissed the rod that made thee smart.—
To work, then, happy Muse, and contradict

[16] Beauty.
[17] *i.e.* Skill.

What Sannazar hath in his envy writ.   [*Writes.*

"Love's measure is the mean, sweet his annoys,

His pleasures life, and his reward all joys."

Had Annabella lived when Sannazar

Did, in his brief Encomium,[18] celebrate

Venice, that queen of cities, he had left

That verse which gained him such a sum of gold,

And for one only look from Annabel

Had writ of her and her diviner cheeks.

O, how my thoughts are—

   Vasques. [*Within*] Pray, forbear; in rules of civility, let me give notice on't: I shall be taxed of my neglect of duty and service.

   Soranzo. What rude intrusion interrupts my peace? Can I be no where private?

   Vasques. [*Within*] Troth, you wrong your modesty.

   Soranzo. What's the matter, Vasques? who is't?

Enter HIPPOLITA *and* VASQUES.

   Hippolita.   'Tis I;

Do you know me now? Look, perjured man, on her

Whom thou and thy distracted lust have wronged.

Thy sensual rage of blood hath made my youth

A scorn to men and angels; and shall I

Be now a foil to thy unsated change?

Thou know'st, false wanton, when my modest fame

Stood free from stain or scandal, all the charms

Of hell or sorcery could not prevail

Against the honour of my chaster bosom.

Thine eyes did plead in tears, thy tongue in oaths,

Such and so many, that a heart of steel

Would have been wrought to pity, as was mine:

And shall the conquest of my lawful bed,

---

[18] This is the well-known epigram, beginning

> "Viderat Hadriacis Venetam Neptunus in undis
> Stare urbem," &c.

It is given by Coryat, who thus speaks of it: "I heard in Venice that a certaine Italian poet, called Jacobus Sannazarius, had a hundred crownes bestowed upon him by the Senate of Venice for each of these verses following. I would to God my poeticall friend Master Benjamin Johnson were so well rewarded for his poems here in England, seeing he hath made many as good verses (in my opinion) as these of Sannazarius."—*Gifford.*

My husband's death, urged on by his disgrace,
My loss of womanhood, be ill-rewarded
With hatred and contempt? No; know, Soranzo,
I have a spirit doth as much distaste
The slavery of fearing thee, as thou
Dost loathe the memory of what hath passed.

   Soranzo. Nay, dear Hippolita,—

   Hippolita.   Call me not dear,
Nor think with supple words to smooth the grossness
Of my abuses: 'tis not your new mistress,
Your goodly madam-merchant, shall triumph
On my dejection; tell her thus from me,
My birth was nobler and by much more free.

   Soranzo. You are too violent.

   Hippolita.   You are too double
In your dissimulation. Seest thou this,
This habit, these black mourning weeds of care?
'Tis thou art cause of this; and hast divorced
My husband from his life, and me from him,
And made me widow in my widowhood.

   Soranzo. Will you yet hear?

   Hippolita.   More of thy perjuries?
Thy soul is drowned too deeply in those sins;
Thou need'st not add to the number.

   Soranzo.   Then I'll leave you;
You're past all rules of sense.

   Hippolita.   And thou of grace.

   Vasques. Fie, mistress, you are not near the limits of
reason: if my lord had a resolution as noble as virtue itself,
you take the course to unedge it all.—Sir, I beseech you do
not perplex her; griefs, alas, will have a vent: I dare undertake Madam Hippolita will now freely hear you.

   Soranzo. Talk to a woman frantic!—Are these the fruits
of your love?

   Hippolita. They are the fruits of thy untruth, false man!
Didst thou not swear, whilst yet my husband lived,
That thou wouldst wish no happiness on earth
More than to call me wife? didst thou not vow,
When he should die, to marry me? for which
The devil in my blood, and thy protests,

Caused me to counsel him to undertake
A voyage to Ligorne, for that we heard
His brother there was dead, and left a daughter
Young and unfriended, who, with much ado,
I wished him to bring hither: he did so,
And went; and, as thou know'st, died on the way.
Unhappy man, to buy his death so dear,
With my advice! yet thou, for whom I did it,
Forgett'st thy vows, and leav'st me to my shame.

    Soranzo. Who could help this?

    Hippolita.   Who! perjured man, thou couldst,
If thou hadst faith or love.

    Soranzo.   You are deceived:
The vows I made, if you remember well,
Were wicked and unlawful; 'twere more sin
To keep them than to break them: as for me,
I cannot mask my penitence. Think thou
How much thou hast digressed from honest shame
In bringing of a gentleman to death
Who was thy husband; such a one as he,
So noble in his quality, condition,
Learning, behaviour, entertainment, love,
As Parma could not show a braver man.

    Vasques. You do not well; this was not your promise.

    Soranzo. I care not; let her know her monstrous life.
Ere I'll be servile to so black a sin,
I'll be a curse.—Woman, come here no more;
Learn to repent, and die; for, by my honour,
I hate thee and thy lust: you've been too foul.   [*Exit.*

    Vasques. [*Aside*] This part has been scurvily played.

    Hippolita. How foolishly this beast contemns his fate,
And shuns the use of that which I more scorn
Than I once loved, his love! But let him go;
My vengeance shall give comfort to his woe.[19]   [*Going.*

    Vasques. Mistress, mistress, Madam Hippolita! pray, a
word or two.

    Hippolita. With me, sir?

    Vasques. With you, if you please.

    Hippolita. What is't?

---

[19] *i.e.* To the woe occasioned by his falsehood.

Vasques. I know you are infinitely moved now, and you think you have cause: some I confess you have, but sure not so much as you imagine.

Hippolita. Indeed!

Vasques. O, you were miserably bitter, which you followed even to the last syllable; 'faith, you were somewhat too shrewd: by my life, you could not have took my lord in a worse time since I first knew him; to-morrow you shall find him a new man.

Hippolita. Well, I shall wait his leisure.

Vasques. Fie, this is not a hearty patience; it comes sourly from you: 'troth, let me persuade you for once.

Hippolita. [*Aside*] I have it, and it shall be so; thanks, opportunity!—Persuade me! to what?

Vasques. Visit him in some milder temper. O, if you could but master a little your female spleen, how might you win him!

Hippolita. He will never love me. Vasques, thou hast been a too trusty servant to such a master, and I believe thy reward in the end will fall out like mine.

Vasques. So perhaps too.

Hippolita. Resolve[20] thyself it will. Had I one so true, so truly honest, so secret to my counsels, as thou hast been to him and his, I should think it a slight acquittance, not only to make him master of all I have, but even of myself.

Vasques. O, you are a noble gentlewoman!

Hippolita. Wilt thou feed always upon hopes? well, I know thou art wise, and seest the reward of an old servant daily, what it is.

Vasques. Beggary and neglect.

Hippolita. True; but, Vasques, wert thou mine, and wouldst be private to me and my designs, I here protest, myself and all what I can else call mine should be at thy dispose.

Vasques. [*Aside*] Work you that way, old mole? then I have the wind of you.—I were not worthy of it by any desert that could lie within my compass: if I could—

Hippolita. What then?

---

[20] Assure.

Vasques. I should then hope to live in these my old years
with rest and security.

Hippolita. Give me thy hand: now promise but thy si-
lence,
And help to bring to pass a plot I have,
And here, in sight of heaven, that being done,
I make thee lord of me and mine estate.

Vasques. Come, you are merry; this is such a happiness
that I can neither think or believe.

Hippolita. Promise thy secrecy, and 'tis confirmed.

Vasques. Then here I call our good genii for witnesses,
whatsoever your designs are, or against whomsoever, I will
not only be a special actor therein, but never disclose it till
it be effected.

Hippolita. I take thy word, and, with that, thee for mine;
Come, then, let's more confer of this anon.—
On this delicious bane my thoughts shall banquet;
Revenge shall sweeten what my griefs have tasted.

[*Aside, and exit with* VASQUES.

SCENE III—*The Street*

Enter RICHARDETTO *and* PHILOTIS.

Richardetto. Thou seest, my lovely niece, these strange
mishaps,
How all my fortunes turn to my disgrace;
Wherein I am but as a looker-on,
Whiles others act my shame, and I am silent.

Philotis. But, uncle, wherein can this borrowed shape
Give you content?

Richardetto. I'll tell thee, gentle niece:
Thy wanton aunt in her lascivious riots
Lives now secure, thinks I am surely dead
In my late journey to Ligorne for you,—
As I have caused it to be rumoured out.
Now would I see with what an impudence
She gives scope to her loose adultery,
And how the common voice allows hereof:
Thus far I have prevailed.

Philotis.   Alas, I fear
You mean some strange revenge.
    Richardetto.   O, be not troubled;
Your ignorance shall plead for you in all:
But to our business.—What! you learned for certain
How Signor Florio means to give his daughter
In marriage to Soranzo?
    Philotis.   Yes, for certain.
    Richardetto. But how find you young Annabella's love
Inclined to him?
    Philotis.   For aught I could perceive,
She neither fancies him or any else.
    Richardetto. There's mystery in that, which time must
        show.
She used you kindly?
    Philotis.   Yes.
    Richardetto.   And craved your company?
    Philotis. Often.
    Richardetto.   'Tis well; it goes as I could wish.
I am the doctor now; and as for you,
None knows you: if all fail not, we shall thrive.—
But who comes here? I know him; 'tis Grimaldi.
A Roman and a soldier, near allied
Unto the Duke of Montferrato, one
Attending on the nuncio of the pope
That now resides in Parma; by which means
He hopes to get the love of Annabella.

                    Enter GRIMALDI.

    Grimaldi. Save you, sir.
    Richardetto.   And you, sir.
    Grimaldi.   I have heard
Of your approvèd skill, which through the city
Is freely talked of, and would crave your aid.
    Richardetto. For what, sir?
    Grimaldi. Marry, sir, for this—
But I would speak in private.
    Richardetto. Leave us, cousin.[21]   [*Exit* PHILOTIS.
    Grimaldi. I love fair Annabella, and would know

21 "Cousin" was frequently used for nephew or niece.

Whether in art there may not be receipts
To move affection.

   Richardetto.   Sir, perhaps there may;
But these will nothing profit you.

   Grimaldi.   Not me?

   Richardetto. Unless I be mistook, you are a man
Greatly in favour with the cardinal.

   Grimaldi. What of that?

   Richardetto.   In duty to his grace,
I will be bold to tell you, if you seek
To marry Florio's daughter, you must first
Remove a bar 'twixt you and her.

   Grimaldi.   Who's that?

   Richardetto. Soranzo is the man that hath her heart;
And while he lives, be sure you cannot speed.

   Grimaldi. Soranzo! what, mine enemy? is't he?

   Richardetto. Is he your enemy?

   Grimaldi.   The man I hate
Worse than confusion; I will to him straight.

   Richardetto. Nay, then, take mine advice,
Even for his grace's sake the cardinal:
I'll find a time when he and she do meet,
Of which I'll give you notice; and, to be sure
He shall not 'scape you, I'll provide a poison
To dip your rapier's point in: if he had
As many heads as Hydra had, he dies.

   Grimaldi. But shall I trust thee, doctor?

   Richardetto.   As yourself;
     Doubt not in aught. [*Exit* GRIMALDI.]—Thus shall the
        fates decree
     By me Soranzo falls, that ruined me.   [*Exit*.

SCENE IV—*Another part of the Street*

Enter DONADO *with a letter,* BERGETTO, *and* POGGIO.

   Donado. Well, sir, I must be content to be both your
secretary and your messenger myself. I cannot tell what
this letter may work; but, as sure as I am alive, if thou come

once to talk with her, I fear thou wilt mar whatsoever I make.

Bergetto. You make, uncle! why, am not I big enough to carry mine own letter, I pray?

Donado. Ay, ay, carry a fool's head o' thy own! why, thou dunce, wouldst thou write a letter, and carry it thyself?

Bergetto. Yes, that I would, and read it to her with my own mouth; for you must think, if she will not believe me myself when she hears me speak, she will not believe another's handwriting. O, you think I am a blockhead, uncle. No, sir, Poggio knows I have indited a letter myself; so I have.

Poggio. Yes, truly, sir; I have it in my pocket.

Donado. A sweet one, no doubt; pray let's see't.

Bergetto. I cannot read my own hand very well, Poggio; read it, Poggio.

Donado. Begin.

Poggio. [*Reads*] "Most dainty and honey-sweet mistress; I could call you fair, and lie as fast as any that loves you; but my uncle being the elder man, I leave it to him, as more fit for his age and the colour of his beard. I am wise enough to tell you I can bourd [22] where I see occasion; or if you like my uncle's wit better than mine you shall marry me; if you like mine better than his, I will marry you, in spite of your teeth. So, commending my best parts to you, I rest

Yours upwards and downwards, or you may choose,
                                        Bergetto."

Bergetto. Ah, ha! here's stuff, uncle!

Donado. Here's stuff indeed—to shame us all. Pray, whose advice did you take in this learned letter?

Poggio. None, upon my word, but mine own.

Bergetto. And mine, uncle, believe it, nobody's else; 'twas mine own brain, I thank a good wit for't.

Donado. Get you home, sir, and look you keep within doors till I return.

Bergetto. How! that were a jest indeed! I scorn it, i'faith.

Donado. What! you do not?

Bergetto. Judge me, but I do now.

Poggio. Indeed, sir, 'tis very unhealthy.

22 Jest.

Donado. Well, sir, if I hear any of your apish running to motions[23] and fopperies, till I come back, you were as good no; look to't.   [*Exit.*

Bergetto. Poggio, shall's steal to see this horse with the head in's tail?

Poggio. Ay, but you must take heed of whipping.

Bergetto. Dost take me for a child, Poggio? Come, honest Poggio.   [*Exeunt.*

SCENE V—Friar Bonaventura's *Cell*

Enter Friar *and* Giovanni.

Friar. Peace! thou hast told a tale whose every word
Threatens eternal slaughter to the soul;
I'm sorry I have heard it: would mine ears
Had been one minute deaf, before the hour
That thou cam'st to me! O young man, castaway,
By the religious number[24] of mine order,
I day and night have waked my agèd eyes
Above my strength, to weep on thy behalf;
But Heaven is angry, and be thou resolved [25]
Thou art a man remarked [26] to taste a mischief.
Look for't; though it come late, it will come sure.

Giovanni. Father, in this you are uncharitable;
What I have done I'll prove both fit and good.
It is a principle which you have taught,
When I was yet your scholar, that the frame
And composition of the mind doth follow
The frame and composition of the body:
So, where the body's furniture is beauty,
The mind's must needs be virtue; which allowed,
Virtue itself is reason but refined,
And love the quintessence of that: this proves,
My sister's beauty being rarely fair
Is rarely virtuous; chiefly in her love,

---

[23] Puppet-shows.
[24] Gifford proposed "founder."
[25] Satisfied.
[26] Marked out.

And chiefly in that love, her love to me:
If hers to me, then so is mine to her;
Since in like causes are effects alike.

Friar. O ignorance in knowledge! Long ago,
How often have I warned thee this before!
Indeed, if we were sure there were no Deity,
Nor Heaven nor Hell, then to be led alone
By Nature's light—as were philosophers
Of elder times—might instance some defence.
But 'tis not so: then, madman, thou wilt find
That Nature is in Heaven's positions blind.

Giovanni. Your age o'errules you; had you youth like
      mine,
You'd make her love your heaven, and her divine.

Friar. Nay, then I see thou'rt too far sold to hell:
It lies not in the compass of my prayers
To call thee back, yet let me counsel thee;
Persuade thy sister to some marriage.

Giovanni. Marriage! why, that's to damn her; that's to
      prove
Her greedy variety of lust.

Friar. O, fearful! if thou wilt not, give me leave
To shrive her, lest she should die unabsolved.

Giovanni. At your best leisure, father: then she'll tell you
How dearly she doth prize my matchless love;
Then you will know what pity 'twere we two
Should have been sundered from each other's arms.
View well her face, and in that little round
You may observe a world of variety;
For colour, lips; for sweet perfumes, her breath;
For jewels, eyes; for threads of purest gold,
Hair; for delicious choice of flowers, cheeks;
Wonder in every portion of that form.[27]
Hear her but speak, and you will swear the spheres
Make music to the citizens in Heaven.
But, father, what is else for pleasure framed
Lest I offend your ears, shall go unnamed.

Friar. The more I hear, I pity thee the more,

---

[27] "Throne" in the old edition.

That one so excellent should give those parts
All to a second death. What I can do
Is but to pray; and yet—I could advise thee,
Wouldst thou be ruled.

   Giovanni.   In what?

   Friar.   Why leave her yet;
The throne of mercy is above your trespass;
Yet time is left you both—

   Giovanni.   To embrace each other,
Else let all time be struck quite out of number:
She is like me, and I like her, resolved.

   Friar. No more! I'll visit her.—This grieves me most,
       Things being thus, a pair of souls are lost. [*Exeunt.*

SCENE VI—*A Room in* FLORIO'S *House*

Enter FLORIO, DONADO, ANNABELLA, *and* PUTANA.

   Florio. Where's Giovanni?

   Annabella.   Newly walked abroad,
And, as I heard him say, gone to the friar,
His reverend tutor.

   Florio.   That's a blessèd man,
A man made up of holiness: I hope
He'll teach him how to gain another world.

   Donado. Fair gentlewoman, here's a letter sent
To you from my young cousin; I dare swear
He loves you in his soul: would you could hear
Sometimes what I see daily, sighs and tears,
As if his breast were prison to his heart!

   Florio. Receive it, Annabella.

   Annabella. Alas, good man!   [*Takes the letter.*

   Donado. What's that she said?

   Putana. An't please you, sir, she said, "Alas, good man!"
Truly I do commend him to her every night before her
first sleep, because I would have her dream of him; and
she hearkens to that most religiously.

   Donado. Sayest so? God-a'-mercy, Putana! there's something for thee [*Gives her money*]: and prithee do what

thou canst on his behalf; 'shall not be lost labour, take
my word for't.

Putana. Thank you most heartily, sir: now I have a feeling of your mind, let me alone to work.

Annabella. Guardian,—

Putana. Did you call?

Annabella. Keep this letter.

Donado. Signior Florio, in any case bid her read it instantly.

Florio. Keep it! for what? pray, read it me hereright.

Annabella. I shall, sir.   [*She reads the letter.*

Donado. How d'ye find her inclined, signior?

Florio. Troth, sir, I know not how; not all so well
As I could wish.

Annabella. Sir, I am bound to rest your cousin's debtor.
The jewel I'll return; for if he love,
I'll count that love a jewel.

Donado.   Mark you that?
Nay, keep them both, sweet maid.

Annabella.   You must excuse me,
Indeed I will not keep it.

Florio.   Where's the ring,
That which your mother, in her will, bequeathed,
And charged you on her blessing not to give 't
To any but your husband? send back that.

Annabella. I have it not.

Florio.   Ha! have it not! where is't?

Annabella. My brother in the morning took it from me,
Said he would wear't to day.

Florio.   Well, what do you say
To young Bergetto's love? are you content to
Match with him? speak.

Donado.   There is the point, indeed.

Annabella. [*Aside*] What shall I do? I must say something now.

Florio. What say? why d'ye not speak?

Annabella.   Sir, with your leave—
Please you to give me freedom?

Florio.   Yes, you have it.

Annabella. Signior Donado, if your nephew mean
To raise his better fortunes in his match,
The hope of me will hinder such a hope:
Sir, if you love him, as I know you do,
Find one more worthy of his choice than me:
In short, I'm sure I shall not be his wife.

Donado. Why, here's plain dealing; I commend thee
for't;
And all the worst I wish thee is, Heaven bless thee!
Your father yet and I will still be friends:—
Shall we not, Signior Florio?

Florio.   Yes; why not?
Look, here your cousin comes.

Enter BERGETTO *and* POGGIO.

Donado. [*Aside*] O, coxcomb! what doth he make here?

Bergetto. Where's my uncle, sirs?

Donado. What's the news now?

Bergetto. Save you, uncle, save you!—You must not think
I come for nothing, masters.—And how, and how is't?
what, you have read my letter? ah, there I—tickled you,
i'faith.

Poggio. [*Aside to* BERGETTO] But 'twere better you had
tickled her in another place.

Bergetto. Sirrah sweetheart, I'll tell thee a good jest; and
riddle what 'tis.

Annabella. You say you'll tell me.

Bergetto. As I was walking just now in the street, I met a
swaggering fellow would needs take the wall of me; and
because he did thrust me, I very valiantly called him rogue.
He hereupon bade me draw; I told him I had more wit
than so; but when he saw that I would not, he did so
maul me with the hilts of his rapier, that my head sung
whilst my feet capered in the kennel.

Donado. [*Aside*] Was ever the like ass seen!

Annabella. And what did you all this while?

Bergetto. Laugh at him for a gull, till I saw the blood run
about mine ears, and then I could not choose but find in
my heart to cry; till a fellow with a broad beard—they say

he is a new-come doctor—called me into his house, and
gave me a plaster, look you, here 'tis:—and, sir, there was
a young wench washed my face and hands most excellently;
i' faith, I shall love her as long as I live for't.—Did she not,
Poggio?

Poggio. Yes, and kissed him too.

Bergetto. Why, la, now, you think I tell a lie, uncle, I
warrant.

Donado. Would he that beat thy blood out of thy head
had beaten some wit into it! for I fear thou never wilt have
any.

Bergetto. O, uncle, but there was a wench would have
done a man's heart good to have looked on her.—By this
light, she had a face methinks worth twenty of you,
Mistress Annabella.

Donado. [*Aside*] Was ever such a fool born!

Annabella. I am glad she liked [28] you sir.

Bergetto. Are you so? by my troth, I thank you, forsooth.

Florio. Sure, 'twas the doctor's niece, that was last day
with us here.

Bergetto. 'Twas she, 'twas she.

Donado. How do you know that, simplicity?

Bergetto. Why, does not he say so? if I should have said
no, I should have given him the lie, uncle, and so have
deserved a dry beating again: I'll none of that.

Florio. A very modest well-behaved young maid
As I have seen.

Donado. Is she indeed?

Florio. Indeed she is, if I have any judgment.

Donado. Well, sir, now you are free: you need not care
for sending letters now; you are dismissed, your mistress
here will none of you.

Bergetto. No! why, what care I for that? I can have
wenches enough in Parma for half-a-crown a-piece:—cannot
I, Poggio?

Poggio. I'll warrant you, sir.

Donado. Signior Florio,
I thank you for your free recourse you gave
For my admittance: and to you, fair maid,

28 *i.e.* Pleased.

That jewel I will give you 'gainst your marriage.—
Come, will you go, sir?

Bergetto. Ay, marry, will I.—Mistress, farewell, mistress;
I'll come again to-morrow; farewell, mistress.

> [*Exeunt* DONADO, BERGETTO, *and* POGGIO.

Enter GIOVANNI.

Florio. Son, where have you been? what, alone, alone
still?
I would not have it so; you must forsake
This over-bookish humour. Well, your sister
Hath shook the fool off.

Giovanni.   'Twas no match for her.

Florio. 'Twas not indeed; I meant it nothing less;
Soranzo is the man I only like:—
Look on him, Annabella.—Come, 'tis supper-time,
And it grows late.   [*Exit.*

Giovanni. Whose jewel's that?

Annabella. Some sweetheart's.

Giovanni.   So I think.

Annabella.   A lusty youth,
Signior Donado, gave it me to wear
Against my marriage.

Giovanni.   But you shall not wear it:
Send it him back again.

Annabella.   What, you are jealous?

Giovanni. That you shall know anon, at better leisure.
Welcome sweet night! the evening crowns the day.

> [*Exeunt.*

ACT THE THIRD

SCENE I—*A Room in* DONADO's *House*

Enter BERGETTO *and* POGGIO.

BERGETTO. Does my uncle think to make me a baby still?
No, Poggio; he shall know I have a sconce [29] now.

---

[29] Head.

Poggio. Ay, let him not bob you off like an ape with an apple.

Bergetto. 'Sfoot, I will have the wench, if he were ten uncles, in despite of his nose, Poggio.

Poggio. Hold him to the grindstone, and give not a jot of ground: she hath in a manner promised you already.

Bergetto. True, Poggio; and her uncle, the doctor, swore I should marry her.

Poggio. He swore; I remember.

Bergetto. And I will have her, that's more: didst see the codpiece-point she gave me and the box of marmalade?

Poggio. Very well; and kissed you, that my chops watered at the sight on't. There's no way but to clap-up a marriage in hugger-mugger.

Bergetto. I will do't; for I tell thee, Poggio, I begin to grow valiant methinks, and my courage begins to rise.

Poggio. Should you be afraid of your uncle?

Bergetto. Hang him, old doting rascal! no: I say I will have her.

Poggio. Lose no time, then.

Bergetto. I will beget a race of wise men and constables that shall cart whores at their own charges; and break the duke's peace ere I have done myself. Come away.

[*Exeunt.*

SCENE II—*A Room in* Florio's *House*

Enter Florio, Giovanni, Soranzo, Annabella,
Putana, *and* Vasques.

Florio. My Lord Soranzo, though I must confess
The proffers that are made me have been great
In marriage of my daughter, yet the hope
Of your still rising honours have prevailed
Above all other jointures: here she is;
She knows my mind; speak for yourself to her,—
And hear, you, daughter, see you use him nobly:
For any private speech I'll give you time.—
Come, son, and you the rest; let them alone;
Agree they as they may.

Soranzo.   I thank you, sir.
Giovanni. [*Aside to* ANNABELLA]. Sister, be not all
    woman; think on me.
Soranzo. Vasques,—
Vasques.   My lord?
Soranzo.   Attend me without.
        [*Exeunt all but* SORANZO *and* ANNABELLA.
Annabella. Sir, what's your will with me?
Soranzo.   Do you not know
What I should tell you?
Annabella.   Yes; you'll say you love me.
Soranzo. And I will swear it too; will you believe it?
Annabella. 'Tis no point of faith.

     Enter GIOVANNI *in the Gallery above.*

Soranzo.   Have you not will to love?
Annabella. Not you.
Soranzo. Whom then?
Annabella.   That's as the fates infer.
Giovanni. [*Aside*] Of those I'm regent now.
Soranzo.   What mean you, sweet?
Annabella. To live and die a maid.
Soranzo.   O, that's unfit.
Giovanni. [*Aside*] Here's one can say that's but a
    woman's note.
Soranzo. Did you but see my heart, then would you
    swear—
Annabella. That you were dead.
Giovanni. [*Aside*]   That's true, or somewhat near it.
Soranzo. See you these true love's tears?
Annabella.   No.
Giovanni. [*Aside*]   Now she winks.
Soranzo. They plead to you for grace.
Annabella.   Yet nothing speak.
Soranzo. O, grant my suit!
Annabella.   What is it?
Soranzo.   To let me live—
Annabella. Take it.
Soranzo.   Still yours.
Annabella.   That is not mine to give.

Giovanni. [*Aside*] One such another word would kill his hopes.

Soranzo. Mistress, to leave those fruitless strifes of wit,
Know I have loved you long and loved you truly:
Not hope of what you have, but what you are,
Hath drawn me on; then let me not in vain

Still feel the rigour of your chaste disdain:
I'm sick, and sick to the heart.

    Annabella.   Help, aqua-vitæ!

    Soranzo. What mean you?

    Annabella.   Why, I thought you had been sick.

    Soranzo. Do you mock my love?

    Giovanni. [*Aside*]   There, sir, she was too nimble.

    Soranzo. [*Aside*] 'Tis plain she laughs at me.—These
        scornful taunts
Neither become your modesty or years.

    Annabella. You are no looking-glass: or if you were,
I'd dress my language by you.

    Giovanni. [*Aside*]   I'm confirmed.

    Annabella. To put you out of doubt, my lord, methinks
Your common sense should make you understand
That if I loved you, or desired your love,
Some way I should have given you better taste:
But since you are a nobleman, and one
I would not wish should spend his youth in hopes,
Let me advise you to forbear your suit,
And think I wish you well, I tell you this.

    Soranzo. Is't you speak this?

    Annabella.   Yes, I myself; yet know,—
Thus far I give you comfort,—if mine eyes
Could have picked out a man amongst all those
That sued to me to make a husband of,
You should have been that man: let this suffice;
Be noble in your secrecy and wise.

    Giovanni. [*Aside*] Why, now I see she loves me.

    Annabella.   One word more.
As ever virtue lived within your mind,
As ever noble courses were your guide,
As ever you would have me know you loved me,
Let not my father know hereof by you:

If I hereafter find that I must marry,
It shall be you or none.

   Soranzo.   I take that promise.

   Annabella. O, O my head!

   Soranzo. What's the matter? not well?

   Annabella. O, I begin to sicken!

   Giovanni.   Heaven forbid!

                   [Aside, and exit from above.

   Soranzo. Help, help, within there, ho!

Re-enter FLORIO, GIOVANNI, *and* PUTANA.

Look to your daughter, Signior Florio.

   Florio. Hold her up, she swoons.

   Giovanni. Sister, how d'ye?

   Annabella.   Sick,—brother, are you there?

   Florio. Convey her to her bed instantly, whilst I send for
a physician: quickly, I say.

   Putana. Alas, poor child!   *[Exeunt all but* SORANZO.

Re-enter VASQUES.

   Vasques. My lord,—

   Soranzo. O, Vasques, now I doubly am undone
Both in my present and my future hopes!
She plainly told me that she could not love,
And thereupon soon sickened; and I fear
Her life's in danger.

   Vasques. [*Aside*] By'r lady, sir, and so is yours, if you
knew all.—'Las, sir, I am sorry for that: may be 'tis but
the maid's-sickness, an over-flux of youth; and then, sir,
there is no such present remedy as present marriage. But
hath she given you an absolute denial?

   Soranzo. She hath, and she hath not; I'm full of grief:
But what she said I'll tell thee as we go.   [*Exeunt.*

SCENE III—*Another Room in the same*

Enter GIOVANNI *and* PUTANA.

   Putana. O, sir, we are all undone, quite undone, utterly
undone, and shamed for ever! your sister, O, your sister!

Giovanni. What of her? for Heaven's sake, speak; how does she?

Putana. O, that ever I was born to see this day!

Giovanni. She is not dead, ha? is she?

Putana. Dead! no, she is quick; 'tis worse, she is with child. You know what you have done; Heaven forgive ye! 'tis too late to repent now, Heaven help us!

Giovanni. With child? how dost thou know't?

Putana. How do I know't! am I at these years ignorant what the meanings of qualms and water-pangs be? of changing of colours, queasiness of stomachs, pukings, and another thing that I could name? Do not, for her and your credit's sake, spend the time in asking how, and which way, 'tis so: she is quick, upon my word: if you let a physician see her water, you're undone.

Giovanni. But in what case is she?

Putana. Prettily amended: 'twas but a fit, which I soon espied, and she must look for often henceforward.

Giovanni. Commend me to her, bid her take no care;[30]
Let not the doctor visit her, I charge you;
Make some excuse, till I return.—O, me!
I have a world of business in my head.—
Do not discomfort her.—
How do these news perplex me!—If my father
Come to her, tell him she's recovered well;
Say 'twas but some ill diet—d'ye hear, woman?
Look you to't.

Putana. I will, sir.   [*Exeunt.*

SCENE IV—*Another Room in the same*

Enter FLORIO *and* RICHARDETTO.

Florio. And how d'ye find her, sir?

Richardetto.   Indifferent well;
I see no danger, scarce perceive she's sick,
But that she told me she had lately eaten
Melons, and, as she thought, those disagreed
With her young stomach.

---

[30] Not be too anxious.

Florio.   Did you give her aught?

Richardetto. An easy surfeit-water, nothing else.

You need not doubt her health: I rather think
Her sickness is a fulness of the blood,—
You understand me?

Florio.   I do; you counsel well;
And once, within these few days, will so order't
She shall be married ere she know the time.

Richardetto. Yet let not haste, sir, make unworthy choice;
That were dishonour.

Florio.   Master Doctor, no;
I will not do so neither: in plain words,
My Lord Soranzo is the man I mean.

Richardetto. A noble and a virtuous gentleman.

Florio. As any is in Parma. Not far hence
Dwells Father Bonaventure, a grave friar,
Once tutor to my son: now at his cell
I'll have 'em married.

Richardetto.   You have plotted wisely.

Florio. I'll send one straight to speak with him to-night.

Richardetto. Soranzo's wise; he will delay no time.

Florio. It shall be so.

Enter Friar *and* GIOVANNI.

Friar.   Good peace be here and love!

Florio. Welcome, religious friar; you are one
That still bring blessing to the place you come to.

Giovanni. Sir, with what speed I could, I did my best
To draw this holy man from forth his cell
To visit my sick sister; that with words
Of ghostly comfort, in this time of need,
He might absolve her, whether she live or die.

Florio. 'Twas well done, Giovanni; thou herein
Hast showed a Christian's care, a brother's love.
Come, father, I'll conduct you to her chamber,
And one thing would entreat you.

Friar.   Say on, sir.

Florio. I have a father's dear impression
And wish, before I fall into my grave,
That I might see her married, as 'tis fit:

A word from you, grave man, will win her more
Than all our best persuasions.

Friar.   Gentle sir,
All this I'll say, that Heaven may prosper her.   [*Exeunt.*

SCENE V—*A Room in* RICHARDETTO'S *House*

Enter GRIMALDI.

Grimaldi. Now if the doctor keep his word, Soranzo,
Twenty to one you miss your bride. I know
'Tis an unnoble act, and not becomes
A soldier's valour; but in terms of love,
Where merit cannot sway, policy must:
I am resolved, if this physician
Play not on both hands, then Soranzo falls.

Enter RICHARDETTO.

Richardetto. You're come as I could wish; this very night
Soranzo, 'tis ordained, must be affied [31]
To Annabella, and, for aught I know,
Married.

Grimaldi. How!

Richardetto.   Yet your patience:—
The place, 'tis Friar Bonaventure's cell.
Now I would wish you to bestow this night
In watching thereabouts; 'tis but a night:
If you miss now, to-morrow I'll know all.

Grimaldi. Have you the poison?

Richardetto.   Here 'tis, in this box:
Doubt nothing, this will do't; in any case,
As you respect your life, be quick and sure.

Grimaldi. I'll speed him.

Richardetto.   Do.—Away; for 'tis not safe
You should be seen much here. Ever my love!

Grimaldi. And mine to you.   [*Exit.*

Richardetto. So! if this hit, I'll laugh and hug revenge;
And they that now dream of a wedding-feast

[31] Contracted.

May chance to mourn the lusty bridegroom's ruin.
But to my other business.—Niece Philotis!

Enter PHILOTIS.

Philotis. Uncle?
Richardetto. My lovely niece!
You have bethought ye?
Philotis.   Yes,—and, as you counselled,
Fashioned my heart to love him: but he swears
He will to-night be married: for he fears
His uncle else, if he should know the drift,
Will hinder all, and call his coz to shrift.
Richardetto. To-night! why, best of all: but, let me see—
Ay—ha! yes, so it shall be—in disguise
We'll early to the friar's; I have thought on't.
Philotis. Uncle, he comes.

Enter BERGETTO *and* POGGIO.

Richardetto.   Welcome, my worthy coz.
Bergetto. Lass, pretty lass, come buss, lass!—A-ha, Poggio!
                                              [*Kisses her.*
Richardetto. [*Aside*] There's hope of this yet.—
You shall have time enough; withdraw a little;
We must confer at large.
Bergetto. Have you not sweetmeats or dainty devices for
me?
Philotis. You shall have enough, sweetheart.
Bergetto. Sweetheart! mark that, Poggio.—By my troth, I
cannot choose but kiss thee once more for that word,
"sweetheart."—Poggio, I have a monstrous swelling about
my stomach, whatsoever the matter be.
Poggio. You shall have physic for't, sir.
Richardetto. Time runs apace.
Bergetto. Time's a blockhead.
Richardetto. Be ruled: when we have done what's fit to do,
Then you may kiss your fill, and bed her too.   [*Exeunt.*

SCENE VI—ANNABELLA'S *Chamber*

A table with wax lights; ANNABELLA *at confession before
the* Friar; *she weeps and wrings her hands.*

Friar. I'm glad to see this penance; for, believe me,
You have unripped a soul so foul and guilty,
As, I must tell you true, I marvel how
The earth hath borne you up: but weep, weep on,
These tears may do you good; weep faster yet,
Whiles I do read a lecture.

   Annabella.   Wretched creature!

   Friar. Ay, you are wretched, miserably wretched,
Almost condemned alive. There is a place,—
List, daughter!—in a black and hollow vault,
Where day is never seen; there shines no sun,
But flaming horror of consuming fires,
A lightless sulphur, choked with smoky fogs
Of an infected darkness: in this place
Dwell many thousand thousand sundry sorts
Of never-dying deaths: there damnèd souls
Roar without pity; there are gluttons fed
With toads and adders; there is burning oil
Poured down the drunkard's throat; the usurer
Is forced to sup whole draughts of molten gold;
There is the murderer for ever stabbed,
Yet can he never die; there lies the wanton
On racks of burning steel, whiles in his soul
He feels the torment of his raging lust.

   Annabella. Mercy! O, mercy!

   Friar.   There stand these wretched things
Who have dreamed out whole years in lawless sheets
And secret incests, cursing one another.
Then you will wish each kiss your brother gave
Had been a dagger's point; then you shall hear
How he will cry, "O, would my wicked sister
Had first been damned, when she did yield to lust!"—
But soft, methinks I see repentance work
New motions in your heart: say, how is't with you?

Annabella. Is there no way left to redeem my miseries?

Friar. There is, despair not; Heaven is merciful,
And offers grace even now. 'Tis thus agreed:
First, for your honour's safety, that you marry
My Lord Soranzo; next, to save your soul,
Leave off this life, and henceforth live to him.

Annabella. Ay me!

Friar.   Sigh not; I know the baits of sin
Are hard to leave; O, 'tis a death to do't:
Remember what must come. Are you content?

Annabella. I am.

Friar.   I like it well; we'll take the time.—
Who's near us there?

Enter FLORIO *and* GIOVANNI.

Florio.   Did you call, father?

Friar. Is Lord Soranzo come?

Florio.   He stays below.

Friar. Have you acquainted him at full?

Florio.   I have,
And he is overjoyed.

Friar.   And so are we.
Bid him come near.

Giovanni. [*Aside*] My sister weeping! Ha!
I fear this friar's falsehood.—I will call him.   [*Exit*

Florio. Daughter, are you resolved?

Annabella.   Father, I am.

Re-enter GIOVANNI *with* SORANZO *and* VASQUES.

Florio. My Lord Soranzo, here
Give me your hand; for that I give you this.
                                        [*Joins their hands.*

Soranzo. Lady, say you so too?

Annabella.   I do, and vow
To live with you and yours.

Friar.   Timely resolved:
My blessing rest on both! More to be done,
You may perform it on the morning sun.   [*Exeunt.*

SCENE VII—*The Street before the Monastery*

Enter GRIMALDI *with his rapier drawn and a dark lantern.*

Grimaldi. 'Tis early night as yet, and yet too soon
To finish such a work; here I will lie
To listen who comes next.   [*He lies down.*

Enter BERGETTO *and* PHILOTIS *disguised, followed at a
    short distance by* RICHARDETTO *and* POGGIO.

Bergetto. We are almost at the place, I hope, sweetheart.
Grimaldi. [*Aside*] I hear them near, and heard one say
    "sweetheart."
'Tis he; now guide my hand, some angry justice,
Home to his bosom!—Now have at you, sir!
                     [*Stabs* BERGETTO *and exit.*
Bergetto. O, help, help! here's a stitch fallen in my guts:
O for a flesh-tailor quickly!—Poggio!
Philotis. What ails my love?
Bergetto. I am sure I cannot piss forward and backward,
and yet I am wet before and behind.—Lights! lights! ho,
lights!
Philotis. Alas, some villain here has slain my love!
Richardetto. O, Heaven forbid it!—Raise up the next
    neighbours
Instantly, Poggio, and bring lights.   [*Exit* POGGIO.
How is't, Bergetto? slain! It cannot be;
Are you sure you're hurt?
Bergetto. O, my belly seethes like a porridge-pot! Some
cold water, I shall boil over else; my whole body is in a
sweat, that you may wring my shirt; feel here.—Why,
Poggio!

Re-enter POGGIO *with* Officers *and lights.*

Poggio. Here. Alas, how do you?
Richardetto. Give me a light.—What's here? all blood!—
    O, sirs,
Signior Donado's nephew now is slain.
Follow the murderer with all the haste

Up to the city, he cannot be far hence:
Follow, I beseech you.

Officers.   Follow, follow, follow!   [*Exeunt.*

Richardetto. Tear off thy linen, coz, to stop his wounds.—
Be of good comfort, man.

Bergetto. Is all this mine own blood? nay, then, good
night with me.—Poggio, commend me to my uncle, dost
hear? bid him, for my sake, make much of this wench.—O,
I am going the wrong way sure, my belly aches so.—O,
farewell, Poggio!—O, O!   [*Dies.*

Philotis. O, he is dead!

Poggio.   How! dead!

Richardetto.   He's dead indeed;
'Tis now too late to weep: let's have him home,
And with what speed we may find out the murderer.

Poggio. O, my master! my master! my master!

        [*Exeunt.*

SCENE VIII—*A Room in* HIPPOLITA'S *House*

Enter VASQUES *and* HIPPOLITA.

Hippolita. Betrothed?

Vasques. I saw it.

Hippolita. And when's the marriage-day?

Vasques.   Some two days hence.

Hippolita. Two days! why, man, I would but wish two
        hours
To send him to his last and lasting sleep;
And, Vasques, thou shalt see I'll do it bravely.

Vasques. I do not doubt your wisdom, nor, I trust, you
my secrecy; I am infinitely yours.

Hippolita. I will be thine in spite of my disgrace.—
So soon? O wicked man, I durst be sworn
He'd laugh to see me weep.

Vasques. And that's a villanous fault in him.

Hippolita. No, let him laugh; I'm armed in my resolves:
Be thou still true.

Vasques. I should get little by treachery against so hopeful
a preferment as I am like to climb to.

Hippolita. Even to—my bosom, Vasques. Let my youth
Revel in these new pleasures: if we thrive,
He now hath but a pair of days to live.   [*Exeunt.*

SCENE IX—*The Street before the* Cardinal's *Gates*

Enter FLORIO, DONADO, RICHARDETTO, POGGIO, *and* Officers.

Florio. 'Tis bootless now to show yourself a child,
Signior Donado; what is done, is done:
Spend not the time in tears, but seek for justice.

Richardetto. I must confess somewhat I was in fault
That had not first acquainted you what love
Passed 'twixt him and my niece; but, as I live,
His fortune grieves me as it were mine own.

Donado. Alas, poor creature! he meant no man harm,
That I am sure of.

Florio.   I believe that too.
But stay, my masters: are you sure you saw
The murderer pass here?

1st Officer. An it please you, sir, we are sure we saw a
ruffian, with a naked weapon in his hand all bloody, get into
my lord cardinal's grace's gate; that we are sure of; but for
fear of his grace—bless us!—we durst go no farther.

Donado. Know you what manner of man he was?

1st Officer. Yes, sure, I know the man; they say he is a
soldier; he that loved your daughter, sir, an't please ye; 'twas
he for certain.

Florio. Grimaldi, on my life!

1st Officer.   Ay, ay, the same.

Richardetto. The cardinal is noble; he no doubt
Will give true justice.

Donado.   Knock some one at the gate.

Poggio. I'll knock, sir.   [*Knocks.*

Servant. [*Within.*] What would ye?

Florio. We require speech with the lord cardinal
About some present business: pray inform
His grace that we are here.

Enter the Cardinal, *followed by* GRIMALDI.

Cardinal. Why, how now, friends! what saucy mates are
     you
That know nor duty nor civility?
Are we a person fit to be your host;
Or is our house become your common inn,
To beat our doors at pleasure? What such haste
Is yours, as that it cannot wait fit times?
Are you the masters of this commonwealth,
And know no more discretion? O, your news
Is here before you; you have lost a nephew,
Donado, last night by Grimaldi slain:
Is that your business? well, sir, we have knowledge on't;
Let that suffice.
     Grimaldi.   In presence of your grace,
In thought I never meant Bergetto harm:
But, Florio, you can tell with how much scorn
Soranzo, backed with his confederates,
Hath often wronged me; I to be revenged,—
For that I could not win him else to fight,—
Had thought by way of ambush to have killed him,
But was unluckily therein mistook;
Else he had felt what late Bergetto did:
And though my fault to him were merely chance,
Yet humbly I submit me to your grace,   [*Kneeling.*
To do with me as you please.
     Cardinal.   Rise up, Grimaldi.—[*He rises.*
You citizens of Parma, if you seek
For justice, know, as nuncio from the pope,
For this offence I here receive Grimaldi
Into his holiness' protection:
He is no common man, but nobly born,
Of princes' blood, though you, Sir Florio,
Thought him too mean a husband for your daughter.
If more you seek for, you must go to Rome,
For he shall thither: learn more wit, for shame.—
Bury your dead.—Away, Grimaldi; leave 'em!
                         [*Exeunt* Cardinal *and* GRIMALDI.

Donado. Is this a churchman's voice? dwells justice here?

Florio. Justice is fled to Heaven, and comes no nearer.
Soranzo!—was't for him? O, impudence!
Had he the face to speak it, and not blush?
  Come, come, Donado, there's no help in this,
  When cardinals think murder's not amiss.
  Great men may do their wills, we must obey;
  But Heaven will judge them for't another day.   [*Exeunt.*

ACT THE FOURTH

SCENE I—*A Room in* FLORIO'S *House*

A banquet set out; hautboys. Enter the Friar, GIOVANNI,
ANNABELLA, PHILOTIS, SORANZO, DONADO, FLORIO,
RICHARDETTO, PUTANA, *and* VASQUES.

FRIAR. These holy rites performed, now take your times
To spend the remnant of the day in feast:
Such fit repasts are pleasing to the saints,
Who are your guests, though not with mortal eyes
To be beheld.—Long prosper in this day,
You happy couple, to each other's joy!

  Soranzo. Father, your prayer is heard; the hand of good-
      ness
Hath been a shield for me against my death:
And, more to bless me, hath enriched my life
With this most precious jewel; such a prize
As earth hath not another like to this.—
Cheer up, my love:—and, gentlemen my friends,
Rejoice with me in mirth: this day we'll crown
With lusty cups to Annabella's health.

  Giovanni. [*Aside*] O torture! were the marriage yet un-
      done,
Ere I'd endure this sight, to see my love
Clipt[32] by another, I would dare confusion,
And stand the horror of ten thousand deaths.

[32] Embraced.

Vasques. Are you not well, sir?

Giovanni.   Prithee, fellow, wait;
I need not thy officious diligence.

Florio. Signior Donado, come, you must forget
Your late mishaps, and drown your cares in wine.

Soranzo. Vasques!

Vasques.   My lord?

Soranzo.   Reach me that weighty bowl.
Here, brother Giovanni, here's to you;
Your turn come next, though now a bachelor;
Here's to your sister's happiness and mine!

                         [*Drinks and offers him the bowl.*

Giovanni. I cannot drink.

Soranzo.   What!

Giovanni.   'Twill indeed offend me.

Annabella. Pray, do not urge him, if he be not willing.

                                        [*Hautboys.*

Florio. How now! what noise[33] is this?

Vasques. O, sir, I had forgot to tell you; certain young
maidens of Parma, in honour to Madam Annabella's marriage, have sent their loves to her in a Masque, for which
they humbly crave your patience and silence.

Soranzo. We are much bound to them; so much the more
As it comes unexpected: guide them in.

Enter HIPPOLITA, *followed by* Ladies *in white robes with
    garlands of willows, all masked. Music and a dance.*

Thanks, lovely virgins! now might we but know
To whom we've been beholding for this love,
We shall acknowledge it.

Hippolita.   Yes, you shall know. [*Unmasks.*
What think you now?

All.   Hippolita!

Hippolita.   'Tis she;
Be not amazed; nor blush, young lovely bride;
I come not to defraud you of your man:
'Tis now no time to reckon-up the talk.
What Parma long hath rumoured of us both:
Let rash report run on; the breath that vents it

[33] Music.

Will, like a bubble, break itself at last.
But now to you, sweet creature; lend's your hand;—
Perhaps it hath been said that I would claim
Some interest in Soranzo, now your lord;
What I have right to do, his soul knows best:
But in my duty to your noble worth,
Sweet Annabella, and my care of you,—
Here, take, Soranzo, take this hand from me;
I'll once more join what by the holy church
Is finished and allowed.—Have I done well?

  Soranzo. You have too much engaged us.

  Hippolita.   One thing more..
That you may know my single[34] charity,
Freely I here remit all interest
I e'er could claim, and give you back your vows;
And to confirm't,—reach me a cup of wine,—

                    [VASQUES *gives her a poisoned cup.*
My Lord Soranzo, in this draught I drink
Long rest t'ye! [*She drinks*].—[*Aside to* VASQUES] Look
    to it, Vasques.

  Vasques. [*Aside to* HIPPOLITA] Fear nothing.

  Soranzo. Hippolita, I thank you; and will pledge
This happy union as another life.—
Wine, there!

  Vasques. You shall have none; neither shall you pledge
her.

  Hippolita. How!

  Vasques. Know now, Mistress She-devil, your own mis-
chievous treachery hath killed you; I must not marry you.

  Hippolita. Villain!

  All. What's the matter?

  Vasques. Foolish woman, thou art now like a firebrand
that hath kindled others and burnt thyself:—*troppo sperar,
inganna,*[35]—thy vain hope hath deceived thee; thou art but
dead; if thou hast any grace, pray.

  Hippolita. Monster!

  Vasques. Die in charity, for shame.—This thing of malice,
this woman, had privately corrupted me with promise of

---

34 Single-minded.
35 Too much hope brings disappointment.

marriage, under this politic reconciliation, to poison my lord,
whiles she might laugh at his confusion on his marriage-day.
I promised her fair; but I knew what my reward should
have been, and would willingly have spared her life, but
that I was acquainted with the danger of her disposition;
and now have fitted her a just payment in her own coin:
there she is, she hath yet[36]——and end thy days in peace, vile
woman; as for life, there's no hope; think not on't.

 All. Wonderful justice!

 Richardetto. Heaven, thou art righteous.

 Hippolita.   O, 'tis true;
I feel my minute coming. Had that slave
Kept promise,—O, my torment!—thou this hour
Hadst died, Soranzo;—heat above hell-fire!—
Yet, ere I pass away,—cruel, cruel flames!—
Take here my curse amongst you: may thy bed
Of marriage be a rack unto thy heart,
Burn blood, and boil in vengeance;—O, my heart,
My flame's intolerable!—mayst thou live
To father bastards; may her womb bring forth
Monsters,—and die together in your sins,
Hated, scorned, and unpitied!—O, O!   [*Dies.*

 Florio. Was e'er so vile a creature!

 Richardetto.   Here're the end
Of lust and pride.

 Annabella.   It is a fearful sight.

 Soranzo. Vasques, I know thee now a trusty servant,
And never will forget thee.—Come, my love,
We'll home, and thank the heavens for this escape.—
Father and friends, we must break up this mirth;
It is too sad a feast.

 Donado.   Bear hence the body.

 Friar. [*Aside to* GIOVANNI] Here's an ominous change!
Mark this, my Giovanni, and take heed—!
 I fear the event: that marriage seldom's good
Where the bride-banquet so begins in blood. [*Exeunt.*

---

[36] The old copy has a considerable double break here, probably from some defect
in the MS.

SCENE II—*A Room in* RICHARDETTO's *House*

Enter RICHARDETTO *and* PHILOTIS.

Richardetto. My wretched wife, more wretched in her
　　shame
Than in her wrongs to me, hath paid too soon
The forfeit of her modesty and life.
And I am sure, my niece, though vengeance hover,
Keeping aloof yet from Soranzo's fall,
Yet he will fall, and sink with his own weight.
I need not now—my heart persuades me so—
To further his confusion; there is One
Above begins to work: for, as I hear,
Debates already 'twixt his wife and him
Thicken and run to head; she, as 'tis said,
Slightens his love, and he abandons hers:
Much talk I hear. Since things go thus, my niece,
In tender love and pity of your youth,
My counsel is, that you should free your years
From hazard of these woes by flying hence
To fair Cremona, there to vow your soul
In holiness, a holy votaress:
Leave me to see the end of these extremes.
All human worldly courses are uneven;
No life is blessèd but the way to Heaven.
　　Philotis. Uncle, shall I resolve to be a nun?
　　Richardetto. Ay, gentle niece; and in your hourly prayers
Remember me, your poor unhappy uncle.
Hie to Cremona now, as fortune leads,
Your home your cloister, your best friends your beads:
Your chaste and single life shall crown your birth:
Who dies a virgin lives a saint on earth.
　　Philotis. Then farewell, world, and worldly thoughts,
　　adieu!
Welcome, chaste vows; myself I yield to you.　　[*Exeunt.*

SCENE III—*A Chamber in* SORANZO's *House*

Enter SORANZO *unbraced, and dragging in* ANNABELLA.

Soranzo. Come, strumpet, famous whore! were every drop
Of blood that runs in thy adulterous veins
A life, this sword—dost see't?—should in one blow
Confound them all. Harlot, rare, notable harlot,
That with thy brazen face maintain'st thy sin,
Was there no man in Parma to be bawd
To your loose cunning whoredom else but I?
Must your hot itch and plurisy of lust,
The heyday of your luxury,[37] be fed
Up to a surfeit, and could none but I
Be picked out to be cloak to your close tricks,
Your belly sports? Now I must be the dad
To all that gallimaufry that is stuffed
In thy corrupted bastard-bearing womb!
Say, must I?
     Annabella. Beastly man! why, 'tis thy fate.
I sued not to thee; for, but that I thought
Your over-loving lordship would have run
Mad on denial, had ye lent me time,
I would have told ye in what case I was:
But you would needs be doing.
     Soranzo.   Whore of whores!
Darest thou tell me this?
     Annabella.   O, yes; why not?
You were deceived in me; 'twas not for love
I chose you, but for honour: yet know this,
Would you be patient yet, and hide your shame,
I'd see whether I could love you.
     Soranzo.   Excellent quean!
Why, art thou not with child?
     Annabella.   What needs all this,
When 'tis superfluous? I confess I am.

---

[37] Luxury was commonly used in the sense of lust.

Soranzo. Tell me by whom.

Annabella.   Soft! 'twas not in my bargain.
Yet somewhat, sir, to stay your longing stomach,
I am content t' acquaint you with; the man,
The more than man, that got this sprightly boy,—
For 'tis a boy, and therefore glory, sir,
Your heir shall be a son—

Soranzo.   Damnable monster!

Annabella. Nay, an you will not hear, I'll speak no more.

Soranzo. Yes, speak, and speak thy last.

Annabella.   A match! a match!
This noble creature was in every part
So angel-like, so glorious, that a woman
Who had not been but human, as was I,
Would have kneeled to him, and have begged for love.—
You! why, you are not worthy once to name
His name without true worship, or, indeed,
Unless you kneeled, to hear another name him.

Soranzo. What was he called?

Annabella.   We are not come to that;
Let it suffice that you shall have the glory
To father what so brave a father got.
In brief, had not this chance fall'n out as't doth,
I never had been troubled with a thought
That you had been a creature:—but for marriage,
I scarce dream yet of that.

Soranzo.   Tell me his name.

Annabella. Alas, alas, there's all! will you believe?

Soranzo. What?

Annabella.   You shall never know.

Soranzo.   How!

Annabella.   Never: if
You do, let me be cursed!

Soranzo. Not know it, strumpet! I'll rip up thy heart,
And find it there.

Annabella.   Do, do.

Soranzo.   And with my teeth
Tear the prodigious lecher joint by joint.

Annabella. Ha, ha, ha! the man's merry.

Soranzo.   Dost thou laugh?
Come, whore, tell me your lover, or, by truth,
I'll hew thy flesh to shreds; who is't?

Annabella. [*Sings*] *Che morte più dolce che morire per
    amore?* [38]

Soranzo. Thus will I pull thy hair, and thus I'll drag
Thy lust-be-lepered body through the dust.

                    [*Hales her up and down.*
Yet tell his name.

Annabella. [*Sings*] *Morendo in grazia dee morire senza
    dolore.*[39]

Soranza. Dost thou triúmph? The treasures of the earth
Shall not redeem thee; were there kneeling kings
Did beg thy life, or angels did come down
To plead in tears, yet should not all prevail
Against my rage: dost thou not tremble yet?

Annabella. At what? to die! no, be a gallant hangman;[40]
I dare thee to the worst: strike, and strike home;
I leave revenge behind, and thou shalt feel't.

Soranzo. Yet tell me ere thou diest, and tell me truly,
Knows thy old father this?

Annabella.   No, by my life.

Soranzo. Wilt thou confess, and I will spare thy life?

Annabella. My life! I will not buy my life so dear.

Soranzo. I will not slack my vengeance.

                              [*Draws his sword.*

                    Enter VASQUES.

Vasques.   What d'ye mean, sir?

Soranzo. Forbear, Vasques; such a damnèd whore
Deserves no pity.

Vasques.   Now the gods forfend!
And would you be her executioner, and kill her in your rage
too? O, 'twere most unmanlike. She is your wife: what
faults have been done by her before she married you were
not against you: alas, poor lady, what hath she committed,
which any lady in Italy, in the like case, would not? Sir,

---

[38] What death sweeter than to die for love?
[39] To die in grace is to die without sorrow.
[40] Executioner.

you must be ruled by your reason, and not by your fury;
that were unhuman and beastly.

Soranzo. She shall not live.

Vasques. Come, she must. You would have her confess
the author of her present misfortunes, I warrant ye; 'tis an
unconscionable demand, and she should lose the estimation
that I, for my part, hold of her worth, if she had done it:
why, sir, you ought not, of all men living, to know it. Good
sir, be reconciled: alas, good gentlewoman!

Annabella. Pish, do not beg for me; I prize my life
As nothing; if the man will needs be mad,
Why, let him take it.

Soranzo.   Vasques, hear'st thou this?

Vasques. Yes, and commend her for it; in this she shows
the nobleness of a gallant spirit, and beshrew my heart, but
it becomes her rarely.—[*Aside to* Soranzo] Sir, in any case,
smother your revenge; leave the scenting-out your wrongs to
me: be ruled, as you respect your honour, or you mar all.—
[*Aloud*] Sir, if ever my service were of any credit with you,
be not so violent in your distractions: you are married now;
what a triumph might the report of this give to other
neglected suitors! 'Tis as manlike to bear extremities as god-
like to forgive.

Soranzo. O, Vasques, Vasques, in this piece of flesh,
This faithless face of hers, had I laid up
The treasure of my heart!—Hadst thou been virtuous,
Fair, wicked woman, not the matchless joys
Of life itself had made me wish to live
With any saint but thee: deceitful creature,
How hast thou mocked my hopes, and in the shame
Of thy lewd womb even buried me alive!
I did too dearly love thee.

Vasques. [*Aside to* Soranzo] This is well; follow this
temper with some passion: be brief and moving; 'tis for the
purpose.

Soranzo. Be witness to my words thy soul and thoughts;
And tel! me, didst not think that in my heart
I did too superstitiously adore thee?

Annabella. I must confess I know you loved me well.

Soranzo. And wouldst thou use me thus! O Annabella,

Be thou assured, whoe'er the villain was
That thus hath tempted thee to this disgrace,
Well he might lust, but never loved like me:
He doted on the picture that hung out
Upon thy cheeks to please his humorous eye;
Not on the part I loved, which was thy heart,
And, as I thought, thy virtues.

   Annabella.   O, my lord!
These words wound deeper than your sword could do.

   Vasques. Let me not ever take comfort, but I begin to
weep myself, so much I pity him: why, madam, I knew,
when his rage was over-past, what it would come to.

   Soranzo. Forgive me, Annabella. Though thy youth
Hath tempted thee above thy strength to folly,
Yet will not I forget what I should be,
And what I am—a husband; in that name
Is hid divinity: if I do find
That thou wilt yet be true, here I remit
All former faults, and take thee to my bosom.

   Vasques. By my troth, and that's a point of noble charity.

   Annabella. Sir, on my knees,—

   Soranzo.   Rise up, you shall not kneel.
Get you to your chamber; see you make no show
Of alteration; I'll be with you straight:
My reason tells me now that " 'tis as common
To err in frailty as to be a woman."
Go to your chamber.   [*Exit* ANNABELLA.

   Vasques. So! this was somewhat to the matter: what do
you think of your heaven of happiness now, sir?

   Soranzo. I carry hell about me; all my blood
Is fired in swift revenge.

   Vasques. That may be; but know you how, or on whom?
Alas, to marry a great woman, being made great in the
stock to your hand, is a usual sport in these days; but to
know what ferret it was that hunted your cony-berry,—
there's the cunning.

   Soranzo. I'll make her tell herself, or—

   Vasques. Or what? you must not do so; let me yet persuade your sufferance a little while: go to her, use her

mildly; win her, if it be possible, to a voluntary, to a weeping tune: for the rest, if all hit, I will not miss my mark.
Pray, sir, go in: the next news I tell you shall be wonders.

Soranzo. Delay in vengeance gives a heavier blow. [*Exit.*

Vasques. Ah, sirrah, here's work for the nonce! I had a
suspicion of a bad matter in my head a pretty whiles ago;
but after my madam's scurvy looks here at home, her
waspish perverseness and loud fault-finding, then I remembered the proverb, that "where hens crow, and cocks hold
their peace, there are sorry houses." 'Sfoot, if the lower parts
of a she-tailor's cunning can cover such a swelling in the
stomach, I'll never blame a false stitch in a shoe whiles I
live again. Up, and up so quick? and so quickly too? 'twere
a fine policy to learn by whom: this must be known; and I
have thought on't:—

Enter PUTANA *in tears.*

Here's the way, or none.—What, crying, old mistress! alas,
alas, I cannot blame ye; we have a lord, Heaven help us, is
so mad as the devil himself, the more shame for him.

Putana. O, Vasques, that ever I was born to see this day!
Doth he use thee so too sometimes, Vasques?

Vasques. Me? why he makes a dog of me: but if some
were of my mind, I know what we would do. As sure as I
am an honest man, he will go near to kill my lady with un-
kindness: say she be with child, is that such a matter for a
young woman of her years to be blamed for?

Putana. Alas, good heart, it is against her will full sore.

Vasques. I durst be sworn all his madness is for that she
will not confess whose 'tis, which he will know; and when
he doth know it, I am so well acquainted with his humour,
that he will forget all straight. Well, I could wish she would
in plain terms tell all, for that's the way, indeed.

Putana. Do you think so?

Vasques. Foh, I know't; provided that he did not win her
to 't by force. He was once in a mind that you could tell,
and meant to have wrung it out of you; but I somewhat
pacified him for that: yet, sure, you know a great deal.

Putana. Heaven forgive us all! I know a little, Vasques.

Vasques. Why should you not? who else should? Upon my conscience, she loves you dearly; and you would not betray her to any affliction for the world.

Putana. Not for all the world, by my faith and troth, Vasques.

Vasques. 'Twere pity of your life if you should; but in this you should both relieve her present discomforts, pacify my lord, and gain yourself everlasting love and preferment.

Putana. Dost think so, Vasques?

Vasques. Nay, I know't; sure 'twas some near and entire friend.

Putana. 'Twas a dear friend indeed; but—

Vasques. But what? fear not to name him; my life between you and danger: 'faith, I think 'twas no base fellow.

Putana. Thou wilt stand between me and harm?

Vasques. 'Ud's pity, what else? you shall be rewarded too, trust me.

Putana. 'Twas even no worse than her own brother.

Vasques. Her brother Giovanni, I warrant ye!

Putana. Even he, Vasques; as brave a gentleman as ever kissed fair lady. O, they love most perpetually.

Vasques. A brave gentleman indeed! why, therein I commend her choice.—[*Aside*] Better and better.—You are sure 'twas he?

Putana. Sure; and you shall see he will not be long from her too.

Vasques. He were to blame if he would: but may I believe thee?

Putana. Believe me! why, dost think I am a Turk or a Jew? No, Vasques, I have known their dealings too long to belie them now.

Vasques. Where are you there? within, sirs!

Enter Banditti.

Putana. How now! what are these?

Vasques. You shall know presently.—Come, sirs, take me this old damnable hag, gag her instantly, and put out her eyes, quickly, quickly!

Putana. Vasques! Vasques!—

Vasques. Gag her, I say; 'sfoot, d'ye suffer her to prate?

what d'ye fumble about? let me come to her. I'll help your
old gums, you toad-bellied bitch! [*They gag her.*] Sirs, carry
her closely into the coal-house, and put out her eyes instantly; if she roars, slit her nose: d'ye hear, be speedy and
sure.   [*Exeunt* Banditti *with* PUTANA.
Why, this is excellent and above expectation—her own
brother! O, horrible! to what a height of liberty in damnation hath the devil trained our age! her brother, well!
there's yet but a beginning; I must to my lord, and tutor
him better in his points of vengeance: now I see how a
smooth tale goes beyond a smooth tail.—But soft! what
thing comes next? Giovanni! as I would wish: my belief is
strengthened, 'tis as firm as winter and summer.

Enter GIOVANNI.

Giovanni. Where's my sister?

Vasques. Troubled with a new sickness, my lord; she's
somewhat ill.

Giovanni. Took too much of the flesh, I believe.

Vasques. Troth, sir, and you, I think, have e'en hit it:
but my virtuous lady—

Giovanni. Where's she?

Vasques. In her chamber; please you visit her; she is
alone. [GIOVANNI *gives him money.*] Your liberality hath
doubly made me your servant, and ever shall, ever.

                    [*Exit* GIOVANNI.

Re-enter SORANZO.

Sir, I am made a man; I have plied my cue with cunning
and success: I beseech you let's be private.

Soranzo. My lady's brother's come; now he'll know all.

Vasques. Let him know't; I have made some of them fast
enough. How have you dealt with my lady?

Soranzo. Gently, as thou hast counselled; O, my soul
Runs circular in sorrow for revenge:
But, Vasques, thou shalt know—

Vasques. Nay, I will know no more, for now comes your
turn to know: I would not talk so openly with you.—
[*Aside*] Let my young master take time enough, and go

at pleasure; he is sold to death, and the devil shall not ransom him.—Sir, I beseech you, your privacy.

Soranzo. No conquest can gain glory of my fear. [*Exeunt.*

ACT THE FIFTH

SCENE I—*The Street before* SORANZO's *House*

ANNABELLA *appears at a window above.*

ANNABELLA. Pleasures, farewell, and all ye thriftless minutes
Wherein false joys have spun a weary life!
To these my fortunes now I take my leave.
Thou, precious Time, that swiftly rid'st in post
Over the world, to finish-up the race
Of my last fate, here stay thy restless course,
And bear to ages that are yet unborn
A wretched, woeful woman's tragedy!
My conscience now stands up against my lust
With depositions charactered in guilt,

Enter Friar *below.*

And tells me I am lost: now I confess
Beauty that clothes the outside of the face
Is cursèd if it be not clothed with grace.
Here like a turtle mewed-up in a cage,
Unmated, I converse with air and walls,
And descant on my vile unhappiness.
O, Giovanni, thou hast had the spoil
Of thine own virtues and my modest fame,
Would thou hadst been less subject to those stars
That luckless reigned at my nativity!
O, would the scourge due to my black offence
Might pass from thee, that I alone might feel
The torment of an uncontrollèd flame!

Friar [*Aside*] What's this I hear?

Annabella.   That man, that blessèd friar,
Who joined in ceremonial knot my hand
To him whose wife I now am, told me oft

I trod the path to death, and showed me how.
But they who sleep in lethargies of lust
Hug their confusion, making Heaven unjust;
And so did I.

    Friar [*Aside*] Here's music to the soul!

    Annabella. Forgive me, my good genius, and this once
Be helpful to my ends: let some good man
Pass this way, to whose trust I may commit
This paper, double-lined with tears and blood;
Which being granted, here I sadly vow
Repentance, and a leaving-of that life
I long have died in.

    Friar.   Lady, Heaven hath heard you,
And hath by providence ordained that I
Should be his minister for your behoof.

    Annabella. Ha, what are you?

    Friar.   Your brother's friend, the friar;
Glad in my soul that I have lived to hear
This free confession 'twixt your peace and you.
What would you, or to whom? fear not to speak.

    Annabella. Is Heaven so bountiful? then I have found
More favour than I hoped. Here, holy man:

                      [*Throws down a letter.*

Commend me to my brother; give him that,
That letter; bid him read it, and repent.
Tell him that I, imprisoned in my chamber,
Barred of all company, even of my guardian,—
Who gives me cause of much suspect,—have time
To blush at what hath passed; bid him be wise,
And not believe the friendship of my lord:
I fear much more than I can speak: good father,
The place is dangerous, and spies are busy.
I must break off. You'll do't?

    Friar.   Be sure I will,
And fly with speed. My blessing ever rest
With thee, my daughter; live, to die more blest!   [*Exit.*

    Annabella. Thanks to the heavens, who have prolonged
      my breath
To this good use! now I can welcome death.

                  [*Withdraws from the window.*

SCENE II—*A Room in* SORANZO's *House*

Enter SORANZO *and* VASQUES.

Vasques. Am I to be believed now? first marry a strumpet, that cast herself away upon you but to laugh at your horns, to feast on your disgrace, riot in your vexations, cuckold you in your bride-bed, waste your estate upon panders and bawds!—

Soranzo. No more, I say, no more!

Vasques. A cuckold is a goodly tame beast, my lord.

Soranzo. I am resolved; urge not another word;
My thoughts are great, and all as resolute
As thunder: in mean time I'll cause our lady
To deck herself in all her bridal robes;
Kiss her, and fold her gently in my arms.
Begone,—yet, hear you, are the banditti ready
To wait in ambush.

Vasques. Good sir, trouble not yourself about other business than your own resolution: remember that time lost cannot be recalled.

Soranzo. With all the cunning words thou canst, invite
The states[41] of Parma to my birthday's feast:
Haste to my brother-rival and his father,
Entreat them gently, bid them not to fail.
Be speedy, and return.

Vasques. Let not your pity betray you till my coming back; think upon incest and cuckoldry.

Soranzo. Revenge is all the ambition I aspire;
To that I'll climb or fall: my blood's on fire.   [*Exeunt.*

SCENE III—*A Room in* FLORIO's *House*

Enter GIOVANNI.

Giovanni. Busy opinion is an idle fool,
That, as a school-rod keeps a child in awe,
Frights the unexperienced temper of the mind:

[41] *i.e.* Nobles.

So did it me, who, ere my precious sister
Was married, thought all taste of love would die
In such a contract; but I find no change
Of pleasure in this formal law of sports.
She is still one to me, and every kiss
As sweet and as delicious as the first
I reaped, when yet the privilege of youth
Entitled her a virgin. O, the glory
Of two united hearts like hers and mine!
Let poring book-men dream of other worlds;
My world and all of happiness is here,
And I'd not change it for the best to come:
A life of pleasure is elysium.

Enter Friar.

Father, you enter on the jubilee
Of my retired delights: now I can tell you,
The hell you oft have prompted is nought else
But slavish and fond superstitious fear;
And I could prove it too—
    Friar.   Thy blindness slays thee:
Look there, 'tis writ to thee.   [*Gives him the letter.*
    Giovanni. From whom?
    Friar. Unrip the seals and see;
The blood's yet seething hot, that will anon
Be frozen harder than congealèd coral.—
Why d'ye change colour, son?
    Giovanni.   'Fore Heaven, you make
Some petty devil factor 'twixt my love
And your religion-maskèd sorceries.
Where had you this?
    Friar.   Thy conscience, youth, is seared,
Else thou wouldst stoop to warning.
    Giovanni.   'Tis her hand,
I know't; and 'tis all written in her blood.
She writes I know not what. Death! I'll not fear
An armèd thunderbolt aimed at my heart.
She writes, we are discovered:—Pox on dreams
Of low faint-hearted cowardice!—discovered?
The devil we are! which way is't possible?

Are we grown traitors to our own delights?
Confusion take such dotage! 'tis but forged:
This is your peevish chattering, weak old man!

Enter VASQUES.

Now, sir, what brings you?

Vasques. My lord, according to his yearly custom, keeping
this day a feast in honour of his birthday, by me invites you
thither. Your worthy father, with the pope's reverend
nuncio, and other magnificoes of Parma, have promised
their presence: will't please you to be of the number?

Giovanni. Yes, tell him I dare come.

Vasques. "Dare come!"

Giovanni. So I said; and tell him more, I will come.

Vasques. These words are strange to me.

Giovanni. Say, I will come.

Vasques. You will not miss?

Giovanni. Yet more! I'll come, sir. Are you answered?

Vasques. So I'll say.—My service to you.   [*Exit.*

Friar. You will not go, I trust.

Giovanni.   Not go! for what?

Friar. O, do not go: this feast, I'll gage my life,
Is but a plot to train you to your ruin.
Be ruled, you shall not go.

Giovanni.   Not go! stood Death
Threatening his armies of confounding plagues,
With hosts of dangers hot as blazing stars,
I would be there: not go! yes, and resolve
To strike as deep in slaughter as they all;
For I will go.

Friar.   Go where thou wilt: I see
The wildness of thy fate draws to an end,
To a bad fearful end. I must not stay
To know thy fall: back to Bononia I
With speed will haste, and shun this coming blow.—
Parma, farewell; would I had never known thee,
Or aught of thine!—Well, young man, since no prayer
Can make thee safe, I leave thee to despair.   [*Exit.*

Giovanni. Despair, or tortures of a thousand hells;

All's one to me: I have set up my rest.[42]
Now, now, work serious thoughts on baneful plots;
Be all a man, my soul; let not the curse
Of old prescription rend from me the gall
Of courage, which enrols a glorious death:
If I must totter like a well-grown oak,
Some under-shrubs shall in my weighty fall
Be crushed to splits; with me they all shall perish!   [*Exit.*

SCENE IV—*A Hall in* Soranzo's *House*

Enter Soranzo, Vasques *with masks, and* Banditti.

Soranzo. You will not fail, or shrink in the attempt?

Vasques. I will undertake for their parts.—Be sure, my
masters, to be bloody enough, and as unmerciful as if you
were preying upon a rich booty on the very mountains of
Liguria: for your pardons trust to my lord; but for reward
you shall trust none but your own pockets.

Banditti. We'll make a murder.

Soranzo. Here's gold [*Gives them money*]; here's more;
          want nothing; what you do
Is noble, and an act of brave revenge:
I'll make ye rich, banditti, and all free.

Banditti. Liberty! liberty!

Vasques. Hold, take every man a vizard [*Gives them
masks*]: when ye are withdrawn, keep as much silence as
you can possibly. You know the watchword; till which be
spoken, move not; but when you hear that, rush in like a
stormy flood; I need not instruct ye in your own profession.

Banditti. No, no, no.

Vasques. In, then: your ends are profit and preferment:
away!   [*Exeunt* Banditti.

Soranzo. The guests will all come, Vasques?

Vasques. Yes, sir. And now let me a little edge your
resolution: you see nothing is unready to this great work,
but a great mind in you; call to your remembrance your
disgraces, your loss of honour, Hippolita's blood, and arm

[42] *i.e.* I have taken my resolution.

your courage in your own wrongs; so shall you best right
those wrongs in vengeance, which you may truly call your
own.

Soranzo. 'Tis well: the less I speak, the more I burn.
And blood shall quench that flame.

Vasques. Now you begin to turn Italian. This beside:—
when my young incest-monger comes, he will be sharp set
on his old bit: give him time enough, let him have your
chamber and bed at liberty; let my hot hare have law ere
he be hunted to his death, that, if it be possible, he post to
hell in the very act of his damnation.

Soranzo. It shall be so; and see, as we would wish,
He comes himself first.

Enter GIOVANNI.

                        Welcome, my much-loved brother:
Now I perceive you honour me; you're welcome.
But where's my father?

Giovanni.   With the other states,[43]
Attending on the nuncio of the pope,
To wait upon him hither. How's my sister?

Soranzo.   Like a good housewife, scarcely ready yet;
You're best walk to her chamber.

Giovanni.   If you will.

Soranzo. I must expect my honourable friends;
Good brother, get her forth.

Giovanni.   You're busy, sir.   [*Exit.*

Vasques. Even as the great devil himself would have it!
let him go and glut himself in his own destruction.—
[*Flourish.*] Hark, the nuncio is at hand: good sir, be ready
to receive him.

Enter Cardinal, FLORIO, DONADO, RICHARDETTO, and Attendants.

Soranzo. Most reverend lord, this grace hath made me
       proud,
That you vouchsafe my house; I ever rest
Your humble servant for this noble favour.

Cardinal. You are our friend, my lord: his holiness

---

[43] Nobles.

Shall understand how zealously you honour
Saint Peter's vicar in his substitute:
Our special love to you.

 Soranzo.   Signiors, to you
My welcome, and my ever best of thanks
For this so memorable courtesy.—
Pleaseth your grace walk near?

 Cardinal.   My lord, we come
To celebrate your feast with civil mirth,
As ancient custom teacheth: we will go.

 Soranzo. Attend his grace there!—Signiors, keep your
  way.   [*Exeunt.*

SCENE V—ANNABELLA's *Bed-chamber in the same*

ANNABELLA *richly dressed and* GIOVANNI *discovered
lying on a bed.*

 Giovanni. What, changed so soon! hath your new
  sprightly lord
Found out a trick in night-games more than we
Could know in our simplicity? Ha! is't so?
Or does the fit come on you, to prove treacherous
To your past vows and oaths?

 Annabella.   Why should you jest
At my calamity, without all sense
Of the approaching dangers you are in?

 Giovanni. What danger's half so great as thy revolt?
Thou art a faithless sister, else thou know'st,
Malice, or any treachery beside,
Would stoop to my bent brows: why, I hold fate
Clasped in my fist, and could command the course
Of time's eternal motion, hadst thou been
One thought more steady than an ebbing sea.
And what? you'll now be honest, that's resolved?

 Annabella. Brother, dear brother, know what I have been,
And know that now there's but a dining-time
'Twixt us and our confusion: let's not waste
These precious hours in vain and useless speech.

Alas, these gay attires were not put on
But to some end; this sudden solemn feast
Was not ordained to riot in expense;
I, that have now been chambered here alone,
Barred of my guardian or of any else,
Am not for nothing at an instant freed
To fresh access. Be not deceived, my brother;
This banquet is an harbinger of death
To you and me; resolve yourself it is,
And be prepared to welcome it.

    Giovanni.   Well, then;
The schoolmen teach that all this globe of earth
Shall be consumed to ashes in a minute.

    Annabella. So I have read too.

    Giovanni.   But 'twere somewhat strange
To see the waters burn: could I believe
This might be true, I could believe as well
There might be hell or Heaven.

    Annabella.   That's most certain.

    Giovanni. A dream, a dream! else in this other world
We should know one another.

    Annabella.   So we shall.

    Giovanni. Have you heard so?

    Annabella.   For certain.

    Giovanni.   But d'ye think
That I shall see you there?—You look on me.—
May we kiss one another, prate or laugh,
Or do as we do here?

    Annabella.   I know not that.
But, brother, for the present, what d'ye mean
To free yourself from danger? some way think
How to escape: I'm sure the guests are come.

    Giovanni. Look up, look here; what see you in my face?

    Annabella. Distraction and a troubled conscience.

    Giovanni. Death, and a swift repining wrath:—yet look;
What see you in mine eyes?

    Annabella.   Methinks you weep.

    Giovanni. I do indeed: these are the funeral tears
Shed on your grave; these furrowed-up my cheeks
When first I loved and knew not how to woo.

Fair Annabella, should I here repeat
The story of my life, we might lose time.
Be record all the spirits of the air,
And all things else that are, that day and night,
Early and late, the tribute which my heart
Hath paid to Annabella's sacred love
Hath been these tears, which are her mourners now!
Never till now did Nature do her best
To show a matchless beauty to the world,
Which in an instant, ere it scarce was seen,
The jealous Destinies required again.
Pray, Annabella, pray! Since we must part,
Go thou, white in thy soul, to fill a throne
Of innocence and sanctity in Heaven.
Pray, pray, my sister!

Annabella.   Then I see your drift.—
Ye blessèd angels, guard me!

Giovanni.   So say I.
Kiss me. If ever after-times should hear
Of our fast-knit affections, though perhaps
The laws of conscience and of civil use
May justly blame us, yet when they but know
Our loves, that love will wipe away that rigour
Which would in other incests be abhorred.
Give me your hand: how sweetly life doth run
In these well-coloured veins! how constantly
These palms do promise health! but I could chide
With Nature for this cunning flattery.
Kiss me again:—forgive me.

Annabella.   With my heart.

Giovanni. Farewell!

Annabella.   Will you be gone?

Giovanni.   Be dark, bright sun,
And make this mid-day night, that thy gilt rays
May not behold a deed will turn their splendour
More sooty than the poets feign their Styx!—
One other kiss, my sister.

Annabella.   What means this?

Giovanni. To save thy fame, and kill thee in a kiss.
                                    [*Stabs her.*

Thus die, and die by me, and by my hand!
Revenge is mine; honour doth love command.

   Annabella. O, brother, by your hand!

   Giovanni.   When thou art dead
I'll give my reasons for't; for to dispute
With thy—even in thy death—most lovely beauty,
Would make me stagger to perform this act,
Which I most glory in.

   Annabella. Forgive him, Heaven—and me my sins! Fare-
      well,
Brother unkind, unkind—Mercy, great Heaven!
O, O!   [*Dies.*

   Giovanni. She's dead, alas, good soul! The hapless fruit
That in her womb received its life from me
Hath had from me a cradle and a grave.
I must not dally. This sad marriage-bed,
In all her best, bore her alive and dead.
Soranzo, thou hast missed thy aim in this:
I have prevented now thy reaching plots,
And killed a love, for whose each drop of blood
I would have pawned my heart.—Fair Annabella,
How over-glorious art thou in thy wounds,
Triumphing over infamy and hate!—
Shrink not, courageous hand, stand up, my heart,
And boldly act my last and greater part!
                                     [*The scene closes.*

SCENE VI—*A Banqueting-room*[44] *in the same*

A banquet set out. Enter the Cardinal, FLORIO, DONADO,
   SORANZO, RICHARDETTO, VASQUES, *and* Attendants.

   Vasques. [*Aside to* SORANZO] Remember, sir, what you
have to do; be wise and resolute.

   Soranzo. [*Aside to* VASQUES] Enough: my heart is fixed.
   —Pleaseth your grace
To taste these coarse confections: though the use
Of such set entertainments more consists

---

[44] They had dined in another room, and, according to the usual practice, repaired
to the apartment in which the confectionery was set out.—*Gifford.*

In custom than in cause, yet, reverend sir,
I am still made your servant by your presence.
   Cardinal. And we your friend.
   Soranzo. But where's my brother Giovanni?

     Enter GIOVANNI *with a heart upon his dagger.*

   Giovanni. Here, here, Soranzo! trimmed in reeking blood,
That triumphs over death, proud in the spoil
Of love and vengeance! Fate, or all the powers
That guide the motions of immortal souls,
Could not prevent me.
   Cardinal. What means this?
   Florio. Son Giovanni!
   Soranzo. [*Aside*] Shall I be forestalled?
   Giovanni. Be not amazed: if your misgiving hearts
Shrink at an idle sight, what bloodless fear
Of coward passion would have seized your senses,
Had you beheld the rape of life and beauty
Which I have acted!—My sister, O, my sister!
   Florio. Ha! what of her?
   Giovanni.   The glory of my deed
Darkened the mid-day sun, made noon as night.
You came to feast, my lords, with dainty fare:
I came to feast too; but I digged for food
In a much richer mine than gold or stone
Of any value balanced; 'tis a heart,
A heart, my lords, in which is mine entombed:
Look well upon't; d'ye know't?
   Vasques. [*Aside*] What strange riddle's this?
   Giovanni. 'Tis Annabella's heart, 'tis:—why d'ye star-
     tle?—
I vow 'tis hers: this dagger's point ploughed up
Her fruitful womb, and left to me the fame
Of a most glorious executioner.
   Florio. Why, madman, art thyself?
   Giovanni. Yes, father; and, that times to come may know
How, as my fate, I honoured my revenge,
List, father; to your ears I will yield up
How much I have deserved to be your son.
   Florio. What is't thou say'st?

Giovanni.   Nine moons have had their changes
Since I first throughly viewed and truly loved
Your daughter and my sister.
     Florio.   How!—Alas, my lords,
He is a frantic madman!
     Giovanni.   Father, no.
For nine months' space in secret I enjoyed
Sweet Annabella's sheets; nine months I lived
A happy monarch of her heart and her.—
Soranzo, thou know'st this: thy paler cheek
Bears the confounding print of thy disgrace;
For her too-fruitful womb too soon bewrayed
The happy passage of our stol'n delights,
And made her mother to a child unborn.
     Cardinal. Incestuous villain!
     Florio.   O, his rage belies him.
     Giovanni. It does not, 'tis the oracle of truth;
I vow it is so.
     Soranzo.   I shall burst with fury,—
Bring the strumpet forth!
     Vasques. I shall, sir.   [*Exit.*
     Giovanni.   Do, sir.—Have you all no faith
To credit yet my triumphs? Here I swear
By all that you call sacred, by the love
I bore my Annabella whilst she lived,
These hands have from her bosom ripped this heart.

Re-enter VASQUES.

Is't true, or no, sir?
     Vasques.   'Tis most strangely true.
     Florio. Cursèd man!—Have I lived to—   [*Dies.*
     Cardinal.   Hold up, Florio.—
Monster of children! see what thou hast done,
Broke thy old father's heart.—Is none of you
Dares venture on him?
     Giovanni.   Let 'em!—O, my father,
How well his death becomes him in his griefs!
Why, this was done with courage: now survives
None of our house but I, gilt in the blood
Of a fair sister and a hapless father.

Soranzo. Inhuman scorn of men, hast thou a thought
T' outlive thy murders?   [*Draws.*

Giovanni.   Yes, I tell thee, yes;
For in my fists I bear the twists of life.
Soranzo, see this heart, which was thy wife's;
Thus I exchange it royally for thine.   [*They fight.*
And thus, and thus!   [SORANZO *falls.*
                Now brave revenge is mine.

Vasques. I cannot hold any longer.—You, sir, are you
grown insolent in your butcheries? have at you!

Giovanni. Come, I am armed to meet thee. [*They fight.*

Vasques. No! will it not be yet? if this will not, another
shall. Not yet? I shall fit you anon.—Vengeance!

The Banditti *rush in.*

Giovanni. Welcome! come more of you; whate'er you be,
I dare your worst.   [*They surround and wound him.*
O, I can stand no longer! feeble arms,
Have you so soon lost strength?   [*Falls.*

Vasques. Now you are welcome, sir!—[*Aside to* Banditti.]
Away, my masters, all is done; shift for yourselves, your
reward is your own; shift for yourselves.

Banditti. Away, away!   [*Exeunt.*

Vasques. How d'ye, my lord?—See you this? [*Pointing
to* GIOVANNI.] How is't?

Soranzo. Dead; but in death well pleased that I have lived
To see my wrongs revenged on that black devil.
O, Vasques, to thy bosom let me give
My last of breath; let not that lecher live.
O!   [*Dies.*

Vasques. The reward of peace and rest be with him, my
ever dearest lord and master!

Giovanni. Whose hand gave me this wound?

Vasques. Mine, sir; I was your first man: have you
enough?

Giovanni. I thank thee; thou hast done for me
But what I would have else done on myself.
Art sure thy lord is dead?

Vasques.   O, impudent slave!
As sure as I am sure to see thee die.

Cardinal. Think on thy life and end, and call for mercy.

Giovanni. Mercy! why, I have found it in this justice.

Cardinal. Strive yet to cry to Heaven.

Giovanni.   O, I bleed fast!
Death, thou'rt a guest long looked for; I embrace
Thee and thy wounds: O, my last minute comes!
Where'er I go, let me enjoy this grace,
Freely to view my Annabella's face.   [*Dies*.

Donado. Strange miracle of justice!

Cardinal. Raise up the city; we shall be murdered all!

Vasques. You need not fear, you shall not: this strange
task being ended, I have paid the duty to the son which I
have vowed to the father.

Cardinal. Speak, wretched villain, what incarnate fiend
Hath led thee on to this?

Vasques. Honesty, and pity of my master's wrongs: for
know, my lord, I am by birth a Spaniard, brought forth
my country in my youth by Lord Soranzo's father, whom
whilst he lived I served faithfully: since whose death I have
been to this man as I was to him. What I have done was
duty, and I repent nothing, but that the loss of my life had
not ransomed his.

Cardinal. Say, fellow, know'st thou any yet unnamed
Of counsel in this incest?

Vasques. Yes, an old woman, sometimes[45] guardian to
this murdered lady.

Cardinal. And what's become of her?

Vasques. Within this room she is! whose eyes, after her
confession, I caused to be put out, but kept alive, to confirm
what from Giovanni's own mouth you have heard. Now,
my lord, what I have done you may judge of; and let your
own wisdom be a judge in your own reason.

Cardinal. Peace!—First this woman, chief in these effects,
My sentence is, that forthwith she be ta'en
Out of the city, for example's sake,
There to be burnt to ashes.

Donado.   'Tis most just.

Cardinal. Be it your charge, Donado, see it done.

Donado. I shall.

---

[45] *i.e.* Formerly.

Vasques. What for me? if death, 'tis welcome: I have
been honest to the son, as I was to the father.

Cardinal. Fellow, for thee, since what thou didst was done
Not for thyself, being no Italian,
We banish thee for ever; to depart
Within three days: in this we do dispense
With grounds of reason, not of thine offence.

Vasques. 'Tis well: this conquest is mine, and I rejoice
that a Spaniard outwent an Italian in revenge.   [*Exit.*

Cardinal. Take up these slaughtered bodies, see them
And all the gold and jewels, or whatsoever,   [buried;
Confiscate by the canons of the church,
We seize upon to the pope's proper use.

Richardetto. [*Discovers himself.*] Your grace's pardon:
    thus long I lived disguised,
To see the effect of pride and lust at once
Brought both to shameful ends.

Cardinal. What! Richardetto, whom we thought for
    dead?

Donado. Sir, was it you—

Richardetto.   Your friend.

Cardinal.   We shall have time
To talk at large of all: but never yet
Incest and murder have so strangely met.
Of one so young, so rich in nature's store,
Who could not say, 'Tis PITY SHE'S A WHORE?

                                    [*Exeunt.*

THE BROKEN HEART

No account remains of the first appearance of this play, or of its success. It was acted by the King's servants at the Blackfriars Theatre, and was published in 1633. It is said in the Prologue that the story—the scene of which is curiously placed in Sparta—had some foundation in fact. It may have been taken from an Italian novel.

To the most worthy deserver of the noblest titles in honour,

WILLIAM, LORD CRAVEN, BARON OF HAMPSTEAD-MARSHALL[1]

My Lord,

THE glory of a great name, acquired by a greater glory of action, hath in all ages lived the truest chronicle to his own memory. In the practice of which argument your growth to perfection, even in youth, hath appeared so sincere, so unflattering a penman, that posterity cannot with more delight read the merit of noble endeavours than noble endeavours merit thanks from posterity to be read with delight. Many nations, many eyes have been witnesses of your deserts, and loved them: be pleased, then, with the freedom of your own name, to admit *one* amongst all, particularly into the list of such as honour a fair example of nobility. There is a kind of humble ambition, not uncommendable, when the silence of study breaks forth into discourse, coveting rather encouragement than applause; yet herein censure commonly is too severe an auditor, without the moderation of an able patronage. I have ever been slow in courtship of greatness, not ignorant of such defects as are frequent to opinion: but the justice of your inclination to industry emboldens my weakness of confidence to relish an experience of your mercy, as many brave dangers have tasted of your courage. Your Lordship strove to be known to the world, when the world knew you least, by voluntary but excellent attempts: like allowance I plead of being known to your Lordship (in this low presumption), by tendering, to a favourable entertainment, a devotion offered from a heart that can be as truly sensible of any least respect as ever profess the owner in my best, my readiest services, a lover of your natural love to virtue.

JOHN FORD

[1] "William, first Baron and Earl Craven" (according to Collins's *Peerage*), "the eldest son of Sir W. Craven, Lord Mayor, was much affected with military exercises from his youth, and signalised himself in Germany and in the Netherlands under Henry, Prince of Orange. In which valiant adventures he gained such honour, that on his return he was first knighted at Newmarket, March 4, 1626, and in the year after deservedly raised to the dignity of Lord Craven of Hampstead-Marshall. In 1631 he was one of the commanders of those forces sent to the assistance of the great Gustavus Adolphus, and was wounded in the assault upon the strong fortress of Kreutznach. He died, after a very active and chequered life, April 9, 1697, at the advanced age of 88. He is now chiefly remembered for his romantic attachment to the Queen of Bohemia, daughter of James I., to whom it is generally supposed he was privately married." "One may be pardoned for remembering," Ward adds, "that the chivalrous knight-errant and (as is thought) secret husband of Elizabeth of Bohemia survived her for nearly a quarter of a century."

PROLOGUE

Our scene is Sparta. He whose best of art
Hath drawn this piece calls it *The Broken Heart.*
The title lends no expectation here
Of apish laughter, or of some lame jeer
At place or persons; no pretended clause
Of jests fit for a brothel courts applause
From vulgar admiration: such low songs,
Tuned to unchaste ears, suit not modest tongues.
The virgin-sisters then deserved fresh bays
When innocence and sweetness crowned their lays;
Then vices gasped for breath, whose whole commérce
Was whipped to exile by unblushing verse.
This law we keep in our presentment now,
Not to take freedom more than we allow;
What may be here thought Fiction, when time's youth
Wanted some riper years, was known a Truth:
In which, if words have clothed the subject right,
You may partake a pity with delight.

DRAMATIS PERSONÆ

AMYCLAS, King of Laconia
ITHOCLES, a Favourite
ORGILUS, Son of Crotolon
BASSANES, a jealous Nobleman
ARMOSTES, a Counsellor of State
CROTOLON, another Counsellor
PROPHILUS, Friend of Ithocles
NEARCHUS, Prince of Argos
TECNICUS, a Philosopher
HEMOPHIL, }
GRONEAS, } Courtiers
AMELUS, Friend of Nearchus
PHULAS, Servant to Bassanes
Lords, Courtiers, Officers, Attendants, &c.

CALANTHA, Daughter of Amyclas
PENTHEA, Sister of Ithocles and Wife of Bassanes
EUPHRANEA, Daughter of Crotolon, a Maid of honour
CHRISTALLA, }
PHILEMA, } Maids of honour
GRAUSIS, Overseer of Penthea

SCENE—SPARTA

THE BROKEN HEART

ACT THE FIRST

SCENE I—*A Room in* CROTOLON's *House*

Enter CROTOLON *and* ORGILUS.

CROTOLON. Dally not further; I will know the reason
That speeds thee to this journey.
   Orgilus.   Reason! good sir,
I can yield many.
   Crotolon.   Give me one, a good one;
Such I expect, and ere we part must have:
Athens! pray, why to Athens? you intend not
To kick against the world, turn cynic, stoic,
Or read the logic-lecture, or become
An Areopagite, and judge in cases
Touching the commonwealth; for, as I take it,
The budding of your chin cannot prognosticate
So grave an honour.
   Orgilus.   All this I acknowledge.
   Crotolon. You do! then, son, if books and love of knowl-
      edge
Inflame you to this travel, here in Sparta
You may as freely study.
   Orgilus.   'Tis not that, sir.
   Crotolon. Not that, sir! As a father, I command thee
T' acquaint me with the truth.
   Orgilus.   Thus I obey ye.
After so many quarrels as dissension,
Fury, and rage had broached in blood, and sometimes
With death to such confederates as sided
With now-dead Thrasus and yourself, my lord;
Our present king, Amyclas, reconciled
Your eager swords and sealed a gentle peace:
Friends you professed yourselves; which to confirm,
A resolution for a lasting league
171

Betwixt your families was entertained,
By joining in a Hymenean bond
Me and the fair Penthea, only daughter
To Thrasus.
    Crotolon. What of this?
    Orgilus.   Much, much, dear sir.
A freedom of convérse, an interchange
Of holy and chaste love, so fixed our souls
In a firm growth of union, that no time
Can eat into the pledge: we had enjoyed
The sweets our vows expected, had not cruelty
Prevented all those triumphs we prepared for,
By Thrasus his untimely death.
    Crotolon.   Most certain.
    Orgilus. From this time sprouted-up that poisonous stalk
Of aconite, whose ripened fruit hath ravished
All health, all comfort of a happy life;
For Ithocles, her brother, proud of youth,
And prouder in his power, nourished closely
The memory of former discontents,
To glory in revenge. By cunning partly,
Partly by threats, he woos at once, and forces
His virtuous sister to admit a marriage
With Bassanes, a nobleman, in honour
And riches, I confess, beyond my fortunes.
    Crotolon. All this is no sound reason to impórtune
My leave for thy departure.
    Orgilus.   Now it follows.
Beauteous Penthea, wedded to this torture
By an insulting brother, being secretly
Compelled to yield her virgin freedom up
To him, who never can usurp her heart,
Before contracted mine, is now so yoked
To a most barbarous thraldrom, misery,
Affliction, that he savours not humanity,
Whose sorrow melts not into more than pity
In hearing but her name.
    Crotolon.   As how, pray?
    Orgilus.   Bassanes,
The man that calls her wife, considers truly

What heaven of perfections he is lord of
By thinking fair Penthea his: this thought
Begets a kind of monster-love, which love
Is nurse unto a fear so strong and servile
As brands all dotage with a jealousy:
All eyes who gaze upon that shrine of beauty
He doth resolve[1] do homage to the miracle;
Some one, he is assured, may now or then,
If opportunity but sort, prevail:
So much, out of a self-unworthiness,
His fears transport him; not that he finds cause
In her obedience, but his own distrust.

   Crotolon. You spin-out your discourse.
   Orgilus.   My griefs are violent:
For, knowing how the maid was heretofore
Courted by me, his jealousies grow wild
That I should steal again into her favours,
And undermine her virtues; which the gods
Know I nor dare nor dream of. Hence, from hence,
I undertake a voluntary exile;
First, by my absence to take off the cares
Of jealous Bassanes; but chiefly, sir,
To free Penthea from a hell on earth;
Lastly, to lose the memory of something
Her presence makes to live in me afresh.

   Crotolon. Enough, my Orgilus, enough. To Athens,
I give a full consent.—Alas, good lady!—
We shall hear from thee often?

   Orgilus.   Often.
   Crotolon.   See,
Thy sister comes to give a farewell.

Enter EUPHRANEA.

   Euphranea.   Brother!
   Orgilus. Euphranea, thus upon thy cheeks I print
A brother's kiss; more careful of thine honour,
Thy health, and thy well-doing, than my life.
Before we part, in presence of our father,
I must prefer a suit t' ye.

[1] *i.e.* Convince himself.

Euphranea.   You may style it,
My brother, a command.
   Orgilus.   That you will promise
Never to pass to any man, however
Worthy, your faith, till, with our father's leave,
I give a free consent.
   Crotolon.   An easy motion!
I'll promise for her, Orgilus.
   Orgilus.   Your pardon;
Euphranea's oath must yield me satisfaction.
   Euphranea. By Vesta's sacred fires I swear.
   Crotolon.   And I,
By great Apollo's beams, join in the vow,
Not without thy allowance to bestow her
On any living.
   Orgilus.   Dear Euphranea,
Mistake me not: far, far 'tis from my thought,
As far from any wish of mine, to hinder
Preferment to an honourable bed
Or fitting fortune; thou art young and handsome;
And 'twere injustice,—more, a tyranny,—
Not to advance thy merit: trust me, sister,
It shall be my first care to see thee matched
As may become thy choice and our contents.
I have your oath.
   Euphranea.   You have. But mean you, brother,
To leave us, as you say?
   Crotolon.   Ay, ay, Euphranea:
He has just grounds direct him. I will prove
A father and a brother to thee.
   Euphranea.   Heaven
Does look into the secrets of all hearts:
Gods, you have mercy with ye, else—
   Crotolon.   Doubt nothing;
Thy brother will return in safety to us.
   Orgilus. Souls sunk in sorrows never are without 'em;
They change fresh airs, but bear their griefs about 'em.
                                        [*Exeunt.*

SCENE II—*A Room in the Palace*

Flourish. Enter AMYCLAS, ARMOSTES, PROPHILUS,
Courtiers, *and* Attendants.

Amyclas. The Spartan gods are gracious; our humility
Shall bend before their altars, and perfume
Their temples with abundant sacrifice.
See, lords, Amyclas, your old king, is entering
Into his youth again! I shall shake off
This silver badge of age, and change this snow
For hairs as gay as are Apollo's locks;
Our heart leaps in new vigour.
  Armostes.   May old time
Run back to double your long life, great sir!
  Amyclas. It will, it must, Armostes: thy bold nephew,
Death-braving Ithocles, brings to our gates
Triumphs and peace upon his conquering sword.
Laconia is a monarchy at length;
Hath in this latter war trod under foot
Messene's pride; Messene bows her neck
To Lacedæmon's royalty. O, 'twas
A glorious victory, and doth deserve
More than a chronicle—a temple, lords,
A temple to the name of Ithocles.—
Where didst thou leave him, Prophilus?
  Prophilus.   At Pephon,
Most gracious sovereign; twenty of the noblest
Of the Messenians there attend your pleasure,
For such conditions as you shall propose
In settling peace, and liberty of life.
  Amyclas. When comes your friend the general?
  Prophilus.   He promised
To follow with all speed convenient.

Enter CALANTHA, EUPHRANEA; CHRISTALLA *and*
PHILEMA *with a garland; and* CROTOLON.

Amyclas. Our daughter!—Dear Calantha, the happy news,

The conquest of Messene, hath already
Enriched thy knowledge.

    Calantha.   With the circumstance
And manner of the fight, related faithfully
By Prophilus himself.—But, pray, sir, tell me
How doth the youthful general demean
His actions in these fortunes?

    Prophilus.   Excellent princess,
Your own fair eyes may soon report a truth
Unto your judgment, with what moderation,
Calmness of nature, measure, bounds, and limits
Of thankfulness and joy, he doth digest
Such amplitude of his success as would
In others, moulded of a spirit less clear,
Advance 'em to comparison with heaven:
But Ithocles—

    Calantha.   Your friend—

    Prophilus.   He is so, madam,
In which the period of my fate consists:
He, in this firmament of honour, stands
Like a star fixed, not moved with any thunder
Of popular applause or sudden lightning
Of self-opinion; he hath served his country,
And thinks 'twas but his duty.

    Crotolon.   You describe
A miracle of man.

    Amyclas.   Such, Crotolon,
On forfeit of a king's word, thou wilt find him.—

                                 [*Flourish.*

Hark, warning of his coming! all attend him.

Enter ITHOCLES, *ushered in by the* Lords, *and followed by*
HEMOPHIL *and* GRONEAS.

Return into these arms, thy home, thy sanctuary,
Delight of Sparta, treasure of my bosom,
Mine own, own Ithocles!

    Ithocles.   Your humblest subject.

    Armostes. Proud of the blood I claim an interest in,
As brother to thy mother, I embrace thee,
Right noble nephew.

Ithocles.   Sir, your love's too partial.

Crotolon. Our country speaks by me, who by thy valour,
Wisdom, and service, shares in this great action;
Returning thee, in part of thy due merits,
A general welcome.

Ithocles.   You exceed in bounty.

Calantha. Christalla, Philema, the chaplet. [*Takes the
          chaplet from them.*]—Ithocles,
Upon the wings of fame the singular
And chosen fortune of an high attempt
Is borne so past the view of common sight,
That I myself with mine own hands have wrought,
To crown thy temples, this provincial garland [2]:
Accept, wear, and enjoy it as our gift
Deserved, not purchased.

Ithocles.   You're a royal maid.

Amyclas. She is in all our daughter.

Ithocles.   Let me blush,
Acknowledging how poorly I have served,
What nothings I have done, compared with the honours
Heaped on the issue of a willing mind;
In that lay mine ability, that only:
For who is he so sluggish from his birth,
So little worthy of a name or country,
That owes not out of gratitude for life
A debt of service, in what kind soever
Safety or counsel of the commonwealth
Requires, for payment?

Calantha.   He speaks truth.

Ithocles.   Whom heaven
Is pleased to style victorious, there to such
Applause runs madding, like the drunken priests
In Bacchus' sacrifices, without reason
Voicing the leader-on a demi-god;
Whenas, indeed, each common soldier's blood
Drops down as current coin in that hard purchase
As his whose much more delicate condition
Hath sucked the milk of ease: judgment commands,
But resolution executes. I use not,

---

[2] *i.e.* The laurel wreath conferred on those who added a province to the empire.

Before this royal presence, these fit slights[3]
As in contempt of such as can direct;
My speech hath other end; not to attribute
All praise to one man's fortune, which is strengthened
By many hands: for instance, here is Prophilus,
A gentleman—I cannot flatter truth—
Of much desert; and, though in other rank,
Both Hemophil and Groneas were not missing
To wish their country's peace; for, in a word,
All there did strive their best, and 'twas our duty.

    Amyclas. Courtiers turn soldiers!—We vouchsafe our
        hand.   [HEMOPHIL *and* GRONEAS *kiss his hand.*
Observe our great example.
    Hemophil.   With all diligence.
    Groneas. Obsequiously and hourly.
    Amyclas.   Some repose
After these toils is needful. We must think on
Conditions for the conquered; they expect 'em.
On!—Come, my Ithocles.
    Euphranea.   Sir, with your favour,
I need not a supporter.
    Prophilus.   Fate instructs me.

        [*Exit* AMYCLAS *attended,* ITHOCLES, CALANTHA,
          &c. *As* CHRISTALLA *and* PHILEMA *are follow-*
          ing CALANTHA *they are detained by* HEMOPHIL
          and GRONEAS.

    Christalla. With me?
    Philema.   Indeed I dare not stay.
    Hemophil.   Sweet lady.
Soldiers are blunt,—your lip.   [*Kisses her.*
    Christalla.   Fie, this is rudeness:
You went not hence such creatures.
    Groneas.   Spirit of valour
Is of a mounting nature.
    Philema.   It appears so.—
Pray, in earnest, how many men apiece
Have you two been the death of?
    Groneas.   'Faith, not many;
We were composed of mercy.

[3] *i.e.* Slight words fitting slight services.

Hemophil.   For our daring,
You heard the general's approbation
Before the king.
 Christalla.   You "wished your country's peace;"
That showed your charity: where are your spoils,
Such as the soldier fights for?
 Philema.   They are coming.
 Christalla. By the next carrier, are they not?
 Groneas.   Sweet Philema,
When I was in the thickest of mine enemies,
Slashing off one man's head, another's nose,
Another's arms and legs,—
 Philema.   And all together.
 Groneas. Then would I with a sigh remember thee,
And cry "Dear Philema, 'tis for thy sake
I do these deeds of wonder!"—dost not love me
With all thy heart now?
 Philema.   Now as heretofore.
I have not put my love to use; the principal
Will hardly yield an interest.
 Groneas.   By Mars,
I'll marry thee!
 Philema.   By Vulcan, you're forsworn,
Except my mind do alter strangely.
 Groneas.   One word.
 Christalla. You lie beyond all modesty: forbear me.
 Hemophil. I'll make thee mistress of a city; 'tis
Mine own by conquest.
 Christalla.   By petition; sue for't
In formâ pauperis.—City! kennel.—Gallants!
Off with your feathers, put on aprons, gallants;
Learn to reel, thrum,[4] or trim a lady's dog,
And be good quiet souls of peace, hobgoblins!
 Hemophil. Christalla!
 Christalla.   Practise to drill hogs, in hope
To share in the acorns.—Soldiers! corncutters,
But not so valiant; they ofttimes draw blood,
Which you durst never do. When you have practised
More wit or more civility, we'll rank ye

[4] Weave. Thrum is, properly, the tuft at the end of the warp.

I' the list of men: till then, brave things-at-arms,
Dare not to speak to us,—most potent Groneas!—
  Philema. And Hemophil the hardy!—at your services.

                    [*Exeunt* CHRISTALLA *and* PHILEMA.
  Groneas. They scorn us, as they did before we went.
  Hemophil. Hang 'em! let us scorn them, and be revenged.
  Groneas. Shall we?
  Hemophil.   We will: and when we slight them thus,
Instead of following them, they'll follow us;
It is a woman's nature.
  Groneas.   'Tis a scurvy one.   [*Exeunt.*

SCENE III—*The Gardens of the Palace. A Grove.*

Enter TECNICUS, *and* ORGILUS *disguised like one of his*
                    Scholars.

  Tecnicus. Tempt not the stars; young man, thou canst not
With the severity of fate: this change   [play
Of habit and disguise in outward view
Hides not the secrets of thy soul within thee
From their quick-piercing eyes, which dive at all times
Down to thy thoughts: in thy aspéct I note
A consequence of danger.
  Orgilus.   Give me leave,
Grave Tecnicus, without foredooming destiny,
Under thy roof to ease my silent griefs,
By applying to my hidden wounds the balm
Of thy oraculous lectures. If my fortune
Run such a crookèd by-way as to wrest
My steps to ruin, yet thy learnèd precepts
Shall call me back and set my footings straight.
I will not court the world.
  Tecnicus.   Ah, Orgilus,
Neglects in young men of delights and life
Run often to extremities; they care not
For harms to others who contemn their own.
  Orgilus. But I, most learnèd artist, am not so much
At odds with nature that I grudge the thrift
Of any true deserver; nor doth malice

Of present hopes so check them with despair
As that I yield to thought of more affliction
Than what is incident to frailty: wherefore
Impute not this retirèd course of living
Some little time to any other cause
Than what I justly render,—the information
Of an unsettled mind; as the effect
Must clearly witness.

 Tecnicus.   Spirit of truth inspire thee!
On these conditions I conceal thy change,
And willingly admit thee for an auditor.—
I'll to my study.

 Orgilus.   I to contemplations
In these delightful walks.   [*Exit* Tecnicus.
        Thus metamorphosed,
I may without suspicion hearken after
Penthea's usage and Euphranea's faith.
Love, thou art full of mystery! the deities
Themselves are not secure[5] in searching out
The secrets of those flames, which, hidden, waste
A breast made tributary to the laws
Of beauty: physic yet hath never found
A remedy to cure a lover's wound.—
Ha! who are those that cross yon private walk
Into the shadowing grove in amorous foldings?

   Prophilus *passes by, supporting* Euphranea *and
        whispering.*

My sister! O, my sister! 'tis Euphranea
With Prophilus: supported too! I would
It were an apparition! Prophilus
Is Ithocles his friend: it strangely puzzles me.

   Re-enter Prophilus *and* Euphranea.

Again! help me, my book; this scholar's habit
Must stand my privilege: my mind is busy,
Mine eyes and ears are open.

     [*Walks aside, pretending to read.*
 Prophilus.   Do not waste

[5] Certain.

The span of this stol'n time, lent by the gods
For precious use, in niceness.[6] Bright Euphranea,
Should I repeat old vows, or study new,
For purchase of belief to my desires,—

 Orgilus. [*Aside*] Desires!
 Prophilus.   My service, my integrity,—
 Orgilus. [*Aside*] That's better.
 Prophilus.   I should but repeat a lesson
Oft conned without a prompter but thine eyes:
My love is honourable.

 Orgilus. [*Aside*]   So was mine
To my Penthea, chastely honourable.

 Prophilus. Nor wants there more addition to my wish
Of happiness than having thee a wife;
Already sure of Ithocles, a friend
Firm and unalterable.

 Orgilus. [*Aside*]   But a brother
More cruel than the grave.

 Euphranea.   What can you look for,
In answer to your noble protestations,
From an unskilful maid, but language suited
To a divided mind?

 Orgilus. [*Aside*] Hold out, Euphranea!

 Euphranea. Know, Prophilus, I never undervalued,
From the first time you mentioned worthy love,
Your merit, means, or person: it had been
A fault of judgment in me, and a dulness
In my affections, not to weigh and thank
My better stars that offered me the grace
Of so much blissfulness. For, to speak truth,
The law of my desires kept equal pace
With yours; nor have I left that resolution:
But only, in a word, whatever choice
Lives nearest in my heart must first procure
Consent both from my father and my brother,
Ere he can own me his.

 Orgilus. [*Aside*]   She is forsworn else.
 Prophilus. Leave me that task.

---

[6] Preciseness.

Euphranea.　　　　　　　　　My brother, ere he parted
To Athens, had my oath.

Orgilus. [*Aside*]　　　Yes, yes, he had, sure.

Prophilus. I doubt not, with the means the court supplies,
But to prevail at pleasure.

Orgilus. [*Aside*]　　　Very likely!

Prophilus. Meantime, best, dearest, I may build my hopes
On the foundation of thy constant sufferance
In any opposition.

Euphranea.　　　Death shall sooner
Divorce life and the joys I have in living
Than my chaste vows from truth.

Prophilus.　　　　　　　On thy fair hand
I seal the like.

Orgilus. [*Aside*] There is no faith in woman.
Passion, O, be contained! my very heart-strings
Are on the tenters.

Euphranea.　　　Sir, we are overheard.
Cupid protect us! 'twas a stirring,
Of some one near.

Prophilus.　　　Your fears are needless, lady;
None have access into these private pleasures
Except some near in court, or bosom-student
From Tecnicus his oratory, granted
By special favour lately from the king
Unto the grave philosopher.

Euphranea.　　　　　　Methinks
I hear one talking to himself,—I see him.

Prophilus. 'Tis a poor scholar, as I told you, lady.

Orgilus. [*Aside*] I am discovered.—[*Half aloud to himself, as if studying*] Say it; is it possible,
With a smooth tongue, a leering countenance,
Flattery, or force of reason—I come t'ye, sir—
To turn or to appease the raging sea?
Answer to that.—Your art! what art? to catch
And hold fast in a net the sun's small atoms?
No, no; they'll out, they'll out: ye may as easily
Outrun a cloud driven by a northern blast
As fiddle-faddle so! Peace, or speak sense.

Euphranea. Call you this thing a scholar? 'las, he's lunatic.

Prophilus. Observe him, sweet; 'tis but his recreation.

Orgilus. But will you hear a little? You're so tetchy,
You keep no rule in argument: philosophy
Works not upon impossibilities,
But natural conclusions.—Mew!—absurd!
The metaphysics are but speculations
Of the celestial bodies, or such accidents
As not mixed perfectly, in the air engendered,
Appear to us unnatural; that's all.
Prove it; yet, with a reverence to your gravity,
I'll balk illiterate sauciness, submitting
My sole opinion to the touch of writers.

Prophilus. Now let us fall in with him.

                               [*They come forward.*

Orgilus.   Ha, ha, ha!
These apish boys, when they but taste the grammates
And principles of theory, imagine
They can oppose their teachers. Confidence
Leads many into errors.

Prophilus.   By your leave, sir.

Euphranea. Are you a scholar, friend?

Orgilus.   I am, gay creature,
With pardon of your deities, a mushroom
On whom the dew of heaven drops now and then;
The sun shines on me too, I thank his beams!
Sometime I feel their warmth; and eat and sleep.

Prophilus. Does Tecnicus read to thee?

Orgilus.   Yes, forsooth,
He is my master surely; yonder door
Opens upon his study.

Prophilus.   Happy creatures!
Such people toil not, sweet, in heats of state,
Nor sink in thaws of greatness; their affections
Keep order with the limits of their modesty;
Their love is love of virtue.—What's thy name?

Orgilus. Aplotes, sumptuous master, a poor wretch.

Euphranea. Dost thou want anything?

Orgilus.   Books, Venus, books.

Prophilus. Lady, a new conceit comes in my thought,
And most available for both our comforts.

Euphranea. My lord,—

Prophilus.   Whiles I endeavour to deserve
Your father's blessing to our loves, this scholar
May daily at some certain hours attend,
What notice I can write of my success,
Here in this grove, and give it to your hands;
The like from you to me: so can we never,
Barred of our mutual speech, want sure intelligence,
And thus our hearts may talk when our tongues cannot.

Euphranea. Occasion is most favourable; use it.

Prophilus. Aplotes, wilt thou wait us twice a-day,
At nine i' the morning and at four at night,
Here in this bower, to convey such letters
As each shall send to other? Do it willingly,
Safely, and secretly, and I will furnish
Thy study, or what else thou canst desire.

Orgilus. Jove, make me thankful, thankful, I beseech
          thee,
Propitious Jove! I will prove sure and trusty:
You will not fail me books?

Prophilus.   Nor aught besides
Thy heart can wish. This lady's name's Euphranea,
Mine Prophilus.

Orgilus.   I have a pretty memory;
It must prove my best friend. I will not miss
One minute of the hours appointed.

Prophilus.   Write
The books thou wouldst have bought thee in a note,
Or take thyself some money.

Orgilus.   No, no, money;
Money to scholars is a spirit invisible,
We dare not finger it: or books, or nothing.

Prophilus. Books of what sort thou wilt: do not forget
Our names.

Orgilus. I warrant ye, I warrant ye.

Prophilus. Smile, Hymen, on the growth of our desires;
We'll feed thy torches with eternal fires!

          [*Exeunt* PROPHILUS *and* EUPHRANEA.

Orgilus. Put out thy torches, Hymen, or their light
Shall meet a darkness of eternal night!
Inspire me, Mercury, with swift deceits.
Ingenious Fate has leapt into mine arms,
Beyond the compass of my brain. Mortality
Creeps on the dung of earth, and cannot reach
The riddles which are purposed by the gods.
Great arts best write themselves in their own stories;
They die too basely who outlive their glories.   [*Exit.*

ACT THE SECOND

SCENE I—*A Room in* BASSANES' *House*

Enter BASSANES *and* PHULAS.

BASSANES. I'll have that window next the street dammed up;
It gives too full a prospect to temptation,
And courts a gazer's glances: there's a lust
Committed by the eye, that sweats and travails,
Plots, wakes, contrives, till the deformèd bear-whelp,
Adultery, be licked into the act,
The very act: that light shall be dammed up;
D'ye hear, sir?
　　Phulas.　　　　I do hear, my lord; a mason
Shall be provided suddenly.
　　Bassanes.　　　　　　　Some rogue,
Some rogue of your confederacy,—factor
For slaves and strumpets!—to convey close packets
From this spruce springal [7] and the t'other youngster;
That gaudy earwig, or my lord your patron,
Whose pensioner you are.—I'll tear thy throat out,
Son of a cat, ill-looking hound's-head, rip-up
Thy ulcerous maw, if I but scent a paper,
A scroll, but half as big as what can cover
A wart upon thy nose, a spot, a pimple,
Directed to my lady; it may prove
A mystical preparative to lewdness.

[7] Youth.

Phulas. Care shall be had: I will turn every thread
About me to an eye.—[*Aside*] Here's a sweet life!

Bassanes. The city housewives, cunning in the traffic
Of chamber merchandise, set all at price
By wholesale; yet they wipe their mouths and simper,
Cull,[8] kiss, and cry "sweetheart," and stroke the head
Which they have branched; and all is well again!
Dull clods of dirt, who dare not feel the rubs
Stuck on their foreheads.

Phulas.   'Tis a villainous world;
One cannot hold his own in't.

Bassanes.   Dames at court,
Who flaunt in riots, run another bias;
Their pleasure heaves the patient ass that suffers
Up on the stilts of office, titles, incomes;
Promotion justifies the shame, and sues for't.
Poor honour, thou art stabbed, and bleed'st to death
By such unlawful hire! The country mistress
Is yet more wary, and in blushes hides
Whatever trespass draws her troth to guilt.
But all are false: on this truth I am bold,
No woman but can fall, and doth, or would.—
Now for the newest news about the city;
What blab the voices, sirrah?

Phulas.   O, my lord,
The rarest, quaintest, strangest, tickling news
That ever—

Bassanes. Hey-day! up and ride me, rascal!
What is't?

Phulas. Forsooth, they say the king has mewed [9]
All his gray beard, instead of which is budded
Another of a pure carnation colour,
Speckled with green and russet.

Bassanes.   Ignorant block!

Phulas. Yes, truly; and 'tis talked about the streets,
That since Lord Ithocles came home, the lions
Never left roaring, at which noise the bears
Have danced their very hearts out.

---

[8] Embrace.
[9] Shed. A term in falconry.

Bassanes.   Dance out thine too.

Phulas. Besides, Lord Orgilus is fled to Athens
Upon a fiery dragon, and 'tis thought
He never can return.

Bassanes.   Grant it, Apollo!

Phulas. Moreover, please your lordship, 'tis reported
For certain, that whoever is found jealous
Without apparent proof that's wife is wanton
Shall be divorced: but this is but she-news;
I had it from a midwife. I have more yet.

Bassanes. Antic, no more! idiots and stupid fools
Grate my calamities. Why to be fair
Should yield presumption of a faulty soul—
Look to the doors.

Phulas.   The horn of plenty crest him!

                                      [*Aside, and exit.*

Bassanes. Swarms of confusion huddle in my thoughts
In rare distemper.—Beauty! O, it is
An unmatched blessing or a horrid curse.
She comes, she comes! so shoots the morning forth,
Spangled with pearls of transparent dew.—
The way to poverty is to be rich,
As I in her am wealthy; but for her,
In all contents a bankrupt.

              Enter PENTHEA *and* GRAUSIS.

                      Loved Penthea!
How fares my heart's best joy?

Grausis.   In sooth, not well,
She is so over-sad.

Bassanes.   Leave chattering, magpie.—
Thy brother is returned, sweet, safe, and honoured
With a triumphant victory; thou shalt visit him:
We will to court, where, if it be thy pleasure,
Thou shalt appear in such a ravishing lustre
Of jewels above value, that the dames
Who brave it there, in rage to be outshined,
Shall hide them in their closets, and unseen
Fret in their tears; whiles every wondering eye
Shall crave none other brightness but thy presence.

Choose thine own recreations; be a queen
Of what delights thou fanciest best, what company,
What place, what times; do anything, do all things
Youth can command, so thou wilt chase these clouds
From the pure firmament of thy fair looks.

    Grausis. Now 'tis well said, my lord.—What, lady! laugh,
Be merry; time is precious.

    Bassanes. [*Aside*]   Furies whip thee!

    Penthea. Alas, my lord, this language to your hand-maid
Sounds as would music to the deaf; I need
No braveries nor cost of art to draw
The whiteness of my name into offence:
Let such, if any such there are, who covet
A curiosity of admiration,
By laying-out their plenty to full view,
Appear in gaudy outsides; my attires
Shall suit the inward fashion of my mind;
From which, if your opinion, nobly placed,
Change not the livery your words bestow,
My fortunes with my hopes are at the highest.

    Bassanes. This house, methinks, stands somewhat **too**
        much inward,
It is too melancholy; we'll remove
Nearer the court: or what thinks my Penthea
Of the delightful island we command?
Rule me as thou canst wish.

    Penthea.   I am no mistress:
Whither you please, I must attend; all ways
Are alike pleasant to me.

    Grausis.   Island! prison;
A prison is as gaysome: we'll no islands;
Marry, out upon 'em! whom shall we see there?
Sea-gulls, and porpoises, and water-rats,
And crabs, and mews, and dog-fish; goodly gear
For a young lady's dealing,—or an old one's!
On no terms islands; I'll be stewed first.

    Bassanes. [*Aside to* GRAUSIS]   Grausis,
You are a juggling bawd.—This sadness, sweetest,
Becomes not youthful blood.—[*Aside to* GRAUSIS] I'll have
        you pounded.—

For my sake put on a more cheerful mirth;
Thou'lt mar thy cheeks, and make me old in griefs.—
[*Aside to* GRAUSIS] Damnable bitch-fox!

Grausis.   I am thick of hearing,
Still, when the wind blows southerly.—What think ye,
If your fresh lady breed young bones, my lord!
Would not a chopping boy d'ye good at heart?
But, as you said—

Bassanes. [*Aside to* GRAUSIS] I'll spit thee on a stake,
Or chop thee into collops!

Grausis.   Pray, speak louder.
Sure, sure the wind blows south still.

Penthea.   Thou prat'st madly.

Bassanes. 'Tis very hot; I sweat extremely.

Re-enter PHULAS.

                                                        Now?

Phulas. A herd of lords, sir.

Bassanes.   Ha!

Phulas.   A flock of ladies.

Bassanes. Where?

Phulas.   Shoals of horses.

Bassanes.   Peasant, how?

Phulas.   Caroches[10]
In drifts; the one enter, the other stand without, sir:
And now I vanish.   [*Exit.*

Enter PROPHILUS, HEMOPHIL, GRONEAS, CHRISTALLA,
                    and PHILEMA.

Prophilus.   Noble Bassanes!

Bassanes. Most welcome, Prophilus; ladies, gentlemen,
To all my heart is open; you all honour me,—
[*Aside*] A tympany swells in my head already,—
Honour me bountifully.—[*Aside*] How they flutter,
Wagtails and jays together!

Prophilus.   From your brother
By virtue of your love to him, I require
Your instant presence, fairest.

Penthea.   He is well, sir?

---

[10] Coaches.

Prophilus. The gods preserve him ever! Yet, dear beauty,
I find some alteration in him lately,
Since his return to Sparta.—My good lord,
I pray, use no delay.

Bassanes.   We had not needed
An invitation, if his sister's health
Had not fall'n into question.—Haste, Penthea,
Slack not a minute.—Lead the way, good Prophilus;
I'll follow step by step.

Prophilus.   Your arm, fair madam.

          [*Exeunt all but* BASSANES *and* GRAUSIS.

Bassanes. One word with your old bawdship: th' hadst
          been better
Railed at the sins[11] thou worshipp'st than have thwarted
My will: I'll use thee cursedly.

Grausis.   You dote,
You are beside yourself. A politician
In jealousy? no, you're too gross, too vulgar.
Pish, teach not me my trade; I know my cue:
My crossing you sinks me into her trust,
By which I shall know all; my trade's a sure one.

Bassanes. Forgive me, Grausis, 'twas consideration
I relished not; but have a care now.

Grausis.   Fear not,
I am no new-come-to't.

Bassanes.   Thy life's upon it,
And so is mine. My agonies are infinite.   [*Exeunt.*

SCENE II—*The Palace.* ITHOCLES' *Apartment.*

Enter ITHOCLES.

Ithocles. Ambition! 'tis of vipers' breed: it gnaws
A passage through the womb that gave it motion.
Ambition, like a seelèd[12] dove, mounts upward,
Higher and higher still, to perch on clouds,
But tumbles headlong down with heavier ruin.
So squibs and crackers fly into the air,

[11] Altered by Gifford to "saints."
[12] Blinded by sewing up the eye-lids.

Then, only breaking with a noise, they vanish
In stench and smoke. Morality, applied
To timely practice, keeps the soul in tune,
At whose sweet music all our actions dance:
But this is formed of books and school-tradition;
It physics not the sickness of a mind
Broken with griefs: strong fevers are not eased
With counsel, but with best receipts and means;
Means, speedy means and certain; that's the cure.

Enter ARMOSTES *and* CROTOLON.

Armostes. You stick, Lord Crotolon, upon a point
Too nice and too unnecessary; Prophilus
Is every way desertful. I am confident
Your wisdom is too ripe to need instruction
From your son's tutelage.

   Crotolon.   Yet not so ripe,
My Lord Armostes, that it dare to dote
Upon the painted meat of smooth persuasion,
Which tempts me to a breach of faith.

   Ithocles.   Not yet
Resolved, my lord? Why, if your son's consent
Be so available, we'll write to Athens
For his repair to Sparta: the king's hand
Will join with our desires; he has been moved to't.

   Armostes. Yes, and the king himself impórtuned Crotolon
For a dispatch.

   Crotolon.   Kings may command; their wills
Are laws not to be questioned.

   Ithocles.   By this marriage
You knit an union so devout, so hearty,
Between your loves to me and mine to yours,
As if mine own blood had an interest in it;
For Prophilus is mine, and I am his.

   Crotolon. My lord, my lord!—

   Ithocles.   What, good sir? speak your thought.

   Crotolon. Had this sincerity been real once,
My Orgilus had not been now unwived,
Nor your lost sister buried in a bride-bed:
Your uncle here, Armostes, knows this truth;

For had your father Thrasus lived,—but peace
Dwell in his grave! I've done.
   Armostes.   You're bold and bitter.
   Ithocles. [*Aside*] He presses home the injury; it smarts.—
No reprehensions, uncle; I deserve 'em,
Yet, gentle sir, consider what the heat
Of an unsteady youth, a giddy brain,
Green indiscretion, flattery of greatness,
Rawness of judgment, wilfulness in folly,
Thoughts vagrant as the wind and as uncertain,
Might lead a boy in years to:—'twas a fault,
A capital fault; for then I could not dive
Into the secrets of commanding love;
Since when experience, by the extremes in others,
Hath forced me collect—and, trust me, Crotolon,
I will redeem those wrongs with any service
Your satisfaction can require for current.
   Armostes. The acknowledgment is satisfaction:
What would you more?
   Crotolon.   I'm conquered: if Euphranea
Herself admit the motion, let it be so;
I doubt not my son's liking.
   Ithocles.   Use my fortunes,
Life, power, sword, and heart,—all are your own.
   Armostes. The princess, with your sister.

   Enter CALANTHA, PENTHEA, EUPHRANEA, CHRISTALLA,
     PHILEMA, GRAUSIS, BASSANES, *and* PROPHILUS.

   Calantha.   I present ye
A stranger here in court, my lord; for did not
Desire of seeing you draw her abroad,
We had not been made happy in her company.
   Ithocles. You are a gracious princess.—Sister, wedlock
Holds too severe a passion in your nature,
Which can engross all duty to your husband,
Without attendance on so dear a mistress.—
[*To* BASSANES] 'Tis not my brother's pleasure, I presume,
T' immure her in a chamber.
   Bassanes.   'Tis her will;
She governs her own hours. Noble Ithocles,

We thank the gods for your success and welfare:
Our lady has of late been indisposed,
Else we had waited on you with the first.

Ithocles. How does Penthea now?

Penthea.   You best know, brother,
From whom my health and comforts are derived.

Bassanes. [*Aside*] I like the answer well; 'tis sad and
  modest.
There may be tricks yet, tricks.—Have an eye, Grausis!

Calantha. Now, Crotolon, the suit we joined in must not
Fall by too long demur.

Crotolon.   'Tis granted, princess,
For my part.

Armostes. With condition, that his son
Favour the contract.

Calantha.   Such delay is easy.—
The joys of marriage make thee, Prophilus,
A proud deserver of Euphranea's love,
And her of thy desert!

Prophilus.   Most sweetly gracious!

Bassanes. The joys of marriage are the heaven on earth,
Life's paradise, great princess, the soul's quiet,
Sinews of concord, earthly immortality,
Eternity of pleasures;—no restoratives
Like to a constant woman!—[*Aside*] But where is she?
'Twould puzzle all the gods but to create
Such a new monster.—I can speak by proof,
For I rest in Elysium; 'tis my happiness.

Crotolon. Euphranea, how are you resolved, speak freely,
In your affections to this gentleman?

Euphranea. Nor more nor less than as his love assures me;
Which—if your liking with my brother's warrants—
I cannot but approve in all points worthy.

Crotolon. So, so!—[*To* PROPHILUS] I know your answer.

Ithocles.   'T had been pity
To sunder hearts so equally consented.

Enter HEMOPHIL.

Hemophil. The king, Lord Ithocles, commands your presence;—

And, fairest princess, yours.
    Calantha.   We will attend him.

Enter GRONEAS.

    Groneas. Where are the lords? all must unto the king
Without delay: the Prince of Argos—
    Calantha.   Well, sir?
    Groneas. Is coming to the court, sweet lady.
    Calantha.   How
The Prince of Argos?
    Groneas.   'Twas my fortune, madam,
T' enjoy the honour of these happy tidings.
    Ithocles. Penthea!—
    Penthea.   Brother?
    Ithocles.   Let me an hour hence
Meet you alone within the palace-grove;
I have some secret with you.—Prithee, friend,
Conduct her thither, and have special care
The walks be cleared of any to disturb us.
    Prophilus. I shall.
    Bassanes. [*Aside*] How's that?
    Ithocles.   Alone, pray be alone.—
I am your creature, princess.—On, my lords!
                   [*Exeunt all but* BASSANES.
    Bassanes. Alone! alone! what means that word "alone"?
Why might not I be there?—hum!—he's her brother.
Brothers and sisters are but flesh and blood,
And this same whoreson court-ease is temptation
To a rebellion in the veins;—besides,
His fine friend Prophilus must be her guardian:
Why may not he dispatch a business nimbly
Before the other come?—or—pandering, pandering
For one another,—be't to sister, mother,
Wife, cousin, anything,—'mongst youths of mettle
Is in request; it is so—stubborn fate!
But if I be a cuckold, and can know it,
I will be fell, and fell.

Re-enter GRONEAS.

    Groneas.   My lord, you're called for.

Bassanes. Most heartily I thank ye. Where's my wife,
   pray?

Groneas. Retired amongst the ladies.

Bassanes.   Still I thank ye.
There's an old waiter with her; saw you her too?

Groneas. She sits i' the presence-lobby fast asleep, sir.

Bassanes. Asleep! asleep, sir!

Groneas.   Is your lordship troubled?
You will not to the king?

Bassanes.   Your humblest vassal.

Groneas. Your servant, my good lord.

Bassanes.   I wait your footsteps.
                                          [*Exeunt.*

SCENE III—*The Gardens of the Palace. A Grove.*

Enter PROPHILUS *and* PENTHEA.

Prophilus. In this walk, lady, will your brother find you:
And, with your favour, give me leave a little
To work a preparation. In his fashion
I have observed of late some kind of slackness
To such alacrity as nature once
And custom took delight in; sadness grows
Upon his recreations, which he hoards
In such a willing silence, that to question
The grounds will argue little skill in friendship,
And less good manners.

Penthea.   Sir, I'm not inquisitive
Of secrecies without an invitation.

Prophilus. With pardon, lady, not a syllable
Of mine implies so rude a sense; the drift—

Enter ORGILUS, *disguised as before.*

[*To Orgilus.*] Do thy best
To make this lady merry for an hour.

Orgilus. Your will shall be a law, sir.   [*Exit* PROPHILUS.

Penthea.   Prithee, leave me;
I have some private thoughts I would account with;
Use thou thine own.

   Orgilus.   Speak on, fair nymph; our souls
Can dance as well to music of the spheres
As any's who have feasted with the gods.
   Penthea. Your school-terms are too troublesome.
   Orgilus.   What Heaven
Refines mortality from dross of earth
But such as uncompounded beauty hallows
With glorified perfection?
   Penthea.   Set thy wits
In a less wild proportion.
   Orgilus.   Time can never
On the white table of unguilty faith
Write counterfeit dishonour; turn those eyes,
The arrows of pure love, upon that fire,
Which once rose to a flame, perfumed with vows
As sweetly scented as the incense smoking
On Vesta's altars, ...[13]
. . . the holiest odours, virgin's tears,
. . . . sprinkled, like dews, to feed them
And to increase their fervour.
   Penthea.   Be not frantic.
   Orgilus. All pleasures are but mere imagination,
Feeding the hungry appetite with steam
And sight of banquet, whilst the body pines,
Not relishing the real taste of food:
Such is the leanness of a heart divided
From intercourse of troth-contracted loves;
No horror should deface that precious figure
Sealed with the lively stamp of equal souls.
   Penthea. Away! some Fury hath bewitched thy tongue:
The breath of ignorance, that flies from thence,
Ripens a knowledge in me of afflictions
Above all sufferance.—Thing of talk, begone!
Begone, without reply!
   Orgilus.   Be just, Penthea,
In thy commands; when thou send'st forth a doom

---

[13] This passage is corrupt; it was amended by Gifford; the old copy reads,

> "as the incense smoking
> The holiest artars, virgin tears (like
> On Vesta's odours) sprinkled dews to feed 'em,
> And to increase," &c.

Of banishment, know first on whom it lights.
Thus I take off the shroud, in which my cares
Are folded up from view of common eyes.

> [*Throws off his* Scholar's *dress.*

What is thy sentence next?
  Penthea.   Rash man! thou lay'st
A blemish on mine honour, with the hazard
Of thy too-desperate life: yet I profess,
By all the laws of ceremonious wedlock,
I have not given admittance to one thought
Of female change since cruelty enforced
Divorce betwixt my body and my heart.
Why would you fall from goodness thus?
  Orgilus.   O, rather
Examine me, how I could live to say
I have been much, much wronged. 'Tis for thy sake
I put on this imposture: dear Penthea,
If thy soft bosom be not turned to marble,
Thou'lt pity our calamities; my interest
Confirms me thou art mine still.
  Penthea.   Lend your hand;
With both of mine I clasp it thus, thus kiss it,
Thus kneel before ye.   [PENTHEA *kneels.*
  Orgilus.   You instruct my duty. [ORGILUS *kneels.*
  Penthea. We may stand up. [*They rise*] Have you aught
       else to urge
Of new demand? as for the old, forget it;
'Tis buried in an everlasting silence,
And shall be, shall be ever: what more would ye?
  Orgilus. I would possess my wife; the equity
Of very reason bids me.
  Penthea.   Is that all?
  Orgilus. Why, 'tis the all of me, myself.
  Penthea.   Remove
Your steps some distance from me:—at this space
A few words I dare change; but first put on
Your borrowed shape.
  Orgilus.   You are obeyed; 'tis done.

> [*He resumes his disguise.*

  Penthea. How, Orgilus, by promise I was thine

The heavens do witness; they can witness too
A rape done on my truth: how I do love thee
Yet, Orgilus, and yet, must best appear
In tendering thy freedom; for I find
The constant preservation of thy merit,
By thy not daring to attempt my fame
With injury of any loose conceit,
Which might give deeper wounds to discontents.
Continue this fair race: then, though I cannot
Add to thy comfort, yet I shall more often
Remember from what fortune I am fall'n,
And pity mine own ruin.—Live, live happy,—
Happy in thy next choice, that thou mayst people
This barren age with virtues in thy issue!
And O, when thou art married, think on me
With mercy, not contempt! I hope thy wife,
Hearing my story, will not scorn my fall.—
Now let us part.

   Orgilus.   Part! yet advise thee better:
Penthea is the wife to Orgilus,
And ever shall be.

   Penthea.   Never shall nor will.

   Orgilus. How!

   Penthea.   Hear me; in a word I'll tell thee why.
The virgin-dowry which my birth bestowed
Is ravished by another; my true love
Abhors to think that Orgilus deserved
No better favours than a second bed.

   Orgilus. I must not take this reason.

   Penthea.   To confirm it;
Should I outlive my bondage, let me meet
Another worse than this and less desired,
If, of all men alive, thou shouldst but touch
My lip or hand again!

   Orgilus.   Penthea, now
I tell ye, you grow wanton in my sufferance:
Come, sweet, thou'rt mine.

   Penthea.   Uncivil sir, forbear!
Or I can turn affection into vengeance;
Your reputation, if you value any,

Lies bleeding at my feet. Unworthy man,
If ever henceforth thou appear in language,
Message, or letter, to betray my frailty,
I'll call thy former protestations lust,
And curse my stars for forfeit of my judgment.
Go thou, fit only for disguise, and walks,
To hide thy shame: this once I spare thy life.
I laugh at mine own confidence; my sorrows
By thee are made inferior to my fortunes.
If ever thou didst harbour worthy love,
Dare not to answer. My good genius guide me,
That I may never see thee more!—Go from me!

   Orgilus. I'll tear my veil of politic French off,
And stand up like a man resolved to do:
Action, not words, shall show me.—O Penthea!   [*Exit.*

   Penthea. He sighed my name, sure, as he parted from me:
I fear I was too rough. Alas, poor gentleman!
He looked not like the ruins of his youth,
But like the ruins of those ruins. Honour,
How much we fight with weakness to preserve thee!

                                        [*Walks aside.*

                Enter BASSANES *and* GRAUSIS.

   Bassanes. Fie on thee! damn thee, rotten maggot, damn
      thee!
Sleep? sleep at court? and now? Aches,[14] convulsions,
Imposthumes, rheums, gouts, palsies, clog thy bones
A dozen years more yet!
   Grausis.   Now you're in humours.
   Bassanes. She's by herself, there's hope of that; she's sad
      too;
She's in strong contemplation; yes, and fixed:
The signs are wholesome.
   Grausis.   Very wholesome, truly.
   Bassanes. Hold your chops, nightmare!—Lady, come; your
      brother
Is carried to his closet; you must thither.
   Penthea. Not well, my lord?

---

[14] The word was pronounced as a dissyllable. *aitches.*

    Bassanes.   A sudden fit; 'twill off!
Some surfeit or disorder.—How dost, dearest?
    Penthea. Your news is none o' the best.

Re-enter PROPHILUS.

    Prophilus.   The chief of men,
The excellentest Ithocles, desires
Your presence, madam.
    Bassanes.   We are hasting to him.
    Penthea. In vain we labour in this course of life
To piece our journey out at length, or crave
Respite of breath: our home is in the grave.
    Bassanes. Perfect philosophy!
    Penthea.   Then let us care
To live so, that our reckonings may fall even
When we're to make account.
    Prophilus.   He cannot fear
Who builds on noble grounds: sickness or pain
Is the deserver's exercise; and such
Your virtuous brother to the world is known.
Speak comfort to him, lady; be all gentle:
Stars fall but in the grossness of our sight;
A good man dying, the earth doth lose a light.

[Exeunt.

ACT THE THIRD

SCENE I—*The Study of* TECNICUS

Enter TECNICUS, *and* ORGILUS *in his usual dress.*

TECNICUS. Be well advised; let not a resolution
Of giddy rashness choke the breath of reason.
    Orgilus. It shall not, most sage master.
    Tecnicus.   I am jealous;[15]
For if the borrowed shape so late put on
Inferred a consequence, we must conclude

---

[15] Suspicious.

Some violent design of sudden nature
Hath shook that shadow off, to fly upon
A new-hatched execution. Orgilus,
Take heed thou hast not, under our integrity,
Shrouded unlawful plots; our mortal eyes
Pierce not the secrets of your heart, the gods
Are only privy to them.

   Orgilus.   Learnèd Tecnicus,
Such doubts are causeless; and, to clear the truth
From misconceit, the present state commands me.
The Prince of Argos comes himself in person
In quest of great Calantha for his bride,
Our kingdom's heir; besides, mine only sister,
Euphranea, is disposed to Prophilus;
Lastly, the king is sending letters for me
To Athens, for my quick repair to court:
Please to accept these reasons.

   Tecnicus.   Just ones, Orgilus,
Not to be contradicted: yet beware
Of an unsure foundation; no fair colours
Can fortify a building faintly jointed.
I have observed a growth in thy aspéct
Of dangerous extent, sudden, and—look to't—
I might add, certain—

   Orgilus.   My aspéct! could art
Run through mine inmost thoughts, it should not sift
An inclination there more than what suited
With justice of mine honour.

   Tecnicus.   I believe it.
But know then, Orgilus, what honour is:
Honour consists not in a bare opinion
By doing any act that feeds content,
Brave in appearance, 'cause we think it brave;
Such honour comes by accident, not nature,
Proceeding from the vices of our passion,
Which makes our reason drunk: but real honour
Is the reward of virtue, and acquired
By justice, or by valour which for basis
Hath justice to uphold it. He then fails
In honour, who for lucre or revenge

Commits thefts, murders, treasons, and adulteries,
With suchlike, by intrenching on just laws,
Whose sovereignty is best preserved by justice.
Thus, as you see how honour must be grounded
On knowledge, not opinion,—for opinion
Relies on probability and accident,
But knowledge on necessity and truth,—
I leave thee to the fit consideration
Of what becomes the grace of real honour,
Wishing success to all thy virtuous meanings.

Orgilus. The gods increase thy wisdom, reverend oracle,
And in thy precepts make me ever thrifty!

Tecnicus. I thank thy wish.   [*Exit* ORGILUS.
                    Much mystery of fate
Lies hid in that man's fortunes; curiosity
May lead his actions into rare attempts:—
But let the gods be moderators still;
No human power can prevent their will.

Enter ARMOSTES *with a casket.*

From whence come ye?

Armostes.   From King Amyclas,—pardon
My interruption of your studies.—Here,
In this sealed box, he sends a treasure to you,
Dear to him as his crown: he prays your gravity,
You would examine, ponder, sift, and bolt
The pith and circumstance of every tittle
The scroll within contains.

Tecnicus.   What is 't, Armostes?

Armostes. It is the health of Sparta, the king's life,
Sinews and safety of the commonwealth;
The sum of what the oracle delivered
When last he visited the prophetic temple
At Delphos: what his reasons are, for which,
After so long a silence, he requires
Your counsel now, grave man, his majesty
Will soon himself acquaint you with.

Tecnicus.   Apollo [*He takes the casket.*
Inspire my intellect!—The Prince of Argos
Is entertained?

Armostes.   He is; and has demanded
Our princess for his wife; which I conceive
One special cause the king impórtunes you
For resolution of the oracle.
    Tecnicus. My duty to the king, good peace to Sparta,
And fair day to Armostes!
    Armostes.   Like to Tecnicus!   [*Exeunt.*

SCENE II—*The Palace.* ITHOCLES' *Apartment.*

Soft music. A song within, during which PROPHILUS, BAS-
    SANES, PENTHEA, *and* GRAUSIS *pass over the stage.* BASSANES
    and GRAUSIS *re-enter softly, and listen in different places.*

SONG.

Can you paint a thought? or number
Every fancy in a slumber?
Can you count soft minutes roving
From a dial's point by moving?
Can you grasp a sigh? or, lastly,
Rob a virgin's honour chastely?
    No, O, no! yet you may
Sooner do both that and this,
This and that, and never miss,
    Than by any praise display
Beauty's beauty; such a glory,
As beyond all fate, all story,
        All arms, all arts,
        All loves, all hearts,
Greater than those or they,
Do, shall, and must obey.

Bassanes. All silent, calm, secure.—Grausis, no creaking?
No noise? dost hear nothing?
    Grausis.   Not a mouse,
Or whisper of the wind.
    Bassanes.   The floor is matted;
The bedposts sure are steel or marble.—Soldiers
Should not affect, methinks, strains so effeminate:

Sounds of such delicacy are but fawnings
Upon the sloth of luxury, they heighten
Cinders of covert lust up to a flame.

    Grausis. What do you mean, my lord?—speak low; that
        gabbling
Of yours will but undo us.

    Bassanes.   Chamber-combats
Are felt, not heard.

    Prophilus. [*Within*] He wakes.

    Bassanes.   What's that?

    Ithocles. [*Within*]   Who's there?
Sister?—All quit the room else.

    Bassanes.   'Tis consented!

Re-enter PROPHILUS.

    Prophilus. Lord Bassanes, your brother would be private,
We must forbear; his sleep hath newly left him.
Please ye withdraw.

    Bassanes.   By any means; 'tis fit.

    Prophilus. Pray, gentlewoman, walk too.

    Grausis.   Yes, I will, sir. [*Exeunt.*

The scene opens; ITHOCLES *is discovered in a chair, and*
PENTHEA *beside him.*

    Ithocles. Sit nearer, sister to me; nearer yet:
We had one father, in one womb took life,
Were brought up twins together, yet have lived
At distance, like two strangers: I could wish
That the first pillow whereon I was cradled
Had proved to me a grave.

    Penthea.   You had been happy:
Then had you never known that sin of life
Which blots all following glories with a vengeance,
For forfeiting the last will of the dead,
From whom you had your being.

    Ithocles.   Sad Penthea,
Thou canst not be too cruel; my rash spleen
Hath with a violent hand plucked from thy bosom
A love-blest heart, to grind it into dust;
For which mine's now a-breaking.

Penthea.   Not yet, Heaven.
I do beseech thee! first let some wild fires
Scorch, not consume it! may the heat be cherished
With desires infinite, but hopes impossible!
   Ithocles. Wronged soul, thy prayers are heard.
   Penthea.   Here, lo, I breathe.
A miserable creature, led to ruin
By an unnatural brother!
   Ithocles.   I consume
In languishing affections for that trespass;
Yet cannot die.
   Penthea.   The handmaid to the wages
Of country toil drinks the untroubled streams
With leaping kids and with the bleating lambs,
And so allays her thirst secure; whiles I
Quench my hot sighs with fleetings of my tears.
   Ithocles. The labourer doth eat his coarsest bread,
Earned with his sweat, and lies him down to sleep;
While every bit I touch turns in digestion
To gall as bitter as Penthea's curse.
Put me to any penance for my tyranny.
And I will call thee merciful.
   Penthea.   Pray kill me,
Rid me from living with a jealous husband;
Then we will join in friendship, be again
Brother and sister.—Kill me, pray; nay, will ye?
   Ithocles. How does thy lord esteem thee?
   Penthea.   Such an one
As only you have made me; a faith-breaker,
A spotted whore:—forgive me, I am one—
In act, not in desires, the gods must witness.
   Ithocles. Thou dost belie thy friend.
   Penthea.   I do not, Ithocles;
For she that's wife to Orgilus, and lives
In known adultery with Bassanes,
Is at the best a whore. Wilt kill me now?
The ashes of our parents will assume
Some dreadful figure, and appear to charge
Thy bloody guilt, that hast betrayed their name
To infamy in this reproachful match.

Ithocles. After my victories abroad, at home
I meet despair; ingratitude of nature
Hath made my actions monstrous: thou shalt stand
A deity, my sister, and be worshipped
For thy resolvèd martyrdom; wrongèd maids
And married wives shall to thy hallowed shrine
Offer their orisons, and sacrifice
Pure turtles, crowned with myrtle; if thy pity
Unto a yielding brother's pressure lend
One finger but to ease it.

 Penthea.   O, no more!

 Ithocles. Death waits to waft me to the Stygian banks,
And free me from this chaos of my bondage;
And till thou wilt forgive, I must endure.

 Penthea. Who is the saint you serve?

 Ithocles.   Friendship, or nearness
Of birth to any but my sister, durst not
Have moved that question; 'tis a secret, sister,
I dare not murmur to myself.

 Penthea.   Let me,
By your new protestations I conjure ye,
Partake her name.

 Ithocles. Her name?—'tis—'tis—I dare not.

 Penthea. All your respects are forged.

 Ithocles.   They are not.—Peace!
Calantha is—the princess—the king's daughter—
Sole heir of Sparta.—Me, most miserable!
Do I now love thee? for my injuries
Revenge thyself with bravery, and gossip
My treasons to the king's ears, do:—Calantha
Knows it not yet, nor Prophilus, my nearest.

 Penthea. Suppose you were contracted to her, would it
  not
Split even your very soul to see her father
Snatch her out of your arms against her will,
And force her on the Prince of Argos?

 Ithocles.   Trouble not
The fountains of mine eyes with thine own story;
I sweat in blood for't.

 Penthea.   We are reconciled.

Alas, sir, being children, but two branches
Of one stock, 'tis not fit we should divide:
Have comfort, you may find it.

    Ithocles.   Yes, in thee;
Only in thee, Penthea mine.

    Penthea.   If sorrows
Have not too much dulled my infected brain,
I'll cheer invention for an active strain.

    Ithocles. Mad man! why have I wronged a maid so
        excellent!

BASSANES *rushes in with a poniard, followed by* PROPHILUS,
    GRONEAS, HEMOPHIL, *and* GRAUSIS.

    Bassanes. I can forbear no longer; more, I will not:
Keep off your hands, or fall upon my point.—
Patience is tired; for, like a slow-paced ass,
Ye ride my easy nature, and proclaim
My sloth to vengeance a reproach and property.

    Ithocles. The meaning of this rudeness?

    Prophilus.   He's distracted.

    Penthea. O, my grieved lord!—

    Grausis.   Sweet lady, come not near him;
He holds his perilous weapon in his hand
To prick he cares not whom nor where,—see, see, see!

    Bassanes. My birth is noble: though the popular blast
Of vanity, as giddy as thy youth,
Hath reared thy name up to bestride a cloud,
Or progress[16] in the chariot of the sun,
I am no clod of trade, to lackey pride,
Nor, like your slave of expectation, wait
The bawdy hinges of your doors, or whistle
For mystical conveyance to your bed-sports.

    Groneas. Fine humours! they become him.

    Hemophil.   How he stares,
Struts, puffs, and sweats! most admirable lunacy!

---

[16] This passage is not without curiosity as tending to prove that some of the
words now supposed to be Americanisms were in use among our ancestors, and
crossed the Atlantic with them. It is not generally known that Ford's county
(Devonshire) suppled a very considerable number of the earlier settlers in the
Colonies.—*Gifford.*

Ithocles. But that I may conceive the spirit of wine
Has took possession of your soberer custom,
I'd say you were unmannerly.
   Penthea.   Dear brother!—
   Bassanes. Unmannerly!—mew, kitling!—smooth formality
Is usher to the rankness of the blood,
But impudence bears up the train. Indeed, sir,
Your fiery mettle, or your springal blaze
Of huge renown, is no sufficient royalty
To print upon my forehead the scorn, "cuckold."
   Ithocles. His jealousy has robbed him of his wits;
He talks he knows not what.
   Bassanes.   Yes, and he knows
To whom he talks; to one that franks his lust
In swine-security[17] of bestial incest.
   Ithocles. Ha, devil!
   Bassanes.   I will haloo't; though I blush more
To name the filthiness than thou to act it.
   Ithocles. Monster!   [*Draws his sword.*
   Prophilus.   Sir, by our friendship—
   Penthea.   By our bloods—
Will you quite both undo us, brother?
   Grausis.   Out on him!
These are his megrims, firks,[18] and melancholies.
   Hemophil. Well said, old touch-hole.
   Groneas.   Kick him out of doors.
   Penthea. With favour, let me speak.—My lord, what slack-
       ness
In my obedience hath deserved this rage?
Except humility and silent duty
Have drawn on your unquiet, my simplicity
Ne'er studied your vexation.
   Bassanes.   Light of beauty,
Deal not ungently with a desperate wound!
No breach of reason dares make war with her
Whose looks are sovereignty, whose breath is balm:

---

[17] Bassanes alludes to the small enclosures—"franks," as distinguished from
"styes"—in which boars were fattened. As these animals were dangerous when full-
fed, it was necessary to shut them up alone.—*Gifford.*
[18] Freaks.

O, that I could preserve thee in fruition
As in devotion!
  Penthea. Sir, may every evil
Locked in Pandora's box shower, in your presence,
On my unhappy head, if, since you made me
A partner in your bed, I have been faulty
In one unseemly thought against your honour!
  Ithocles. Purge not his griefs, Penthea.
  Bassanes.   Yes, say on,
Excellent creature!—[*To* ITHOCLES.] Good, be not a hin-
   drance
To peace and praise of virtue.—O, my senses
Are charmed with sounds celestial!—On, dear, on:
I never gave you one ill word; say, did I?
Indeed I did not.
  Penthea. Nor, by Juno's forehead,
Was I e'er guilty of a wanton error.
  Bassanes. A goddess! let me kneel.
  Grausis.   Alas, kind animal!
  Ithocles. No; but for penance.
  Bassanes.   Noble sir, what is it?
With gladness I embrace it; yet, pray let not
My rashness teach you to be too unmerciful.
  Ithocles. When you shall show good proof that manly
   wisdom,
Not overswayed by passion or opinion,
Knows how to lead your judgment, then this lady,
Your wife, my sister, shall return in safety
Home, to be guided by you; but, till first
I can out of clear evidence approve it,
She shall be my care.
  Bassanes. Rip my bosom up,
I'll stand the execution with a constancy;
This torture is insufferable.
  Ithocles.   Well, sir,
I dare not trust her to your fury.
  Bassanes.   But
Penthea says not so.
  Penthea. She needs no tongue

To plead excuse who never purposed wrong.

        [Exit with ITHOCLES *and* PROPHILUS.

  Hemophil. Virgin of reverence and antiquity,

Stay you behind.   *[To* GRAUSIS, *who is following* PENTHEA.

  Groneas. The court wants not your diligence.

        [Exeunt HEMOPHIL *and* GRONEAS.

  Grausis. What will you do, my lord? my lady's gone;

I am denied to follow.

  Bassanes.   I may see her,

Or speak to her once more?

  Grausis.   And feel her too, man;

Be of good cheer, she's your own flesh and bone.

  Bassanes. Diseases desperate must find cures alike.

She swore she has been true.

  Grausis.   True, on my modesty.

  Bassanes. Let him want truth who credits not her vows!

Much wrong I did her, but her brother infinite;

Rumour will voice me the contempt of manhood,

Should I run on thus: some way I must try

To outdo art, and jealousy decry.   *[Exeunt.*

SCENE III—*A Room in the Palace*

Flourish. Enter AMYCLAS, NEARCHUS, *leading* CALANTHA,
ARMOSTES, CROTOLON, EUPHRANEA, CHRISTALLA, PHILEMA,
and AMELUS.

  Amyclas. Cousin of Argos, what the heavens have pleased,

In their unchanging counsels, to conclude

For both our kingdoms' weal, we must submit to:

Nor can we be unthankful to their bounties,

Who, when we were even creeping to our grave,

Sent us a daughter, in whose birth our hope

Continues of succession. As you are

In title next, being grandchild to our aunt,

So we in heart desire you may sit nearest

Calantha's love; since we have ever vowed

Not to enforce affection by our will,

But by her own choice to confirm it gladly.

Nearchus. You speak the nature of a right just father.
I come not hither roughly to demand
My cousin's thraldom, but to free mine own:
Report of great Calantha's beauty, virtue,
Sweetness, and singular perfections, courted
All ears to credit what I find was published
By constant truth; from which, if any service
Of my desert can purchase fair construction,
This lady must command it.

  Calantha.   Princely sir,
So well you know how to profess observance,
That you instruct your hearers to become
Practitioners in duty; of which number
I'll study to be chief.

  Nearchus.   Chief, glorious virgin,
In my devotion, as in all men's wonder.

  Amyclas. Excellent cousin, we deny no liberty;
Use thine own opportunities.—Armostes,
We must consult with the philosophers;
The business is of weight.

  Armostes.   Sir, at your pleasure.

  Amyclas. You told me, Crotolon, your son's returned
From Athens: wherefore comes he not to court,
As we commanded?

  Crotolon.   He shall soon attend
Your royal will, great sir.

  Amyclas.   The marriage
Between young Prophilus and Euphranea
Tastes of too much delay.

  Crotolon.   My lord,—

  Amyclas.   Some pleasures
At celebration of it would give life
To the entertainment of the prince our kinsman;
Our court wears gravity more than we relish.

  Armostes. Yet the heavens smile on all your high attempts,
Without a cloud.

  Crotolon.   So may the gods protect us!

  Calantha. A prince a subject?

Nearchus.   Yes, to beauty's sceptre;
As all hearts kneel, so mine.
    Calantha.   You are too courtly.

    Enter ITHOCLES, ORGILUS, *and* PROPHILUS.

    Ithocles. Your safe return to Sparta is most welcome:
I joy to meet you here, and, as occasion
Shall grant us privacy, will yield you reasons
Why I should covet to deserve the title
Of your respected friend; for, without compliment,
Believe it, Orgilus, 'tis my ambition.
    Orgilus. Your lordship may command me, your poor
        servant.
    Ithocles. [*Aside*] So amorously close!—so soon!—my
        heart!
    Prophilus. What sudden change is next?
    Ithocles.   Life to the king!
To whom I here present this noble gentleman,
New come from Athens: royal sir, vouchsafe
Your gracious hand in favour of his merit.
                    [*The* King *gives* ORGILUS *his hand to kiss.*
    Crotolon. [*Aside*] My son preferred by Ithocles!
    Amyclas.   Our bounties
Shall open to thee, Orgilus; for instance,—
Hark in thine ear,—if, out of those inventions
Which flow in Athens, thou hast there engrossed
Some rarity of wit, to grace the nuptials
Of thy fair sister, and renown our court
In the eyes of this young prince, we shall be debtor
To thy conceit: think on't.
    Orgilus.   Your highness honours me.
    Nearchus. My tongue and heart are twins.
    Calantha.   A noble birth,
Becoming such a father.—Worthy Orgilus,
You are a guest most wished for.
    Orgilus.   May my duty
Still rise in your opinion, sacred princess!
    Ithocles. Euphranea's brother, sir; a gentleman
Well worthy of your knowledge.

Nearchus.   We embrace him,
Proud of so dear acquaintance.
 Amyclas.   All prepare
For revels and disport; the joys of Hymen,
Like Phœbus in his lustre, put to flight
All mists of dulness, crown the hours with gladness:
No sounds but music, no discourse but mirth!
 Calantha. Thine arm, I prithee, Ithocles.—Nay, good
My lord, keep on your way; I am provided.
 Nearchus. I dare not disobey.
 Ithocles.   Most heavenly lady!

              [Exeunt.

SCENE IV—*A Room in the House of* CROTOLON

Enter CROTOLON *and* ORGILUS.

Crotolon. The king hath spoke his mind.
 Orgilus.   His will he hath;
But were it lawful to hold plea against
The power of greatness, not the reason, haply
Such undershrubs as subjects sometimes might
Borrow of nature justice, to inform
That license sovereignty holds without check
Over a meek obedience.
 Crotolon.   How resolve you
Touching your sister's marriage? Prophilus
Is a deserving and a hopeful youth.
 Orgilus. I envy not his merit, but applaud it;
Could wish him thrift in all his best desires,
And with a willingness inleague our blood
With his, for purchase of full growth in friendship.
He never touched on any wrong that maliced
The honour of our house nor stirred our peace:
Yet, with your favour, let me not forget
Under whose wing he gathers warmth and comfort,
Whose creature he is bound, made, and must live so.
 Crotolon. Son, son, I find in thee a harsh condition;[19]
No courtesy can win it, 'tis too rancorous.

---

[19] *i.e.* Disposition.

Orgilus. Good sir, be not severe in your construction;
I am no stranger to such easy calms
As sit in tender bosoms: lordly Ithocles
Hath graced my entertainment in abundance;
Too humbly hath descended from that height
Of arrogance and spleen which wrought the rape
On grieved Penthea's purity; his scorn
Of my untoward fortunes is reclaimed
Unto a courtship, almost to a fawning:—
I'll kiss his foot, since you will have it so.

Crotolon. Since I will have it so! friend, I will have it so,
Without our ruin by your politic plots,
Or wolf of hatred snarling in your breast.
You have a spirit, sir, have ye? a familiar
That posts i' the air for your intelligence?
Some such hobgoblin hurried you from Athens,
For yet you come unsent for.

Orgilus.   If unwelcome,
I might have found a grave there.

Crotolon.   Sure, your business
Was soon dispatched, or your mind altered quickly.

Orgilus. 'Twas care, sir, of my health cut short my jour-
     ney;
For there a general infection
Threatens a desolation.

Crotolon.   And I fear
Thou hast brought back a worse infection with thee,—
Infection of thy mind; which, as thou say'st,
Threatens the desolation of our family.

Orgilus. Forbid it, our dear genius! I will rather
Be made a sacrifice on Thrasus' monument,
Or kneel to Ithocles his son in dust,
Than woo a father's curse. My sister's marriage
With Prophilus is from my heart confirmed;
May I live hated, may I die despised,
If I omit to further it in all
That can concern me!

Crotolon.   I have been too rough.
My duty to my king made me so earnest;
Excuse it, Orgilus.

Orgilus.   Dear sir!—
Crotolon.   Here comes
Euphranea, with Prophilus and Ithocles.

Enter PROPHILUS, EUPHRANEA, ITHOCLES, GRONEAS *and*
HEMOPHIL.

Orgilus. Most honoured!—ever famous!
Ithocles.   Your true friend;
On earth not any truer.—With smooth eyes
Look on this worthy couple; your consent
Can only make them one.
Orgilus.   They have it.—Sister,
Thou pawnedst to me an oath, of which engagement
I never will release thee, if thou aim'st
At any other choice than this.
Euphranea.   Dear brother,
At him, or none.
Crotolon.   To which my blessing's added.
Orgilus. Which, till a greater ceremony perfect,—
Euphranea, lend thy hand,—here, take her, Prophilus:
Live long a happy man and wife; and further,
That these in presence may conclude an omen.
Thus for a bridal song I close my wishes:

  (*Sings*) Comforts lasting, loves increasing,
           Like soft hours never ceasing:
           Plenty's pleasure, peace complying,
           Without jars, or tongues envying;
           Hearts by holy union wedded,
           More than theirs by custom bedded;
           Fruitful issues; life so graced,
           Not by age to be defaced,
           Budding, as the year ensu'th,
           Every spring another youth:
           All what thought can add beside
           Crown this bridegroom and this bride!

Prophilus. You have sealed joy close to my soul.—Eupra-
    nea
Now I may call thee mine.

Ithocles.   I but exchange
One good friend for another.
    Orgilus.   If these gallants
Will please to grace a poor invention
By joining with me in some slight device,
I'll venture on a strain my younger days
Have studied for delight.
    Hemophil.   With thankful willingness
I offer my attendance.
    Groneas.   No endeavour
Of mine shall fail to show itself.
    Ithocles.   We will
All join to wait on thy directions, Orgilus.
    Orgilus. O, my good lord, your favours flow towards
A too unworthy worm;—but as you please;
I am what you will shape me.
    Ithocles.   A fast friend.
    Crotolon. I think thee, son, for this acknowledgement;
It is a sight of gladness.
    Orgilus   But my duty.   [*Exeunt.*

SCENE V—CALANTHA'S *Apartment in the Palace*

Enter CALANTHA, PENTHEA, CHRISTALLA, *and* PHILEMA.

    Calantha. Whoe'er would speak with us, deny his en-
        trance;
Be careful of our charge.
    Christalla.   We shall, madam.
    Calantha. Except the king himself, give none admittance;
Not any.
    Philema. Madam, it shall be our care.
                    [*Exeunt* CHRISTALLA *and* PHILEMA.
    Calantha. Being alone, Penthea, you have granted
The opportunity you sought, and might
At all times have commanded.
    Penthea.   'Tis a benefit
Which I shall owe your goodness even in death for:
My glass of life, sweet princess, hath few minutes

Remaining to run down; the sands are spent;
For by an inward messenger I feel
The summons of departure short and certain.

   Calantha. You feel too much your melancholy.

   Penthea.   Glories
Of human greatness are but pleasing dreams
And shadows soon decaying: on the stage
Of my mortality my youth hath acted
Some scenes of vanity, drawn out at length
By varied pleasures, sweetened in the mixture,
But tragical in issue: beauty, pomp,
With every sensuality our giddiness
Doth frame an idol, are unconstant friends,
When any troubled passion makes assault
On the unguarded castle of the mind.

   Calantha. Contemn not your condition for the proof
Of bare opinion only: to what end
Reach all these moral texts?

   Penthea.   To place before ye
A perfect mirror, wherein you may see
How weary I am of a lingering life,
Who count the best a misery.

   Calantha.   Indeed
You have no little cause; yet none so great
As to distrust a remedy.

   Penthea.   That remedy
Must be a winding-sheet, a fold of lead,
And some untrod-on corner in the earth.—
Not to detain your expectation, princess,
I have an humble suit.

   Calantha.   Speak; I enjoy it.

   Penthea. Vouchsafe, then, to be my executrix,
And take that trouble on ye to dispose
Such legacies as I bequeath impartially;
I have not much to give, the pains are easy;
Heaven will reward your piety, and thank it
When I am dead; for sure I must not live;
I hope I cannot.

   Calantha.   Now, beshrew thy sadness,
Thou turn'st me too much woman.   [*Weeps.*

Penthea. [*Aside*]   Her fair eyes
Melt into passion.—Then I have assurance
Encouraging my boldness. In this paper
My will was charactered; which you, with pardon,
Shall now know from mine own mouth.
    Calantha.   Talk on, prithee;
It is a pretty earnest.
    Penthea.   I have left me
But three poor jewels to bequeath. The first is
My youth; for though I am much old in griefs,
In years I am a child.
    Calantha.   To whom that jewel?
    Penthea. To virgin-wives, such as abuse not wedlock
By freedom of desires, but covet chiefly
The pledges of chaste beds for ties of love,
Rather than ranging of their blood; and next
To married maids, such as prefer the number
Of honourable issue in their virtues
Before the flattery of delights by marriage:
May those be ever young!
    Calantha.   A second jewel
You mean to part with?
    Penthea.   'Tis my fame, I trust
By scandal yet untouched: this I bequeath
To Memory, and Time's old daughter, Truth.
If ever my unhappy name find mention
When I am fall'n to dust, may it deserve
Beseeming charity without dishonour!
    Calantha. How handsomely thou play'st with harmless
        sport
Of mere imagination! speak the last.
I strangely like thy will.
    Penthea.   This jewel, madam,
Is dearly precious to me; you must use
The best of your discretion to employ
This gift as I intend it.
    Calantha.   Do not doubt me.
    Penthea. 'Tis long agone since first I lost my heart:
Long I have lived without it, else for certain
I should have given that too; but instead

Of it, to great Calantha, Sparta's heir,
By service bound and by affection vowed,
I do bequeath, in holiest rites of love,
Mine only brother, Ithocles.
    Calantha.   What saidst thou?
    Penthea. Impute not, heaven-blest lady, to ambition
A faith as humbly perfect as the prayers
Of a devoted suppliant can endow it:
Look on him, princess, with an eye of pity;
How like the ghost of what he late appeared
He moves before you.
    Calantha.   Shall I answer here,
Or lend my ear too grossly?
    Penthea.   First his heart
Shall fall in cinders, scorched by your disdain,
Ere he will dare, poor man, to ope an eye
On these divine looks, but with low-bent thoughts
Accusing such presumption; as for words,
He dares not utter any but of service:
Yet this lost creature loves ye.—Be a princess
In sweetness as in blood; give him his doom,
Or raise him up to comfort.
    Calantha.   What new change
Appears in my behaviour, that thou dar'st
Tempt my displeasure?
    Penthea.   I must leave the world
To revel in Elysium, and 'tis just
To wish my brother some advantage here;
Yet, by my best hopes, Ithocles is ignorant
Of this pursuit: but if you please to kill him,
Lend him one angry look or one harsh word,
And you shall soon conclude how strong a power
Your absolute authority holds over
His life and end.
    Calantha.   You have forgot, Penthea,
How still I have a father.
    Penthea.   But remember
I am a sister, though to me this brother
Hath been, you know, unkind, O, most unkind!

Calantha. Christalla, Philema, where are ye?—Lady,
Your check lies in my silence.

Re-enter CHRISTALLA *and* PHILEMA.

Christalla and Philema.   Madam, here.
Calantha. I think ye sleep, ye drones: wait on Penthea
Unto her lodging.—[*Aside*] Ithocles? wronged lady!
     Penthea. My reckonings are made even; death or fate
Can now nor strike too soon nor force too late.

                                   [*Exeunt.*

ACT THE FOURTH

SCENE I—*The Palace.* ITHOCLES' *Apartment.*

Enter ITHOCLES *and* ARMOSTES.

ITHOCLES. Forbear your inquisition: curiosity
Is of too subtle and too searching nature,
In fears of love too quick, too slow of credit.—
I am not what you doubt me.
     Armostes.   Nephew, be, then,
As I would wish;—all is not right.—Good heaven
Confirm your resolutions for dependence
On worthy ends, which may advance your quiet!
     Ithocles. I did the noble Orgilus much injury,
But grieved Penthea more: I now repent it,—
Now, uncle, now; this "now" is now too late.
So provident is folly in sad issue,
That after-wit, like bankrupts' debts, stands tallied,
Without all possibilities of payment.
Sure, he's an honest, very honest gentleman;
A man of single[20] meaning.
     Armostes.   I believe it:
Yet, nephew, 'tis the tongue informs our ears;
Our eyes can never pierce into the thoughts,
For they are lodged too inward:—but I question
No truth in Orgilus.—The princess, sir.

[20] Sincere.

Ithocles. The princess! ha!

Armostes.   With her the Prince of Argos.

Enter NEARCHUS, *leading* CALANTHA; AMELUS,
CHRISTALLA, PHILEMA.

Nearchus. Great fair one, grace my hopes with any in-
stance
Of livery,[21] from the allowance of your favour;
This little spark—[*Attempts to take a ring from her finger.*
Calantha.   A toy!

Nearchus.   Love feasts on toys,
For Cupid is a child;—vouchsafe this bounty:
It cannot be denied.

Calantha.   You shall not value,
Sweet cousin, at a price, what I count cheap;
So cheap, that let him take it who dares stoop for't,
And give it at next meeting to a mistress:
She'll thank him for't, perhaps.

         [*Casts the ring before* ITHOCLES, *who takes it up.*
Amelus.   The ring, sir, is
The princess's; I could have took it up.

Ithocles. Learn manners, prithee.—To the blessèd owner,
Upon my knees—   [*Kneels and offers it to* CALANTHA.
Nearchus.   You're saucy.

Calantha.   This is pretty!
I am, belike, "a mistress"—wondrous pretty!—
Let the man keep his fortune, since he found it;
He's worthy on't.—On, cousin!

         [*Exeunt* NEARCHUS, CALANTHA, CHRISTALLA, *and*
PHILEMA.

Ithocles [*to* AMELUS]   Follow, spaniel;
I'll force ye to a fawning else.

Amelus.   You dare not.   [*Exit.*

Armostes. My lord, you were too forward.

Ithocles.   Look ye, uncle,
Some such there are whose liberal contents
Swarm without care in every sort of plenty;
Who after full repasts can lay them down

---

21 This was the language of courtship, and was derived from the practice of dis-
tinguishing the followers and retainers of great families by the badge or crest of
the house.—*Gifford.*

To sleep; and they sleep, uncle: in which silence
Their very dreams present 'em choice of pleasures,
Pleasures—observe me, uncle—of rare object;
Here heaps of gold, there increments of honours,
Now change of garments, then the votes of people;
Anon varieties of beauties, courting,
In flatteries of the night, exchange of dalliance:
Yet these are still but dreams. Give me felicity
Of which my senses waking are partakers,
A real, visible, material happiness;
And then, too, when I stagger in expectance
Of the least comfort that can cherish life.—
I saw it, sir, I saw it; for it came
From her own hand.

  Armostes.   The princess threw it t'ye.

  Ithocles. True; and she said—well I remember what—
Her cousin prince would beg it.

  Armostes.   Yes, and parted
In anger at your taking on't.

  Ithocles.   Penthea,
O, thou hast pleaded with a powerful language!
I want a fee to gratify thy merit;
But I will do—

  Armostes.   What is't you say?

  Ithocles.   In anger!
In anger let him part; for could his breath,
Like whirlwinds, toss such servile slaves as lick
The dust his footsteps print into a vapour,
It durst not stir a hair of mine, it should not;
I'd rend it up by the roots first. To be anything
Calantha smiles on, is to be a blessing
More sacred than a petty prince of Argos
Can wish to equal or in worth or title.

  Armostes. Contain yourself, my lord: Ixion, aiming
To embrace Juno, bosomed but a cloud,
And begat Centaurs; 'tis an useful moral:
Ambition hatched in clouds of mere opinion
Proves but in birth a prodigy.

  Ithocles.   I thank ye;
Yet, with your license, I should seem uncharitable

To gentler fate, if, relishing the dainties
Of a soul's settled peace, I were so feeble
Not to digest it.
  Armostes. He deserves small trust
Who is not privy-counsellor to himself.

   Re-enter NEARCHUS *and* AMELUS, *with* ORGILUS.

  Nearchus. Brave me?
  Orgilus.   Your excellence mistakes his temper;
For Ithocles in fashion of his mind
Is beautiful, soft, gentle, the clear mirror
Of absolute perfection.
  Amelus.   Was't your modesty
Termed any of the prince's servants "spaniel"?
Your nurse, sure, taught you other language.
  Ithocles.   Language!
  Nearchus. A gallant man-at-arms is here, a doctor
In feats of chivalry, blunt and rough-spoken,
Vouchsafing not the fustian of civility,
Which less rash spirits style good manners.
  Ithocles.   Manners!
  Orgilus. No more, illustrious sir; 'tis matchless Ithocles.
  Nearchus. You might have understood who I am.
  Ithocles.   Yes,
I did; else—but the presence calmed the affront—
You're cousin to the princess.
  Nearchus.   To the king too;
A certain instrument that lent supportance
To your colossic greatness—to that king too,
You might have added.
  Ithocles.   There is more divinity
In beauty than in majesty.
  Armostes.   O fie, fie!
  Nearchus. This odd youth's pride turns heretic in loyalty.
Sirrah! low mushrooms never rival cedars.
         [*Exeunt* NEARCHUS *and* AMELUS.
  Ithocles. Come back!—What pitiful dull thing am I
So to be tamely scolded at! come back!—
Let him come back, and echo once again
That scornful sound of mushroom! painted colts—

Like heralds' coats gilt o'er with crowns and sceptres—
May bait a muzzled lion.

   Armostes.   Cousin, cousin,
Thy tongue is not thy friend.

   Orgilus.   In point of honour
Discretion knows no bounds. Amelus told me
'Twas all about a little ring.

   Ithocles.   A ring
The princess threw away, and I took up:
Admit she threw't to me, what arm of brass
Can snatch it hence? No; could he grind the hoop
To powder, he might sooner reach my heart
Than steal and wear one dust on't.—Orgilus,
I am extremely wronged.

   Orgilus.   A lady's favour
Is not to be so slighted.

   Ithocles.   Slighted!

   Armostes.   Quiet
These vain unruly passions, which will render ye
Into a madness.

   Orgilus.   Griefs will have their vent.

Enter TECNICUS *with a scroll*.

   Armostes. Welcome; thou com'st in season, reverend man,
To pour the balsam of a suppling patience
Into the festering wound of ill-spent fury.

   Orgilus. [*Aside*] What makes he here?

   Tecnicus.   The hurts are yet but mortal,
Which shortly will prove deadly. To the king,
Armostes, see in safety thou deliver
This sealed-up counsel; bid him with a constancy
Peruse the secrets of the gods.—O Sparta,
O Lacedæmon! double-named, but one
In fate: when kingdoms reel,—mark well my saw,—
Their heads must needs be giddy. Tell the king
That henceforth he no more must inquire after
My agèd head; Apollo wills it so:
I am for Delphos.

   Armostes.   Not without some conference
With our great master?

Tecnicus.   Never more to see him:
A greater prince commands me.—Ithocles,
   "When youth is ripe, and age from time doth part,
      The lifeless trunk shall wed the broken heart."
Ithocles. What's this, if understood?
Tecnicus.   List, Orgilus;
Remember what I told thee long before,
These tears shall be my witness.
   Armostes.   'Las, good man!
Tecnicus. "Let craft with courtesy a while confer,
      Revenge proves its own executioner."
Orgilus. Dark sentences are for Apollo's priests;
I am not Œdipus.
   Tecnicus.   My hour is come;
Cheer up the king; farewell to all.—O Sparta,
O Lacedæmon!   [*Exit.*
   Armostes.   If prophetic fire
Have warmed this old man's bosom, we might construe
His words to fatal sense.
   Ithocles.   Leave to the powers
Above us the effects of their decrees;
My burthen lies within me: servile fears
Prevent no great effects—Divine Calantha!
   Armostes. The gods be still propitious!
                        [*Exeunt* ITHOCLES *and* ARMOSTES.
   Orgilus.   Something oddly
The book-man prated, yet he talked it weeping;
   "Let craft with courtesy a while confer,
      Revenge proves its own executioner."
Con it again;—for what? It shall not puzzle me;
'Tis dotage of a withered brain.—Penthea
Forbade me not her presence; I may see her,
And gaze my fill. Why see her, then, I may,
When, if I faint to speak—I must be silent.   [*Exit.*

SCENE II—*A Room in* BASSANES' *House*

Enter BASSANES, GRAUSIS, *and* PHULAS.

Bassanes. Pray, use your recreations, all the service
I will expect is quietness amongst ye;
Take liberty at home, abroad, at all times,
And in your charities appease the gods,
Whom I, with my distractions, have offended.

    Grausis. Fair blessings on thy heart!

    Phulas. [*Aside*]   Here's a rare change!
My lord, to cure the itch, is surely gelded;
The cuckold in conceit hath cast his horns.

    Bassanes. Betake ye to your several occasions;
And wherein I have heretofore been faulty,
Let your constructions mildly pass it over;
Henceforth I'll study reformation,—more
I have not for employment.

    Grausis.   O, sweet man!
Thou art the very "Honeycomb of Honesty."

    Phulas. The "Garland of Good-will." [22]—Old lady, hold
        up
Thy reverend snout, and trot behind me softly,
As it becomes a moil [23] of ancient carriage.

                    [*Exeunt* GRAUSIS *and* PHULAS.

    Bassanes. Beasts, only capable of sense, enjoy
The benefit of food and ease with thankfulness;
Such silly creatures, with a grudging, kick not
Against the portion nature hath bestowed:
But men, endowed with reason and the use
Of reason, to distinguish from the chaff
Of abject scarcity the quintessence,
Soul, and elixir of the earth's abundance,
The treasures of the sea, the air, nay, heaven,
Repining at these glories of creation
Are verier beasts than beasts; and of those beasts

---

[22] The *Honeycomb of Honesty*, like the *Garland of Goodwill*, was probably one
of the popular miscellanies of the day.—*Gifford.*
[23] *i.e.* Mule.

The worst am I: I, who was made a monarch
Of what a heart could wish for,—a chaste wife,—
Endeavoured what in me lay to pull down
That temple built for adoration only,
And level't in the dust of causeless scandal.
But, to redeem a sacrilege so impious,
Humility shall pour, before the deities
I have incensed, a largess of more patience
Than their displeasèd altars can require:
No tempests of commotion shall disquiet
The calms of my composure.

Enter ORGILUS.

  Orgilus.   I have found thee,
Thou patron of more horrors than the bulk
Of manhood, hooped about with ribs of iron,
Can cram within thy breast: Penthea, Bassanes,
Cursed by thy jealousies,—more, by thy dotage,—
Is left a prey to words.

  Bassanes.   Exercise
Your trials for addition to my penance;
I am resolved.

  Orgilus.   Play not with misery
Past cure: some angry minister of fate hath
Deposed the empress of her soul, her reason,
From its most proper throne; but, what's the miracle
More new, I, I have seen it, and yet live!

  Bassanes. You may delude my senses, not my judgment;
'Tis anchored into a firm resolution;
Dalliance of mirth or wit can ne'er unfix it:
Practise[24] yet further.

  Orgilus.   May thy death of love to her
Damn all thy comforts to a lasting fast
From every joy of life! Thou barren rock,
By thee we have been split in ken of harbour.

Enter PENTHEA with her hair loose, ITHOCLES, ARMOSTES,
PHILEMA, and CHRISTALLA.

  Ithocles. Sister, look up; your Ithocles, your brother,

---

[24] *i.e.* Practise on my patience.

Speaks t'ye; why do you weep? dear, turn not from me.—
Here is a killing sight; lo, Bassanes,
A lamentable object!
 Orgilus.   Man, does see't?
Sports are more gamesome; am I yet in merriment?
Why dost not laugh?
 Bassanes.   Divine and best of ladies,
Please to forget my outrage; mercy ever
Cannot but lodge under a roof so excellent:
I have cast off that cruelty of frenzy
Which once appeared imposture, and then juggled
To cheat my sleeps of rest.
 Orgilus.   Was I in earnest?
 Penthea. Sure, if we were all Sirens, we should sing piti-
  fully,
And 'twere a comely music, when in parts
One sung another's knell: the turtle sighs
When he hath lost his mate; and yet some say
He must be dead first: 'tis a fine deceit
To pass away in a dream! indeed, I've slept
With mine eyes open a great while. No falsehood
Equals a broken faith; there's not a hair
Sticks on my head but, like a leaden plummet,
It sinks me to the grave: I must creep thither;
The journey is not long.
 Ithocles.   But thou, Penthea,
Hast many years, I hope, to number yet,
Ere thou canst travel that way.
 Bassanes.   Let the sun first
Be wrapped up in an everlasting darkness,
Before the light of nature, chiefly formed
For the whole world's delight, feel an eclipse
So universal!
 Orgilus. Wisdom, look ye, begins
To rave!—art thou mad too, antiquity?
 Penthea. Since I was first a wife, I might have been
Mother to many pretty prattling babes;
They would have smiled when I smiled, and for certain
I should have cried when they cried:—truly, brother,
My father would have picked me out a husband,

And then my little ones had been no bastards;
But 'tis too late for me to marry now,
I am past child-bearing; 'tis not my fault.

   Bassanes. Fall on me, if there be a burning Ætna,
And bury me in flames! sweats hot as sulphur
Boil through my pores! affliction hath in store
No torture like to this.

   Orgilus.   Behold a patience!
Lay-by thy whining gray dissimulation,[25]
Do something worth a chronicle; show justice
Upon the author of this mischief; dig out
The jealousies that hatched this thraldom first
With thine own poniard: every antic rapture
Can roar as thine does.

   Ithocles.   Orgilus, forbear.

   Bassanes. Disturb him not; it is a talking motion[26]
Provided for my torment. What a fool am I
To bandy passion! ere I'll speak a word,
I will look on and burst.

   Penthea.   I loved you once.   [*To* ORGILUS.

   Orgilus. Thou didst, wronged creature: in despite of
       malice,
For it I love thee ever.

   Penthea.   Spare your hand;
Believe me, I'll not hurt it.

   Orgilus.   My heart too.

   Penthea. Complain not though I wring it hard: I'll kiss it;
O, 'tis a fine soft palm!—hark, in thine ear;
Like whom do I look, prithee?—nay, no whispering.
Goodness! we had been happy; too much happiness
Will make folk proud, they say—but that is he—
                  [*Pointing to* ITHOCLES.
And yet he paid for't home; alas, his heart
Is crept into the cabinet of the princess;
We shall have points[27] and bride-laces. Remember,

---

[25] Gifford remarks that this beautiful expression is happily adopted by Milton,
the great plunderer of the poetical hive of our old dramatists;
        "He ended here; and Satan, bowing low
         His gray dissimulation," &c. *Par. Reg.*

[26] Puppet.

[27] Tagged laces.

When we last gathered roses in the garden,
I found my wits; but truly you lost yours.
That's he, and still 'tis he. [*Again pointing to* ITHOCLES.
  Ithocles.   Poor soul, how idly
Her fancies guide her tongue!
  Bassanes. [*Aside*]   Keep in, vexation,
And break not into clamour.
  Orgilus. [*Aside*]   She has tutored me,
Some powerful inspiration checks my laziness.—
Now let me kiss your hand, grieved beauty.
  Penthea.   Kiss it.—
Alack, alack, his lips be wondrous cold;
Dear soul, 'has lost his colour: have ye seen
A straying heart? all crannies! every drop
Of blood is turnèd to an amethyst,
Which married bachelors hang in their ears.
  Orgilus. Peace usher her into Elysium!—
If this be madness, madness is an oracle.

                        [*Aside, and exit.*
  Ithocles. Christalla, Philema, when slept my sister,
Her ravings are so wild?
  Christalla.   Sir, not these ten days.
  Philema. We watch by her continually; besides,
We can not any way pray her to eat.
  Bassanes. O, misery of miseries!
  Penthea.   Take comfort;
You may live well, and die a good old man:
By yea and nay, an oath not to be broken,
If you had joined our hands once in the temple,—
'Twas since my father died, for had he lived
He would have done't,—I must have called you father.—
O, my wrecked honour! ruined by those tyrants,
A cruel brother and a desperate dotage.
There is no peace left for a ravished wife
Widowed by lawless marriage; to all memory
Penthea's, poor Penthea's name is strumpeted:
But since her blood was seasoned by the forfeit
Of noble shame with mixtures of pollution,
Her blood—'tis just—be henceforth never heightened
With taste of sustenance! starve; let that fulness

Whose plurisy hath fevered faith and modesty—
Forgive me; O, I faint!

　　　　　　　　[Falls into the arms of her Attendants.

　Armostes.　　　　　Be not so wilful,
Sweet niece, to work thine own destruction.

　Ithocles.　　　　　　　　　　　Nature
Will call her daughter monster!—What! not eat?
Refuse the only ordinary means
Which are ordained for life? Be not, my sister,
A murderess to thyself.—Hear'st thou this, Bassanes?

　Bassanes. Foh! I am busy; for I have not thoughts
Enow to think: all shall be well anon.
'Tis tumbling in my head; there is a mastery
In art to fatten and keep smooth the outside,
Yes, and to comfort-up the vital spirits
Without the help of food, fumes or perfumes,
Perfumes or fumes. Let her alone; I'll search out
The trick on't.

　Penthea.　　Lead me gently; heavens reward ye.
Griefs are sure friends; they leave without control
Nor cure nor comforts for a leprous soul.

　　　　　　[Exit, supported by CHRISTALLA *and* PHILEMA.

　Bassanes. I grant ye; and will put in practice instantly
What you shall still admire: 'tis wonderful,
'Tis super-singular, not to be matched;
Yet, when I've done't, I've done't:—ye shall all thank me.

　　　　　　　　　　　　　　　　[Exit.

　Armostes. The sight is full of terror.

　Ithocles.　　　　　　　　On my soul
Lies such an infinite clog of massy dulness,
As that I have not sense enough to feel it.—
See, uncle, the angry thing returns again;
Shall's welcome him with thunder? we are haunted,
And must use exorcism to conjure down
This spirit of malevolence.

　Armostes.　　　　　　Mildly, nephew.

　　　　　Enter NEARCHUS *and* AMELUS.

　Nearchus. I come not, sir, to chide your late disorder,
Admitting that the inurement to a roughness

In soldiers of your years and fortunes, chiefly
So lately prosperous, hath not yet shook off
The custom of the war in hours of leisure;
Nor shall you need excuse, since you're to render
Account to that fair excellence, the princess,
Who in her private gallery expects it
From your own mouth alone: I am a messenger
But to her pleasure.

 Ithocles.   Excellent Nearchus,
Be prince still of my services, and conquer
Without the combat of dispute; I honour ye.

 Nearchus. The king is on a sudden indisposed,
Physicians are called for; 'twere fit, Armostes,
You should be near him.

 Armostes.   Sir, I kiss your hands.
        [*Exeunt* ITHOCLES *and* ARMOSTES.

 Nearchus. Amelus, I perceive Calantha's bosom
Is warmed with other fires than such as can
Take strength from any fuel of the love
I might address to her: young Ithocles,
Or ever I mistake, is lord ascendant
Of her devotions; one, to speak him truly,
In every disposition nobly fashioned.

 Amelus. But can your highness brook to be so rivalled,
Considering the inequality of the persons?

 Nearchus. I can, Amelus; for affections injured
By tyranny or rigour of compulsion,
Like tempest-threatened trees unfirmly rooted,
Ne'er spring to timely growth: observe, for instance,
Life-spent Penthea and unhappy Orgilus.

 Amelus. How does your grace determine?

 Nearchus.   To be jealous
In public of what privately I'll further;
And though they shall not know, yet they shall find it.
              [*Exeunt.*

SCENE III—*An Apartment in the Palace*

Enter AMYCLAS, *led by* HEMOPHIL *and* GRONEAS, *followed by* ARMOSTES *with a box,* CROTOLON, *and* PROPHILUS. AMYCLAS *is placed in a chair.*

Amyclas. Our daughter is not near?
Armostes.   She is retired, sir,
Into her gallery.
Amyclas.   Where's the prince our cousin?
Prophilus. New walked into the grove, my lord.
Amyclas.   All leave us
Except Armostes, and you, Crotolon;
We would be private.
Prophilus.   Health unto your majesty!
          [*Exeunt* PROPHILUS, HEMOPHIL, *and* GRONEAS.
Amyclas. What! Tecnicus is gone?
Armostes.   He is to Delphos;
And to your royal hands presents this box.
Amyclas. Unseal it, good Armostes; therein lie
The secrets of the oracle; out with it:
                    [ARMOSTES *takes out the scroll.*
Apollo live our patron! Read, Armostes.
Armostes. [*Reads*] "The plot in which the vine takes root
    Begins to dry from head to foot;
    The stock, soon withering, want of sap
    Doth cause to quail the budding grape;
    But from the neighbouring elm a dew
    Shall drop, and feed the plot anew."
Amyclas. That is the oracle: what exposition
Makes the philosopher?
Armostes.   This brief one only.
[*Reads*] "The plot is Sparta, the dried vine the king;
    The quailing grape his daughter; but the thing
    Of most importance, not to be revealed,
    Is a near prince, the elm: the rest concealed.
                              TECNICUS."
Amyclas. Enough; although the opening of this riddle
Be but itself a riddle, yet we construe

How near our labouring age draws to a rest:
But must Calantha quail too? that young grape
Untimely budded! I could mourn for her;
Her tenderness hath yet deserved no rigour
So to be crossed by fate.

    Armostes.   You misapply, sir,—
With favour let me speak it,—what Apollo
Hath clouded in hid sense: I here conjecture
Her marriage with some neighbouring prince, the dew
Of which befriending elm shall ever strengthen
Your subjects with a sovereignty of power.

    Crotolon. Besides, most gracious lord, the pith of oracles
Is to be then digested when the events
Expound their truth, not brought as soon to light
As uttered; Truth is child of Time: and herein
I find no scruple, rather cause of comfort,
With unity of kingdoms.

    Amyclas.   May it prove so,
For weal of this dear nation!—Where is Ithocles?—
Armostes, Crotolon, when this withered vine
Of my frail carcass, on the funeral pile
Is fired into its ashes, let that young man
Be hedged about still with your cares and loves:
Much owe I to his worth, much to his service.—
Let such as wait come in now.

    Armostes.   All attend here!

    Enter CALANTHA, ITHOCLES, PROPHILUS, ORGILUS,
        EUPHRANEA, HEMOPHIL, *and* GRONEAS.

    Calantha. Dear sir! king! father!
    Ithocles.   O, my royal master!
    Amyclas. Cleave not my heart, sweet twins of my life's
      solace,
With your forejudging fears; there is no physic
So cunningly restorative to cherish
The fall of age, or call back youth and vigour,
As your consents in duty: I will shake off
This languishing disease of time, to quicken
Fresh pleasures in these drooping hours of sadness.
Is fair Euphranea married yet to Prophilus?

Crotolon. This morning, gracious lord.

Orgilus.   This very morning;
Which, with your highness' leave, you may observe too.
Our sister looks, methinks, mirthful and sprightly,
As if her chaster fancy could already
Expound the riddle of her gain in losing
A trifle maids know only that they know not.
Pish! prithee, blush not; 'tis but honest change
Of fashion in the garment, loose for strait,
And so the modest maid is made a wife:
Shrewd business—is't not, sister?

Euphranea.   You are pleasant.

Amyclas. We thank thee, Orgilus; this mirth becomes
    thee.
But wherefore sits the court in such a silence?
A wedding without revels is not seemly.

Calantha. Your late indisposition, sir, forbade it.

Amyclas. Be it thy charge, Calantha, to set forward
The bridal sports, to which I will be present;
If not, at least consenting.—Mine own Ithocles,
I have done little for thee yet.

Ithocles.   You've built me
To the full height I stand in.

Calantha. [*Aside*]   Now or never!—
May I propose a suit?

Amyclas.   Demand, and have it.

Calantha. Pray, sir, give me this young man, and no
    further
Account him yours than he deserves in all things
To be thought worthy mine: I will esteem him
According to his merit.

Amyclas.   Still thou'rt my daughter,
Still grow'st upon my heart.—[*To* Ithocles] Give me thine
    hand;—
Calantha, take thine own: in noble actions
Thou'lt find him firm and absolute.—I would not
Have parted with thee, Ithocles, to any
But to a mistress who is all what I am.

Ithocles. A change, great king, most wished for, 'cause
    the same.

Calantha. [*Aside to* ITHOCLES] Thou'rt mine. Have I now
 kept my word?

Ithocles. [*Aside to* CALANTHA]   Divinely.

Orgilus. Rich fortunes guard, the favour of a princess
Rock thee, brave man, in ever-crownèd plenty!
You're minion of the time; be thankful for it.—
[*Aside*] Ho! here's a swing in destiny—apparent!
The youth is up on tiptoe, yet may stumble.

Amyclus. On to your recreations.—Now convey me
Unto my bed-chamber: none on his forehead
Wear a distempered look.

All.   The gods preserve ye!

Calantha. [*Aside to* ITHOCLES] Sweet, be not from my
 sight.

Ithocles. [*Aside to* CALANTHA] My whole felicity!
      [AMYCLUS *is carried out. Exeunt all but*
      ITHOCLES, *who is detained by* ORGILUS.

Orgilus. Shall I be bold, my lord?

Ithocles.   Thou canst not, Orgilus.
Call me thine own; for Prophilus must henceforth
Be all thy sister's: friendship, though it cease not
In marriage, yet is oft at less command
Than when a single freedom can dispose it.

Orgilus. Most right, my most good lord, my most great
 lord,
My gracious princely lord, I might add, royal.

Ithocles. Royal! a subject royal?

Orgilus.   Why not, pray, sir?
The sovereignty of kingdoms in their nonage
Stooped to desert, not birth; there's as much merit
In clearness of affection as in puddle
Of generation: you have conquered love
Even in the loveliest; if I greatly err not,
The son of Venus hath bequeathed his quiver
To Ithocles his manage, by whose arrows
Calantha's breast is opened.

Ithocles.   Can't be possible?

Orgilus. I was myself a piece of suitor once,
And forward in preferment too; so forward,
That, speaking truth, I may without offence, sir,

Presume to whisper that my hopes, and—hark ye—
My certainty of marriage stood assured
With as firm footing—by your leave—as any's
Now at this very instant—but—

   Ithocles.   'Tis granted:
And for a league of privacy between us,
Read o'er my bosom and partake a secret;
The princess is contracted mine.

   Orgilus.   Still, why not?
I now applaud her wisdom: when your kingdom
Stands seated in your will secure and settled,
I dare pronounce you will be a just monarch;
Greece must admire and tremble.

   Ithocles.   Then the sweetness
Of so imparadised a comfort, Orgilus!
It is to banquet with the gods.

   Orgilus.   The glory
Of numerous children, potency of nobles,
Bent knees, hearts paved to tread on!

   Ithocles.   With a friendship
So dear, so fast as thine.

   Orgilus.   I am unfitting
For office; but for service—

   Ithocles.   We'll distinguish
Our fortunes merely in the title; partners
In all respects else but the bed.

   Orgilus.   The bed!
Forfend it Jove's own jealousy!—till lastly
We slip down in the common earth together;
And there our beds are equal; save some monument
To show this was the king, and this the subject.—

                            [*Soft sad music.*

List, what sad sounds are these,—extremely sad ones?

   Ithocles. Sure, from Penthea's lodgings.

   Orgilus.   Hark! a voice too.

               Song *within.*

      O, no more, no more, too late
        Sighs are spent; the burning tapers
      Of a life as chaste as fate,

Pure as are unwritten papers,
Are burnt out: no heat, no light
Now remains; 'tis ever night.

Love is dead; let lovers' eyes,
Locked in endless dreams,
Th' extremes of all extremes,
Ope no more, for now Love dies,
Now Love dies,—implying
Love's martyrs must be ever, ever dying.

Ithocles. O, my misgiving heart!

Orgilus.   A horrid stillness
Succeeds this deathful air; let's know the reason:
Tread softly; there is mystery in mourning.   [*Exeunt.*

SCENE IV—PENTHEA'S *Apartment in the Palace*

PENTHEA *discovered in a chair, veiled;* CHRISTALLA *and*
PHILEMA *at her feet mourning. Enter two* Servants *with
two other chairs, one with an engine.*[28]

Enter ITHOCLES *and* ORGILUS.

1st Servant. [*Aside to* ORGILUS] 'Tis done; that on her
right hand.

Orgilus.   Good: begone.

                                        [*Exeunt Servants.*

Ithocles. Soft peace enrich this room!

Orgilus.   How fares the lady?

Philema. Dead!

Christalla.   Dead!

Philema.   Starved!

---

[28] This "engine," as it is here called, in correspondence with the homely proper-
ties of our old theatres, was merely a couple of movable arms added to the
common chair. The contrivance itself is of early date, and, if Pausanias (*Attica,*
c. 20) is to be trusted, of celestial origin. Vulcan, he tells us, in order to be
revenged of Juno for turning him out of heaven, insidiously presented her with
a golden throne with hidden springs, which prevented her, after being seated
upon it, from rising up again. Ford, however, brought no golden chair from
Olympus: he found his simple contrivance not only on the stage, but (where his
predecessors probably found it) in Bandello, Nov. i. Parte iv. vol. ix. p. 13, ed.
Milano, 1814, where it is described at length, and Deodati is entrapped by il
Turchi, precisely as Ithocles is here by Orgilus, and then stabbed with a dagger.
—*Gifford.*

Christalla.   Starved!
Ithocles.   Me miserable!
Orgilus.   Tell us
How parted she from life.
   Philema.   She called for music,
And begged some gentle voice to tune a farewell
To life and griefs: Christalla touched the lute;
I wept the funeral song.
   Christalla.   Which scarce was ended
But her last breath sealed-up these hollow sounds,
"O, cruel Ithocles and injured Orgilus!"
So down she drew her veil, so died.
   Ithocles.   So died!
   Orgilus. Up! you are messengers of death; go from us;

              [CHRISTALLA *and* PHILEMA *rise.*

Here's woe enough to court without a prompter:
Away; and—hark ye—till you see us next,
No syllable that she is dead.—Away,
Keep a smooth brow.

            [*Exeunt* CHRISTALLA *and* PHILEMA.
        My lord,—
   Ithocles.   Mine only sister!
Another is not left me.
   Orgilus.   Take that chair;
I'll seat me here in this: between us sits
The object of our sorrows; some few tears
We'll part among us: I perhaps can mix
One lamentable story to prepare 'em.—
There, there; sit there, my lord.
   Ithocles.   Yes, as you please.

        [*Sits down, the chair closes upon him.*

What means this treachery?
   Orgilus.   Caught! you are caught,
Young master; 'tis thy throne of coronation,
Thou fool of greatness! See, I take this veil off;
Survey a beauty withered by the flames
Of an insulting Phaëton, her brother.
   Ithocles. Thou mean'st to kill me basely?
   Orgilus.   I foreknew
The last act of her life, and trained thee hither

To sacrifice a tyrant to a turtle.
You dreamt of kingdoms, did ye? how to bosom
The delicacies of a youngling princess;
How with this nod to grace that subtle courtier,
How with that frown to make this noble tremble,
And so forth; whiles Penthea's groans and tortures,
Her agonies, her miseries, afflictions,
Ne'er touched upon your thought: as for my injuries,
Alas, they were beneath your royal pity;
But yet they lived, thou proud man, to confound thee.
Behold thy fate; this steel!   [*Draws a dagger.*

   Ithocles.   Strike home! A courage
As keen as thy revenge shall give it welcome:
But prithee faint not; if the wound close up,
Tent[29] it with double force, and search it deeply.
Thou look'st that I should whine and beg compassion,
As loth to leave the vainness of my glories;
A statelier resolution arms my confidence,
To cozen thee of honour; neither could I
With equal trial of unequal fortune
By hazard of a duel; 'twere a bravery
Too mighty for a slave intending murder.
On to the execution, and inherit
A conflict with thy horrors.

   Orgilus.   By Apollo,
Thou talk'st a goodly language! for requital
I will report thee to thy mistress richly:
And take this peace along; some few short minutes
Determined, my resolves shall quickly follow
Thy wrathful ghost; then, if we tug for mastery,
Penthea's sacred eyes shall lend new courage.
Give me thy hand: be healthful in thy parting
From lost mortality! thus, thus I free it.   [*Stabs him.*

   Ithocles. Yet, yet, I scorn to shrink.

   Orgilus.   Keep up thy spirit:
I will be gentle even in blood; to linger
Pain, which I strive to cure, were to be cruel.

                          [*Stabs him again.*

   Ithocles. Nimble in vengeance, I forgive thee. Follow

29 Probe.

Safety, with best success: O, may it prosper!—
Penthea, by thy side thy brother bleeds;
The earnest of his wrongs to thy forced faith.
Thoughts of ambition, or delicious banquet
With beauty, youth, and love, together perish
In my last breath, which on the sacred altar
Of a long-looked-for peace—now—moves—to heaven.
                                                                        [*Dies.*

  Orgilus. Farewell, fair spring of manhood! henceforth
    welcome
Best expectation of a noble sufferance.
I'll lock the bodies safe, till what must follow
Shall be approved.—Sweet twins, shine stars for ever!—
  In vain they build their hopes whose life is shame:
  No monument lasts but a happy name.
                                                      [*Locks the door, and exit.*

ACT THE FIFTH

SCENE I—*A Room in* BASSANES' *House*

Enter BASSANES.

BASSANES. Athens—to Athens I have sent, the nursery
Of Greece for learning and the fount of knowledge;
For here in Sparta there's not left amongst us
One wise man to direct; we're all turned madcaps.
'Tis said Apollo is the god of herbs,
Then certainly he knows the virtue of 'em:
To Delphos I have sent too. If there can be
A help for nature, we are sure yet.

Enter ORGILUS.

  Orgilus.   Honour
Attend thy counsels ever!
  Bassanes.   I beseech thee
With all my heart, let me go from thee quietly;
I will not aught to do with thee, of all men.
The doubles of a hare,—or, in a morning,

Salutes from a splay-footed witch,—to drop
Three drops of blood at th' nose just and no more,—
Croaking of ravens, or the screech of owls,
Are not so boding mischief as thy crossing
My private meditations: shun me, prithee;
And if I cannot love thee heartily,
I'll love thee as well as I can.

   Orgilus.   Noble Bassanes,
Mistake me not.

   Bassanes.   Phew! then we shall be troubled.
Thou wert ordained my plague—heaven make me thankful,
And give me patience too, heaven, I beseech thee.

   Orgilus. Accept a league of amity; for henceforth,
I vow, by my best genius, in a syllable,
Never to speak vexation: I will study
Service and friendship, with a zealous sorrow
For my past incivility towards ye.

   Bassanes. Hey-day, good words, good words! I must
        believe 'em,
And be a coxcomb for my labour.

   Orgilus.   Use not
So hard a language; your misdoubt is causeless:
For instance, if you promise to put on
A constancy of patience, such a patience
As chronicle or history ne'er mentioned,
As follows not example, but shall stand
A wonder and a theme for imitation,
The first, the index[30] pointing to a second,
I will acquaint ye with an unmatched secret,
Whose knowledge to your griefs shall set a period.

   Bassanes. Thou canst not, Orgilus; 'tis in the power
Of the gods only: yet, for satisfaction,
Because I note an earnest in thine utterance,
Unforced and naturally free, be resolute[31]
The virgin-bays shall not withstand the lightning
With a more careless danger than my constancy
The full of thy relation; could it move
Distraction in a senseless marble statue,

[30] *i.e.* The index-hand common on the margin of old books.
[31] Satisfied.

It should find me a rock: I do expect now
Some truth of unheard moment.

 Orgilus.   To your patience
You must add privacy, as strong in silence
As mysteries locked-up in Jove's own bosom.

 Bassanes. A skull hid in the earth a treble age
Shall sooner prate.

 Orgilus.   Lastly, to such direction
As the severity of a glorious action
Deserves to lead your wisdom and your judgment,
You ought to yield obedience.

 Bassanes.   With assurance
Of will and thankfulness.

 Orgilus.   With manly courage
Please, then, to follow me.

 Bassanes.   Where'er, I fear not. [*Exeunt.*

SCENE II [32]—*A State-room in the Palace*

A floursh. Enter EUPHRANEA, *led by* GRONEAS *and* HEMO-
PHIL; PROPHILUS, *led by* CHRISTALLA *and* PHILEMA; NEAR-
CHUS *supporting* CALANTHA; CROTOLON *and* AMELUS.

 Calantha. We miss our servant Ithocles and Orgilus;
On whom attend they?

 Crotolon.   My son, gracious princess,
Whispered some new device, to which these revels
Should be but usher: wherein I conceive
Lord Ithocles and he himself are actors.

 Calantha. A fair excuse for absence: as for Bassanes,
Delights to him are troublesome: Armostes
Is with the king?

 Crotolon.   He is.

 Calantha.   On to the dance!—
Dear cousin, hand you the bride; the bridegroom must be
Intrusted to my courtship. Be not jealous,
Euphranea; I shall scarcely prove a temptress.—
Fall to our dance.

---

[32] Hazlitt pointed out that this scene was suggested by the mask-scene in
Marston's *Malcontent.*

The Revels.

Music. NEARCHUS *dances with* EUPHRANEA, PROPHILUS *with* CALANTHA, CHRISTALLA *with* HEMOPHIL, PHILEMA *with* GRONEAS.

They dance the first change; during which ARMOSTES *enters.*

Armostes. [*Whispers* CALANTHA] The king your father's dead.

Calantha. To the other change.

Armostes.   Is't possible?

They dance the second change.

Enter BASSANES.

Bassanes. [*Whispers* CALANTHA]   O, madam!
Penthea, poor Penthea's starved.

Calantha.   Beshrew thee!—
Lead to the next.

Bassanes.   Amazement dulls my senses.

They dance the third change.

Enter ORGILUS.

Orgilus. [*Whispers* CALANTHA] Brave Ithocles is murdered, murdered cruelly.

Calantha. How dull this music sounds! Strike up more sprightly;
Our footings are not active like our hearts,
Which treads the nimbler measure.

Orgilus.   I am thunderstruck.

The last change.

Calantha. So! let us breathe awhile.   [*Music ceases.*]—
                         Hath not this motion
Raised fresher colour on our cheeks?

Nearchus.   Sweet princess,
A perfect purity of blood enamels
The beauty of your white.

Calantha.   We all look cheerfully:
And, cousin, 'tis methinks a rare presumption
In any who prefer our lawful pleasures

Before their own sour censure, t' interrupt
The custom of this ceremony bluntly.

   Nearchus. None dares, lady.

   Calantha. Yes, yes; some hollow voice delivered to me
How that the king was dead.

   Armostes.   The king is dead:
That fatal news was mine; for in mine arms
He breathed his last, and with his crown bequeathed ye
Your mother's wedding-ring; which here I tender.

   Crotolon. Most strange!

   Calantha. Peace crown his ashes! We are queen, then.

   Nearchus. Long live Calantha! Sparta's sovereign queen!

   All. Long live the queen!

   Calantha.   What whispered Bassanes?

   Bassanes. That my Penthea, miserable soul,
Was starved to death.

   Calantha.   She's happy; she hath finished
A long and painful progress.—A third murmur
Pierced mine unwilling ears.

   Orgilus.   That Ithocles
Was murdered;—rather butchered, had not bravery
Of an undaunted spirit, conquering terror,
Proclaimed his last act triumph over ruin.

   Armostes. How! murdered!

   Calantha.   By whose hand?

   Orgilus.   By mine; this weapon
Was instrument to my revenge: the reasons
Are just, and known; quit him of these, and then
Never lived gentleman of greater merit,
Hope or abiliment to steer a kingdom.

   Crotolon. Fie, Orgilus!

   Euphranea.   Fie, brother!

   Calantha.   You have done it?

   Bassanes. How it was done let him report, the forfeit
Of whose allegiance to our laws doth covet
Rigour of justice; but that done it is
Mine eyes have been an evidence of credit
Too sure to be convinced.[33] Armostes, rend not
Thine arteries with hearing the bare cricumstances

---

  [33] *i.e.* Confuted.

Of these calamities; thou'st lost a nephew,
A niece, and I a wife: continue man still;
Make me the pattern of digesting evils,
Who can outlive my mighty ones, not shrinking
At such a pressure as would sink a soul
Into what's most of death, the worst of horrors.
But I have sealed a covenant with sadness,
And entered into bonds without condition,
To stand these tempests calmly; mark me, nobles,
I do not shed a tear, not for Penthea!
Excellent misery!
 Calantha. We begin our reign
With a first act of justice: thy confession,
Unhappy Orgilus, dooms thee a sentence;
But yet thy father's or thy sister's presence
Shall be excused.—Give, Crotolon, a blessing
To thy lost son;—Euphranea, take a farewell;—
And both be gone.
 Crotolon. [*To* ORGILUS.] Confirm thee noble sorrow
In worthy resolution!
 Euphranea. Could my tears speak,
My griefs were slight.
 Orgilus. All goodness dwell amongst ye!
Enjoy my sister, Prophilus: my vengeance
Aimed never at thy prejudice.
 Calantha. Now withdraw.
   [*Exeunt* CROTOLON, PROPHILUS, *and* EUPHRANEA.
Bloody relater of thy stains in blood,
For that thou hast reported him, whose fortunes
And life by thee are both at once snatched from him,
With honourable mention, make thy choice
Of what death likes thee best; there's all our bounty.—
But to excuse delays, let me, dear cousin,
Intreat you and these lords see execution
Instant before ye part.
 Nearchus. Your will commands us.
 Orgilus. One suit, just queen, my last: vouchsafe your
  clemency,
That by no common hand I be divided
From this my humble frailty.

Calantha.   To their wisdoms
Who are to be spectators of thine end
I make the reference: those that are dead
Are dead; had they not now died, of necessity
They must have paid the debt they owed to nature
One time or other.—Use dispatch, my lords;
We'll suddenly prepare our coronation.

        [*Exeunt* CALANTHA, PHILEMA, *and* CHRISTALLA.

  Armostes. 'Tis strange these tragedies should never touch
     on
Her female pity.

  Bassanes.   She has a masculine spirit;
And wherefore should I pule, and, like a girl,
Put finger in the eye? let's be all toughness,
Without distinction betwixt sex and sex.

  Nearchus. Now, Orgilus, thy choice?

  Orgilus.   To bleed to death.

  Armostes. The executioner?

  Orgilus.   Myself, no surgeon;
I am well skilled in letting blood. Bind fast
This arm, that so the pipes may from their conduits
Convey a full stream;[34] here's a skilful instrument:

        [*Shows his dagger*

Only I am a beggar to some charity
To speed me in this execution
By lending th' other prick to the tother arm,
When this is bubbling life out.

  Bassanes.   I am for ye;
It most concerns my art, my care, my credit.—
Quick fillet both his arms.

  Orgilus.   Grammercy, friendship!
Such courtesies are real which flow cheerfully
Without an expectation of requital.
Reach me a staff in this hand.   [*They give him a staff.*]
           —If a proneness
Or custom in my nature from my cradle

---

[34] In performing the operation of bleeding, formerly so common, the arm was
bound above the spot selected in order to distend the veins. For the same reason
the patient grasped a staff.

Had been inclined to fierce and eager bloodshed,
A coward guilt, hid in a coward quaking,
Would have betrayed me to ignoble flight
And vagabond pursuit of dreadful safety:
But look upon my steadiness, and scorn not
The sickness of my fortune, which since Bassanes
Was husband to Penthea had lain bed-rid.
We trifle time in words:—thus I show cunning
In opening of a vein too full, too lively.

> [*Pierces the vein with his dagger.*

Armostes. Desperate courage!
Nearchus.   Honourable infamy!
Hemophil. I tremble at the sight.
Groneas.   Would I were loose!
Bassanes. It sparkles like a lusty wine new broached;
The vessel must be sound from which it issues.—
Grasp hard this other stick—I'll be as nimble—
But prithee, look not pale—have at ye! stretch out
Thine arm with vigour and with unshook virtue.

> [*Opens the vein.*

Good! O, I envy not a rival, fitted
To conquer in extremities: this pastime
Appears majestical; some high-tuned poem
Hereafter shall deliver to posterity
The writer's glory and his subject's triumph.
How is't, man?—droop not yet.
Orgilus.   I feel no palsies.
On a pair-royal do I wait in death;
My sovereign, as his liegeman; on my mistress,
As a devoted servant; and on Ithocles,
As if no brave, yet no unworthy enemy:
Nor did I use an engine to entrap
His life, out of a slavish fear to combat
Youth, strength, or cunning;[35] but for that I durst not
Engage the goodness of a cause on fortune,
By which his name might have outfaced my vengeance.
O, Tecnicus, inspired with Phœbus' fire!
I call to mind thy augury, 'twas perfect;

[35] Skill.

"Revenge proves its own executioner."
When feeble man is bending to his mother,
The dust he was first framed on, thus he totters.

    Bassanes. Life's fountain is dried up.

    Orgilus.   So falls the standard
Of my prerogative in being a creature!
A mist hangs o'er mine eyes, the sun's bright splendour
Is clouded in an everlasting shadow;
Welcome, thou ice, that sitt'st about my heart
No heat can ever thaw thee.   [*Dies.*

    Nearchus.   Speech hath left him.

    Bassanes. He has shook hands with time; his funeral urn
Shall be my charge: remove the bloodless body.
The coronation must require attendance;
That past, my few days can be but one mourning.

                             [*Exeunt.*

SCENE III—*A Temple*

*An altar covered with white; two lights of virgin wax upon
it. Recorders*[36] *play, during which enter* Attendants *bear-
ing* ITHOCLES *on a hearse (in a rich robe, with a crown
on his head) and place him on one side of the altar. Afterwards enter* CALANTHA *in white, crowned attended by*
EUPHRANEA, PHILEMA, *and* CHRISTALLA, *also in white;*
NEARCHUS, ARMOSTES, CROTOLON, PROPHILUS, AMELUS,
BASSANES, HEMOPHIL, *and* GRONEAS.

CALANTHA *kneels before the altar, the* Ladies *kneeling behind
her, the rest stand off. The recorders cease during her
devotions. Soft music.* CALANTHA *and the rest rise, doing
obeisance to the altar.*

    Calantha. Our orisons are heard; the gods are merciful.—
Now tell me, you whose loyalties pay tribute
To us your lawful sovereign, how unskilful
Your duties or obedience is to render
Subjection to the sceptre of a virgin,
Who have been ever fortunate in princes
Of masculine and stirring composition.

---

[36] A kind of flutes or flageolets.

A woman has enough to govern wisely
Her own demeanours, passions, and divisions.
A nation warlike and inured to practice
Of policy and labour cannot brook
A feminate authority: we therefore
Command your counsel, how you may advise us
In choosing of a husband, whose abilities
Can better guide this kingdom.

    Nearchus.   Royal lady,
Your law is in your will.

    Armostes.   We have seen tokens
Of constancy too lately to mistrust it.

    Crotolon. Yet, if your highness settle on a choice
By your own judgment both allowed and liked of,
Sparta may grow in power, and proceed
To an increasing height.

    Calantha.   Hold you the same mind?

    Bassanes. Alas, great mistress, reason is so clouded
With the thick darkness of my infinite woes,
That I forecast nor dangers, hopes, or safety.
Give me some corner of the world to wear out
The remnant of the minutes I must number,
Where I may hear no sounds but sad complaints
Of virgins who have lost contracted partners;
Of husbands howling that their wives were ravished
By some untimely fate; of friends divided
By churlish opposition; or of fathers
Weeping upon their children's slaughter'd carcases;
Or daughters groaning o'er their fathers' hearses;
And I can dwell there, and with these keep consort
As musical as theirs. What can you look for
From an old, foolish, peevish, doting man
But craziness of age?

    Calantha. Cousin of Argos,—

    Nearchus.   Madam?

    Calantha.   Were I presently
To choose you for my lord, I'll open freely
What articles I would propose to treat on
Before our marriage.

    Nearchus.   Name them, virtuous lady.

Calantha. I would presume you would retain the royalty
Of Sparta in her own bounds; then in Argos
Armostes might be viceroy; in Messene
Might Crotolon bear sway; and Bassanes—

Bassanes. I, queen! alas, what I?

Calantha.   Be Sparta's marshal:
The multitudes of high employments could not
But set a peace to private griefs. These gentlemen,
Groneas and Hemophil, with worthy pensions,
Should wait upon your person in your chamber.—
I would bestow Christalla on Amelus.
She'll prove a constant wife; and Philema
Should into Vesta's Temple.

Bassanes.   This is a testament!
It sounds not like conditions on a marriage.

Nearchus. All this should be performed.

Calantha.   Lastly, for Prophilus,
He should be, cousin, solemnly invested
In all those honours, titles, and preferments
Which his dear friend and my neglected husband
Too short a time enjoyed.

Prophilus.   I am unworthy
To live in your remembrance.

Euphranea.   Excellent lady!

Nearchus. Madam, what means that word, "neglected
       husband"?

Calantha. Forgive me:—now I turn to thee, thou shadow
Of my contracted lord! Bear witness all,
I put my mother's wedding-ring upon
His finger; 'twas my father's last bequest.

                      [*Places a ring on the finger of* ITHOCLES.
Thus I new-marry him whose wife I am;
Death shall not separate us. O, my lords,
I but deceived your eyes with antic gesture,
When one news straight came huddling on another
Of death! and death! and death! still I danced forward;
But it struck home, and here, and in an instant.
Be such mere women, who with shrieks and outcries
Can vow a present end to all their sorrows,

Yet live to court new pleasures, and outlive them:
They are the silent griefs which cut the heart-strings;
Let me die smiling.

    Nearchus.   'Tis a truth too ominous.

    Calantha. One kiss on these cold lips, my last! [*Kisses*
    ITHOCLES.]—Crack, crack!—
Argos now's Sparta's king.—Command the voices
Which wait at the altar now to sing the song
I fitted for my end.

    Nearchus.   Sirs, the song!

DIRGE.

    Chorus. Glories, pleasures, pomps, delights, and ease,
             Can but please
          The outward senses, when the mind
          Is or untroubled or by peace refined.

  1st. Voice. Crowns may flourish and decay,
          Beauties shine, but fade away.

 2nd Voice. Youth may revel, yet it must
          Lie down in a bed of dust.

 3rd Voice. Earthly honours flow and waste,
          Time alone doth change and last.

    Chorus. Sorrows mingled with contents prepare
             Rest far care;
          Love only reigns in death; though art
          Can find no comfort for a broken heart.

                           [CALANTHA *dies.*

    Armostes. Look to the queen!

    Bassanes.   Her heart is broke indeed.
O, royal maid, would thou hadst missed this part!
Yet 'twas a brave one. I must weep to see
Her smile in death.

    Armostes.   Wise Tecnicus! thus said he;
"When youth is ripe, and age from time doth part,
The Lifeless Trunk shall wed the Broken Heart."
'Tis here fulfilled.

    Nearchus.   I am your king.

    All.   Long live
Nearchus, King of Sparta!

Nearchus.   Her last will
Shall never be digressed from: wait in order
Upon these faithful lovers, as becomes us.—
The counsels of the gods are never known
Till men can call the effects of them their own.   [*Exeunt.*

EPILOGUE

WHERE noble judgments and clear eyes are fixed
To grace endeavour, there sits truth, not mixed
With ignorance; those censures may command
Belief which talk not till they understand.
Let some say, "This was flat;" some, "Here the scene
Fell from its height;" another, "That the mean
Was ill observed in such a growing passion
As it transcended either state or fashion:"
Some few may cry, " 'Twas pretty well," or so,
"But—" and there shrug in silence: yet we know
Our writer's aim was in the whole addrest
Well to deserve of all, but please the best;
Which granted, by the allowance of this strain
The *Broken Heart* may be pieced-up again.

LOVE'S SACRIFICE

LOVE'S SACRIFICE was acted at the Phœnix in Drury Lane, and published in 1633, as "a tragedy received generally well." The source of the story is unknown. The passages in which D'Avolos excites the jealousy of the Duke were evidently suggested by *Othello*. The words in which D'Avolos bids farewell to his judges resemble, as Ward points out, those of Marinelli in Lessing's *Emilia Galotti*.

To my Friend, Master John Ford.

Unto this altar, rich with thy own spice,
I bring one grain to thy *Love's Sacrifice;*
And boast to see thy flames ascending, while
Perfumes enrich our air from thy sweet pile.
Look here, thou that hast malice to the stage,
And impudence enough for the whole age;
"Voluminously"-ignorant, be vext
To read this tragedy, and thy own be next.

JAMES SHIRLEY

Thou cheat'st us, Ford: mak'st one seem two by art:
What is Love's Sacrifice but the Broken Heart?

RICHARD CRASHAW[1]

[1] This appeared in Crashaw's *Delights of the Muses* (1646). It is interesting to note the evident regard which the religious poet and mystic felt for the dramatist.

To my Truest Friend, my Worthiest Kinsman,

JOHN FORD, OF GRAY'S INN, Esq.

THE title of this little work, my good cousin, is in sense but the argument of a dedication; which being in most writers a custom, in many a compliment, I question not but your clear knowledge of my intents will, in me, read as the earnest of affection. My ambition herein aims at a fair flight, borne up on the double wings of gratitude for a received, and acknowledgment for a continued love. It is not so frequent to number many kinsmen, and amongst them some friends, as to presume on some friends, and amongst them little friendship. But in every fulness of these particulars I do not more partake through you, my cousin, the delight than enjoy the benefit of them. This inscription to your name is only a faithful deliverance to memory of the truth of my respects to virtue, and to the equal in honour with virtue, desert. The contempt thrown on studies of this kind by such as dote on their own singularity[1] hath almost so outfaced invention and proscribed judgment, that it is more safe, more wise, to be suspectedly silent than modestly confident of opinion herein. Let me be bold to tell the severity of censurers how willingly I neglect their practice, so long as I digress from no becoming thankfulness. Accept, then, my cousin, this witness to posterity of my constancy to your merits; for no ties of blood, no engagements of friendship, shall more justly live a precedent than the sincerity of both in the heart of

JOHN FORD

[1] Here is an allusion to Prynne, also referred to by Shirley in the verses prefixed to this play. Prynne had just produced his *Histriomastix, or Actor's Tragedy,* and was at this time before the Star-Chamber for a supposed insult to the Queen by his reflection on women-players. A few days before *Histriomastix* appeared the Queen and her ladies had acted in a pastoral at Whitehall.

DRAMATIS PERSONÆ

PHILIPPO CARAFFA, Duke of Pavia
PAULO BAGLIONE, Uncle of the Duchess
FERNANDO, Favourite of the Duke
FERENTES, a wanton Courtier
ROSEILLI, a young Nobleman
PETRUCHIO, } two Counsellors of State
NIBRASSA, }
RODERICO D'AVOLOS, Secretary to the Duke
MAURUCCIO, an old Buffoon
GIACOPO, Servant to Mauruccio
Abbot of Monaco
Courtiers, Officers, Friars, Attendants, &c.

BIANCA, the Duchess
FIORMONDA, the Duke's Sister
COLONA, Daughter of Petruchio
JULIA, Daughter of Nibrassa
MORONA, a Widow

SCENE—PAVIA

LOVE'S SACRIFICE

ACT THE FIRST

SCENE I—*A Room in the Palace*

Enter ROSEILLI *and* RODERICO D'AVOLOS.

ROSEILLI. Depart the court?

D'Avolos. Such was the duke's command.

Roseilli. You're secretary to the state and him,
Great in his counsels, wise, and, I think, honest.
Have you, in turning over old recórds,
Read but one name descended of the house
Of Lesui in his loyalty remiss?

D'Avolos. Never, my lord.

Roseilli. Why, then, should I now, now when glorious
       peace
Triumphs in change of pleasures, be wiped off,
Like to a useless moth, from courtly ease?—
And whither must I go?

D'Avolos. You have the open world before you.

Roseilli. Why, then 'tis like I'm banished?

D'Avolos. Not so: my warrant is only to command you
from the court; within five hours to depart after notice
taken, and not to live within thirty miles of it, until it be
thought meet by his excellence to call you back. Now
I have warned you, my lord, at your peril be it, if you
disobey. I shall inform the duke of your discontent.   [*Exit.*

Roseilli. Do, politician, do! I scent the plot
Of this disgrace; 'tis Fiormonda, she,
That glorious widow, whose commanding check
Ruins my love: like foolish beasts, thus they
Find danger that prey too near the lions' den.

Enter FERNANDO *and* PETRUCHIO.

Fernando. My noble lord, Roseilli!

Roseilli.   Sir, the joy

261

I should have welcomed you with is wrapt up
In clouds of my disgrace; yet, honoured sir,
Howsoe'er frowns of great ones cast me down,
My service shall pay tribute in my lowness
To your uprising virtues.

   Fernando.   Sir, I know
You are so well acquainted with your own,
You need not flatter mine: trust me, my lord,
I'll be a suitor for you.

   Petruchio.   And I'll second
My nephew's suit with importunity.

   Roseilli. You are, my Lord Fernando, late returned
From travels; pray instruct me:—since the voice
Of most supreme authority commands
My absence, I determine to bestow
Some time in learning languages abroad;
Perhaps the change of air may change in me
Remembrance of my wrongs at home: good sir,
Inform me; say I meant to live in Spain,
What benefit of knowledge might I treasure?

   Fernando. Troth, sir, I'll freely speak as I have found.
In Spain you lose experience; 'tis a climate
Too hot to nourish arts;[1] the nation proud,
And in their pride unsociable; the court
More pliable to glorify itself
Than do a stranger grace: if you intend
To traffic like a merchant, 'twere a place
Might better much your trade; but as for me,
I soon took surfeit on it.

   Roseilli.   What for France?

   Fernando. France I more praise and love. You are, my
      lord,
Yourself for horsemanship much famed; and there
You shall have many proofs to show your skill.[2]

---

[1] It was the age of Velasquez and Calderon, but Spain was not popular in England at this period. Ford was probably indebted in part to Howell for this description.

[2] It seems that about this period the English were surpassed by most nations in this noble art: nor was it till James I. wisely encouraged horse-races, that we thought of improving the old, heavy, short-winded breed of horses, by the introduction of Barbary and other stallions.—*Gifford.*

The French are passing courtly, ripe of wit,
Kind, but extreme dissemblers; you shall have
A Frenchman ducking lower than your knee,
At the instant mocking even your very shoe-ties.
To give the country due, it is on earth
A paradise; and if you can neglect
Your own appropriaments, but praising that
In others wherein you excel yourself,
You shall be much beloved there.

    Roseilli.   Yet methought
I heard you and the duchess, two night since,
Discoursing of an island thereabouts,
Called—let me think—'twas—

    Fernando.   England?

    Roseilli.   That: pray, sir—
You have been there, methought I heard you praise it.

    Fernando. I'll tell you what I found there; men as neat,
As courtly as the French, but in condition[3]
Quite opposite. Put case that you, my lord,
Could be more rare on horseback than you are,
If there—as there are many—one excelled
You in your art as much as you do others,
Yet will the English think their own is nothing
Compared with you, a stranger; in their habits
They are not more fantastic than uncertain;
In short, their fair abundance, manhood, beauty,
No nation can disparage but itself.

    Roseilli. My lord, you have much eased me; I resolve.

    Fernando. And whither are you bent?

    Roseilli.   My lord, for travel;
To speed or England.

    Fernando.   No, my lord, you must not:
I have yet some private conference
T' impart unto you for your good; at night
I'll meet you at my Lord Petruchio's house:
Till then be secret.

    Roseilli.   Dares my cousin trust me?

    Petruchio. Dare I, my lord! yes, 'less your fact were greater
Than a bold woman's spleen.

[3] Disposition.

Roseilli.   The duke's at hand,
And I must hence: my service to your lordships.   [*Exit.*

   Petruchio. Now, nephew, as I told you, since the duke
Hath held the reins of state in his own hand,
Much altered from the man he was before,—

   .   .   .   .   .   .

As if he were transformèd in his mind,[4]
To soothe him in his pleasures, amongst whom
Is fond Ferentes; one whose pride takes pride
In nothing more than to delight his lust;
And he—with grief I speak it—hath, I fear,
Too much besotted my unhappy daughter,
My poor Colona; whom, for kindred's sake,
As you are noble, as you honour virtue,
Persuade to love herself: a word from you
May win her more than my entreaties or frowns.

   Fernando. Uncle, I'll do my best: meantime, pray tell me,
Whose mediation wrought the marriage
Betwixt the duke and duchess,—who was agent.

   Petruchio. His roving eye and her enchanting face,
The only dower nature had ordained
T' advance her to her bride-bed. She was daughter
Unto a gentleman of Milán—no better—
Preferred to serve i' the Duke of Milan's court;
Where for her beauty she was greatly famed:
And passing late from thence to Monaco
To visit there her uncle, Paul Baglione
The Abbot, Fortune—queen to such blind matches—
Presents her to the duke's eye, on the way,
As he pursues the deer: in short, my lord,
He saw her, loved her, wooed her, won her, matched her;
No counsel could divert him.

   Fernando.   She is fair.

   Petruchio. She is; and, to speak truth, I think right noble
In her conditions.

   Fernando.   If, when I should choose,

---

[4] One or more lines, the purport of which may easily be gathered, have dropped out here.

Beauty and virtue were the fee proposed,
I should not pass[5] for parentage.

Petruchio.   The duke
Doth come.

Fernando. Let's break-off talk.—[*Aside*] If ever, now,
Good angel of my soul, protect my truth!

Enter the Duke, BIANCA, FIORMONDA, NIBRASSA,
FERENTES, JULIA, *and* D'AVOLOS.

Duke. Come, my Bianca, revel in mine arms;
Whiles I, wrapt in my admiration, view
Lilies and roses growing in thy cheeks.—
Fernando! O, thou half myself! no joy
Could make my pleasure full without thy presence:
I am a monarch of felicity,
Proud in a pair of jewels, rich and beautiful,—
A perfect friend, a wife above compare.

Fernando. Sir, if a man so low in rank may hope,
By loyal duty and devoted zeal,
To hold a correspondency in friendship
With one so mighty as the Duke of Pavy,[6]
My uttermost ambition is to climb
To those deserts may give the style of servant.

Duke. Of partner in my dukedom, in my heart,
As freely as the privilege of blood
Hath made them mine; Philippo and Fernando
Shall be without distinction.—Look, Bianca,
On this good man; in all respects to him
Be as to me: only the name of husband,
And reverent observance of our bed,
Shall differ us in person, else in soul
We are all one.

Bianca.   I shall, in best of love,
Regard the bosom-partner of my lord.

Fiormonda. [*Aside to* FERENTES] Ferentes,—

Ferentes. [*Aside to* FIORMONDA]   Madam?

---

[5] *i.e.* Care.
[6] Pavia.

Fiormonda. [*Aside to* FERENTES] You are one loves court-
  ship
He hath some change of words,[7] 'twere no lost labour
To stuff your table-books;[8] the man speaks wisely!
  Ferentes. [*Aside to* FIORMONDA] I'm glad your highness
  is so pleasant.
Duke.   Sister,—
Fiormonda. My lord and brother?
Duke.   You are too silent,
Quicken[9] your sad remembrance, though the loss
Of your dead husband be of more account
Than slight neglect, yet 'tis a sin against
The state of princes to exceed a mean
In mourning for the dead.
  Fiormonda.   Should form, my lord,
Prevail above affection? no, it cannot.
You have yourself here a right noble duchess,
Virtuous at least; and should your grace now pay—
Which Heaven forbid!—the debt you owe to nature,
I dare presume she'd not so soon forget
A prince that thus advanced her.—Madam, could you?
  D'Avolos. [*Aside*] Bitter and shrewd.
  Bianca. Sister, I should too much bewray my weakness,
To give a resolution on a passion
I never felt nor feared.
  Nibrassa.   A modest answer.
  Fernando. If credit may be given to a face,
My lord, I'll undertake on her behalf;
Her words are trusty heralds to her mind.
  Fiormonda. [*Aside to* D'AVOLOS] Exceeding good; the
  man will "undertake"!
Observe it, D'Avolos.
  D'Avolos. [*Aside to* FIORMONDA] Lady, I do;
'Tis a smooth praise.
  Duke. Friend, in thy judgment I approve thy love,
And love thee better for thy judging mine.
Though my gray-headed senate in the laws

---

[7] *i.e.* He is a ready talker.
[8] Memorandum book.
[9] Enliven.

Of strict opinion and severe dispute
Would tie the limits of our free affects,[10]—
Like superstitious Jews,—to match with none
But in a tribe of princes like ourselves,
Gross-nurtured slaves, who force their wretched souls
To crouch to profit; nay, for trash and wealth
Dote on some crookèd or misshapen form;
Hugging wise nature's lame deformity,
Begetting creatures ugly as themselves:—
But why should princes do so, that command
The storehouse of the earth's hid minerals?—
No, my Bianca, thou'rt to me as dear
As if thy portion had been Europe's riches;
Since in thine eyes lies more than these are worth.
Set on; they shall be strangers to my heart
That envy thee thy fortunes.—Come, Fernando,
My but divided self; what we have done
We are only debtor to Heaven for.—On!

Fiormonda. [*Aside to* D'AVOLOS.] Now take thy time, or
        never, D'Avolos;
Prevail, and I will raise thee high in grace.

D'Avolos. [*Aside to* FIORMONDA.] Madam, I will omit no
    art.

        [*Exeunt all but* D'AVOLOS, *who recalls* FERNANDO.
My honoured Lord Fernando!

Fernando.   To me, sir?

D'Avolos. Let me beseech your lordship to excuse me, in
the nobleness of your wisdom, if I exceed good manners:
I am one, my lord, who in the admiration of your perfect
virtues do so truly honour and reverence your deserts, that
there is not a creature bears life shall more faithfully study
to do you service in all offices of duty and vows of due respect.

Fernando. Good sir, you bind me to you: is this all?

D'Avolos. I beseech your ear a little; good my lord, what
I have to speak concerns your reputation and best fortune.

Fernando. How's that! my reputation? lay aside
Superfluous ceremony; speak; what is't?

D'Avolos. I do repute myself the blessedest man alive,

[10] *i.e.* Affections.

that I shall be the first gives your lordship news of your
perpetual comfort.

Fernando. As how?

D'Avolos. If singular beauty, unimitable virtues, honour,
youth, and absolute goodness be a fortune, all those are at
once offered to your particular choice.

Fernando. Without delays, which way?

D'Avolos. The great and gracious Lady Fiormonda loves
you, infinitely loves you.—But, my lord, as ever you tendered a servant to your pleasures, let me not be revealed
that I gave you notice on't.

Fernando. Sure, you are strangely out of tune, sir.

D'Avolos. Please but to speak to her; be but courtly-
ceremonious with her, use once but the language of affection, if I misreport aught besides my knowledge, let me
never have place in your good opinion. O, these women,
my lord, are as brittle metal as your glasses, as smooth,
as slippery,—their very first substance was quicksands:[11]
let 'em look never so demurely, one fillip chokes them.
My lord, she loves you; I know it.—But I beseech your
lordship not to discover me; I would not for the world
she should that you know it by me.

Fernando. I understand you, and to thank your care
Will study to requite it; and I vow
She never shall have notice of your news
By me or by my means. And, worthy sir,
Let me alike enjoin you not to speak
A word of that I understand her love;
And as for me, my word shall be your surety
I'll not as much as give her cause to think
I ever heard it.

D'Avolos. Nay, my lord, whatsoever I infer, you may
break with her in it, if you please; for, rather than silence
should hinder you one step to such a fortune, I will expose
myself to any rebuke for your sake, my good lord.

Fernando. You shall not indeed, sir; I am still your friend,
and will prove so. For the present I am forced to attend
the duke: good hours befall ye! I must leave you.   [*Exit.*

[11] In allusion to the traditionary stories of the first discovery of glass by the
Phœnician mariners in consequence of their lighting a fire on the sand.—*Gifford.*

D'Avolos. Gone already? 'sfoot, I ha' marred all! this is worse and worse; he's as cold as hemlock. If her highness knows how I have gone to work she'll thank me scurvily: a pox of all dull brains! I took the clean contrary course. There is a mystery in this slight carelessness of his; I must sift it, and I will find it. Ud's me, fool myself out of my wit! well, I'll choose some fitter opportunity to inveigle him, and till then smooth her up that he is a man overjoyed with the report.   [*Exit.*

SCENE II—*Another Room in the Palace*

Enter FERENTES *and* COLONA.

Ferentes. Madam, by this light I vow myself your servant; only yours, in especially yours. Time, like a turncoat, may order and disorder the outward fashions of our bodies, but shall never enforce a change on the constancy of my mind. Sweet Colona, fair Colona, young and sprightful lady, do not let me in the best of my youth languish in my earnest affections.

Colona. Why should you seek, my lord, to purchase glory
By the disgrace of a silly maid.

Ferentes. That I confess too. I am every way so unworthy of the first-fruits of thy embraces, so far beneath the riches of thy merit, that it can be no honour to thy fame to rank me in the number of thy servants; yet prove me how true, how firm I will stand to thy pleasures, to thy command; and, as time shall serve, be ever thine. Now, prithee, dear Colona,—

Colona. Well, well, my lord, I have no heart of flint;
Or if I had, you know by cunning words
How to outwear it:—but—

Ferentes. But what? do not pity thy own gentleness, lovely Colona. Shall I? Speak, shall I?—say but ay, and our wishes are made up.

Colona. How shall I say ay, when my fears say no?

Ferentes. You will not fail to meet me two hours hence, sweet?

Colona. No;

Yes, yes, I would have said: how my tongue trips!

Ferentes. I take that promise and that double "yes" as an assurance of thy faith. In the grove; good sweet, remember; in any case alone,—d'ye mark, love?—not as much as your duchess' little dog;—you'll not forget?—two hours hence—think on't, and miss not: till then—

Colona. O, if you should prove false, and love another!

Ferentes. Defy me, then! I'll be all thine, and a servant only to thee, only to thee. [*Exit* COLONA]—Very passing good! three honest women in our courts here of Italy are enough to discredit a whole nation of that sex. He that is not a cuckold or a bastard is a strangely happy man; for a chaste wife, or a mother that never stepped awry, are wonders, wonders in Italy. 'Slife! I have got the feat on't, and am every day more active in my trade: 'tis a sweet sin, this slip of mortality, and I have tasted enough for one passion of my senses.—Here comes more work for me

Enter JULIA.

And how does my own Julia? Mew upon this sadness! what's the matter you are melancholy?—Whither away, wench?

Julia. 'Tis well; the time has been when your smooth tongue
Would not have mocked my griefs; and had I been
More chary of mine honour, you had still
Been lowly as you were.

Ferentes. Lowly! why, I am sure I cannot be much more lowly than I am to thee; thou bringest me on my bare knees, wench, twice in every four-and-twenty hours, besides half-turns instead of bevers.[12] What must we next do, sweetheart?

Julia. Break vows on your side; I expect no other,
But every day look when some newer choice
May violate your honour and my trust.

Ferentes. Indeed, forsooth! how say ye by that, la? I hope I neglect no opportunity to your *nunquam satis,* to be called

---

[12] A slight repast, usually between breakfast and dinner.

in question for. Go, thou art as fretting as an old grogram:[13]
by this hand, I love thee for't; it becomes thee so prettily to
be angry. Well, if thou shouldst die, farewell all love with
me for ever! go; I'll meet thee soon in thy lady's back-
lobby, I will, wench; look for me.

Julia. But shall I be resolved [14] you will be mine?

Ferentes. All thine; I will reserve my best ability, my
heart, my honour only to thee, only to thee. Pity of my
blood, away! I hear company coming on: remember, soon
I am all thine, I will live perpetually only to thee: away!
[*Exit* JULIA] 'Sfoot! I wonder about what time of the year
I was begot; sure, it was when the moon was in conjunction,
and all the other planets drunk at a morris-dance: I am
haunted above patience; my mind is not as infinite to do as
my occasions are proffered of doing. Chastity! I am an
eunuch if I think there be any such thing; or if there be,
'tis amongst us men, for I never found it in a woman
thoroughly tempted yet. I have a shrewd hard task coming
on; but let it pass.—Who comes now? My lord, the duke's
friend! I will strive to be inward with him.

Enter FERNANDO.

My noble Lord Fernando!—

Fernando. My Lord Ferentes, I should change some words
Of consequence with you; but since I am,
For this time, busied in more serious thoughts,
I'll pick some fitter opportunity.

Ferentes. I will wait your pleasure, my lord. Good-day to
your lordship.   [*Exit.*

Fernando. Traitor to friendship, whither shall I run,
That, lost to reason, cannot sway the float
Of the unruly faction in my blood?
The duchess, O, the duchess! in her smiles
Are all my joys abstracted.—Death to my thoughts!
My other plague comes to me.

---

[13] A coarse kind of silk taffety, usually stiffened with gum, and easily losing its
gloss.
[14] Assured.

Enter FIORMONDA *and* JULIA.

Fiormonda. My Lord Fernando, what, so hard at study!
You are a kind companion to yourself,
That love to be alone so.
    Fernando.   Madam, no;
I rather chose this leisure to admire
The glories of this little world, the court,
Where, like so many stars, on several thrones
Beauty and greatness shine in proper orbs;
Sweet matter for my meditation.
    Fiormonda. So, so, sir!—Leave us, Julia [*Exit* JULIA]—
        your own proof,
By travel and prompt observation,
Instructs you how to place the use of speech.—
But since you are at leisure, pray let's sit:
We'll pass the time a little in discourse.
What have you seen abroad?
    Fernando.   No wonders, lady,
Like these I see at home.
    Fiormonda.   At home! as how?
    Fernando. Your pardon, if my tongue, the voice of truth,
Report but what is warranted by sight.
    Fiormonda. What sight?
    Fernando.   Look in your glass, and you shall see
A miracle.
    Fiormonda. What miracle?
    Fernando.   Your beauty,
So far above all beauties else abroad
As you are in your own superlative.
    Fiormonda. Fie, fie! your wit hath too much edge.
    Fernando.   Would that,
Or any thing that I could challenge mine,
Were but of value to express how much
I serve in love the sister of my prince!
    Fiormonda. 'Tis for your prince's sake, then, not for
        mine?
    Fernando. For you in him, and much for him in you.
I must acknowledge, madam, I observe

In your affects[15] a thing to me most strange,
Which makes me so much honour you the more.
   Fiormonda. Pray, tell it.
   Fernando. Gladly, lady:
I see how opposite to youth and custom
You set before you, in the tablature
Of your remembrance, the becoming griefs
Of a most loyal lady for the loss
Of so renowned a prince as was your lord.
   Fiormonda. Now, good my lord, no more of him.
   Fernando.   Of him!
I know it is a needless task in me
To set him forth in his deservèd praise;
You better can record it; for you find
How much more he exceeded other men
In most heroic virtues of account,
So much more was your loss in losing him.
Of him! his praise should be a field too large,
Too spacious, for so mean an orator
As I to range in.
   Fiormonda.   Sir, enough: 'tis true
He well deserved your labour. On his deathbed
This ring he gave me, bade me never part
With this but to the man I loved as dearly
As I loved him: yet since you know which way
To blaze his worth so rightly, in return
To your deserts wear this for him and me.
                           [*Offers him the ring.*
   Fernando. Madam!
   Fiormonda.   'Tis yours.
   Fernando.   Methought you said he charged you
Not to impart it but to him you loved
As dearly as you loved him.
   Fiormonda.   True, I said so.
   Fernando. O, then, far be it my unhallowed hand
With any rude intrusion should annul
A testament enacted by the dead!
   Fiormonda. Why, man, that testament is disannulled
And cancelled quite by us that live. Look here,

[15] Affections.

My blood is not yet freezed; for better instance,
Be judge yourself; experience is no danger—
Cold are my sighs; but, feel, my lips are warm.

[*Kisses him.*

Fernando. What means the virtuous marquess?
Fiormonda.   To new-kiss
The oath to thee, which whiles he lived was his:
Hast thou yet power to love?
Fernando.   To love!
Fiormonda.   To meet
Sweetness of language in discourse as sweet?
Fernando. Madam, 'twere dulness past the ignorance
Of common blockheads not to understand
Whereto this favour tends; and 'tis a fortune
So much above my fate, that I could wish
No greater happiness on earth: but know
Long since I vowed to live a single life.
Fiormonda. What was't you said?
Fernando.   I said I made a vow—

Enter BIANCA, PETRUCHIO, COLONA, *and* D'AVOLOS.

[*Aside*] Blessèd deliverance!
Fiormonda. [*Aside*] Prevented? mischief on this interrup-
  tion!
Bianca. My Lord Fernando, you encounter fitly
I have a suit t'ye.
Fernando.   'Tis my duty, madam,
To be commanded.
Bianca.   Since my lord the duke
Is now disposed to mirth, the time serves well
For mediation, that he would be pleased
To take the Lord Roseilli to his grace.
He is a noble gentleman; I dare
Engage my credit, loyal to the state;—
And, sister, one that ever strove, methought,
By special service and obsequious care,
To win respect from you: it were a part
Of gracious favour, if you pleased to join
With us in being suitors to the duke
For his return to court.

Fiormonda.   To court! indeed,
You have some cause to speak; he undertook,
Most champion-like, to win the prize at tilt,
In honour of your picture; marry, did he.
There's not a groom o' the querry could have matched
The jolly riding-man: pray, get him back;
I do not need his service, madam, I.

Bianca. Not need it, sister? why, I hope you think
'Tis no necessity in me to move it,
More than respect of honour.

Fiormonda.   Honour! puh!
Honour is talked of more than known by some.

Bianca. Sister, these words I understand not.

Fernando. [*Aside*] Swell not, unruly thoughts!—
Madam, the motion you propose proceeds
From the true touch of goodness; 'tis a plea
Wherein my tongue and knee shall jointly strive
To beg his highness for Roseilli's cause.
Your judgment rightly speaks him; there is not
In any court of Christendom a man
For quality or trust more absolute.

Fiormonda. [*Aside*] How! is't even so?

Petruchio.   I shall for ever bless
Your highness for your gracious kind esteem
Of my disheartened kinsman; and to add
Encouragement to what you undertake,
I dare affirm 'tis no important fault
Hath caused the duke's distaste.

Bianca.   I hope so too.

D'Avolos. Let your highness, and you all, my lords, take
advice how you motion his excellency on Roseilli's behalf;
there is more danger in that man than is fit to be publicly
reported. I could wish things were otherwise for his own
sake; but I'll assure ye, you will exceedingly alter his excellency's disposition he now is in, if you but mention the
name of Roseilli to his ear; I am so much acquainted in the
process of his actions.

Bianca. If it be so, I am the sorrier, sir:
I'm loth to move my lord unto offence;
Yet I'll adventure chiding.

Fernando. [*Aside*] O, had I India's gold, I'd give it all
T' exchange one private word, one minute's breath,
With this heart-wounding beauty!

Enter the Duke, FERENTES, *and* NIBRASSA.

Duke. Prithee, no more, Ferentes; by the faith
I owe to honour, thou hast made me laugh
Beside my spleen.[16]—Fernando, hadst thou heard
The pleasant humour of Mauruccio's dotage
Discoursed, how in the winter of his age
He is become a lover, thou wouldst swear
A morris-dance were but a tragedy
Compared to that: well, we will see the youth.—
What council hold you now, sirs?

Bianca.   We, my lord,
Were talking of the horsemanship in France,
Which, as your friend reports, he thinks exceeds
All other nations.

Duke.   How! why, have not we
As gallant riders here?

Fernando.   None that I know.

Duke. Pish, your affection leads you; I dare wage
A thousand ducats, not a man in France
Outrides Roseilli.

Fiormonda. [*Aside*] I shall quit this wrong.

Bianca. I said as much, my lord.

Fernando.   I have not seen
His practice since my coming back.

Duke.   Where is he?
How is't we see him not?

Petruchio. [*Aside*]   What's this? what's this?

Fernando. I hear he was commanded from the court.

D'Avolos. [*Aside*] O, confusion on this villainous occasion!

Duke. True; but we meant a day or two at most
Should be his furthest term. Not yet returned?
Where's D'Avolos?

D'Avolos. [*Advancing*] My lord?

---

[16] *i.e.* Beyond my nature, the spleen being regarded as the source of any sudden
and violent ebullition.

Duke.   You know our mind:
How comes it thus to pass we miss Roseilli?

D'Avolos. My lord, in a sudden discontent I hear he
departed towards Benevento, determining, as I am given
to understand, to pass to Seville, minding to visit his cousin,
Don Pedro de Toledo, in the Spanish court.

Duke. The Spanish court! now by the blessèd bones
Of good Saint Francis, let there posts be sent
To call him back, or I will post thy head
Beneath my foot: ha, you! you know my mind;
Look that you get him back: the Spanish court!
And without our commission!—

Petruchio. [*Aside*]   Here's fine juggling!

Bianca. Good sir, be not so moved.

Duke.   Fie, fie, Bianca,
'Tis such a gross indignity; I'd rather
Have lost seven years' revenue:—the Spanish court!—
How now, what ails our sister?

Fiormonda.   On the sudden
I fall a-bleeding; 'tis an ominous sign,
Pray Heaven it turn to good!—Your highness' leave. [*Exit.*

Duke. Look to her.—Come, Fernando,—come, Bianca,—
Let's strive to overpass this choleric heat.—
Sirrah, see that you trifle not. [*To* D'Avolos]—How we
Who sway the manage of authority
May be abused by smooth officious agents!—
But look well to our sister.

                         [*Exeunt all but* Petruchio *and* Fernando.

Petruchio.   Nephew, please you
To see your friend to-night?

Fernando.   Yes, uncle, yes. [*Exit* Petruchio.
Thus bodies walk unsouled! mine eyes but follow
My heart entombed in yonder goodly shrine:
Life without her is but death's subtle snares,
And I am but a coffin to my cares.   [*Exit.*

ACT THE SECOND

SCENE I—*A Room in* MAURUCCIO'S *House*

MAURUCCIO *looking in a glass, trimming his beard;*
GIACOPO *brushing him.*

MAURUCCIO. Beard, be confined to neatness, that no hair
May stover up[17] to prick my mistress' lip,
More rude than bristles of a porcupine.—Giacopo!
   Giacopo.   My lord?
   Mauruccio.   Am I all sweet behind?
   Giacopo. I have no poulterer's nose; but your apparel sits
about you most debonairly.
   Mauruccio. But, Giacopo, with what grace do my words
proceed out of my mouth? Have I a moving countenance?
is there harmony in my voice? canst thou perceive, as it
were, a handsomeness of shape in my very breath, as it is
formed into syllables, Giacopo?

Enter above Duke, BIANCA, FIORMONDA, FERNANDO,
Courtiers, *and* Attendants.

   Giacopo. Yes, indeed, sir, I do feel a savour as pleasant as
—a glister-pipe[18] [*Aside*]—calamus, or civet.
   Duke. Observe him, and be silent.
   Mauruccio. Hold thou the glass, Giacopo, and mark me
with what exceeding comeliness I could court the lady
marquess, if it come to the push.
   Duke. Sister, you are his aim.
   Fiormonda.   A subject fit
To be the stale of laughter! [19]
   Bianca.   That's your music.
   Mauruccio. Thus I reverse my pace, and thus stalking in
courtly gait, I advance one, two, and three.—Good! I kiss
my hand, make my congee, settle my countenance, and thus
begin.—Hold up the glass higher, Giacopo.
   Giacopo. Thus high, sir?

---

17 Bristle up: a west country word.
18 Enema syringe.
19 Laughing stock.

Mauruccio. 'Tis well; now mark me.

> "Most excellent marquéss, most fair la-dy,
>   Let not old age or hairs that are sil-vér
> Disparage my desire; for it may be
>   I am than other green youth nimblé-er.
> Since I am your gra-cé's servánt so true,
>   Great lady, then, love me for my vir-tue."

O, Giacopo, Petrarch was a dunce, Dante a jig-maker,
Sanazzar a goose, and Ariosto a puck-fist,[20] to me! I tell
thee, Giacopo, I am rapt with fury; and have been for these
six nights together drunk with the pure liquor of Helicon.

Giacopo. I think no less, sir; for you look as wild, and
talk as idly, as if you had not slept these nine years.

Duke. What think you of this language, sister?

Fiormonda.   Sir,
I think in princes' courts no age nor greatness
But must admit the fool; in me 'twere folly
To scorn what greater states[21] than I have been.

Bianca. O, but you are too general—

Fiormonda.   A fool!
I thank your highness: many a woman's wit
Have thought themselves much better was much worse.

Bianca. You still mistake me.

Duke.   Silence! note the rest.

Mauruccio. God-a'mercy, brains! Giacopo, I have it.

Giacopo. What, my lord?

Mauruccio. A conceit, Giacopo, and a fine one—down on
thy knees, Giacopo, and worship my wit. Give me both thy
ears. Thus it is; I will have my picture drawn most com-
posituously, in a square table[22] of some two foot long, from
the crown of the head to the waist downward, no further.

Giacopo. Then you'll look like a dwarf, sir, being cut off
by the middle.

Mauruccio. Speak not thou, but wonder at the conceit
that follows. In my bosom, on my left side, I will have a

---

[20] *i.e.* An empty boaster, from the fungus better known as puffball.
[21] *i.e.* Persons of state.
[22] The board or canvas on which the picture was to be painted.

leaf of blood-red crimson velvet—as it were part of my
doublet—open; which being opened, Giacopo,—now mark!
—I will have a clear and most transparent crystal in the
form of a heart.—Singular-admirable!—When I have framed
this, I will, as some rare outlandish piece of workmanship,
bestow it on the most fair and illustrious Lady Fiormonda.

Giacopo. But now, sir, for the conceit.

Mauruccio. Simplicity and ignorance, prate no more!
blockhead, dost not understand yet? Why, this being to her
instead of a looking-glass, she shall no oftener powder her
hair, surfel [23] her cheeks, cleanse her teeth, or conform the
hairs of her eyebrows, but having occasion to use this glass
—which for the rareness and richness of it she will hourly
do—but she shall as often gaze on my picture, remember
me, and behold the excellence of her excellency's beauty in
the prospective and mirror, as it were, in my heart.

Giacopo. Ay, marry, sir, this is something.

All above except Fiormonda. Ha, ha, ha!

　　　　　　　　　　　　　　　　　　　　[*Exit* FIORMONDA.

Bianca.　　　　　　　　　　　My sister's gone in anger.

Mauruccio. Who's that laughs? search with thine eyes,
Giacopo.

Giacopo. O, my lord, my lord, you have gotten an everlasting fame! the duke's grace, and the duchess' grace, and
my Lord Fernando's grace, with all the rabble of courtiers,
have heard every word; look where they stand! Now you
shall be made a count for your wit, and I lord for my
counsel.

Duke. Beshrew the chance! we are discovered.

Mauruccio. Pity—O, my wisdom! I must speak to them.—
O, duke most great, and most renownèd duchess!
Excuse my apprehension, which not much is;
'Tis love, my lord, that's all the hurt you see;
Angelica herself doth plead for me.

Duke. We pardon you, most wise and learnèd lord;
And, that we may all glorify your wit,
Entreat your wisdom's company to-day

---

[23] To "surfel" or "surphule" the cheeks is to wash them with mercurial or
sulphur water, as it was called, one of those pernicious compounds which, under
the name of cosmetics, found their way to the ladies' toilets. They were generally
rubbed in with Spanish wool or a piece of scarlet cloth.—*Gifford.*

To grace our table with your grave discourse:
What says your mighty eloquence?

Mauruccio. Giacopo, help me; his grace has put me out of
my own bias, and I know not what to answer in form.

Giacopo. Ud's me, tell him you'll come.

Mauruccio. Yes, I will come, my lord the duke, I will.

Duke. We take your word, and wish your honour
      health.—
Away, then! come, Biancia, we have found
A salve for melancholy,—mirth and ease.

                [*Exit the* Duke *followed by all but* BIANCA
                     and FERNANDO.

Bianca. I'll see the jolly lover and his glass
Take leave of one another.

Mauruccio. Are they gone?

Giacopo. O, my lord, I do now smell news.

Mauruccio. What news, Giacopo?

Giacopo. The duke has a smackering towards you, and
you shall clap-up with his sister the widow suddenly.

Mauruccio. She is mine, Giacopo, she is mine! Advance
the glass, Giacopo, that I may practise, as I pass, to walk a
portly grace like a marquis, to which degree I am now
a-climbing.

    Thus do we march to honour's haven of bliss,
    To ride in triumph through Persepolis.[24]

          [*Exit* GIACOPO, *going backward with the glass,*
             followed by MAURUCCIO *complimenting.*[25]

Bianca. Now, as I live, here's laughter
Worthy our presence! I'll not lose him so.   [*Going.*

Fernando. Madam,—

Bianca.   To me, my lord?

Fernando.   Please but to hear
The story of a castaway in love;
And, O, let not the passage of a jest
Make slight a sadder subject, who hath placed
All happiness in your diviner eyes!

Bianca. My lord, the time—

Fernando.   The time! yet hear me speak

---

[24] Mauruccio is here quoting Marlowe's *Tamburlaine.*
[25] *i.e.* Practising the airs of a courtier.

For I must speak or burst: I have a soul
So anchored down with cares in seas of woe,
That passion and the vows I owe to you
Have changed me to a lean anatomy:[26]
Sweet princess of my life,—
   Bianca.   Forbear, or I shall—
   Fernando. Yet, as you honour virtue, do not freeze
My hopes to more discomfort than as yet
My fears suggest; no beauty so adorns
The composition of a well-built mind
As pity: hear me out.
   Bianca.   No more! I spare
To tell you what you are, and must confess
Do almost hate my judgment, that it once
Thought goodness dwelt in you. Remember now,
It is the third time since your treacherous tongue
Hath pleaded treason to my ear and fame;
Yet, for the friendship 'twixt my lord and you,
I have not voiced your follies: if you dare
To speak a fourth time, you shall rue your lust;
'Tis all no better:—learn and love yourself.   [*Exit.*
   Fernando. Gone! O, my sorrows! how am I undone!
Not speak again? no, no, in her chaste breast
Virtue and resolution have discharged
All female weakness: I have sued and sued,
Knelt, wept, and begged; but tears and vows and words
Move her no more than summer-winds a rock.
I must resolve to check this rage of blood,
And will: she is all icy to my fires,
Yet even that ice inflames in me desires.   [*Exit.*

SCENE II—*A Room in* PETRUCHIO'S *House*

Enter PETRUCHIO *and* ROSEILLI.

   Roseilli. Is't possible the duke should be so moved?
   Petruchio. 'Tis true; you have no enemy at court
But her for whom you pine so much in love;

[26] Skeleton.

Then master your affections: I am sorry
You hug your ruin so.—
What say you to the project I proposed?
      Roseilli. I entertain it with a greater joy
Than shame can check.

Enter FERNANDO.

      Petruchio.   You're come as I could wish;
My cousin is resolved.
      Fernando.   Without delay
Prepare yourself, and meet at court anon,
Some half-hour hence; and Cupid bless your joy!
      Roseilli. If ever man was bounden to a friend,—
      Fernando. No more; away!
                    [*Exeunt* PETRUCHIO *and* ROSEILLI.
                              Love's rage is yet unknown;
In his—ay me!—too well I feel my own!—
So, now I am alone; now let me think.
She is the duchess; say she be; a creature
Sewed-up in painted cloth might so be styled;
That's but a name: she's married too; she is,
And therefore better might distinguish love:
She's young and fair; why, madam, that's the bait
Invites me more to hope: she's the duke's wife;
Who knows not this?—she's bosomed to my friend;
There, there, I am quite lost: will not be won;
Still worse and worse: abhors to hear me speak;
Eternal mischief! I must urge no more;
For, were I not be-lepered in my soul,
Here were enough to quench the flames of hell.
What then? pish! if I must not speak, I'll write.
Come, then, sad secretary to my plaints,
Plead thou my faith, for words are turned to sighs.
What says this paper?   [*Takes out a letter, and reads.*

Enter D'AVOLOS *behind with two pictures.*

      D'Avolos. [*Aside*] Now is the time. Alone? reading a
letter? good; how now! striking his breast! what, in the
name of policy, should this mean? tearing his hair! passion;
by all the hopes of my life, plain passion! now I perceive it.

If this be not a fit of some violent affection, I am an ass in understanding; why, 'tis plain,—plainer and plainer; love in the extremest. O, for the party who, now! The greatness of his spirits is too high cherished to be caught with some ordinary stuff, and if it be my Lady Fiormonda, I am strangely mistook. Well, that I have fit occasion soon to understand. I have here two pictures newly drawn, to be sent for a present to the Abbot of Monaco, the duchess' uncle, her own and my lady's: I'll observe which of these may, perhaps, bewray him—he turns about.—My noble lord!—

Fernando. You're welcome, sir; I thank you.

D'Avolos. Me, my lord! for what, my lord?

Fernando. Who's there? I cry you mercy, D'Avolos,
I took you for another; pray, excuse me.
What is't you bear there?

D'Avolos. No secret, my lord, but may be imparted to you: a couple of pictures, my good lord,—please you see them?

Fernando. I care not much for pictures; but whose are they?

D'Avolos. The one is for my lord's sister, the other is the duchess.

Fernando. Ha, D'Avolos! the duchess's?

D'Avolos. Yes, my lord.—[*Aside*] Sure, the word startled him: observe that.

Fernando. You told me, Master Secretary, once,
You owed me love.

D'Avolos. Service, my honoured lord; howsoever you please to term it.

Fernando. 'Twere rudeness to be suitor for a sight;
Yet trust me, sir, I'll be all secret.

D'Avolos. I beseech your lordship;—they are, as I am, constant to your pleasure. [*Shows* FIORMONDA's *picture.*] This, my lord, is the widow marquess's, as it now newly came from the picture-drawer's, the oil yet green: a sweet picture; and, in my judgment, art hath not been a niggard in striving to equal the life. Michael Angelo himself needed not blush to own the workmanship.

Fernando. A very pretty picture; but, kind signior,
To whose use is it?

D'Avolos. For the duke's, my lord, who determines to
send it with all speed as a present to Paul Baglione, uncle
to the duchess, that he may see the riches of two such lustres
as shine in the court of Pavy.

Fernando. Pray, sir, the other?

D'Avolo. [*Shows* BIANCA's *picture*] This, my lord, is for
the duchess Bianca: a wondrous sweet picture, if you well
observe with what singularity the artsman hath strove to set
forth each limb in exquisitest proportion, not missing a
hair.

Fernando. A hair!

D'Avolos. She cannot more formally, or—if it may be
lawful to use the word—more really, behold her own
symmetry in her glass than in taking a sensible view of this
counterfeit. When I first saw it, I verily almost was of a
mind that this was her very lip.

Fernando. Lip!

D'Avolos. [*Aside*] How constantly he dwells upon this
portraiture!—Nay, I'll assure your lordship there is no defect of cunning[27]—[*Aside*] His eye is fixed as if it were
incorporated there.—Were not the party herself alive to
witness that there is a creature composed of flesh and blood
as naturally enriched with such harmony of admirable
beauty as is here artificially counterfeited, a very curious
eye might repute it as an imaginary rapture of some trans-
ported conceit, to aim at an impossibility; whose very first
gaze is of force almost to persuade a substantial love in a
settled heart.

Fernando. Love! heart!

D'Avolos. My honoured lord,—

Fernando. O Heavens!

D'Avolos. [*Aside*] I am confirmed.—What ails your lordship?

Fernando. You need not praise it, sir; itself is praise.—
[*Aside*] How near had I forgot myself!—I thank you.
'Tis such a picture as might well become

[27] Skill.

The shrine of some famed Venus; I am dazzled
With looking on't:—pray, sir, convey it hence.

D'Avolos. I am all your servant.—[*Aside*] Blessed, blessed
discovery!—Please you to command me?

Fernando. No, gentle sir.—[*Aside*] I'm lost beyond my
  senses.—
D'ye hear, sir? good, where dwells the picture-maker?

D'Avolos. By the castle's farther drawbridge, near Gali-
azzo's statue; his name is Alphonso Trinultio.—[*Aside*]
Happy above all fate!

Fernando. You say enough; my thanks t'ye! [*Exit*
  D'Avolos.]—Were that picture
But rated at my lordship, 'twere too cheap.
I fear I spoke or did I know not what;
All sense of providence was in mine eye.

Enter FERENTES, MAURUCCIO, *and* GIACOPO.

Ferentes. [*Aside*] Youth in threescore years and ten!—
Trust me, my Lord Mauruccio, you are now younger in
the judgment of those that compare your former age with
your latter by seven-and-twenty years than you were three
years ago: by all my fidelity, 'tis a miracle! the ladies wonder at you.

Mauruccio. Let them wonder; I am wise as I am courtly.

Giacopo. The ladies, my lord, call him the green broom
of the court,—he sweeps all before him,—and swear he has
a stabbing wit: it is a very glister to laughter.

Mauruccio. Nay, I know I can tickle 'em at my pleasure;
I am stiff and strong, Ferentes.

Giacopo. [*Aside*] A radish-root is a spear of steel in comparison of I know what.

Ferentes. The marquess doth love you.

Mauruccio. She doth love me.

Ferentes. And begins to do you infinite grace, Mauruccio,
infinite grace.

Fernando. I'll take this time.—[*Comes forward*] Good
hour, my lords, to both!

Mauruccio. Right princely Fernando, the best of the Fer-
nandos; by the pith of generation, the man I look for. His

highness hath sent to find you out: he is determined to weather his own proper individual person for two days' space in my Lord Nibrassa's forest, to hunt the deer, the buck, the roe, and eke the barren doe.

Fernando. Is his highness preparing to hunt?

Mauruccio. Yes, my lord, and resolved to lie forth for the breviating the prolixity of some superfluous transmigration of the sun's double cadence to the western horizon, my most perspicuous good lord.

Fernando. O, sir, let me beseech you to speak in your own mother tongue.—[*Aside*] Two days' absence, well.—My Lord Mauruccio, I have a suit t'ye,—

Mauruccio. My Lord Fernando, I have a suit to you.

Fernando. That you will accept from me a very choice token of my love: will you grant it?

Mauruccio. Will you grant mine?

Fernando. What is't?

Mauruccio. Only to know what the suit is you please to prefer to me.

Fernando. Why, 'tis, my lord, a fool.

Mauruccio. A fool!

Fernando. As very a fool as your lordship is—hopeful to see in any time of your life.

Giacopo. Now, good my lord, part not with the fool on any terms.

Mauruccio. I beseech you, my lord, has the fool qualities?

Fernando. Very rare ones: you shall not hear him speak one wise word in a month's converse; passing temperate of diet, for, keep him from meat four-and-twenty hours, and he will fast a whole day and a night together; unless you urge him to swear, there seldom comes an oath from his mouth; and of a fool, my lord, to tell ye the plain truth, had he but half as much wit as you, my lord, he would be in short time three-quarters as arrant wise as your lordship.

Mauruccio. Giacopo, these are very rare elements in a creature of little understanding. O, that I long to see him!

Fernando. A very harmless idiot;—and, as you could wish, look where he comes.

Enter PETRUCHIO, *and* ROSEILLI *dressed like a* Fool.[28]

Petruchio. Nephew, here is the thing you sent for.—Come hither, fool; come, 'tis a good fool.

Fernando. Here, my lord, I freely give you the fool; pray use him well for my sake.

Mauruccio. I take the fool most thankfully at your hands, my lord.—Hast any qualities, my pretty fool? wilt dwell with me?

Roseilli. A, a, a, a, ay.

Petruchio. I never beheld a more natural creature in my life.

Fernando. Uncle, the duke, I hear, prepares to hunt; Let's in and wait.—Farewell, Mauruccio.

[*Exeunt* FERNANDO *and* PETRUCHIO.

Mauruccio. Beast that I am, not to ask the fool's name! 'tis no matter; fool is a sufficient title to call the greatest lord in the court by, if he be no wiser than he.

Giacopo. O, my lord, what an arrant excellent pretty creature 'tis!—Come, honey, honey, honey, come!

Ferentes. You are beholding to my Lord Fernando for this gift.

Mauruccio. True. O, that he could but speak methodically! —Canst speak, fool?

Roseilli. Can speak; de e e e—

Ferentes. 'Tis a present for an emperor. What an excellent instrument were this to purchase a suit or a monopoly from the duke's ear!

Mauruccio. I have it, I am wise and fortunate.—Giacopo, I will leave all conceits, and instead of my picture, offer the lady marquess this mortal man of weak brain.

Giacopo. My lord, you have most rarely bethought you; for so shall she no oftener see the fool but she shall remember you better than by a thousand looking-glasses.

Ferentes. She will most graciously entertain it.

Mauruccio. I may tell you, Ferentes, there's not a great woman amongst forty but knows how to make sport with a fool.—Dost know how old thou art, sirrah?

---

[28] *i.e.* In the long petticoats with which innocents, or idiots, were furnished for the sake of decency.—*Gifford.*

Roseilli. Dud—a clap cheek for nown sake, gaffer; hee e e e e.

Ferentes. Alas, you must ask him no questions, but clap him on the cheek; I understand his language: your fool is the tender-heartedest creature that is.

Enter FIORMONDA *and* D'AVOLOS *in close conversation.*

Fiormonda. No more; thou hast in this discovery
Exceeded all my favours, D'Avolos.
Is't Mistress Madam Duchess? brave revenge!

D'Avolos. But had your grace seen the infinite appetite of lust in the piercing adultery of his eye, you would—

Fiormonda. Or change him, or confound him: prompt
            dissembler!
Is here the bond of his religious vow?
And that, "now when the duke is rid abroad,
My gentleman will stay behind, is sick—or so"?

D'Avolos. "Not altogether in health;"—it was the excuse he made.

Mauruccio. [*Seeing them*] Most fit opportunity! her grace comes just i' the nick; let me study.

Ferendes. Lose no time, my lord.

Giacopo. To her, sir.

Mauruccio. Vouchsafe to stay thy foot, most Cynthian
            hue,
And from a creature ever vowed thy servant
Accept this gift, most rare, most fine, most new;
The earnest penny of a love so fervent.

Fiormonda. What means the jolly youth?

Mauruccio. Nothing, sweet princess, but only to present your grace with this sweet-faced fool; please you to accept him to make you merry: I'll assure your grace he is a very wholesome fool.

Fiormonda. A fool! you might as well ha' given yourself. Whence is he?

Mauruccio. Now, just very now, given me out of special favour by the Lord Fernando, madam.

Fiormonda. By him? well, I accept him; thank you for't:
And, in requital, take that toothpicker;
'Tis yours.

Mauruccio. A toothpicker! I kiss your bounty: no quibble
now?—And, madam,

If I grow sick, to make my spirits quicker,

I will revive them with this sweet toothpicker.

Fiormonda. Make use on't as you list.—Here D'Avolos,
Take in the fool.

D'Avolos. Come, sweetheart, wilt along with me?

Roseilli. U u umh,—u u mh,—wonnot, wonnot—u u umh.

Fiormonda. Wilt go with me, chick?

Roseilli. Will go, te e e—go will go—

Fiormonda. Come D'Avolos, observe to-night; 'tis late:
Or I will win my choice, or curse my fate.

　　　　　[*Exeunt* FIORMONDA, ROSEILLI, *and* D'AVOLOS.

Ferentes. This was wisely done, now. 'Sfoot, you purchase
a favour from a creature, my lord, the greatest king of the
earth would be proud of.

Mauruccio. Giacopo!—

Giacopo. My lord?

Mauruccio. Come behind me, Giacopo: I am big with conceit, and must be delivered of poetry in the eternal commendation of this gracious toothpicker:—but, first, I hold
it a most healthy policy to make a slight supper—

For meat's the food that must preserve our lives,

And now's the time when mortals whet their knives—
on thresholds, shoe-soles, cart-wheels, &c.—Away, Giacopo!

　　　　　　　　　　　　　　　　　　　[*Exeunt.*

SCENE III—*The Palace.* BIANCA'S *Apartment.*

Enter COLONA *with lights,* BIANCA, FIORMONDA, JULIA,
FERNANDO, *and* D'AVOLOS; COLONA *places the lights
on a table, and sets down a chess-board.*

Bianca. 'Tis yet but early night, too soon to sleep:
Sister, shall's have a mate at chess?

Fiormonda.　　　　　　　　　　A mate!

No, madam, you are grown too hard for me;

My Lord Fernando is a fitter match.

Bianca. He's a well-practised gamester: well, I care not

How cunning soe'er he be.—To pass an hour
I'll try your skill, my lord: reach here the chess-board.

D'Avolos. [*Aside*] Are you so apt to try his skill, madam
duchess? Very good!

Fernando. I shall bewray too much my ignorance
In striving with your highness; 'tis a game
I lose at still by oversight.

Bianca.   Well, well,
I fear you not; let's to't.

Fiormonda.   You need not, madam.

D'Avolos. [*Aside to* FIORMONDA] Marry, needs she not;
how gladly will she to't! 'tis a rook to a queen she heaves
a pawn to a knight's place; by'r lady, if all be truly noted,
to a duke's place; and that's beside the play, I can tell ye.

                    [FERNANDO *and* BIANCA *play.*

Fiormonda. Madam, I must entreat excuse; I feel
The temper of my body not in case
To judge the strife.

Bianca.   Lights for our sister, sirs!—
Good rest t'ye; I'll but end my game and follow.

Fiormonda. [*Aside to* D'AVOLOS] Let 'em have time
                enough; and, as thou canst,
Be near to hear their courtship, D'Avolos.

D'Avolos. [*Aside to* FIORMONDA] Madam, I shall observe
'em with all cunning secrecy.

Bianca. Colona, attend our sister to her chamber.

Colona. I shall, madam.

            [*Exit* FIORMONDA, *followed by* COLONA, JULIA,
                and D'AVOLOS.

Bianca. Play.

Fernando. I must not lose the advantage of the game:
Madam, your queen is lost.

Bianca.   My clergy help me!
My queen! and nothing for it but a pawn?
Why, then, the game's lost too: but play.

Fernando.   What, madam?

                    [FERNANDO *often looks about.*

Bianca. You must needs play well, you are so studious.—
Fie upon't! you study past patience:—

What do you dream on? here is demurring
Would weary out a statue!—Good, now, play.

   Fernando. Forgive me; let my knees for ever stick

                                             [*Kneels.*

Nailed to the ground, as earthy as my fears,
Ere I arise, to part away so cursed
In my unbounded anguish as the rage
Of flames beyond all utterance of words
Devour me, lightened by your sacred eyes.

   Bianca. What means the man?

   Fernando.   To lay before your feet
In lowest vassalage the bleeding heart
That sighs the tender of a suit disdained.
Great lady, pity me, my youth, my wounds;
And do not think that I have culled this time
From motion's swiftest measure to unclasp
The book of lust: if purity of love
Have residence in virtue's breast, lo here,
Bent lower in my heart than on my knee,
I beg compassion to a love as chaste
As softness of desire can intimate.

           Re-enter D'AVOLOS *behind.*

   D'Avolos. [*Aside*] At it already! admirable haste!

   Bianca. Am I again betrayed? bad man!—

   Fernando.   Keep in
Bright angel, that severer breath, to cool
That heat of cruelty which sways the temple
Of your too stony breast: you cannot urge
One reason to rebuke my trembling plea,
Which I have not with many nights' expense
Examined; but, O, madam, still I find
No physic strong to cure a tortured mind,
But freedom from the torture it sustains.

   D'Avolos. [*Aside*] Not kissing yet? still on your knees?
O, for a plump bed and clean sheets, to comfort the aching
of his shins! We shall have 'em clip[29] anon and lisp kisses;
here's ceremony with a vengeance!

   Bianca. Rise up; we charge you, rise!   [*He rises.*

[29] Embrace.

Look on our face:
What see you there that may persuade a hope
Of lawless love? Know, most unworthy man,
So much we hate the baseness of thy lust,
As, were none living of thy sex but thee,
We had much rather prostitute our blood
To some envenomed serpent than admit
Thy bestial dalliance. Couldst thou dare to speak
Again, when we forbade? no, wretched thing,
Take this for answer: if thou henceforth ope
Thy leprous mouth to tempt our ear again,
We shall not only certify our lord
Of thy disease in friendship, but revenge
Thy boldness with the forfeit of thy life.
Think on't.

    D'Avolos. [*Aside*] Now, now, now the game is a-foot!
your gray jennet with the white face is curried, forsooth;
—please your lordship leap up into the saddle, forsooth.
—Poor duke, how does thy head ache now!

    Fernando. Stay; go not hence in choler, blessèd woman!
You've schooled me; lend me hearing: though the float
Of infinite desires swell to a tide
Too high so soon to ebb, yet, by this hand,

                    [*Kisses her hand.*
This glorious, gracious hand of yours,—

    D'Avolos. [*Aside*] Ay marry, the match is made; clap
hands and to't, ho!

    Fernando. I swear,
Henceforth I never will as much in word,
In letter, or in syllable, presume
To make a repetition of my griefs.
Good-night t'ye! If, when I am dead, you rip
This coffin of my heart, there shall you read
With constant eyes, what now my tongue defines,
Bianca's name carved out in bloody lines.
For ever, lady, now good-night!

    Bianca.   Good-night!
Rest in your goodness.—Lights there!—

Enter Attendants *with lights.*

Sir, good-night!

[*Exeunt* BIANCA *and* FERNANDO *sundry ways,
with* Attendants.]

D'Avolos. So, via!—To be cuckold—mercy and providence
—is as natural to a married man as to eat, sleep, or wear a
nightcap. Friends!—I will rather trust mine arm in the
throat of a lion, my purse with a courtesan, my neck with
the chance on a die, or my religion in a synagogue of Jews,
than my wife with a friend. Wherein do princes exceed
the poorest peasant that ever was yoked to a sixpenny
strumpet but that the horns of the one are mounted some
two inches higher by a choppine[30] than the other? O Ac-
tæon! the goodliest-headed beast of the forest amongst wild
cattle is a stag; and the goodliest beast among tame fools
in a corporation is a cuckold.

Re-enter FIORMONDA.

Fiormonda. Speak, D'Avolos, how thrives intelligence?

D'Avolos. Above the prevention of fate, madam. I saw
him kneel, make pitiful faces, kiss hands and forefingers,
rise,—and by this time he is up, up, madam. Doubtless the
youth aims to be duke, for he is gotten into the duke's seat
an hour ago.

Fiormonda. Is't true?

D'Avolos. Oracle, oracle! Siege was laid, parley admitted,
composition offered, and the fort entered; there's no interruption. The duke will be at home to-morrow, gentle animal!—what d'ye resolve?

Fiormonda. To stir-up tragedies as black as brave,
And send the lecher panting to his grave.   [*Exeunt.*

---

[30] *i.e.* Clogs or pattens, of cork or light framework covered with leather, and
worn under the shoe. The practice never prevailed in this country, but seems to
have been fashionable at Venice, and places where walking was not required, for
which choppines were totally unfit, as no woman could drag them after her; at
least, if we may trust Lessels, who says that he has often seen them of "a full
half-yard high." Ford's choppines, however, are of a very moderate description,
and do not reach the altitude of the high-heeled shoes which were fashionable
in this country in the last century. They derive their origin, as well as their
name, from Spain, the region of cork.—*Gifford.*

SCENE IV—*A Bedchamber in the Palace*

Enter BIANCA, *her hair loose, in her night-mantle. She draws
a curtain, and* FERNANDO *is discovered in bed, sleeping;
she sets down the candle, and goes to the bedside.*

Bianca. Resolve, and do; 'tis done.—What! are those eyes,
Which lately were so overdrowned in tears,
So easy to take rest? O happy man!
How sweetly sleep hath sealed up sorrows here!
But I will call him.—What, my lord, my lord,
My Lord Fernando!
 Fernando.   Who calls me?
 Bianca.   My lord,
Sleeping or waking?
 Fernando. Ha! who is't?
 Bianca.   'Tis I:
Have you forgot my voice? or is your ear
But useful to your eye?
 Fernando. Madam, the duchess!
 Bianca.   She, 'tis she; sit up,
Sit up and wonder, whiles my sorrows swell:
The nights are short, and I have much to say.
 Fernando. Is't possible 'tis you?
 Bianca.   'Tis possible:
Why do you think I come?
 Fernando.   Why! to crown joys,
And make me master of my best desires.
 Bianca. 'Tis true, you guess aright; sit up and listen.
With shame and passion now I must confess,
Since first mine eyes beheld you, in my heart
You have been only king; if there can be
A violence in love, then I have felt
That tyranny: be record to my soul
The justice which I for this folly fear!
Fernando, in short words, howe'er my tongue
Did often chide thy love, each word thou spak'st
Was music to my ear; was never poor,

Poor wretched woman lived that loved like me,
So truly, so unfeignedly.

    Fernando.   O, madam!

    Bianca. To witness that I speak is truth, look here!
Thus singly[31] I adventure to thy bed,
And do confess my weakness: if thou tempt'st
My bosom to thy pleasures, I will yield.

    Fernando. Perpetual happiness!

    Bianca.   Now hear me out.
When first Caraffa, Pavy's duke, my lord,
Saw me, he loved me; and without respect
Of dower took me to his bed and bosom;
Advanced me to the titles I possess,
Not moved by counsel or removed by greatness;
Which to requite, betwixt my soul and Heaven
I vowed a vow to live a constant wife:
I have done so; nor was there in the world
A man created could have broke that truth
For all the glories of the earth but thou,
But thou, Fernando! Do I love thee now?

    Fernando. Beyond imagination.

    Bianca.   True, I do,
Beyond imagination: if no pledge
Of love can instance what I speak is true
But loss of my best joys, here, here, Fernando,
Be satisfied and ruin me.

    Fernando.   What d'ye mean?

    Bianca. To give my body up to thy embraces,
A pleasure that I never wished to thrive in
Before this fatal minute. Mark me now;
If thou dost spoil me of this robe of shame,
By my best comforts, here I vow again,
To thee, to Heaven, to the world, to time,
Ere yet the morning shall new-christen day,
I'll kill myself!

    Fernando.   How, madam, how!

    Bianca.   I will:
Do what thou wilt, 'tis in thy choice: what say ye?

---

[31] In allusion probably (as Gifford pointed out) not to the absence of attendants, but to the single garment in which she was clad.

Fernando. Pish! do you come to try me? tell me, first,
Will you but grant a kiss?

Bianca.   Yes, take it; that,
Or what thy heart can wish: I am all thine.

                                          [FERNANDO *kisses her.*

Fernando. O, me!—Come, come; how many women, pray,
Were ever heard or read of, granted love,
And did as you protest you will?

Bianca.   Fernando,
Jest not at my calamity. I kneel: [*Kneels.*
By these dishevelled hairs, these wretched tears,
By all that's good, if what I speak my heart
Vows not eternally, then think, my lord,
Was never man sued to me I denied,—
Think me a common and most cunning whore;
And let my sins be written on my grave,
My name rest in reproof! [*Rises.*]—Do as you list.

Fernando. I must believe ye,—yet I hope[32] anon,
When you are parted from me, you will say
I was a good, cold, easy-spirited man,
Nay, laugh at my simplicity: say, will ye?

Bianca. No, by the faith I owe my bridal vows!
But ever hold thee much, much dearer far
Than all my joys on earth, by this chaste kiss.

                                          [*Kisses him.*

Fernando. You have prevailed; and Heaven forbid that I
Should by a wanton appetite profane
This sacred temple! 'tis enough for me
You'll please to call me servant.

Bianca.   Nay, be thine:
Command my power, my bosom; and I'll write
This love within the tables of my heart.

Fernando. Enough: I'll master passion, and triumph
In being conquered; adding to it this,
In you my love as it begun shall end.

Bianca. The latter I new-vow. But day comes on;
What now we leave unfinished of content,
Each hour shall perfect up: sweet, let us part.

Fernando. This kiss,—best life, good rest!   [*Kisses her.*

---

³² Expect.

Bianca.   All mine to thee!
Remember this, and think I speak thy words;
"When I am dead, rip up my heart, and read
With constant eyes, what now my tongue defines,
Fernando's name carved out in bloody lines."
Once more, good rest, sweet!
   Fernando.   Your most faithful servant!
                          [*Exit* BIANCA—*Scene closes.*

ACT THE THIRD

SCENE I—*An Apartment in the Palace*

Enter NIBRASSA *chafing, followed by* JULIA *weeping.*

NIBRASSA. Get from me, strumpet, infamous whore, leprosy
of my blood! make thy moan to ballad-singers and rhymers;
they'll jig-out thy wretchedness and abominations to new
tunes: as for me, I renounce thee; thou'rt no daughter of
mine; I disclaim the legitimation of thy birth, and curse
the hour of thy nativity.

Julia. Pray, sir, vouchsafe me hearing.

Nibrassa. With child! shame to my grave! O, whore,
wretched beyond utterance or reformation, what wouldst
say?

Julia. Sir, by the honour of my mother's hearse,
He has protested marriage, pledged his faith;
If vows have any force, I am his wife.

Nibrassa. His faith! Why, thou fool, thou wickedly-cred-
ulous fool, canst thou imagine luxury[33] is observant of
religion? no, no; it is with a frequent lecher as usual to
forswear as to swear; their piety is in making idolatry a
worship; their hearts and their tongues are as different as
thou, thou whore! and a virgin.

Julia. You are too violent; his truth will prove
His constancy, and so excuse my fault.

Nibrassa. Shameless woman! this belief will damn thee.
How will thy lady marquess justly reprove me for preferring

[33] Lust.

to her service a monster of so lewd and impudent a life!
Look to't; if thy smooth devil leave thee to thy infamy, I
will never pity thy mortal pangs, never lodge thee under my
roof, never own thee for my child; mercy be my witness!

Enter PETRUCHIO, *leading* COLONA.

Petruchio. Hide not thy folly by unwise excuse,
Thou art undone, Colona; no entreaties,
No warning, no persuasion could put off
The habit of thy dotage on that man
Of much deceit, Ferentes. Would thine eyes
Had seen me in my grave, ere I had known
The stain of this thine honour!

Colona.　　　　　　　　　Good my lord,
Reclaim your incredulity: my fault
Proceeds from lawful composition
Of wedlock; he hath sealed his oath to mine
To be my husband.

Nibrassa. Husband! hey-day! is't even so? nay, then, we
have partners in affliction: if my jolly gallant's long clapper
have struck on both sides, all is well.—Petruchio, thou art
not wise enough to be a paritor:[34] come hither, man, come
hither; speak softly; is thy daughter with child?

Petruchio. With child, Nibrassa!

Nibrassa. Foh! do not trick me off; I overheard your
gabbling. Hark in thine ear, so is mine too.

Petruchio. Alas, my lord, by whom?

Nibrassa. Innocent! by whom? what an idle question is
that! One cock hath trod both our hens: Ferentes, Ferentes;
who else? How dost take it? methinks thou art wondrous
patient: why, I am mad, stark mad.

Petruchio. How like you this, Colona? 'tis too true:
Did not this man protest to be your husband?

Colona. Ay me! to me he did.

Nibrassa. What else, what else, Petruchio?—and, madam,
my quondam daughter, I hope h'ave passed some huge
words of matrimony to you too.

Julia. Alas! to me he did.

---

[34] An inferior officer who summoned delinquents (including prostitutes) to a
spiritual court.

Nibrassa. And how many more the great incubus of hell
knows best.—Petruchio, give me your hand; mine own
daughter in this arm,—and yours, Colona, in this:—there,
there, sit ye down together. [JULIA *and* COLONA *sit down.*]
Never rise, as you hope to inherit our blessings, till you have
plotted some brave revenge; think upon it to purpose, and
you shall want no seconds to further it; be secret one to
another.—Come, Petruchio, let 'em alone: the wenches will
demur on't, and for the process we'll give 'em courage.

Petruchio. You counsel wisely; I approve your plot.—
Think on your shames, and who it was that wrought 'em.

Nibrassa. Ay, ay, ay, leave them alone.—To work,
wenches, to work!   [*Exeunt* NIBRASSA *and* PETRUCHIO.

Colona. We are quite ruined.

Julia. True, Colona,
Betrayed to infamy, deceived, and mocked,
By an unconstant villain: what shall's do?
I am with child.

Colona.   Heigh-ho! and so am I:
But what shall's do now?

Julia.   This: with cunning words
First prove his love; he knows I am with child.

Colona. And so he knows I am; I told him on't
Last meeting in the lobby, and, in troth,
The false deceiver laughed.

Julia.   Now, by the stars,
He did the like to me, and said 'twas well
I was so happily sped.

Colona.   Those very words
He used to me: it fretted me to the heart:
I'll be revenged.

Julia.   Peace! here's a noise, methinks.
Let's rise; we'll take a time to talk of this.

                         [*They rise, and walk aside.*

Enter FERENTES *and* MORONA.

Ferentes. Will ye hold? death of my delights, have ye lost
all sense of shame? You're best roar about the court that I
have been your woman's-barber and trimmed ye, kind
Morona.

Morona. Defiance to thy kindness! thou'st robbed me of my good name; didst promise to love none but me, me, only me; sworest like an unconscionable villain, to marry me the twelfth day of the month two months since; didst make my bed thine own, mine house thine own, mine all and everything thine own. I will exclaim to the world on thee, and beg justice of the duke himself, villain! I will.

Ferentes. Yet again? nay, an if you be in that mood, shut up your fore-shop, I'll be your journeyman no longer. Why, wise Madam Dryfist, could your mouldy brain be so addle to imagine I would marry a stale widow at six-and-forty? Marry gip! are there not varieties enough of thirteen? come, stop your clap-dish,[35] or I'll purchase a carting for you. By this light, I have toiled more with this tough carrion hen than with ten quails scarce grown into their first feathers.

Morona. O, treason to all honesty or religion!—Speak, thou perjured, damnable, ungracious defiler of women, who shall father my child which thou hast begotten?

Ferentes. Why, thee, countrywoman; thou'st a larger purse to pay for the nursing. Nay, if you'll needs have the world know how you, reputed a grave, matron-like, motherly madam, kicked up your heels like a jennet whose mark is new come into her mouth, e'en do, do! the worst can be said of me is, that I was ill advised to dig for gold in a coal-pit. Are you answered?

Morona. Answered!

Julia. Let's fall amongst 'em. [*Comes forward with* COLONA]—Love, how is't, chick? ha?

Colona. My dear Ferentes, my betrothèd lord!

Ferentes. [*Aside*] Excellent! O, for three Barbary stone-horses to stop three Flanders mares!—Why, how now, wenches! what means this?

Morona. Out upon me! here's more of his trulls.

Julia. Love, you must go with me.

Colona.   Good love, let's walk.

Ferentes. [*Aside*] I must rid my hands of 'em, or they'll ride on my shoulders.—By your leave, ladies; here's none but is of common counsel one with another; in short, there

---

[35] Two or three centuries ago, diseased or infectious wretches wandered up and down with a clap-dish, a wooden vessel with a movable cover, to give the charitable warning at once of their necessities and their infectious condition.—*Gifford.*

are three of ye with child, you tell me, by me. All of you
I cannot satisfy, nor, indeed, handsomely any of ye. You
all hope I should marry you; which, for that it is impossible
to be done, I am content to have neither of ye: for your
looking big on the matter, keep your own counsels, I'll not
bewray ye! but for marriage,—Heaven bless ye, and me
from ye! This is my resolution.

Colona. How, not me!

Julia. Not me!

Morona. Not me!

Ferentes. Nor you, nor you, nor you: and to give you
some satisfaction, I'll yield ye reasons.—You, Colona, had
a pretty art in your dalliance; but your fault was, you were
too suddenly won.—You, Madam Morona, could have
pleased well enough some three or four-and-thirty years
ago; but you are too old.—You, Julia, were young enough,
but your fault is, you have a scurvy face.—Now, everyone
knowing her proper defect, thank me that I ever vouchsafed
you the honour of my bed once in your lives. If you want
clouts, all I'll promise is to rip up an old shirt or two. So,
wishing a speedy deliverance to all your burdens, I commend you to your patience.   [*Exit.*

Morona. Excellent!

Julia.   Notable!

Colona.   Unmatchèd villain!

Julia. Madam, though strangers, yet we understand
Your wrongs do equal ours; which to revenge,
Please but to join with us, and we'll redeem
Our loss of honour by a brave exploit.

Morona. I embrace your motion, ladies, with gladness,
and will strive by any action to rank with you in any
danger.

Colona. Come, gentlewomen, let's together, then.—
Thrice happy maids that never trusted men!   [*Exeunt.*

SCENE II—*The State-room in the Palace*

Enter the Duke, Bianca *supported by* Fernando, Fiormonda, Petruchio, Nibrassa, Ferentes, *and* D'Avolos.

Duke. Roseilli will not come, then! will not? well;
His pride shall ruin him.—Our letters speak
The duchess' uncle will be here to-morrow,—
To-morrow, D'Avolos.

D'Avolos. To-morrow night, my lord, but not to make
more than one day's abode here; for his Holiness has commanded him to be at Rome the tenth of this month, the
conclave of cardinals not being resolved to sit till his coming.

Duke. Your uncle, sweetheart, at his next return
Must be saluted cardinal.—Ferentes,
Be it your charge to think on some device
To entertain the present[36] with delight.

Fernando. My lord, in honour to the court of Pavy
I'll join with you. Ferentes, not long since
I saw in Brussels, at my being there,
The Duke of Brabant welcome the Archbishop
Of Mentz with rare conceit, even on a sudden,
Performed by knights and ladies of his court,
In nature of an antic;[37] which methought—
For that I ne'er before saw women-antics—
Was for the newness strange, and much commended.

Bianca. Now, good my Lord Fernando, further this
In any wise; it cannot but content.

Fiormonda. [*Aside*] If she entreat, 'tis ten to one the man
Is won beforehand.

Duke.   Friend, thou honour'st me:
But can it be so speedily performed?

Fernando. I'll undertake it, if the ladies please,
To exercise in person only that:
And we must have a fool, or such an one
As can with art well act him.

---

[36] *i.e.* The present time.
[37] *i.e.* Of an anti-masque, which was always of a burlesque character.

Fiormonda.   I shall fit ye;
I have a natural.[38]

Fernando.   Best of all, madam:
Then nothing wants.—You must make one, Ferentes.

Ferentes. With my best service and dexterity,
My lord.

Petruchio. [*Aside to* NIBRASSA] This falls out happily, Nibrassa.

Nibrassa. [*Aside to* PETRUCHIO] We could not wish it
better:
Heaven is an unbribed justice.

Duke. We'll meet our uncle in a solemn grace
Of zealous presence, as becomes the church:
See all the choir be ready, D'Avolos.

D'Avolos. I have already made your highness' pleasure
known to them.

Bianca. Your lip, my lord!

Fernando. Madam?

Bianca. Perhaps your teeth have bled: wipe't with my
handkercher: give me, I'll do't myself.—[*Aside to* FER-
NANDO] Speak, shall I steal a kiss? believe me, my lord,
I long.

Fernando. Not for the world.

Fiormonda. [*Aside*] Apparent impudence!

D'Avolos. Beshrew my heart, but that's not so good.

Duke. Ha, what's that thou mislikest, D'Avolos?

D'Avolos. Nothing, my lord;—but I was hammering a
conceit of my own, which cannot, I find, in so short a time
thrive as a day's practice.

Fiormonda. [*Aside*] Well put off, secretary.

Duke. We are too sad; methinks the life of mirth
Should still be fed where we are: where's Mauruccio?

Ferentes. An't please your highness, he's of late grown
so affectionately inward with my lady marquess's fool, that
I presume he is confident there are few wise men worthy of
his society, who are not as innocently harmless as that creature. It is almost impossible to separate them, and 'tis a
question which of the two is the wiser man.

Duke. 'Would he were here! I have a kind of dulness

---

[38] An idiot.

Hangs on me since my hunting, that I feel
As 'twere a disposition to be sick;
My head is ever aching.

D'Avolos. A shrewd ominous token; I like not that neither.

Duke. Again! what is't you like not?

D'Avolos. I beseech your highness excuse me; I am so busy with this frivolous project, and can bring it to no shape, that it almost confounds my capacity.

Bianca. My lord, you were best to try a set at maw.[39]
I and your friend, to pass away the time,
Will undertake your highness and your sister.

Duke. The game's too tedious.

Fiormonda.   'Tis a peevish play;
Your knave will heave the queen out or your king;
Besides, 'tis all on fortune.

Enter MAURUCCIO *with* ROSEILLI *disguised as before, and* GIACOPO.

Mauruccio. Bless thee, most excellent duke! I here present thee as worthy and learned a gentleman as ever I—and yet I have lived threescore years—conversed with. Take it from me, I have tried him, and he is worthy to be privy-counsellor to the greatest Turk in Christendom; of a most apparent and deep understanding, slow of speech, but speaks to the purpose.—Come forward, sir, and appear before his highness in your own proper elements.

Roseilli. Will—tye—to da new toate sure la now.

Giacopo. A very senseless gentleman, and, please your highness, one that has a great deal of little wit, as they say.

Mauruccio. O, sir, had you heard him, as I did, deliver whole histories in the Tangay tongue, you would swear there were not such a linguist breathed again; and did I but perfectly understand his language, I would be confident in less than two hours to distinguish the meaning of bird, beast, or fish naturally as I myself speak Italian, my lord. Well, he has rare qualities!

[39] A game which bore apparently some resemblance to "reversi," a burlesque of whist.

Duke. Now, prithee, question him, Mauruccio.

Mauruccio. I will, my lord.—

Tell me, rare scholar, which, in thy opinion,

Doth cause the strongest breath, garlic or onion.

Giacopo. Answer him, brother-fool; do, do; speak thy mind, chuck, do.

Roseilli. Have bid seen all da fine knack, and de, e, naghtye tat-tle of da kna-ve, dad la have so.

Duke. We understand him not.

Mauruccio. Admirable, I protest duke; mark, O, duke, mark!—What did I ask him, Giacopo?

Giacopo. What caused the strongest breath, garlic or onions, I take it, sir.

Mauruccio. Right, right, by Helicon! and his answer is, that a knave has a stronger breath than any of 'em: wisdom —or I am an ass—in the highest; a direct figure; put it down, Giacopo.

Duke. How happy is that idiot whose ambition

Is but to eat and sleep, and shun the rod!

Men that have more of wit, and use it ill,

Are fools in proof.

Bianca.   True, my lord, there's many

Who think themselves most wise that are most fools.

D'Avolos. Bitter girds,[40] if all were known;—but—

Duke. But what? speak out; plague on your muttering, grumbling!

I hear you, sir; what is't?

D'Avolos. Nothing, I protest, to your highness pertinent to any moment.

Duke. Well, sir, remember.—Friend, you promised study.—

I am not well in temper.—Come, Bianca.—

Attend our friend, Ferentes.

> [*Exeunt all but* FERNANDO, ROSEILLI, FERENTES *and* MAURUCCIO.

Fernando. Ferentes, take Mauruccio in with you;

He must be one in action.

Ferentes.   Come, my lord,

I shall entreat your help.

[40] *i.e.* Sarcasms.

Fernando.　　　　　　　I'll stay the fool,
And follow instantly.

Mauruccio.　　　　Yes, pray, my lord.

　　　　　　　　　　　[*Exeunt* Ferentes *and* Mauruccio.

Fernando. How thrive your hopes now, cousin?

Roseilli.　　　　　　　　　　　　Are we safe?
Then let me cast myself beneath thy foot,
True, virtuous lord. Know, then, sir, her proud heart
Is only fixed on you, in such extremes
Of violence and passion, that I fear,
Or she'll enjoy you, or she'll ruin you.

Fernando. Me, coz? by all the joys I wish to taste,
She is as far beneath my thought as I
In soul above her malice.

Roseilli.　　　　　　　I observed
Even now a kind of dangerous pretence[41]
In an unjointed phrase from D'Avolos.
I know not his intent; but this I know,
He has a working brain, is minister
To all my lady's counsels; and, my lord,
Pray Heaven there have not anything befall'n
Within the knowledge of his subtle art
To do you mischief!

Fernando.　　　　Pish! should he or hell
Affront me in the passage of my fate,
I'd crush them into atomies.

Roseilli. I do admit you could: meantime, my lord,
Be nearest to yourself; what I can learn,
You shall be soon informed of: here is all
　　We fools can catch the wise in,—to unknot,
　　By privilege of coxcombs, what they plot.　　　[*Exeunt.*

SCENE III—*Another Room in the Palace*

Enter Duke *and* D'Avolos.

Duke. Thou art a traitor: do not think the gloss
Of smooth evasion, by your cunning jests

[41] Design.

And coinage of your politician's brain,
Shall jig me off; I'll know't, I vow I will.
Did not I note your dark abrupted ends
Of words half-spoke? your "wells, if all were known"?
Your short "I like not that"? your girds and "buts"?
Yes, sir, I did; such broken language argues
More matter than your subtlety shall hide:
Tell me, what is't? by honour's self I'll know.

D'Avolos. What would you know, my lord? I confess I
owe my life and service to you, as to my prince; the one
you have, the other you may take from me at your pleasure.
Should I devise matter to feed your distrust, or suggest likeli-
hoods without appearance? what would you have me say?
I know nothing.

Duke. Thou liest, dissembler! on thy brow I read
Distracted horrors figured in thy looks.
On thy allegiance, D'Avolos, as e'er
Thou hop'st to live in grace with us, unfold
What by the parti-halting of thy speech
Thy knowledge can discover. By the faith
We bear to sacred justice, we protest,
Be it or good or evil, thy reward
Shall be our special thanks and love untermed:[42]
Speak, on thy duty; we, thy prince, command.

D'Avolos. O, my disaster! my lord, I am so charmed by
those powerful repetitions of love and duty, that I cannot
conceal what I know of your dishonour.

Duke. Dishonour! then my soul is cleft with fear;
I half presage my misery: say on,
Speak it at once, for I am great with grief.

D'Avolos. I trust your highness will pardon me; yet I will
not deliver a syllable which shall be less innocent than truth
itself.

Duke. By all our wish of joys, we pardon thee.

D'Avolos. Get from me, cowardly servility! my service is
noble, and my loyalty an armour of brass: in short, my lord,
and plain discovery, you are a cuckold.

Duke. Keep in the word,—a "cuckold!"

D'Avolos. Fernando is your rival, has stolen your duchess'

---

[42] Interminable.

heart, murdered friendship, horns your head, and laughs at your horns.

Duke. My heart is split!

D'Avolos. Take courage, be a prince in resolution: I knew it would nettle you in the fire of your composition, and was loth to have given the first report of this more than ridiculous blemish to all patience or moderation: but, O, my lord, what would not a subject do to approve his loyalty to his sovereign? Yet, good sir, take it as quietly as you can: I must needs say 'tis a foul fault; but what man is he under the sun that is free from the career of his destiny? May be she will in time reclaim the errors of her youth; or 'twere a great happiness in you, if you could not believe it; that's the surest way, my lord, in my poor counsel.

Duke. The icy current of my frozen blood
Is kindled up in agonies as hot
As flames of burning sulphur. O, my fate!
A cuckold! had my dukedom's whole inheritance
Been rent, mine honours levelled in the dust,
So she, that wicked woman, might have slept
Chaste in my bosom, 't had been all a sport.
And he, that villain, viper to my heart,
That he should be the man! death above utterance!
Take heed you prove this true.

D'Avolos.   My lord,—

Duke.   If not,
I'll tear thee joint by joint.—Phew! methinks
It should not be:—Bianca! why, I took her
From lower than a bondage:—hell of hells!—
See that you make it good.

D'Avolos. As for that, 'would it were as good as I would make it! I can, if you will temper your distractions, but bring you where you shall see it; no more.

Duke. See it!

D'Avolos. Ay, see it, if that be proof sufficient. I, for my part, will slack no service that may testify my simplicity.

Duke. Enough.

Enter FERNANDO.

What news, Fernando?

Fernando.   Sir, the abbot
Is now upon arrival; all your servants
Attend your presence.
    Duke.   We will give him welcome
As shall befit our love and his respect.
Come, mine own best Fernando, my dear friend.
                                   [*Exit with* FERNANDO.
    D'Avolos. Excellent! now for a horned moon. [*Music
within.*] But I hear the preparation for the entertainment
of this great abbot. Let him come and go, that matters nothing to this; whiles he rides abroad in hope to purchase a
purple hat, our duke shall as earnestly heat the pericranion
of his noddle with a yellow hood at home. I hear 'em
coming.

Loud music. Enter Servants *with torches; then the* Duke,
    followed by FERNANDO, BIANCA, FIORMONDA, PETRUCHIO,
    and NIBRASSA, *at one side; two* Friars, *the* Abbot *and* At-
    tendants *at the other. The* Duke *and* Abbot *meet and
    salute;* BIANCA *and the rest salute, and are saluted; they
    rank themselves, and pass over the stage; the* Choir *sing-
    ing.*

On to your victuals; some of ye, I know, feed upon wormwood.   [*Exit.*

SCENE IV—*Another Apartment in the Palace*

Enter PETRUCHIO *and* NIBRASSA *with napkins, as from
                        supper.*

    Petruchio. The duke's on rising: are you ready? ho!
    [*Within.*] All ready.
    Nibrassa. Then, Petruchio, arm thyself with courage and
resolution; and do not shrink from being stayed on thy
own virtue.
    Petruchio. I am resolved.—Fresh lights!—I hear 'em com-
ing.

Enter Attendants *with lights, before the* Duke, Abbot,
    BIANCA, FIORMONDA, FERNANDO, *and* D'AVOLOS.

    Duke. Right reverend uncle, though our minds be scanted

In giving welcome as our hearts would wish,
Yet we will strive to show how much we joy
Your presence with a courtly show of mirth.
Please you to sit.

    Abbot.   Great duke, your worthy honours
To me shall still have place in my best thanks:
Since you in me so much respect the church,
Thus much I'll promise,—at my next return
His holiness shall grant you an indulgence
Both large and general.

    Duke.   Our humble duty!—
Seat you, my lords.—Now let the masquers enter.

Enter, in an antic fashion, FERENTES, ROSEILLI, *and* MAU-
    RUCCIO *at several doors; they dance a short time. Suddenly
    enter to them* COLONA, JULIA, *and* MORONA *in odd shapes,
    and dance: the men gaze at them, and are invited by the
    women to dance. They dance together sundry changes;
    at last* FERENTES *is closed in,—*MAURUCCIO *and* ROSEILLI
    being shook off, stand at different ends of the stage gazing.
    The women join hands and dance round* FERENTES *with
    divers complimental offers of courtship; at length they
    suddenly fall upon him and stab him; he falls, and they
    run out at several doors. The music ceases.*

    Ferentes. Uncase me; I am slain in jest. A pox upon your
outlandish feminine antics! pull off my visor; I shall bleed
to death ere I have time to feel where I am hurt.—Duke, I
am slain: off with my visor; for heaven's sake, off with my
visor!

    Duke. Slain!—Take his visor off [*They unmask* FEREN-
    TES]:—we are betrayed:
Seize on them! two are yonder: hold Ferentes:
Follow the rest: apparent treachery!

    Abbot. Holy Saint Bennet, what a sight is this!

Re-enter JULIA, COLONA, *and* MORONA *unmasked, each
    with a child in her arms.*

    Julia. Be not amazed, great princes, but vouchsafe
Your audience: we are they have done this deed.
Look here, the pledges of this false man's lust,

Betrayed in our simplicities: he swore,
And pawned his truth, to marry each of us;
Abused us all; unable to revenge
Our public shames but by his public fall,
Which thus we have contrived: nor do we blush
To call the glory of this murder ours;
We did it, and we'll justify the deed;
For when in sad complaints we claimed his vows,
His answer was reproach:—Villain, is't true?

    Colona. I was "too quickly won," you slave!

    Morona. I was "too old," you dog!

    Julia. I,—and I never shall forget the wrong,—
I was "not fair enough;" not fair enough
For thee, thou monster!—let me cut his gall—
Not fair enough! O, scorn! not fair enough!

                       [Stabs him.

    Ferentes. O, O, O!—

    Duke. Forbear, you monstrous women! do not add
Murder to lust: your lives shall pay this forfeit.

    Ferentes. Pox upon all cod-piece extravagancy! I am pep-
pered—O, O, O!—Duke, forgive me!—Had I rid any tame
beasts but Barbary wild colts, I had not been thus jerked
out of the saddle. My forfeit was in my blood; and my life
hath answered it. Vengeance on all wild whores, I say!—O,
'tis true—farewell, generation of hackneys!—O!   *[Dies.*

    Duke. He is dead.
To prison with those monstrous strumpets!

    Petruchio.   Stay;
I'll answer for my daughter.

    Nibrassa.   And I for mine.—
O, well done, girls!

    Fernando.   I for yon gentlewoman, sir.

    Mauruccio. Good my lord, I am an innocent in the busi-
ness.

    Duke. To prison with him! Bear the body hence.

    Abbot. Here's fatal sad presages: but 'tis just
He dies by murder that hath lived in lust.   *[Exeunt.*

ACT THE FOURTH

SCENE I—*An Apartment in the Palace*

Enter Duke, Fiormonda, *and* D'Avolos.

Fiormonda. Art thou Caraffa? is there in thy veins
One drop of blood that issued from the loins
Of Pavy's ancient dukes? or dost thou sit
On great Lorenzo's seat, our glorious father,
And canst not blush to be so far beneath
The spirit of heroic ancestors?
Canst thou engross[43] a slavish shame, which men
Far, far below the region of thy state
Not more abhor than study to revenge?
Thou an Italian! I could burst with rage
To think I have a brother so befooled
In giving patience to a harlot's lust.

D'Avolos. One, my lord, that doth so palpably, so apparently make her adulteries a trophy, whiles the potingstick[44] to her unsatiate and more than goatish abomination jeers at and flouts your sleepish, and more than sleepish, security.

Fiormonda. What is she but the sallow-coloured brat
Of some unlanded bankrupt, taught to catch
The easy fancies of young prodigal bloods
In springes of her stew-instructed art?—
Here's your most virtuous duchess! your rare piece!

D'Avolos. More base in the infiniteness of her sensuality than corruption can infect:—to clip and inveigle your friend too! O, unsufferable!—a friend! how of all men are you most unfortunate!—to pour out your soul into the bosom of such a creature as holds it religion to make your own trust a key to open the passage to your own wife's womb, to be drunk in the privacies of your bed!—think upon that, sir.

---

[43] Possess.

[44] Or poking-stick, a slender rod of bone or steel, for setting the plaits of ruffs, cuffs, &c., after starching.

Duke. Be gentle in your tortures, e'en for pity;
For pity's cause I beg it.

Fiormonda.   Be a prince!
Th'adst better, duke, thou hadst, been born a peasant.
Now boys will sing thy scandal in the streets,
Tune ballads to thy infamy, get money
By making pageants of thee, and invent
Some strangely-shaped man-beast, that may for horns
Resemble thee, and call it Pavy's Duke.

Duke. Endless immortal plague!

D'Avolos. There's the mischief, sir: in the meantime you
shall be sure to have a bastard—of whom you did not so
much as beget a little toe, a left ear, or half the further side
of an upper lip—inherit both your throne and name: this
would kill the soul of very patience itself.

Duke. Forbear; the ashy paleness of my cheek
Is scarleted in ruddy flakes of wrath;
And like some bearded meteor shall suck up,
With swiftest terror, all those dusky mists
That overcloud compassion in our breast.
You've roused a sleeping lion, whom no art,
No fawning smoothness shall reclaim, but blood.
And sister thou, thou, Roderico, thou,
From whom I take the surfeit of my bane,
Henceforth no more so eagerly pursue
To whet my dulness: you shall see Caraffa
Equal his birth, and matchless in revenge.

Fiormonda. Why, now I hear you speak in majesty.

D'Avolos. And it becomes my lord most princely.

Duke. Does it?—Come hither, sister. Thou art near
In nature, and as near to me in love:
I love thee, yes, by yon bright firmament,
I love thee dearly. But observe me well:
If any private grudge or female spleen,
Malice or envy, or such woman's frailty,
Have spurred thee on to set my soul on fire
Without apparent certainty,—I vow,
And vow again, by all our princely blood,
Hadst thou a double soul, or were the lives

Of fathers, mothers, children, or the hearts
Of all our tribe in thine, I would unrip
That womb of bloody mischief with these nails
Where such a cursèd plot as this was hatched.—
But, D'Avolos, for thee—no more; to work
A yet more strong impression in my brain
You must produce an instance to mine eye
Both present and apparent—nay, you shall—or—

    Fiormonda. Or what? you will be mad? be rather wise;
Think on Ferentes first, and think by whom
The harmless youth was slaughtered: had he lived,
He would have told you tales: Fernando feared it;
And to prevent him,—under show, forsooth,
Of rare device,—most trimly cut him off.
Have you yet eyes, duke?

    Duke.   Shrewdly urged,—'tis piercing.

    Fiormonda. For looking on a sight shall split your soul,
You shall not care: I'll undertake myself
To do't some two days hence; for need, to-night,
But that you are in court.

    D'Avolos. Right. Would you desire, my lord, to see them
exchange kisses, sucking one another's lips, nay, begetting
an heir to the dukedom, or practising more than the very
act of adultery itself? Give but a little way by a feigned
absence, and you shall find 'em—I blush to speak doing
what: I am mad to think on't; you are most shamefully,
most sinfully, most scornfully cornuted.

    Duke. D'ye play upon me? as I am your prince,
There's some shall roar for this! Why, what was I,
Both to be thought or made so vile a thing?
Stay, madam marquess,—ho, Roderico, you, sir,—
Bear witness that if ever I neglect
One day, one hour, one minute, to wear out
With toil of plot or practice of conceit
My busy skull, till I have found a death
More horrid than the bull of Phalaris,
Or all the fabling poets' dreaming whips;
If ever I take rest, or force a smile
Which is not borrowed from a royal vengeance,

Before I know which way to satisfy
Fury and wrong,—nay, kneel down [*They kneel*],—let me
    die
More wretched than despair, reproach, contempt,
Laughter, and poverty itself can make me!
Let's rise on all sides friends [*They rise*]:—now all's agreed:
If the moon serve, some that are safe shall bleed.[45]

    Enter BIANCA, FERNANDO, *and* MORONA.

  Bianca. My lord the duke,—
  Duke.   Bianca! ha, how is't?
How is't, Bianca?—What, Fernando!—come,
Shall's shake hands, sirs?—'faith, this is kindly done.
Here's three as one: welcome, dear wife, sweet friend!
  D'Avolos. [*Aside to* FIORMONDA] I do not like this now;
it shows scurvily to me.
  Bianca. My lord, we have a suit; your friend and I—
  Duke. [*Aside*] She puts my friend before, most kindly
    still.
  Bianca. Must join—
  Duke.   What, "must"?
  Bianca.   My lord!—
  Duke.   Must join, you say—
  Bianca. That you will please to set Mauruccio
At liberty; this gentlewoman here
Hath, by agreement made betwixt them two,
Obtained him for her husband: good my lord,
Let me entreat; I dare engage mine honour
He's innocent in any wilful fault.
  Duke. Your honour, madam! now beshrew you for't,
T' engage your honour on so slight a ground:
Honour's a precious jewel, I can tell you;
Nay, 'tis, Bianca; go to!—D'Avolos,
Bring us Mauruccio hither.
  D'Avolos. I shall, my lord.   [*Exit.*
  Morona.   I humbly thank your grace.
  Fernando. And, royal sir, since Julia and Colona,
Chief actors in Ferentes' tragic end,

---

[45] Certain states of the moon were considered especially favourable for the operation of bleeding.

Were, through their ladies' mediation,
Freed by your gracious pardon; I, in pity,
Tendered this widow's friendless misery;
For whose reprieve I shall, in humblest duty,
Be ever thankful.

Re-enter D'AVOLOS *with* MAURUCCIO *in rags, and*
GIACOPO *weeping.*

Mauruccio. Come you, my learnèd counsel, do not roar;
If I must hang, why, then, lament therefore:
You may rejoice, and both, no doubt, be great
To serve your prince, when I am turned worms'-meat.
I fear my lands and all I have is begged;[46]
Else, woe is me, why should I be so ragged?

D'Avolos. Come on, sir; the duke stays for you.

Mauruccio. O, how my stomach doth begin to puke,
When I do hear that only word, the duke!

Duke. You, sir, look on that woman: are you pleased,
If we remit your body from the gaol,
To take her for your wife?

Mauruccio. On that condition, prince, with all my heart.

Morona. Yes, I warrant your grace he is content.

Duke. Why, foolish man, hast thou so soon forgot
The public shame of her abusèd womb,
Her being mother to a bastard's birth?
Or canst thou but imagine she will be
True to thy bed who to herself was false?

Giacopo. [*To* MAURUCCIO] Phew, sir, do not stand upon
that; that's a matter of nothing, you know.

Mauruccio. Nay, an't shall please your good grace, an it
come to that, I care not; as good men as I have lain in foul
sheets, I am sure; the linen has not been much the worse
for the wearing a little: I will have her with all my heart.

Duke. And shalt.—Fernando, thou shalt have the grace
To join their hands; put 'em together, friend.

Bianca. Yes, do, my lord; bring you the bridegroom
hither;
I'll give the bride myself.

D'Avolos. [*Aside*] Here's argument to jealousy as good

46 *i.e.* As a condemned person.

as drink to the dropsy; she will share any disgrace with
him: I could not wish it better.

Duke. Even so: well, do it.

Fernando.   Here, Mauruccio;
Long live a happy couple!

                    [FERNANDO *and* BIANCA *join their hands.*

Duke.   'Tis enough;
Now know our pleasure henceforth. 'Tis our will,
If ever thou, Mauruccio, or thy wife,
Be seen within a dozen miles o' the court,
We will recall our mercy; no entreat
Shall warrant thee a minute of thy life:
We'll have no servile slavery of lust
Shall breathe near us; dispatch, and get ye hence.—
Bianca, come with me.—[*Aside*] O, my cleft soul!

                    [*Exeunt* Duke *and* BIANCA.

Mauruccio. How's that? must I come no more near the
court?

Giacopo. O, pitiful! not near the court, sir!

D'Avolos. Not by a dozen miles, indeed, sir. Your only
course, I can advise you, is to pass to Naples, and set up a
house of carnality: there are very fair and frequent suburbs,
and you need not fear the contagion of any pestilent disease,
for the worst is very proper to the place.

Fernando. 'Tis a strange sentence.

Fiormonda.   'Tis, and sudden too,
And not without some mystery.

D'Avolos.   Will you go, sir?

Mauruccio. Not near the court!

Morona. What matter is it, sweetheart? fear nothing, love;
you shall have new change of apparel, good diet, wholesome attendance;—and we will live like pigeons, my lord.

Mauruccio. Wilt thou forsake me, Giacopo?

Giacopo. I forsake ye! no, not as long as I have a whole
ear on my head, come what will come.

Fiormonda. Mauruccio, you did once proffer true love
To me, but since you are more thriftier sped,
For old affection's sake here take this gold;
Spend it for my sake.

Fernando.   Madam, you do nobly,—
And that's for me, Mauruccio.   [*They give him money.*
D'Avolos.   Will ye go, sir?
Mauruccio. Yes, I will go;—and I humbly thank your
lordship and ladyship.—Pavy, sweet Pavy, farewell!—
Come, wife,—come, Giacopo:

Now is the time that we away must lag,
And march in pomp with baggage and with bag.
O poor Mauruccio! what hast thou misdone,
To end thy life when life was new begun?
Adieu to all; for lords and ladies see
My woeful plight and squires of low degree!

D'Avolos. Away, away, sirs!

　　　　　　　　[*Exeunt all but* FIORMONDA *and* FERNANDO.

Fiormonda. My Lord Fernando,—
Fernando.   Madam?
Fiormonda.   Do you note
My brother's odd distractions? You were wont
To bosom in his counsels: I am sure
You know the ground of it.
Fernando.   Not I, in troth.
Fiormonda. Is't possible? What would you say, my lord
If he, out of some melancholy spleen,
Edged-on by some thank-picking parasite,
Should now prove jealous? I mistrust it shrewdly.
Fernando. What, madam! jealous?
Fiormonda.   Yes; for but observe,
A prince whose eye is chooser to his heart
Is seldom steady in the lists of love,
Unless the party he affects do match
His rank in equal portion or in friends:
I never yet, out of report, or else
By warranted description, have observed
The nature of fantastic jealousy,
If not in him; yet, on my conscience now,
He has no cause.
Fernando.   Cause, madam! by this light,
I'll pledge my soul against a useless rush.
Fiormonda. I never thought her less; yet, trust me, sir,

No merit can be greater than your praise:
Whereat I strangely wonder, how a man
Vowed, as you told me, to a single life,
Should so much deify the saints from whom
You have disclaimed devotion.

 Fernando.   Madam, 'tis true;
From them I have, but from their virtues never.

 Fiormonda. You are too wise, Fernando. To be plain,
You are in love; nay, shrink not, man, you are;
Bianca is your aim: why do you blush?
She is, I know she is.

 Fernando. My aim!

 Fiormonda.   Yes, yours;
I hope I talk no news. Fernando, know
Thou runn'st to thy confusion, if in time
Thou dost not wisely shun that Circe's charm.
Unkindest man! I have too long concealed
My hidden flames, when still in silent signs
I courted thee for love, without respect
To youth or state; and yet thou art unkind.
Fernando, leave that sorceress, if not
For love of me, for pity of thyself.

 Fernando. [*Walks aside*] Injurious woman, I defy thy
lust.
'Tis not your subtle sifting that shall creep
Into the secrets of a heart unsoiled.—
You are my prince's sister, else your malice
Had railed itself to death: but as for me,
 Be record all my fate, I do detest
 Your fury or affection:—judge the rest. [*Exit.*

 Fiormonda. What, gone! well, go thy ways: I see the more
I humble my firm love, the more he shuns
Both it and me. So plain! then 'tis too late
To hope; change, peevish passion, to contempt!
 Whatever rages in my blood I feel,
 Fool, he shall know I was not born to kneel. [*Exit.*

SCENE II—*Another Room in the Palace*

Enter D'AVOLOS *and* JULIA.

D'Avolos. Julia, mine own, speak softly. What, hast thou learned out any thing of this pale widgeon? speak soft; what does she say?

Julia. Foh, more than all; there's not an hour shall pass But I shall have intelligence, she swears. Whole nights—you know my mind; I hope you'll give The gown you promised me.

D'Avolos. Honest Julia, peace; thou'rt a woman worth a kingdom. Let me never be believed now but I think it will be my destiny to be thy husband at last: what though thou have a child,—or perhaps two?

Julia. Never but one, I swear.

D'Avolos. Well, one; is that such a matter? I like thee the better for't! it shows thou hast a good tenantable and fertile womb, worth twenty of your barren, dry, bloodless devourers of youth.—But come, I will talk with thee more privately; the duke has a journey in hand, and will not be long absent: see, he has come already—let's pass away easily.   [*Exeunt.*

Enter Duke *and* BIANCA.

Duke. Troubled? yes, I have cause.—O, Bianca! Here was my fate engraven in thy brow, This smooth, fair, polished table; in thy cheeks Nature summed up thy dower: 'twas not wealth, The miser's god, or royalty of blood, Advanced thee to my bed; but love, and hope Of virtue that might equal those sweet looks: If, then, thou shouldst betray my trust, thy faith, To the pollution of a base desire, Thou wert a wretched woman.

Bianca.   Speaks your love Or fear, my lord?

Duke.   Both, both. Bianca, know, The nightly languish of my dull unrest

Hath stamped a strong opinion; for, methought,—
Mark what I say,—as I in glorious pomp
Was sitting on my throne, whiles I had hemmed
My best-beloved Bianca in mine arms,
She reached my cap of state, and cast it down
Beneath her foot, and spurned it in the dust:
Whiles I—O, 'twas a dream too full of fate!—
Was stooping down to reach it, on my head
Fernando, like a traitor to his vows,
Clapt, in disgrace, a coronet of horns.
But, by the honour of anointed kings,
Were both of you hid in a rock of fire,
Guarded by ministers of flaming hell,
I have a sword—'tis here—should make my way
Through fire, through darkness, death, and hell, and all,
To hew your lust-engendered flesh to shreds,
Pound you to mortar, cut your throats, and mince
Your flesh to mites: I will,—start not,—I will.

   Bianca. Mercy protect me, will ye murder me?

   Duke. Yes.—O, I cry thee mercy!—How the rage
Of my own dreamed-of wrongs made me forget
All sense of sufferance!—Blame me not, Bianca;
One such another dream would quite distract
Reason and self-humanity: yet tell me,
Was't not an ominous vision?

   Bianca.   'Twas, my lord,
Yet but a vision: for did such a guilt
Hang on mine honour, 'twere no blame in you,
If you did stab me to the heart.

   Duke.   The heart!
Nay, strumpet, to the soul; and tear it off
From life, to damn it in immortal death.

   Bianca. Alas! what do you mean, sir?

   Duke.   I am mad.—
Forgive me, good Bianca; still methinks
I dream and dream anew: now, prithee, chide me.
Sickness and these divisions so distract
My senses, that I take things possible
As if they were; which to remove, I mean
To speed me straight to Lucca, where, perhaps,

SCENE II]   LOVE'S SACRIFICE   323

Absence and bathing in those healthful springs
May soon recover me; meantime, dear sweet,
Pity my troubled heart; griefs are extreme:
Yet, sweet, when I am gone, think on my dream.—
Who waits without, ho!

Enter PETRUCHIO, NIBRASSA, FIORMONDA, D'AVOLOS,
ROSEILLI *disguised as before, and* FERNANDO.

                  Is provision ready,
To pass to Lucca?
    Petruchio.   It attends your highness.
    Duke. Friend, hold; take here from me this jewel, this:
                  [*Gives* BIANCA *to* FERNANDO.
Be she your care till my return from Lucca,
Honest Fernando.—Wife, respect my friend.—
Let's go:—but hear ye, wife, think on my dream.
              [*Exeunt all but* ROSEILLI *and* PETRUCHIO.
    Petruchio. Cousin, one word with you: doth not this
      cloud
Acquaint you with strange novelties? The duke
Is lately much distempered: what he means
By journeying now to Lucca, is to me
A riddle; can you clear my doubt?
    Roseilli.   O, Sir,
My fears exceed my knowledge, yet I note
No less than you infer; all is not well;
Would 'twere! whosoe'er thrive, I shall be sure
Never to rise to my unhoped desires.
But, cousin, I shall tell you more anon:
Meantime, pray send my Lord Fernando to me;
I covet much to speak with him.
    Petruchio.   And see,
He comes himself; I'll leave you both together.   [*Exit.*

Re-enter FERNANDO.

    Fernando. The duke is horsed for Lucca. How now, coz,
How prosper you in love?
    Roseilli.   As still I hoped.[47]—
My lord, you are undone.

---

[47] Expected.

Fernando.   Undone! in what?

Roseilli. Lost; and I fear your life is bought and sold;
I'll tell you how. Late in my lady's chamber
As I by chance lay slumbering on the mats,
In comes the lady marquess, and with her
Julia and D'Avolos; where sitting down,
Not doubting me, "Madam," quoth D'Avolos,
"We have discovered now the nest of shame."
In short, my lord,—for you already know
As much as they reported,—there was told
The circumstance of all your private love
And meeting with the duchess; when, at last,
False D'Avolos concluded with an oath,
"We'll make," quoth he, "his heart-strings crack for this."

Fernando. Speaking of me?

Roseilli.   Of you; "Ay," quoth the marquess,
"Were not the duke a baby, he would seek
Swift vengeance; for he knew it long ago."

Fernando. Let him know it; yet I vow
She is as loyal in her plighted faith
As is the sun in Heaven: but put case
She were not, and the duke did know she were not;
This sword lifted up, and guided by this arm,
Shall guard her from an armèd troop of fiends
And all the earth beside.

Roseilli.   You are too safe
In your destruction.

Fernando.   Damn him!—he shall feel—
But peace! who comes?

Enter COLONA.

Colona.   My lord, the duchess craves
A word with you.

Fernando.   Where is she?

Colona.   In her chamber.

Roseilli. Here, have a plum for ie'ee—

Colona. Come, fool, I'll give thee plums enow; come, fool.

Fernando. Let slaves in mind be servile to their fears;
Our heart is high instarred in brighter spheres.

                         [*Exeunt* FERNANDO *and* COLONA.

Roseilli. I see him lost already.
If all prevail not, we shall know too late
No toil can shun the violence of fate.

ACT THE FIFTH

SCENE I—*The Palace. The* Duchess's *Bedchamber.*

BIANCA *discovered in her night-attire, leaning on a cushion at a table, holding* FERNANDO *by the hand. Enter above* FIORMONDA.

FIORMONDA. [*Aside*] Now fly, Revenge, and wound the
        lower earth,
That I, insphered above, may cross the race
Of love despised, and triumph o'er their graves
Who scorn the low-bent thraldom of my heart!
    Bianca. Why shouldst thou not be mine? why should the
        laws,
The iron laws of ceremony, bar
Mutual embraces? what's a vow? a vow?
Can there be sin in unity? could I
As well dispense with conscience as renounce
The outside of my titles, the poor style
Of duchess, I had rather change my life
With any waiting-woman in the land
To purchase one night's rest with thee, Fernando,
Than be Caraffa's spouse a thousand years.
    Fiormonda. [*Aside*] Treason to wedlock! this would
        make you sweat.
    Fernando. Lady of all [48] . . . . . as before,
. . . what I am, . . .
To survive you, or I will see you first
Or widowèd or buried: if the last,
By all the comfort I can wish to taste,
By your fair eyes, that sepulchre that holds
Your coffin shall incoffin me alive;
I sign it with this seal.   [*Kisses her.*

---

[48] This is the largest lacuna in Ford's works. Several lines appear to have fallen out.

Fiormonda. [*Aside*] Ignoble strumpet!

Bianca. You shall not swear; take off that oath again,
Or thus I will enforce it.   [*Kisses him.*

Fernando.   Use that force,
And make me perjurèd; for whiles your lips
Are made the book, it is a sport to swear,
And glory to forswear.

Fiormonda. [*Aside*] Here's fast and loose!
Which, for a ducat, now the game's on foot?

Whilst they are kissing, the Duke *and* D'Avolos, *with their
    swords drawn, appear at the door, followed by* Petruchio,
    Nibrassa, *and a* Guard.

Colona. [*Within*] Help, help! madam, you are betrayed,
madam; help, help!

D'Avolos. [*Aside to* Duke] Is there confidence in credit,
now, sir? belief in your own eyes? do you see? do you see,
sir? can you behold it without lightning?

Colona. [*Within*] Help, madam, help!

Fernando. What noise is that? I heard one cry.

Duke. [*Comes forward*]   Ha, did you?
Know you who I am?

Fernando.   Yes; thou'rt Pavy's duke,
Dressed like a hangman: see, I am unarmed,
Yet do not fear thee; though the coward doubt
Of what I could have done hath made thee steal
The advantage of this time, yet, duke, I dare
Thy worst, for murder sits upon thy cheeks:
To't, man!

Duke.   I am too angry in my rage
To scourge thee unprovided.—Take him hence;
Away with him!   [*The* Guard *seize* Fernando.

Fernando.   Unhand me!

D'Avolos.   You must go, sir.

Fernando. Duke, do not shame thy manhood to lay hands
On that most innocent lady.

Duke.   Yet again!—
Confine him to his chamber.

                    [*Exeunt* D'Avolos *and the* Guard *with* Fernando.
                              Leave us all;

None stay, not one; shut up the doors.

　　　　　　　　　[*Exeunt* PETRUCHIO *and* NIBRASSA.

Fiormonda. Now show thyself my brother, brave Caraffa.

Duke. Woman, stand forth before me;—wretched whore.
What canst thou hope for?

Bianca.　　　　　　　　　Death; I wish no less.
You told me you had dreamt; and, gentle duke,
Unless you be mistook, you're now awaked.

Duke. Strumpet, I am; and in my hand hold up
The edge that must uncut thy twist of life:
Dost thou not shake?

Bianca.　　　　　　　For what? to see a weak,
Faint, trembling arm advance a leaden blade?
Alas, good man! put up, put up; thine eyes
Are likelier much to weep than arms to strike:
What would you do now, pray?

Duke.　　　　　　　　What! shameless harlot!
Rip up the cradle of thy cursèd womb,
In which the mixture of that traitor's lust
Imposthumes for a birth of bastardy.
Yet come, and if thou think'st thou canst deserve
One mite of mercy, ere the boundless spleen
Of just-consuming wrath o'erswell my reason,
Tell me, bad woman, tell me what could move
Thy heart to crave variety of youth.

Bianca. I'll tell ye, if you needs would be resolved;
I held Fernando much the properer man.

Duke. Shameless, intolerable whore!

Bianca.　　　　　　　　　What ails you?
Can you imagine, sir, the name of duke
Could make a crookèd leg, a scambling[49] foot,
A tolerable face, a wearish[50] hand,
A bloodless lip, or such an untrimmed beard
As yours, fit for a lady's pleasure? no:
I wonder you could think 'twere possible,
When I had once but looked on your Fernando,
I ever could love you again; fie, fie!
Now, by my life, I thought that long ago

[49] Sprawling.
[50] Withered.

Y' had known it, and been glad you had a friend
Your wife did think so well of.

Duke.   O my stars!
Here's impudence above all history.
Why, thou detested reprobate in virtue,
Dar'st thou, without a blush, before mine eyes
Speak such immodest language?

Bianca.   Dare! yes, 'faith,
You see I dare: I know what you would say now;
You would fain tell me how exceeding much
I am beholding to you, that vouchsafed
Me, from a simple gentlewoman's place,
The honour of your bed: 'tis true, you did;
But why? 'twas but because you thought I had
A spark of beauty more than you had seen.
To answer this, my reason is the like;
The self-same appetite which led you on
To marry me led me to love your friend:
O, he's a gallant man! if ever yet
Mine eyes beheld a miracle composed
Of flesh and blood, Fernando has my voice.
I must confess, my lord, that for a prince
Handsome enough you are, and—and no more;
But to compare yourself with him! trust me,
You are too much in fault. Shall I advise you?
Hark in your ear; thank Heaven he was so slow
As not to wrong your sheets; for, as I live,
The fault was his, not mine.

Fiormonda.   Take this, take all.

Duke. Excellent, excellent! the pangs of death
Are music to this.—
Forgive me, my good genius; I had thought
I matched a woman, but I find she is
A devil, worser than the worst in hell.—
Nay, nay, since we are in, e'en come, say on;
I mark you to a syllable: you say
The fault was his, not yours; why, virtuous mistress,
Can you imagine you have so much art
Which may persuade me you and your close markman
Did not a little traffic in my right?

Bianca. Look, what I said, 'tis true; for, know it now,—
I must confess I missed no means, no time,
To win him to my bosom; but so much,
So holily, with such religion,
He kept the laws of friendship, that my suit
Was held but, in comparison, a jest;
Nor did I ofter urge the violence
Of my affection, but as oft he urged
The sacred vows of faith 'twixt friend and friend:
Yet be assured, my lord, if ever language
Of cunning servile flatteries, entreaties,
Or what in me is, could procure his love,
I would not blush to speak it.

    Duke.   Such another
As thou art, miserable creature, would
Sink the whole sex of women: yet confess
What witchcraft used the wretch to charm the heart
Of the once spotless temple of thy mind?
For without witchcraft it could ne'er be done.

    Bianca. Phew!—an you be in these tunes, sir, I'll leave;[51]
You know the best and worst and all.

    Duke.   Nay, then,
Thou tempt'st me to thy ruin. Come, black angel,
Fair devil, in thy prayers reckon up
The sum in gross of all thy veinèd [52] follies;
There, amongst others, weep in tears of blood
For one above the rest, adultery!
Adultery, Bianca! such a guilt
As, were the sluices of thine eyes let up,
Tears cannot wash it off: 'tis not the tide
Of trivial wantonness from youth to youth,
But thy abusing of thy lawful bed,
Thy husband's bed; his in whose breast thou sleep'st,
His that did prize thee more than all the trash
Which hoarding worldlings make an idol of.
When thou shalt find the catalogue enrolled
Of thy misdeeds, there shall be writ in text

---

[51] *i.e.* Leave off, say no more.
[52] *i.e.* In the blood.

Thy bastarding the issues of a prince.
Now turn thine eyes into thy hovering soul,
And do not hope for life; would angels sing
A requiem at my hearse but to dispense
With my revenge on thee, 'twere all in vain:
Prepare to die!

    Bianca. [*Opens her bosom*] I do; and to the point
Of thy sharp sword with open breast I'll run
Half way thus naked; do not shrink, Caraffa;
This daunts not me: but in the latter act
Of thy revenge, 'tis all the suit I ask
At my last gasp, to spare thy noble friend;
For life to me without him were a death.

    Duke. Not this; I'll none of this; 'tis not so fit.—
Why should I kill her? she may live and change,
Or—   [*Throws down his sword.*

    Fiormonda. Dost thou halt? faint coward, dost thou wish
To blemish all thy glorious ancestors?
Is this thy courage?

    Duke.   Ha! say you so too?—
Give me thy hand, Bianca.

    Bianca.   Here.

    Duke.   Farewell;
Thus go in everlasting sleep to dwell!

           [*Draws his dagger and stabs her.*
Here's blood for lust, and sacrifice for wrong.

    Bianca. 'Tis bravely done; thou hast struck home at once:
Live to repent too late. Commend my love
To thy true friend, my love to him that owes[53] it;
My tragedy to thee; my heart to—to—Fernando.
O—O!   [*Dies.*

    Duke. Sister, she's dead.

    Fiormonda.   Then, whiles thy rage is warm
Pursue the causer of her trespass.

    Duke.   Good:
I'll slack no time whiles I am hot in blood.

           [*Takes up his sword and exit.*

    Fiormonda. Here's royal vengeance! this becomes the state
Of his disgrace and my unbounded hate.   [*Exit above.*

---

53 Owns.

SCENE II—*An Apartment in the Palace*

Enter FERNANDO, NIBRASSA, *and* PETRUCHIO.

Petruchio. May we give credit to your words, my lord?
Speak, on your honour.

Fernando.   Let me die accursed,
If ever, through the progress of my life,
I did as much as reap the benefit
Of any favour from her save a kiss:
A better woman never blessed the earth.

Nibrassa. Beshrew my heart, young lord, but I believe
thee: alas, kind lady, 'tis a lordship to a dozen of points[54]
but the jealous madman will in his fury offer her some
violence.

Petruchio. If it be thus, 'twere fit you rather kept
A guard about you for your own defence
Than to be guarded for security
Of his revenge; he is extremely moved.

Nibrassa. Passion of my body, my lord, if he come in his
odd fits to you, in the case you are, he might cut your
throat ere you could provide a weapon of defence: nay,
rather than it shall be so, hold, take my sword in your hand;
'tis none of the sprucest, but 'tis a tough fox[55] will not fail
his master, come what will come. Take it; I'll answer't, I:
in the mean time Petruchio and I will back to the duchess'
lodging.   [*Gives* FERNANDO *his sword.*

Petruchio. Well thought on;—and, despite of all his rage,
Rescue the virtuous lady.

Nibrassa. Look to yourself, my lord! the duke comes.

Enter the Duke, *a sword in one hand, and a bloody dagger
in the other.*

Duke. Stand, and behold thy executioner,
Thou glorious traitor! I will keep no form
Of ceremonious law to try thy guilt:
Look here, 'tis written on my poniard's point,

---

[54] Tagged laces.
[55] Sword.

The bloody evidence of thy untruth,
Wherein thy conscience and the wrathful rod
Of Heaven's scourge for lust at once give up
The verdict of thy crying villainies.
I see thou'rt armed: prepare, I crave no odds
Greater than is the justice of my cause;
Fight, or I'll kill thee.

    Fernando.   Duke, I fear thee not:
But first I charge thee, as thou art a prince,
Tell me how hast thou used thy duchess?

    Duke.   How!
To add affliction to thy trembling ghost,
Look on my dagger's crimson dye, and judge.

    Fernando. Not dead?

    Duke. Not dead! yes, by my honour's truth: why, fool,
Dost think I'll hug my injuries? no, traitor!
I'll mix your souls together in your deaths,
As you did both your bodies in her life.—
Have at thee!

    Fernando. Stay; I yield my weapon up.

                               [He drops his sword.
Here, here's my bosom: as thou art a duke,
Dost honour goodness, if the chaste Bianca
Be murdered, murder me.

    Duke.   Faint-hearted coward,
Art thou so poor in spirit! Rise and fight;
Or, by the glories of my house and name,
I'll kill thee basely.

    Fernando.   Do but hear me first:
Unfortunate Caraffa, thou hast butchered
An innocent, a wife as free from lust
As any terms of art can deify.

    Duke. Pish, this is stale dissimulation;
I'll hear no more.

    Fernando.   If ever I unshrined
The altar of her purity, or tasted
More of her love than what without control
Or blame a brother from a sister might,
Rack me to atomies. I must confess
I have too much abused thee; did exceed

In lawless courtship; 'tis too true, I did:
But, by the honour which I owe to goodness,
For any actual folly I am free.

   Duke. 'Tis false: as much in death for thee she spake.

   Fernando. By yonder starry roof, 'tis true. O duke!
Couldst thou rear up another world like this,
Another like to that, and more, or more,
Herein thou art most wretched; all the wealth
Of all those worlds could not redeem the loss
Of such a spotless wife. Glorious Bianca,
Reign in the triumph of thy martyrdom;
Earth was unworthy of thee!

   Nibrassa and Petruchio. Now, on our lives, we both be-
      lieve him.

   Duke. Fernando, dar'st thou swear upon my sword
To justify thy words?

   Fernando.   I dare; look here. [*Kisses the sword.*
'Tis not the fear of death doth prompt my tongue,
For I would wish to die; and thou shalt know,
Poor miserable duke, since she is dead,
I'll hold all life a hell.

   Duke. Bianca chaste!

   Fernando.   As virtue's self is good.

   Duke. Chaste, chaste, and killed by me! to her
I offer up this remnant of my—

      [*Offers to stab himself, and is stayed by* FERNANDO.

   Fernando.   Hold!
Be gentler to thyself.

   Petruchio.   Alas, my lord,
Is this a wise man's carriage?

   Duke.   Whither now
Shall I run from the day, where never man,
Nor eye, nor eye of Heaven may see a dog
So hateful as I am? Bianca chaste!
Had not the fury of some hellish rage
Blinded all reason's sight, I must have seen
Her clearness in her confidence to die.
Your leave—

      [*Kneels, holds up his hands, and, after speaking
      to himself a little, rises.*

'Tis done: come, friend, now for her love,
Her love that praised thee in the pangs of death,
I'll hold thee dear.—Lords, do not care for me,
I am too wise to die yet.—O, Bianca!

Enter D'AVOLOS.

D'Avolos. The Lord Abbot of Monaco, sir, is, in his return from Rome, lodged last night late in the city very
privately; and hearing the report of your journey, only intends to visit your duchess to-morrow.

Duke. Slave, torture me no more!—note him, my lords;
If you would choose a devil in the shape
Of man, an arch-arch-devil, there stands one.—
We'll meet our uncle.—Order straight, Petruchio,
Our duchess may be coffined; 'tis our will
She forthwith be interred, with all the speed
And privacy you may, i' the college-church
Amongst Caraffa's ancient monuments:
Some three days hence we'll keep her funeral.—
Damned villain! bloody villain!—O, Bianca!—
   No counsel from our cruel wills can win us;
   But ills once done, we bear our guilt within us.
                              [*Exeunt all but* D'AVOLOS.

D'Avolos. Good b'wi'ye! "Arch-arch-devil!" why, I am
paid. Here's bounty for good service! beshrew my heart, it
is a right princely reward. Now must I say my prayers,
that I have lived to so ripe an age to have my head stricken
off. I cannot tell; 't may be my Lady Fiormonda will stand
on my behalf to the duke: that's but a single hope; a dis-
graced courtier oftener finds enemies to sink him when he
is falling than friends to relieve him. I must resolve to stand
to the hazard of all brunts now. Come what may, I will not
die like a coward; and the world shall know it.   [*Exit.*

SCENE III—*Another Apartment in the Palace*

Enter FIORMONDA, *and* ROSEILLI *discovering himself.*

Roseilli. Wonder not, madam; here behold the man
Whom your disdain hath metamorphosèd.

Thus long have I been clouded in this shape,
Led on by love; and in that love, despair:
If not the sight of our distracted court,
Nor pity of my bondage, can reclaim
The greatness of your scorn, yet let me know
My latest doom from you.
    Fiormonda.   Strange miracle!
Roseilli, I must honour thee: thy truth,
Like a transparent mirror, represents
My reason with my errors. Noble lord,
That better dost deserve a better fate,
Forgive me: if my heart can entertain
Another thought of love, it shall be thine.
    Roseilli. Blessèd, for ever blessèd be the words!
In death you have revived me.

Enter D'AVOLOS.

    D'Avolos. [*Aside*] Whom have we here? Roseilli, the
supposed fool? 'tis he; nay, then, help me a brazen face!—
My honourable lord!—
    Roseilli. Bear off, bloodthirsty man! come not near me.
    D'Avolos. Madam, I trust the service—
    Fiormonda. Fellow, learn to new-live: the way to thrift
For thee in grace is a repentant shrift.
    Roseilli. Ill has thy life been, worse will be thy end:
Men fleshed in blood know seldom to amend.

Enter Servant.

    Servant. His highness commends his love to you, and
expects your presence; he is ready to pass to the church,
only staying for my lord abbot to associate him.—Withal,
his pleasure is, that you, D'Avolos, forbear to rank in this
solemnity in the place of secretary; else to be there as a
private man.—Pleaseth you to go?
                        [*Exeunt all but* D'AVOLOS.
    D'Avolos. As a private man! what remedy? This way
they must come; and here I will stand, to fall amongst 'em
in the rear.
*A solemn strain of soft music. The Scene opens, and dis-
covers the Church, with a tomb in the background.*

Enter Attendants *with torches, after them two* Friars; *then
the* Duke *in mourning manner; after him the* Abbot,
FIORMONDA, COLONA, JULIA, ROSEILLI, PETRUCHIO, NI-
BRASSA, *and a* Guard.—D'AVOLOS *follows. When the
procession approaches the tomb they all kneel. The* Duke
goes to the tomb, and lays his hand on it. The music ceases.

Duke. Peace and sweet rest sleep here! Let not the touch
Of this my impious hand profane the shrine
Of fairest purity, which hovers yet
About those blessèd bones inhearsed within.
If in the bosom of this sacred tomb,
Bianca, thy disturbèd ghost doth range,
Behold, I offer up the sacrifice
Of bleeding tears, shed from a faithful spring,
Pouring oblations of a mourning heart
To thee, offended spirit! I confess
I am Caraffa, he, that wretched man,
That butcher, who, in my enragèd spleen,
Slaughtered the life of innocence and beauty.
Now come I to pay tribute to those wounds
Which I digged up, and reconcile the wrongs
My fury wrought and my contrition mourns.
So chaste, so dear a wife was never man
But I enjoyed; yet in the bloom and pride
Of all her years untimely took her life.—
Enough: set ope the tomb, that I may take
My last farewell, and bury griefs with her.

[*The tomb is opened, out of which rises* FERNANDO
*in his winding-sheet, his face only uncovered; as
the* Duke *is going in he puts him back.*

Fernando. Forbear! what art thou that dost rudely press
Into the confines of forsaken graves?
Has death no privilege? Com'st thou, Caraffa,
To practise yet a rape upon the dead?
Inhuman tyrant!—
Whats'ever thou intendest, know this place
Is pointed out for my inheritance;
Here lies the monument of all my hopes:
Had eager lust intrunked my conquered soul,

I had not buried living joys in death.
Go, revel in thy palace, and be proud
To boast thy famous murders; let thy smooth,
Low-fawning parasites renown thy act:
Thou com'st not here.

Duke.   Fernando, man of darkness,
Never till now, before these dreadful sights,
Did I abhor thy friendship: thou hast robbed
My resolution of a glorious name.
Come out, or, by the thunder of my rage,
Thou diest a death more fearful than the scourge
Of death can whip thee with.

Fernando.   Of death!—poor duke!
Why, that's the aim I shoot at; 'tis not threats—
Maugre thy power, or the spite of hell—
Shall rend that honour: let life-hugging slaves,
Whose hands imbrued in butcheries like thine
Shake terror to their souls, be loth to die!
See, I am clothed in robes that fit the grave:
I pity thy defiance.

Duke.   Guard, lay hands,
And drag him out.

Fernando.   Yes, let 'em; here's my shield;
Here's health to victory!

> [*As the* Guard *go to seize him, he drinks-off a
> phial of poison.*

                    Now do thy worst.—
Farewell, duke! once I have outstripped thy plots;
Not all the cunning antidotes of art
Can warrant me twelve minutes of my life:
It works, it works already, bravely! bravely!
Now, now I feel it tear each several joint.
O royal poison! trusty friend! split, split
Both heart and gall asunder, excellent bane!
Roseilli, love my memory.—Well searched out,
Swift, nimble venom! torture every vein.—
I come, Bianca—cruel torment, feast,
Feast on, do—Duke, farewell.—Thus I—hot flames!—
Conclude my love,—and seal it in my bosom!
O!   [*Dies.*

Abbot. Most desperate end!

Duke. None stir;
Who steps a foot steps to his utter ruin.—
And art thou gone, Fernando? art thou gone?
Thou wert a friend unmatched; rest in thy fame.—
Sister, when I have finished my last days,
Lodge me, my wife, and this unequalled friend,
All in one monument.—Now to my vows.
Never henceforth let any passionate[56] tongue
Mention Bianca's and Caraffa's name,
But let each letter in that tragic sound
Beget a sigh, and every sigh a tear;
Children unborn, and widows whose lean cheeks
Are furrowed up by age, shall weep whole nights,
Repeating but the story of our fates;
Whiles in the period, closing up their tale,
They must conclude how for Bianca's love
Caraffa, in revenge of wrongs to her,
Thus on her altar sacrificed his life.   [*Stabs himself.*

Abbot. O, hold the duke's hand!

Fiormonda.   Save my brother, save him!

Duke. Do, do; I was too willing to strike home
To be prevented. Fools, why, could you dream
I would outlive my outrage?—Sprightful flood,
Run out in rivers! O, that these thick streams
Could gather head, and make a standing pool.
That jealous husbands here might bathe in blood!
So! I grow sweetly empty; all the pipes
Of life unvessel life.—Now heavens, wipe out
The writing of my sin!—Bianca, thus
I creep to thee—to thee—to thee, Bi—an—ca.   [*Dies.*

Roseilli. He's dead already, madam.

D'Avolos. [*Aside*] Above hope! here's labour saved; I
could bless the destinies.

Abbot. 'Would I had never seen it!

Fiormonda.   Since 'tis thus,
My Lord Roseilli, in the true requital
Of your continued love, I here possess

---

[56] Sorrowful.

You of the dukedom, and with it of me,
In presence of this holy abbot.
 Abbot.   Lady, then,
From my hand take your husband; long enjoy
           [Joins their hands.
Each to each other's comfort and content!
 All. Long live Roseilli!
 Roseilli. First, thanks to Heaven; next, lady, to your love;
Lastly, my lords, to all: and that the entrance
Into this principality may give
Fair hopes of being worthy of our place,
Our first work shall be justice.—D'Avolos,
Stand forth.
 D'Avolos. My gracious lord!—
 Roseilli.   No, graceless villain!
I am no lord of thine.—Guard, take him hence,
Convey him to the prison's top; in chains
Hang him alive; whosoe'er lends a bit
Of bread to feed him dies.—Speak not against it,
I will be deaf to mercy.—Bear him hence!
 D'Avolos. Mercy, new duke; here's my comfort, I make
but one in the number of the tragedy of princes.
           [He is led off.
 Roseilli. Madam, a second charge is to perform
Your brother's testament; we'll rear a tomb
To those unhappy lovers, which shall tell
Their fatal loves to all posterity.—
Thus, then, for you; henceforth I here dismiss
The mutual comforts of our marriage-bed:
Learn to new-live, my vows unmoved shall stand;
 And since your life hath been so much uneven,
 Bethink in time to make your peace with Heaven.
 Fiormonda. O, me! is this your love?
 Roseilli.   'Tis your desert;
Which no persuasion shall remove.
 Abbot.   'Tis fit;
Purge frailty with repentance.
 Fiormonda.   I embrace it:
 Happy too late, since lust hath made me foul,

Henceforth I'll dress my bride-bed in my soul.
Roseilli. Please you to walk, lord abbot?
Abbot.   Yes, set on.
No age hath heard, nor chronicle can say,
That ever here befell a sadder day.   [*Exeunt*.

PERKIN WARBECK

PERKIN WARBECK was acted at the Phœnix and published in 1634 as "a chronicle history." Ford founded it on Bacon's *Life of Henry VII*.

The play was reprinted in 1714, a period at which there were insurrectionary movements in Scotland. In the memorable year of 1745, when the young Pretender appeared, Ford's play was revived (at the time that two other plays appeared on the same subject, by Macklin and Elderton), at Goodman's Fields Theatre, but so sympathetic a picture of a pretender could scarcely have appealed to the public of that period.

Schiller left behind him the sketch of a drama called *Warbeck*.

To his worthy Friend, Master John Ford, upon his Perkin Warbeck

Let men who are writ poets lay a claim
To the Phœbean hill, I have no name
Nor art in verse: true, I have heard some tell
Of Aganippe, but ne'er knew the well;
Therefore have no ambition with the times
To be in print, for making of ill rhymes;
But love of thee, and justice to thy pen,
Hath drawn me to this bar with other men,
To justify, though against double laws,
Waving the subtle business of his cause,
The glorious Perkin, and thy poet's art,
Equal with his in playing the king's part.

RA. EURE, *baronis primogenitus*[1]

To my Friend and Kinsman, Master John Ford, the Author

Dramatic poets, as the times go now,
Can hardly write what others will allow;
The cynic snarls, the critic howls and barks,
And ravens croak to drown the voice of larks:
Scorn those stage-harpies! This I'll boldly say,
Many may imitate, few match thy play.

JOHN FORD, *Graiensis*[2]

---

[1] The son of William, Lord Eure.
[2] This is the cousin to whom Ford dedicated *Love's Sacrifice*.

To the Rightly Honourable

WILLIAM CAVENDISH,
EARL OF NEWCASTLE, VISCOUNT MANSFIELD, LORD BOLSOVER AND OGLE[1]

My Lord,

OUT of the darkness of a former age,—enlightened by a late both learned and an honourable pen,[2]—I have endeavoured to personate a great attempt, and in it a greater danger. In *other labours* you may read actions of antiquity discoursed; in *this abridgment* find the actors themselves discoursing, in some kind practised as well *what* to speak as speaking *why* to do. Your lordship is a most competent judge in expressions of such credit; commissioned by your known ability in examining, and enabled by your knowledge in determining, the monuments of time. Eminent titles may, indeed, inform *who* their owners are, not often *what*. To yours the addition of that information in both cannot in any application be observed flattery, the authority being established by truth. I can only acknowledge the errors in writing mine own; the worthiness of the subject written being a perfection in the story and of it. The custom of your lordship's entertainments—even to strangers—is rather an example than a fashion: in which consideration I dare not profess a curiosity; but am only studious that your lordship will please, amongst such as best honour your goodness, to admit into your noble construction

JOHN FORD

[1] William Cavendish (nephew to the first Earl of Devonshire), was born in the year 1592, and was early in favour with James I. He continued in favour with Charles I., and engaged on the Royalist side during the civil war. He was created Duke of Newcastle in 1665, and died in 1676, at the advanced age of 84.
[2] *i.e.* That of Lord Bacon.

PROLOGUE

Studies have of this nature been of late
So out of fashion, so unfollowed, that
It is become more justice to revive
The antic follies of the times than strive
To countenance wise industry: no want
Of art doth render wit or lame or scant
Or slothful in the purchase of fresh bays;
But want of truth in them who give the praise
To their self-love, presuming to out-do
The writer, or—for need—the actors too.
But such this author's silence best befits,
Who bids them be in love with their own wits.
From him to clearer judgments we can say
He shows a history couched in a play;
A history of noble mention, known,
Famous, and true; most noble, 'cause our own;
Not forged from Italy, from France, from Spain,
But chronicled at home; as rich in strain
Of brave attempts as ever fertile rage
In action could beget to grace the stage.
We cannot limit scenes, for the whole land
Itself appeared too narrow to withstand
Competitors for kingdoms; nor is here
Unnecessary mirth forced to endear
A multitude: on these two rests the fate
Of worthy expectation,—truth and state.

DRAMATIS PERSONÆ

Henry VII.
Lord Dawbeney
Sir William Stanley, Lord Chamberlain
Earl of Oxford
Earl of Surrey
Fox, Bishop of Durham
Urswick, Chaplain to the King
Sir Robert Clifford
Lambert Simnel
Hialas, a Spanish Agent
James IV., King of Scotland
Earl of Huntley
Earl of Crawford
Lord Dalyell
Marchmont, a Herald
Perkin Warbeck
Stephen Frion, his Secretary
John a-Water, Mayor of Cork
Heron, a Mercer
Skelton, a Tailor
Astley, a Scrivener
Sheriff, Constable, Officers, Messenger, Guards, Soldiers, Masquers, and Attendants

Lady Katherine Gordon
Countess of Crawford
Jane Douglas, Lady Katherine's attendant

SCENE—Partly in England, partly in Scotland

PERKIN WARBECK

ACT THE FIRST

SCENE I—*Westminster. The royal Presence-chamber*

Enter King HENRY, *supported to the throne by the* Bishop
of DURHAM *and* Sir WILLIAM STANLEY; Earls of OXFORD
and SURREY, *and* Lord DAWBENEY. A Guard.

KING HENRY. Still to be haunted, still to be pursued,
Still to be frightened with false apparitions
Of pageant majesty and new-coined greatness,
As if we were a mockery king in state,
Only ordained to lavish sweat and blood,
In scorn and laughter, to the ghosts of York,
Is all below our merits:[1] yet, my lords,
My friends and counsellors, yet we sit fast
In our own royal birthright; the rent face
And bleeding wounds of England's slaughtered people
Have been by us as by the best physician,
At last both throughly cured and set in safety;
And yet, for all this glorious work of peace,
Ourselves is scarce secure.
    Durham.   The rage of malice
Conjures fresh spirits with the spells of York.
For ninety years ten English kings and princes,
Threescore great dukes and earls, a thousand lords
And valiant knights, two hundred fifty thousand
Of English subjects have in civil wars
Been sacrificed to an uncivil thirst
Of discord and ambition: this hot vengeance
Of the just powers above to utter ruin
And desolation had rained on, but that

---

[1] "At this time the king began again to be haunted with sprites by the magic
and curious arts of the Lady Margaret, who raised up the ghost of Richard, Duke
of York, second son to King Edward the Fourth, to walk and vex the king,"
&c.—*Bacon's Henry VII.*

Mercy did gently sheathe the sword of justice,
In lending to this blood-shrunk commonwealth
A new soul, new birth, in your sacred person.
   Dawbeney. Edward the Fourth, after a doubtful fortune,
Yielded to nature, leaving to his sons,
Edward and Richard, the inheritance
Of a most bloody purchase: these young princes,
Richard the tyrant, their unnatural uncle,
Forced to a violent grave:—so just is Heaven,
Him hath your majesty by your own arm,
Divinely strengthened, pulled from his boar's sty,[2]
And struck the black usurper to a carcass.
Nor doth the house of York decay in honours,
Though Lancaster doth repossess his right;
For Edward's daughter is King Henry's queen,—
A blessèd union, and a lasting blessing
For this poor panting island, if some shreds,
Some useless remnant of the house of York
Grudge not at this content.
   Oxford.   Margaret of Burgundy
Blows fresh coals of division.
   Surrey.   Painted fires,
Without or heat to scorch or light to cherish.
   Dawbeney. York's headless trunk, her father; Edward's
      fate,
Her brother, king; the smothering of her nephews
By tyrant Gloster, brother to her nature;
Nor Gloster's own confusion,—all decrees
Sacred in heaven,—can move this woman-monster,
But that she still, from the unbottomed mine
Of devilish policies, doth vent the ore
Of troubles and sedition.
   Oxford.   In her age—
Great sir, observe the wonder[3]—she grows fruitful,

---

[2] An allusion to the armorial bearings of Richard III.
[3] "It is the strangest thing in the world," said Henry's ambassador to the archduke, "that the Lady Margaret should now, when she is old, at the time when other women give-over child-bearing, bring forth two such monsters, being not the births of nine or ten months, but of many years. And whereas other natural mothers bring forth children weak and not able to help themselves, she bringeth forth tall striplings, able soon after their coming into the world to bid battle to mighty kings."

Who in her strength of youth was always barren:
Nor are her births as other mothers' are,
At nine or ten months' end; she has been with child
Eight, or seven years at least; whose twins being born,—
A prodigy in nature,—even the youngest
Is fifteen years of age at his first entrance,
As soon as known i' the world; tall striplings, strong
And able to give battle unto kings,
Idols of Yorkish malice.

　　　Dawbeney.　　　　　　And but idols;
A steely hammer crushes 'em to pieces.

　　　King Henry. Lambert, the eldest, lords, is in our service,
Preferred by an officious care of duty
From the scullery to a falconer;[4] strange example!
Which shows the difference between noble natures
And the base-born: but for the upstart duke,
The new-revived York, Edward's second son,
Murdered long since i' the Tower,—he lives again,
And vows to be your king.

　　　Stanley.　　　　　　The throne is filled, sir.

　　　King Henry. True, Stanley; and the lawful heir sits on it:
A guard of angels and the holy prayers
Of loyal subjects are a sure defence
Against all force and council of intrusion.—
But now, my lords, put case, some of our nobles,
Our great ones, should give countenance and courage
To trim Duke Perkin; you will all confess
Our bounties have unthriftily been scattered
Amongst unthankful men.

　　　Dawbeney.　　　　　　Unthankful beasts,
Dogs, villains, traitors!

　　　King Henry.　　　　Dawbeney, let the guilty
Keep silence; I accuse none, though I know
Foreign attempts against a state and kingdom
Are seldom without some great friends at home.

　　　Stanley. Sir, if no other abler reasons else
Of duty or allegiance could divert
A headstrong resolution, yet the dangers

---

[4] Lambert Simnel, taken prisoner at the battle of Newark, had been made a turn-spit in the king's kitchen, and was afterwards promoted to the office of under-falconer.

So lately passed by men of blood and fortunes
In Lambert Simnel's party must command
More than a fear, a terror to conspiracy.
The high-born Lincoln, son to De la Pole,
The Earl of Kildare,—the Lord Geraldine,—
Francis Lord Lovell, and the German baron
Bold Martin Swart, with Broughton and the rest,—
Most spectacles of ruin, some of mercy,—
Are precedents sufficient to forewarn
The present times, or any that live in them,
What folly, nay, what madness, 'twere to lift
A finger up in all defence but yours,
Which can be but imposturous in a title.

   King Henry. Stanley, we know thou lov'st us, **and thy
      heart**
Is figured on thy tongue; nor think we less
Of any's here.—How closely we have hunted
This cub, since he unlodged, from hole to hole,
Your knowledge is our chronicle: first Ireland,
The common stage of novelty, presented
This gewgaw to oppose us; there the Geraldines
And Butlers once again stood in support
Of this colossic statue: Charles of France
Thence called him into his protection,
Dissembled him the lawful heir of England;
Yet this was all but French dissimulation,
Aiming at peace with us; which being granted
On honourable terms on our part, suddenly
This smoke of straw was packed from France again,
T' infect some grosser air: and now we learn—
Maugre the malice of the bastard Nevill,
Sir Taylor, and a hundred English rebels—
They're all retired to Flanders, to the dam
That nursed this eager whelp, Margaret of Burgundy.
But we will hunt him there too; we will hunt him,
Hunt him to death, even in the beldam's closet,
Though the archduke were his buckler!

   Surrey.   She has styled him
"The fair white rose of England."

   Dawbeney.   Jolly gentleman!

More fit to be a swabber to the Flemish
After a drunken surfeit.

Enter URSWICK *with a paper.*

Urswick.   Gracious sovereign,
Please you peruse this paper.   [*The* King *reads.*
Durham.   The king's countenance
Gathers a sprightly blood.
Dawbeney.   Good news; believe it.
King Henry. Urswick, thine ear.[5] Thou'st lodged him?
Urswick.   Strongly safe, sir.
King Henry. Enough:—is Barley come too?
Urswick.   No, my lord.
King Henry. No matter—phew! he's but a running weed,
At pleasure to be plucked-up by the roots:
But more of this anon.—I have bethought me,
My lords, for reasons which you shall partake,
It is our pleasure to remove our court
From Westminster to the Tower: we will lodge
This very night there; give, Lord Chamberlain,
A present order for 't.
Stanley. [*Aside*]   The Tower!—I shall, sir.
King Henry. Come, my true, best, fast friends: these
    clouds will vanish,
The sun will shine at full; the heavens are clearing.
                    [*Flourish. Exeunt.*

SCENE II—*Edinburgh. An Apartment in the* Earl *of*
HUNTLEY'S *House*

Enter Earl *of* HUNTLEY *and* Lord DALYELL.

Huntley. You trifle time, sir.
Dalyell.   O, my noble lord,
You construe my griefs to so hard a sense,
That where the text is argument of pity,
Matter of earnest love, your gloss corrupts it
With too much ill-placed mirth.

---

[5] Christopher Urswick was at this time almoner to the king. He possessed several
high offices in the Church.

Huntley.   Much mirth! Lord Dalyell;[6]
Not so, I vow. Observe me, sprightly gallant.
I know thou art a noble lad, a handsome,
Descended from an honourable ancestry,
Forward and active, dost resolve to wrestle
And ruffle in the world by noble actions
For a brave mention to posterity:
I scorn not thy affection to my daughter,
Not I, by good Saint Andrew; but this bugbear,
This whoreson tale of honour,—honour, Dalyell!—
So hourly chats and tattles in mine ear
The piece of royalty that is stitched-up
In my Kate's blood,[7] that 'tis as dangerous
For thee, young lord, to perch so near an eaglet
As foolish for my gravity to admit it:
I have spoke all at once.
      Dalyell.   Sir, with this truth
You mix such wormwood, that you leave no hope
For my disordered palate e'er to relish
A wholesome taste again: alas, I know, sir,
What an unequal distance lies between
Great Huntley's daughter's birth and Dalyell's fortunes;
She's the king's kinswoman, placed near the crown,
A princess of the blood, and I a subject.
      Huntley. Right; but a noble subject; put in that too.
      Dalyell. I could add more; and in the rightest line
Derive my pedigree from Adam Mure,
A Scottish knight; whose daughter was the mother
To him who first begot the race of Jameses,
That sway the sceptre to this very day.
But kindreds are not ours when once the date
Of many years have swallowed up the memory
Of their originals; so pasture-fields
Neighbouring too near the ocean are swooped-up,
And known no more; for stood I in my first
And native greatness, if my princely mistress
Vouchsafed me not her servant, 'twere as good

---

[6] There were two persons of the name of Dalzell, William and Robert, grandsons
of Sir John Dalzell.
[7] The Earl of Huntley married Annabella, daughter of James I.

I were reduced to clownery, to nothing,
As to a throne of wonder.

　　Huntley. [*Aside*]　　　　Now, by Saint Andrew,
A spark of mettle! he has a brave fire in him:
I would he had my daughter, so I knew't not.
But 't must not be so, must not.—Well, young lord,
This will not do yet: if the girl be headstrong,
And will not hearken to good counsel, steal her,
And run away with her; dance galliards,[8] do,
And frisk about the world to learn the languages:
'Twill be a thriving trade; you may set up by't.

　　Dalyell. With pardon, noble Gordon, this disdain
Suits not your daughter's virtue or my constancy.

　　Huntley. You're angry.—[*Aside*] Would he would beat
　　　　me, I deserve it.—
Dalyell, thy hand; we're friends: follow thy courtship,
Take thine own time and speak; if thou prevail'st
With passion more than I can with my counsel,
She's thine; nay, she is thine: 'tis a fair match,
Free and allowed. I'll only use my tongue,
Without a father's power; use thou thine:
Self do, self have: no more words; win and wear her.

　　Dalyell. You bless me; I am now too poor in thanks
To pay the debt I owe you.

　　Huntley.　　　　　　Nay, thou'rt poor
Enough.—[*Aside*] I love his spirit infinitely.—
Look ye, she comes: to her now, to her, to her!

　　　　　Enter Lady KATHERINE *and* JANE.

　　Katherine. The king commands your presence, sir.

　　Huntley.　　　　　　　　　The gallant—
This, this, this lord, this servant, Kate, of yours,
Desires to be your master.

　　Katherine.　　　　　I acknowledge him
A worthy friend of mine.

　　Dalyell.　　　　　Your humblest creature.

　　Huntley. [*Aside*] So, so! the game's a-foot; I'm in cold
　　　　hunting;
The hare and hounds are parties.

---

[8] Quick and lively dances.

Dalyell.   Princely lady,
How most unworthy I am to employ
My services in honour of your virtues,
How hopeless my desires are to enjoy
Your fair opinion, and much more your love,—
Are only matter of despair, unless
Your goodness give large warrant to my boldness,
My feeble-winged ambition.
    Huntley. [*Aside*]   This is scurvy.
    Katherine. My lord, I interrupt you not.
    Huntley. [*Aside*]   Indeed!
Now, on my life, she'll court him.—Nay, nay, on, sir.
    Dalyell. Oft have I tuned the lesson of my sorrows
To sweeten discord and enrich your pity;
But all in vain: here had my comforts sunk,
And never risen again to tell a story
Of the despairing lover, had not now,
Even now, the earl your father—
    Huntley. [*Aside*]   He means me, sure.
    Dalyell. After some fit disputes of your condition,
Your highness and my lowness, given a license
Which did not more embolden than encourage
My faulting tongue.
    Huntley.   How, how? how's that? embolden!
Encourage! I encourage ye! d'ye hear, sir?—
A subtle trick, a quaint one:—will you hear, man?
What did I say to you? come, come, to the point.
    Katherine. It shall not need, my lord.
    Huntley.   Then hear me, Kate.—
Keep you on that hand of her, I on this.—
Thou stand'st between a father and a suitor,
Both striving for an interest in thy heart:
He courts thee for affection, I for duty;
He as a servant pleads, but by the privilege
Of nature though I might command, my care
Shall only counsel what it shall not force.
Thou canst but make one choice; the ties of marriage
Are tenures not at will, but during life.
Consider whose thou art, and who; a princess,
A princess of the royal blood of Scotland,

In the full spring of youth and fresh in beauty.
The king that sits upon the throne is young,
And yet unmarried, forward in attempts
On any least occasion to endanger
His person: wherefore, Kate, as I am confident
Thou dar'st not wrong thy birth and education
By yielding to a common servile rage
Of female wantonness, so I am confident
Thou wilt proportion all thy thoughts to side[9]
Thy equals, if not equal thy superiors.
My Lord of Dalyell, young in years, is old
In honours, but nor eminent in titles
Nor in estate, that may support or add to
The expectation of thy fortunes. Settle
Thy will and reason by a strength of judgment;
For, in a word, I give thee freedom; take it.
If equal fates have not ordained to pitch
Thy hopes above my height, let not thy passion
Lead thee to shrink mine honour in oblivion:
Thou art thine own; I have done.
    Dalyell.   O, you're all oracle,
The living stock and root of truth and wisdom!
    Katherine. My worthiest lord and father, the indulgence
Of your sweet composition thus commands
The lowest of obedience; you have granted
A liberty so large, that I want skill
To choose without direction of example:
From which I daily learn, by how much more
You take off from the roughness of a father,
By so much more I am engaged to tender
The duty of a daughter. For respects
Of birth, degrees of title, and advancement,
I nor admire nor slight them; all my studies
Shall ever aim at this perfection only,
To live and die so, that you may not blush
In any course of mine to own me yours.
    Huntley. Kate, Kate, thou grow'st upon my heart like
      peace,
Creating every other hour a jubilee.

[9] *i.e.* Keep pace with.

Katherine. To you, my lord of Dalyell, I address
Some few remaining words: the general fame
That speaks your merit, even in vulgar tongues
Proclaims it clear; but in the best, a precedent.

Huntley. Good wench, good girl, i' faith!

Katherine.   For my part, trust me,
I value mine own worth at higher rate
'Cause you are pleased to prize it: if the stream
Of your protested service—as you term it—
Run in a constancy more than a compliment,
It shall be my delight that worthy love
Leads you to worthy actions, and these guide ye
Richly to wed an honourable name:
So every virtuous praise in after-ages
Shall be your heir, and I in your brave mention
Be chronicled the mother of that issue,
That glorious issue.

Huntley.   O, that I were young again!
Sh'd make me court proud danger, and suck spirit
From reputation.

Katherine.   To the present motion
Here's all that I dare answer: when a ripeness
Of more experience, and some use of time,
Resolves to treat the freedom of my youth
Upon exchange of troths, I shall desire
No surer credit of a match with virtue
Than such as lives in you: mean time my hopes are
Preserved secure in having you a friend.

Dalyell. You are a blessèd lady, and instruct
Ambition not to soar a farther flight
Than in the perfumed air of your soft voice.—
My noble Lord of Huntley, you have lent
A full extent of bounty to this parley;
And for it shall command your humblest servant.

Huntley. Enough: we are still friends, and will continue
A hearty love.—O, Kate, thou art mine own!—
No more:—my Lord of Crawford.

Enter Earl of CRAWFORD.

Crawford.   From the king

I come, my Lord of Huntley, who in council
Requires your present aid.

   Huntley.   Some weighty business?

   Crawford. A secretary from a Duke of York,
The second son to the late English Edward,
Concealed, I know not where, these fourteen years,
Craves audience from our master; and 'tis said
The duke himself is following to the court.

   Huntley. Duke upon duke; 'tis well, 'tis well; here's
      bustling
For majesty.—My lord, I will along with ye.

   Crawford. My service, noble lady!

   Katherine.   Please ye walk, sir?

   Dalyell. [*Aside*] Times have their changes; sorrow makes
      men wise;
The sun itself must set as well as rise;
Then, why not I?—Fair madam, I wait on ye.   [*Exeunt.*

SCENE III—*London. An Apartment in the Tower*

Enter the Bishop of Durham, Sir Robert Clifford, *and*
Urswick. *Lights.*

   Durham. You find, Sir Robert Clifford, how securely
King Henry, our great master, doth commit
His person to your loyalty; you taste
His bounty and his mercy even in this,
That at a time of night so late, a place
So private as his closet, he is pleased
T' admit you to his favour. Do not falter
In your discovery; but as you covet
A liberal grace, and pardon for your follies,
So labour to deserve 't by laying open
All plots, all persons that contrive against it.

   Urswick. Remember not the witchcraft or the magic,
The charms and incantations, which the sorceress
Of Burgundy hath cast upon your reason:
Sir Robert, be your own friend now, discharge
Your conscience freely; all of such as love you
Stand sureties for your honesty and truth.

Take heed you do not dally with the king;
He's wise as he is gentle.

   Clifford.   I am miserable,
If Henry be not merciful.

   Urswick.   The king comes.

Enter King HENRY.

   King Henry. Clifford!

   Clifford. [*Kneels*] Let my weak knees root on the earth,
If I appear as leperous in my treacheries
Before your royal eyes, as to mine own
I seem a monster by my breach of truth.

   King Henry. Clifford, stand up; for instance of thy safety,
I offer thee my hand.

   Clifford.   A sovereign balm
For my bruised soul, I kiss it with a greediness.

               [*Kisses the* King's *hand, and rises.*
Sir, you're a just master, but I—

   King Henry.   Tell me,
Is every circumstance thou hast set down
With thine own hand within this paper true?
Is it a sure intelligence of all
The progress of our enemies' intents
Without corruption?

   Clifford.   True, as I wish Heaven,
Or my infected honour white again.

   King Henry. We know all, Clifford, fully, since this
       meteor,
This airy apparition first discradled
From Tournay into Portugal, and thence
Advanced his fiery blaze for adoration
To the superstitious Irish; since the beard
Of this wild comet, conjured into France,
Sparkled in antic flames in Charles his court;
But shrunk again from thence, and, hid in darkness,
Stole into Flanders flourishing the rag
Of painted power on the shore of Kent,
Whence he was beaten back with shame and scorn,[10]

---

[10] Perkin did not land but sent some of his followers on shore at Sandwich;
they were defeated by the Kentish men. The prisoners, mostly foreigners, were

Contempt, and slaughter of some naked outlaws:
But tell me what new course now shapes Duke Perkin?

   Clifford. For Ireland, mighty Henry; so instructed
By Stephen Frion,[11] sometimes secretary
In the French tongue unto your sacred excellence,
But Perkin's tutor now.

   King Henry.   A subtle villain,
That Frion, Frion,—You, my Lord of Durham,
Knew well the man.

   Durham.   French both in heart and actions.

   King Henry. Some Irish heads work in this mine of treason;
Speak 'em.

   Clifford. Not any of the best; your fortune
Hath dulled their spleens. Never had counterfeit
Such a confusèd rabble of lost bankrupts
For counsellors: first Heron, a broken mercer,
Then John a-Water, sometimes Mayor of Cork,
Skelton a tailor, and a scrivener
Called Astley: and whate'er these list to treat of,
Perkin must hearken to; but Frion, cunning
Above these dull capacities, still prompts him
To fly to Scotland to young James the Fourth.
And sue for aid to him: this is the latest
Of all their resolutions.

   King Henry.   Still more Frion!
Pestilent adder, he will hiss-out poison
As dangerous as infectious: we must match him.
Clifford, thou hast spoke home; we give thee life:
But, Clifford, there are people of our own
Remain behind untold; who are they, Clifford?
Name those, and we are friends, and will to rest;
'Tis thy last task.

   Clifford.   O, sir, here I must break
A most unlawful oath to keep a just one.

   King Henry. Well, well, be brief, be brief.

---

executed, "some of them at London and Wapping, and the rest at divers places
upon the seacoast of Kent, Sussex, and Norfolk, for sea-marks or lighthouses to
teach Perkin's people to avoid the coast."—*Bacon.*
[11] An active agent in the hands of the Duchess of Burgundy.

Clifford.   The first in rank
Shall be John Ratcliffe, Lord Fitzwater, then
Sir Simon Mountford and Sir Thomas Thwaites,
With William Dawbeney, Chessoner, Astwood,
Worseley the Dean of Paul's, two other friars,
And Robert Ratcliffe.[12]

King Henry.   Churchmen are turned devils.
These are the principal?

Clifford.   One more remains
Unnamed, whom I could willingly forget.

King Henry. Ha, Clifford! one more?

Clifford.   Great sir, do not hear him;
For when Sir William Stanley, your lord chamberlain,
Shall come into the list, as he is chief,
I shall lose credit with ye; yet this lord
Last named is first against you.

King Henry.   Urswick, the light!—
View well my face, sirs; is there blood left in it?

Durham. You alter strangely, sir.

King Henry.   Alter, lord bishop!
Why, Clifford stabbed me, or I dreamed he stabbed me.—
Sirrah, it is a custom with the guilty
To think they set their own stains oft by laying
Aspersions on some nobler than themselves;
Lies wait on treasons, as I find it here.
Thy life again is forfeit; I recall
My word of mercy, for I know thou dar'st
Repeat the name no more.

Clifford.   I dare, and once more,
Upon my knowledge, name Sir William Stanley
Both in his counsel and his purse the chief
Assistant to the feignèd Duke of York.

Durham. Most strange!

Urswick.   Most wicked!

King Henry.   Yet again, once more.

Clifford. Sir William Stanley is your secret enemy,
And, if time fit, will openly profess it.

King Henry. Sir William Stanley! Who? Sir William
        Stanley!

---

[12] All these except Worseley and the two Dominicans, perished on the scaffold.

My chamberlain, my counsellor, the love,
The pleasure of my court, my bosom-friend,
The charge and the controlment of my person,
The keys and secrets of my treasury,
The all of all I am! I am unhappy.
Misery of confidence,—let me turn traitor
To mine own person, yield my sceptre up
To Edward's sister and her bastard duke!
    Durham. You lose your constant temper.
    King Henry.   Sir William Stanley!
O, do not blame me; he, 'twas only he,
Who, having rescued me in Bosworth-field
From Richard's bloody sword, snatched from his head
The kingly crown, and placed it first on mine.
He never failed me: what have I deserved
To lose this good man's heart, or he his own?
    Urswick. The night doth waste; this passion ill becomes
        ye;
Provide against your danger.
    King Henry.   Let it be so.
Urswick, command straight Stanley to his chamber;—
'Tis well we are i' the Tower;—set a guard on him.—
Clifford, to bed; you must lodge here to-night;
We'll talk with you to-morrow.—My sad soul
Divines strange troubles.
    Dawbeney. [*Within*] Ho! the king, the king!
I must have entrance.
    King Henry.   Dawbeney's voice; admit him.
What new combustions huddle next, to keep
Our eyes from rest?

        Enter Lord DAWBENEY.

          The news?
    Dawbeney.   Ten thousand Cornish,
Grudging to pay your subsidies, have gathered
A head; led by a blacksmith and a lawyer,
They make for London, and to them is joined
Lord Audley: as they march, their number daily
Increases; they are—
    King Henry.   Rascals!—talk no more;

Such are not worthy of my thoughts to-night.
To bed; and if I cannot sleep, I'll wake.—
When counsels fail, and there's in man no trust,
Even then an arm from Heaven fights for the just.

                                        [*Exeunt.*

ACT THE SECOND

SCENE I—*Edinburgh. The Presence-chamber in the Palace.*

Enter above the Countess of CRAWFORD, Lady KATHERINE, JANE DOUGLAS, *and other* Ladies.

COUNTESS OF CRAWFORD. Come, ladies, here's a solemn preparation
For entertainment of this English prince;
The king intends grace more than ordinary:
'Twere pity now if he should prove a counterfeit.
    Katherine. Bless the young man, our nation would be laughed at
For honest souls through Christendom! My father
Hath a weak stomach to the business, madam,
But that the king must not be crossed.
    Countess of Crawford.   He brings
A goodly troop, they say, of gallants with him;
But very modest people, for they strive not
To fame their names too much; their godfathers
May be beholding to them, but their fathers
Scarce owe them thanks: they are disguisèd princes,
Brought up, it seems, to honest trades; no matter,
They will break forth in season.
    Jane.   Or break out;
For most of 'em are broken by report.—   [*A flourish.*
The king!
    Katherine. Let us observe 'em and be silent.

Enter King JAMES, Earls of HUNTLEY *and* CRAWFORD, Lord DALYELL, *and other* Noblemen.

King James. The right of kings, my lords, extends not
    only
To the safe conservation of their own,
But also to the aid of such allies
As change of time and state hath oftentimes
Hurled down from careful crowns to undergo
An exercise of sufferance in both fortunes:
So English Richard, surnamed Cœur-de-Lion,
So Robert Bruce, our royal ancestor,
Forced by the trial of the wrongs they felt,
Both sought and found supplies from foreign kings,
To repossess their own. Then grudge not, lords,
A much distressèd prince: King Charles of France
And Maximilian of Bohemia both
Have ratified his credit by their letters;
Shall we, then, be distrustful? No; compassion
Is one rich jewel that shines in our crown,
And we will have it shine there.
Huntley.   Do your will, sir.
King James. The young duke is at hand: Dalyell, from us
First greet him, and conduct him on; then Crawford
Shall meet him next; and Huntley, last of all,
Present him to our arms. [*Exit* Lord DALYELL.]—Sound
    sprightly music,
Whilst majesty encounters majesty.   [*Hautboys.*

Re-enter Lord DALYELL *with* PERKIN WARBECK, *followed at
a distance by* FRION, HERON, SKELTON, ASTLEY, *and* JOHN
A-WATER. *The* Earl *of* CRAWFORD *advances, and salutes*
PERKIN *at the door, and afterwards the* Earl *of* HUNTLEY,
who presents him to the King: *they embrace; the* Noblemen *slightly salute his* Followers.

Warbeck. Most high, most mighty king![13] that now there
    stands
Before your eyes, in presence of your peers,
A subject of the rarest kind of pity

---

[13] In Bacon this speech begins thus: "High and mighty king! your grace, and
these your nobles here present, may be pleased benignly to bow your ears to hear
the tragedy of a young man. . . . tossed from misery to misery. . . . You see
here before you the spectacle of a Plantagenet, who hath been carried from the
nursery to the sanctuary, from the sanctuary to the direful prison, from the
prison to the hand of the cruel tormentor," &c.

That hath in any age touched noble hearts,
The vulgar story of a prince's ruin
Hath made it too apparent: Europe knows,
And all the western world, what persecution
Hath raged in malice against us, sole heir
To the great throne of old Plantagenets.
How from our nursery we have been hurried
Unto the sanctuary, from the sanctuary
Forced to the prison, from the prison haled
By cruel hands to the tormentor's fury,
Is registered already in the volume
Of all men's tongues; whose true relation draws
Compassion, melted into weeping eyes
And bleeding souls: but our misfortunes since
Have ranged a larger progress through strange lands,
Protected in our innocence by Heaven.
Edward the Fifth, our brother, in his tragedy
Quenched their hot thirst of blood, whose hire to murder
Paid them their wages of despair and horror;
The softness of my childhood smiled upon
The roughness of their task, and robbed them farther
Of hearts to dare, or hands to execute.
Great king, they spared my life, the butchers spared it;
Returned the tyrant, my unnatural uncle,
A truth of my dispatch: I was conveyed
With secrecy and speed to Tournay; fostered
By obscure means, taught to unlearn myself:
But as I grew in years, I grew in sense
Of fear and of disdain; fear of the tyrant
Whose power swayed the throne then: when disdain
Of living so unknown, in such a servile
And abject lowness, prompted me to thoughts
Of recollecting who I was, I shook off
My bondage, and made haste to let my aunt
Of Burgundy acknowledge me her kinsman,
Heir to the crown of England, snatched by Henry
From Richard's head; a thing scarce known i' the world.
   King James. My lord, it stands not with your counsel now
To fly upon invectives: if you can
Make this apparent what you have discoursed

In every circumstance, we will not study
An answer, but are ready in your cause.

   Warbeck. You are a wise and just king, by the powers
Above reserved, beyond all other aids,
To plant me in mine own inheritance,
To marry these two kingdoms in a love
Never to be divorced while time is time.
As for the manner, first of my escape,
Of my conveyance next, of my life since,
The means and persons who were instruments,
Great sir, 'tis fit I over-pass in silence;
Reserving the relation to the secrecy
Of your own princely ear, since it concerns
Some great ones living yet, and others dead,
Whose issue might be questioned. For your bounty,
Royal magnificence to him that seeks it,
We vow hereafter to demean ourself
As if we were your own and natural brother,
Omitting no occasion in our person
T' express a gratitude beyond example.

   King James. He must be more than subject who can utter
The language of a king, and such is thine.
Take this for answer: be what'er thou art,
Thou never shalt repent that thou hast put
Thy cause and person into my protection.
Cousin of York, thus once more we embrace thee;
Welcome to James of Scotland! for thy safety,
Know, such as love thee not shall never wrong thee.
Come, we will taste a while our court-delights,
Dream hence affliction past, and then proceed
To high attempts of honour. On, lead on!—
Both thou and thine are ours, and we will guard ye.—
Lead on!   *[Exeunt all but the* Ladies *above.*

   Countess of Crawford. I have not seen a gentleman
Of a more brave aspéct or goodlier carriage;
His fortunes move not him.—Madam, you're passionate.[14]

   Katherine. Beshrew me, but his words have touched me
      home,
As if his cause concerned me: I should pity him,

---

[14] Distressed.

If he should prove another than he seems.

Re-enter Earl of CRAWFORD.

Crawford. Ladies, the king commands your presence instantly
For entertainment of the duke.
 Katherine.   The duke
Must, then, be entertained, the king obeyed;
It is our duty.
 Countess of Crawford. We will all wait on him. [*Exeunt.*

SCENE II—*London. The Tower*

A flourish. Enter King HENRY, *the* Earls of Oxford *and*
 Surrey, *and the* Bishop of Durham.

King Henry. Have ye condemned my chamberlain?
 Durham.   His treasons
Condemned him, sir; which were as clear and manifest
As foul and dangerous: besides, the guilt
Of his conspiracy pressed him so nearly,
That it drew from him free confession
Without an importunity.
 King Henry.   O, lord bishop,
This argued shame and sorrow for his folly,
And must not stand in evidence against
Our mercy and the softness of our nature:
The rigour and extremity of law
Is sometimes too-too bitter; but we carry
A chancery of pity in our bosom.
I hope we may reprieve him from the sentence
Of death; I hope we may.
 Durham.   You may, you may;
And so persuade your subjects that the title
Of York is better, nay, more just and lawful,
Than yours of Lancaster! so Stanley holds:
Which if it be not treason in the highest,
Then we are traitors all, perjured and false,
Who have took oath to Henry and the justice

Of Henry's title; Oxford, Surrey, Dawbeney,
With all your other peers of state and church,
Forsworn, and Stanley true alone to Heaven
And England's lawful heir!

Oxford.   By Vere's old honours,
I'll cut his throat dares speak it.

Surrey.   'Tis a quarrel
T' engage a soul in.

King Henry.   What a coil is here
To keep my gratitude sincere and perfect!
Stanley was once my friend, and came in time
To save my life; yet, to say truth, my lords,
The man stayed long enough t' endanger it:—[15]
But I could see no more into his heart
Than what his outward actions did present;
And for 'em have rewarded him so fully,
As that there wanted nothing in our gift
To gratify his merit, as I thought,
Unless I should divide my crown with him,
And give him half; though now I well perceive
'Twould scarce have served his turn without the whole.
But I am charitable, lords; let justice
Proceed in execution, whiles I mourn
The loss of one whom I esteemed a friend.

Durham. Sir, he is coming this way.

King Henry.   If he speak to me,
I could deny him nothing; to prevent it,
I must withdraw. Pray, lords, commend my favours
To his last peace, which I with him will pray for:
That done, it doth concern us to consult
Of other following troubles.   [*Exit.*

Oxford.   I am glad
He's gone: upon my life, he would have pardoned
The traitor, had he seen him.

Surrey.   'Tis a king
Composed of gentleness.

Durham.   Rare and unheard of:

---

[15] "As a little leaven of new distaste doth commonly sour the whole lump of former merits, the king's wit began now to suggest unto his passion that Stanley at Bosworth-field, though he came time enough to save his life, yet he stayed long enough to endanger it."—*Bacon.*

But every man is nearest to himself;
And that the king observes; 'tis fit he should.

   Enter Sir WILLIAM STANLEY, Executioner, Confessor,
     URSWICK, *and* Lord DAWBENEY.

 Stanley. May I not speak with Clifford ere I shake
This piece of frailty off?
 Dawbeney.   You shall; he's sent for.
 Stanley. I must not see the king?
 Durham.   From him, Sir William,
These lords and I am sent; he bade us say
That he commends his mercy to your thoughts;
Wishing the laws of England could remit
The forfeit of your life as willingly
As he would in the sweetness of his nature
Forget your trespass: but howe'er your body
Fall into dust, he vows, the king himself
Doth vow, to keep a requiem for your soul,
As for a friend close treasured in his bosom.
 Oxford. Without remembrance of your errors past,
I come to take my leave, and wish you Heaven.
 Surrey. And I; good angels guard ye!
 Stanley.   O, the king,
Next to my soul, shall be the nearest subject
Of my last prayers. My grave Lord of Durham,
My Lords of Oxford, Surrey, Dawbeney, all,
Accept from a poor dying man a farewell.
I was as you are once,—great, and stood hopeful
Of many flourishing years; but fate and time
Have wheeled about, to turn me into nothing.
 Dawbeney. Sir Robert Clifford comes,—the man, Sir William,
  liam,
You so desire to speak with.
 Durham.   Mark their meeting.

    Enter Sir ROBERT CLIFFORD.

 Clifford. Sir William Stanley, I am glad your conscience
Before your end hath emptied every burthen

Which charged it, as that you can clearly witness
How far I have proceeded in a duty
That both concerned my truth and the state's safety.

    Stanley. Mercy, how dear is life to such as hug it!
Come hither; by this token think on me!

        [Makes a cross on CLIFFORD's *face with his finger.*

    Clifford. This token! What! I am abused?

    Stanley.   You are not.
I wet upon your cheeks a holy sign,—
The cross, the Christian's badge, the traitor's infamy:
Wear, Clifford, to thy grave this painted emblem;
Water shall never wash it off; all eyes
That gaze upon thy face shall read there written
A state-informer's character; more ugly
Stamped on a noble name than on a base.
The heavens forgive thee!—Pray, my lords, no change
Of words; this man and I have used too many.

    Clifford. Shall I be disgraced
Without reply?

    Durham.   Give losers leave to talk;
His loss is irrecoverable.

    Stanley.   Once more,
To all a long farewell! The best of greatness
Preserve the king! My next suit is, my lords,
To be remembered to my noble brother,
Derby, my much-grieved brother: O, persuade him
That I shall stand no blemish to his house
In chronicles writ in another age.
My heart doth bleed for him and for his sighs:
Tell him, he must not think the style of Derby,
Nor being husband to King Henry's mother,
The league with peers, the smiles of fortune, can
Secure his peace above the state of man.
I take my leave, to travel to my dust:
Subjects deserve their deaths whose kings are just.—
Come, confessor.—On with thy axe, friend, on!

                  [He is led off to execution.

    Clifford. Was I called hither by a traitor's breath
To be upbraided? Lords, the king shall know it.

Re-enter King HENRY *with a white staff.*

King Henry. The king doth know it, sir; the king hath
     heard
What he or you could say. We have given credit
To every point of Clifford's information,
The only evidence 'gainst Stanley's head:
He dies for't; are you pleased?
    Clifford.   I pleased, my lord!
    King Henry. No echoes: for your service, we dismiss
Your more attendance on the court, take ease,
And live at home; but, as you love your life,
Stir not from London without leave from us.
We'll think on your reward: away!
    Clifford.   I go, sir.   [*Exit.*
    King Henry. Die all our griefs with Stanley! Take this
     staff
Of office, Dawbeney; henceforth be our chamberlain.
    Dawbeney. I am your humble servant.
    King Henry.   We are followed
By enemies at home, that will not cease
To seek their own confusion: 'tis most true
The Cornish under Audley are marched on
As far as Winchester;—but let them come,
Our forces are in readiness; we'll catch 'em
In their own toils.
    Dawbeney.   Your army, being mustered,
Consists in all, of horse and foot, at least
In number six-and-twenty thousand; men
Daring and able, resolute to fight,
And loyal in their truths.
    King Henry.   We know it, Dawbeney:
For them we order thus; Oxford in chief,
Assisted by bold Essex and the Earl
Of Suffolk, shall lead on the first battalia;
Be that your charge.
    Oxford.   I humbly thank your majesty.
    King Henry. The next division we assign to Dawbeney:
These must be men of action, for on those
The fortune of our fortunes must rely.

The last and main ourself commands in person;
As ready to restore the fight at all times
As to consummate an assurèd victory.
   Dawbeney. The king is still oraculous.
   King Henry.   But, Surrey,
We have employment of more toil for thee:
For our intelligence comes swiftly to us,
That James of Scotland late hath entertained
Perkin the counterfeit with more than common
Grace and respect, nay, courts him with rare favours.
The Scot is young and forward; we must look for
A sudden storm to England from the north;
Which to withstand, Durham shall post to Norham,
To fortify the castle and secure
The frontiers against an invasion there.
Surrey shall follow soon, with such an army
As may relieve the bishop, and encounter
On all occasions the death-daring Scots.
You know your charges all; 'tis now a time
To execute, not talk: Heaven is our guard still.
War must breed peace; such is the fate of kings.   [*Exeunt.*

SCENE III—*Edinburgh. An Apartment in the Palace*

Enter Earl of CRAWFORD *and* Lord DALYELL.

   Crawford. 'Tis more than strange; my reason cannot
      answer
Such argument of fine imposture, couched
In witchcraft of persuasion, that it fashions
Impossibilities, as if appearance
Could cozen truth itself: this dukeling mushroom
Hath doubtless charmed the king.
   Dalyell.   He courts the ladies,
As if his strength of language chained attention
By power of prerogative.
   Crawford.   It madded
My very soul to hear our master's motion:
What surety both of amity and honour
Must of necessity ensue upon

A match betwixt some noble of our nation
And this brave prince, forsooth!

Dalyell.   'Twill prove too fatal;
Wise Huntley fears the threatening. Bless the lady
From such a ruin!

    Crawford.   How the counsel privy
Of this young Phaëthon do screw their faces
Into a gravity their trades, good people,
Were never guilty of! the meanest of 'em
Dreams of at least an office in the state.

    Dalyell. Sure, not the hangman's; 'tis bespoke already
For service to their rogueships—Silence!

Enter King JAMES *and* Earl of HUNTLEY.

    King James.   Do not
Argue against our will; we have descended
Somewhat—as we may term it—too familiarly
From justice of our birthright, to examine
The force of your allegiance,—sir, we have,—
But find it short of duty.

    Huntley.   Break my heart,
Do, do, king! Have my services, my loyalty,—
Heaven knows untainted ever,—drawn upon me
Contempt now in mine age, when I but wanted
A minute of a peace not to be troubled,
My last, my long one? Let me be a dotard,
A bedlam, a poor sot, or what you please
To have me, so you will not stain your blood,
Your own blood, royal sir, though mixed with mine,
By marriage of this girl [16] to a straggler:
Take, take my head, sir; whilst my tongue can wag,
It cannot name him other.

    King James.   Kings are counterfeits
In your repute, grave oracle, not presently
Set on their thrones with sceptres in their fists.

[16] "To put it out of doubt that he took him (Perkin) to be a great prince, and
not a representation only, he (King James) gave consent that this duke should
take to wife the Lady Katherine Gordon, daughter to the Earl of Huntley, being
a near kinswoman to the king himself, and a young virgin of excellent beauty
and virtue."—*Bacon.*

But use your own detraction; 'tis our pleasure
To give our cousin York for wife our kinswoman,
The Lady Katherine: instinct of sovereignty
Designs the honour, though her peevish father
Usurps our resolution.

 Huntley.   O, 'tis well,
Exceeding well! I never was ambitious
Of using congees to my daughter-queen—
A queen! perhaps a quean!—Forgive me, Dalyell,
Thou honourable gentleman;—none here
Dare speak one word of comfort?

 Dalyell.   Cruel misery!

 Crawford. The lady, gracious prince, may-be hath **settled**
Affection on some former choice.

 Dalyell.   Enforcement
Would prove but tyranny.

 Huntley.   I thank ye heartily.
Let any yeoman of our nation challenge
An interest in the girl, then the king
May add a jointure of ascent in titles,
Worthy a free consent; now he pulls down
What old desert hath builded.

 King James.   Cease persuasions.
I violate no pawns of faith, intrude not
On private loves: that I have played the orator
For kingly York to virtuous Kate, her grant
Can justify, referring her contents
To our provision. The Welsh Harry henceforth
Shall therefore know, and tremble to acknowledge,
That not the painted idol of his policy
Shall fright the lawful owner from a kingdom.
We are resolved.

 Huntley. Some of thy subjects' hearts,
King James, will bleed for this.

 King James.   Then shall their bloods
Be nobly spent. No more disputes; he is not
Our friend who contradicts us.

 Huntley.   Farewell, daughter!
My care by one is lessened, thank the king for't:
I and my griefs will dance now.

Enter PERKIN WARBECK, *leading, and complimenting with,*
Lady KATHERINE; Countess of CRAWFORD, JANE DOUGLAS,
FRION, JOHN A-WATER, ASTLEY, HERON, *and* SKELTON.

                                        Look, lords, look;
Here's hand in hand already!
 King James.   Peace, old frenzy!—
How like a king he looks! Lords, but observe
The confidence of his aspect; dross cannot
Cleave to so pure a metal—royal youth!
Plantagenet undoubted!
 Huntley. [*Aside*] Ho, brave!—Youth,
But no Plantagenet, by'r lady, yet,
By red rose or by white.
 Warbeck.   An union this way
Settles possession in a monarchy
Established rightly, as is my inheritance:
Acknowledge me but sovereign of this kingdom,
Your heart, fair princess, and the hand of providence
Shall crown you queen of me and my best fortunes.
 Katherine. Where my obedience is, my lord, a duty
Love owes true service.
 Warbeck.   Shall I?—
 King James.   Cousin, yes,
Enjoy her; from my hand accept your bride;
         [*He joins their hands.*
And may they live at enmity with comfort
Who grieve at such an equal pledge of troths!—
You are the prince's wife now.
 Katherine.   By your gift, sir.
 Warbeck. Thus I take seizure of mine own.
 Katherine.   I miss yet
A father's blessing. Let me find it;—humbly
Upon my knees I seek it.
 Huntley.   I am Huntley,
Old Alexander Gordon, a plain subject,
Nor more nor less; and, lady, if you wish for
A blessing, you must bend your knees to Heaven;
For Heaven did give me you. Alas, alas,
What would you have me say? May all the happiness

My prayers ever sued to fall upon you
Preserve you in your virtues!—Prithee, Dalyell,
Come with me; for I feel thy griefs as full
As mine; let's steal away, and cry together.

Dalyell. My hopes are in their ruins.

     [*Exeunt* Earl of HUNTLEY *and* Lord DALYELL.

King James.   Good, kind Huntley
Is overjoyed: a fit solemnity
Shall perfect these delights.—Crawford, attend
Our order for the preparation.

     [*Exeunt all but* FRION, HERON, SKELTON,
      JOHN A-WATER, *and* ASTLEY.

Frion. Now, worthy gentlemen, have I not followed
My undertakings with success? Here's entrance
Into a certainty above a hope.

Heron. Hopes are but hopes; I was ever confident, when
I traded but in remnants, that my stars had reserved me to
the title of a viscount at least: honour is honour, though
cut out of any stuffs.[17]

Skelton. My brother Heron hath right wisely delivered
his opinion; for he that threads his needle with the sharp
eyes of industry shall in time go through-stitch with the
new suit of preferment.

Astley. Spoken to the purpose, my fine-witted brother
Skelton; for as no indenture but has its counterpane, no
noverint but his condition or defeasance; so no right but
may have claim, no claim but may have possession, any act
of parliament to the contrary notwithstanding.

Frion. You are all read in mysteries of state,
And quick of apprehension, deep in judgment,
Active in resolution; and 'tis pity
Such counsel should lie buried in obscurity.
But why, in such a time and cause of triumph,
Stands the judicious Mayor of Cork so silent?
Believe it, sir, as English Richard prospers,
You must not miss employment of high nature.

John a-Water. If men may be credited in their mortality,
which I dare not peremptorily aver but they may or not be,

---

[17] Heron, or Herne, as Bacon calls him, was a mercer; Skelton was a tailor;
and Astley a scrivener: they were all men of broken fortunes.—*Gifford.*

presumptions by this marriage are then, in sooth, of fruitful
expectation. Or else I must not justify other men's belief,
more than other should rely on mine.

Frion. Pith of experience! those that have borne office
Weigh every word before it can drop from them.
But, noble counsellors, since now the present
Requires in point of honour,—pray, mistake not,—
Some service to our lord, 'tis fit the Scots
Should not engross all glory to themselves
At this so grand and eminent solemnity.

Skelton. The Scots! the motion is defied: I had rather,
for my part, without trial of my country, suffer persecution
under the pressing-iron of reproach; or let my skin be
punched full of eyelet-holes with the bodkin of derision.

Astley. I will sooner lose both my ears on the pillory of
forgery.

Heron. Let me first live a bankrupt, and die in the lousy
Hole[18] of hunger, without compounding for sixpence in the
pound.

John a-Water. If men fail not in their expectations, there
may be spirits also that digest no rude affronts, Master
Secretary Frion, or I am cozened; which is possible, I grant.

Frion. Resolved like men of knowledge: at this feast, then,
In honour of the bride, the Scots, I know,
Will in some show, some masque, or some device,
Prefer their duties: now it were uncomely
That we be found less forward for our prince
Than they are for their lady; and by how much
We outshine them in persons of account,
By so much more will our endeavours meet with
A livelier applause. Great emperors
Have for their recreations undertook
Such kind of pastimes: as for the conceit,
Refer it to my study; the performance
You all shall share a thanks in: 'twill be grateful.

Heron. The motion is allowed: I have stole to a dancing
school when I was a prentice.

Astley. There have been Irish hubbubs, when I have made
one too.

---

[18] That part of the Counter prison in which the poorer prisoners were confined.

Skelton. For fashioning of shapes and cutting a cross-caper, turn me off to my trade again.

John a-Water. Surely there is, if I be not deceived, a kind of gravity in merriment; as there is, or perhaps ought to be, respect of persons in the quality of carriage, which is as it is construed, either so or so.

Frion. Still you come home to me; upon occasion
I find you relish courtship with discretion;
And such are fit for statesmen of your merits.
Pray ye wait the prince, and in his ear acquaint him
With this design; I'll follow and direct ye.

[*Exeunt all but* FRION.

O, the toil
Of humouring this abject scum of mankind,
Muddy-brained peasants! princes feel a misery
Beyond impartial sufferance, whose extremes
Must yield to such abettors:—yet[19] our tide
Runs smoothly, without adverse winds: run on!
   Flow to a full sea! time alone debates
   Quarrels forewritten in the book of fates.   [*Exit.*

ACT THE THIRD

SCENE I—*Westminster. The Palace*

Enter King HENRY, *with his gorget on, his sword, plume of feathers, and truncheon, followed by* URSWICK.

KING HENRY. How runs the time of day?
   Urswick.   Past ten, my lord.
   King Henry. A bloody hour will it prove to some,
Whose disobedience, like the sons o' the earth,
Throws a defiance 'gainst the face of heaven.
Oxford, with Essex and stout De la Pole,
Have quieted the Londoners, I hope,
And set them safe from fear.
   Urswick.   They are all silent.

19 *i.e.* As yet.

King Henry. From their own battlements they may be-
        hold
Saint George's-fields o'erspread with armèd men;
Amongst whom our own royal standard threatens
Confusion to opposers: we must learn
To practise war again in time of peace,
Or lay our crown before our subjects' feet;
Ha, Urswick, must we not?

    Urswick.   The powers who seated
King Henry on his lawful throne will ever
Rise up in his defence.

    King Henry.   Rage shall not fright
The bosom of our confidence: in Kent
Our Cornish rebels, cozened of their hopes,
Met brave resistance by that country's earl,
George Abergeny, Cobham, Poynings, Guilford,
And other loyal hearts; now, if Blackheath
Must be reserved the fatal tomb to swallow
Such stiff-necked abjects as with weary marches
Have travelled from their homes, their wives, and children,
To pay, instead of subsidies, their lives,
We may continue sovereign. Yet, Urswick,
We'll not abate one penny what in parliament
Hath freely been contributed; we must not;
Money gives soul to action. Our competitor,
The Flemish counterfeit, with James of Scotland,
Will prove what courage need and want can nourish,
Without the food of fit supplies:—but, Urswick,
I have a charm in secret that shall loose
The witchcraft wherewith young King James is bound,
And free it at my pleasure without bloodshed.

    Urswick. Your majesty's a wise king, sent from heaven,
Protector of the just.

    King Henry.   Let dinner cheerfully
Be served in; this day of the week is ours,
Our day of providence; for Saturday
Yet never failed in all my undertakings
To yield me rest at night. [*A flourish.*]—What means this
        warning?
Good fate, speak peace to Henry!

Enter Lord DAWBENEY, Earl of OXFORD, *and* Attendants.

Dawbeney.   Live the king,
Triumphant in the ruin of his enemies!

Oxford. The head of strong rebellion is cut off,
The body hewed in pieces.

King Henry.   Dawbeney, Oxford,
Minions to noblest fortunes, how yet stands
The comfort of your wishes?

Dawbeney.   Briefly thus:
The Cornish under Audley, disappointed
Of flattered expectation, from the Kentish—
Your majesty's right-trusty liegemen—flew,
Feathered by rage and heartened by presumption,
To take the field even at your palace-gates,
And face you in your chamber-royal: arrogance
Improved their ignorance; for they, supposing,
Misled by rumour, that the day of battle
Should fall on Monday, rather braved your forces
Than doubted any onset; yet this morning,
When in the dawning I, by your direction,
Strove to get Deptford-strand bridge, there I found
Such a resistance as might show what strength
Could make: here arrows hailed in showers upon us
A full yard long at least; but we prevailed.
My Lord of Oxford, with his fellow peers
Environing the hill, fell fiercely on them
On the one side, I on the other, till, great sir,—
Pardon the oversight,—eager of doing
Some memorable act, I was engaged
Almost a prisoner, but was freed as soon
As sensible of danger: now the fight
Began in heat, which quenched in the blood of
Two thousand rebels, and as many more
Reserved to try your mercy, have returned
A victory with safety.

King Henry.   Have we lost
An equal number with them?

Oxford.   In the total
Scarcely four hundred. Audley, Flammock, Joseph,

The ringleaders of this commotion,
Railèd [20] in ropes, fit ornaments for traitors,
Wait your determinations.

    King Henry.   We must pay
Our thanks where they are only due: O, lords,
Here is no victory, nor shall our people
Conceive that we can triumph in their falls.
Alas, poor souls! let such as are escaped
Steal to the country back without pursuit:
There's not a drop of blood spilt but hath drawn
As much of mine; their swords could have wrought wonders
On their king's part, who faintly were unsheathed
Against their prince, but wounded their own breasts.
Lords, we are debtors to your care; our payment
Shall be both sure and fitting your deserts.

    Dawbeney. Sir, will you please to see those rebels, heads
Of this wild monster-multitude?

    King Henry.   Dear friend,
My faithful Dawbeney, no; on them our justice
Must frown in terror; I will not vouchsafe
An eye of pity to them. Let false Audley
Be drawn upon an hurdle from the Newgate
To Tower-hill in his own coat of arms
Painted on paper, with the arms reversed,
Defaced and torn; there let him lose his head.[21]
The lawyer and the blacksmith shall be hanged,
Quartered; their quarters into Cornwall sent
Examples to the rest, whom we are pleased
To pardon and dismiss from further quest.—
My Lord of Oxford, see it done.

    Oxford.   I shall, sir.

    King Henry. Urswick!

    Urswick.   My lord?

    King Henry.   To Dinham, our high-treasurer,
Say, we command commissions be new granted

---

[20] As the R is very indistinct, I should have been inclined, perhaps, to make "Haled" out of it, had I not found the expression in Bacon; "they were brought to London all railed in ropes, like a team of horses in a cart."—*Gifford.*

[21] "The Lord Audley was led from Newgate to Tower-hill, in a paper coat painted with his own arms, the arms reversed, the coat torn, and at Tower-hill beheaded."—*Bacon.*

For the collection of our subsidies
Through all the west, and that speedily.—
Lords, we acknowledge our engagements due
For your most constant services.

    Dawbeney.   Your soldiers
Have manfully and faithfully acquitted
Their several duties.

    King Henry.   For it we will throw
A largess free amongst them, which shall hearten
And cherish-up their loyalties. More yet
Remains of like employment; not a man
Can be dismissed, till enemies abroad,
More dangerous than these at home, have felt
The puissance of our arms. O, happy kings
Whose thrones are raisèd in their subjects' hearts! [*Exeunt.*

SCENE II—*Edinburgh. The Palace*

Enter Earl of HUNTLEY *and* Lord DALYELL.

    Huntley. Now, sir, a modest word with you, sad gentle-
        man:
Is not this fine, I trow, to see the gambols,
To hear the jigs, observe the frisks, be enchanted
With the rare discord of bells, pipes, and tabors,
Hotch-potch of Scotch and Irish twingle-twangles,
Like to so many quiristers of Bedlam
Trolling a catch! The feasts, the manly stomachs,
The healths in usquebaugh and bonny-clabber,[22]
The ale in dishes never fetched from China,
The hundred-thousand knacks not to be spoken of,—
And all this for King Oberon and Queen Mab,—
Should put a soul into ye. Look ye, good man,
How youthful I am grown: but, by your leave,
This new queen-bride must henceforth be no more
My daughter; no, by'r lady, 'tis unfit:

---

22 A common name for curds-and-whey, or sour buttermilk; a favourite drink
both with the Scotch and Irish.

And yet you see how I do bear this change,
Methinks courageously: then shake off care
In such a time of jollity.

    Dalyell.   Alas, sir,
How can you cast a mist upon your griefs?
Which, howsoe'er you shadow, but present
To any judging eye the perfect substance,
Of which mine are but counterfeits.

    Huntley.   Foh, Dalyell!
Thou interrupt'st the part I bear in music
To this rare bridal-feast; let us be merry,
Whilst flattering calms secure us against storms:
Tempests, when they begin to roar, put out
The light of peace, and cloud the sun's bright eye
In darkness of despair; yet we are safe.

    Dalyell. I wish you could as easily forget
The justice of your sorrows as my hopes
Can yield to destiny.

    Huntley.   Pish! then I see
Thou dost not know the flexible condition
Of my apt nature: I can laugh, laugh heartily,
When the gout cramps my joints; let but the stone
Stop in my bladder, I am straight a-singing;
The quartan-fever, shrinking every limb,
Sets me a-capering straight; do but betray me,
And bind me a friend ever: what! I trust
The losing of a daughter, though I doted
On every hair that grew to trim her head,
Admits not any pain like one of these.
Come, thou'rt deceived in me: give me a blow,
A sound blow on the face, I'll thank thee for't;
I love my wrongs: still thou'rt deceived in me.

    Dalyell. Deceived! O, noble Huntley, my few years
Have learnt experience of too ripe an age
To forfeit fit credulity: forgive
My rudeness, I am bold.

    Huntley.   Forgive me first
A madness of ambition; by example
Teach me humility, for patience scorns
Lectures, which schoolmen use to read to boys

Uncapable of injuries: though old,
I could grow tough in fury, and disclaim
Allegiance to my king; could fall at odds
With all my fellow-peers that durst not stand
Defendants 'gainst the rape done on mine honour:
But kings are earthly gods, there is no meddling
With their anointed bodies; for their actions
They only are accountable to heaven.
Yet in the puzzle of my troubled brain
One antidote's reserved against the poison
Of my distractions; 'tis in thee t' apply it.
 Dalyell. Name it; O, name it quickly, sir!
 Huntley.   **A pardon**
For my most foolish slighting thy deserts;
I have culled out this time to beg it: prithee,
Be gentle; had I been so, thou hadst owned
A happy bride, but now a castaway,
And never child of mine more.
 Dalyell.   Say not so, sir;
It is not fault in her.
 Huntley.   The world would prate
How she was handsome; young I know she was,
Tender, and sweet in her obedience;
But lost now: what a bankrupt am I made
Of a full stock of blessings! Must I hope
A mercy from thy heart?
 Dalyell.   A love, a service,
A friendship to posterity.
 Huntley.   Good angels
Reward thy charity! I have no more
But prayers left me now.
 Dalyell.   I'll lend you mirth, sir,
If you will be in consort.
 Huntley.   Thank you truly:
I must; yes, yes, I must;—here's yet some ease,
A partner in affliction: look not angry.
 Dalyell. Good, noble sir!   [*Flourish.*
 Huntley.   O, hark! we may be quiet,
The King and all the others come; a meeting
Of gaudy sights: this day's the last of revels;

To-morrow sounds of war; then new exchange;
Fiddles must turn to swords.—Unhappy marriage!

A flourish. Enter King JAMES, PERKIN WARBECK *leading*
Lady KATHERINE, Earl of CRAWFORD *and his* Countess;
JANE DOUGLAS, *and other* Ladies. Earl of HUNTLEY *and*
Lord DALYELL *fall in among them.*

   King James. Cousin of York, you and your princely bride
Have liberally enjoyed such soft delights
As a new-married couple could forethink;
Nor has our bounty shortened expectation:
But after all those pleasures of repose,
Of amorous safety, we must rouse the ease
Of dalliance with achievements of more glory
Than sloth and sleep can furnish: yet, for farewell,
Gladly we entertain a truce with time,
To grace the joint endeavours of our servants.
   Warbeck. My royal cousin, in your princely favour
The extent of bounty hath been so unlimited,
As only an acknowledgment in words
Would breed suspicion in our state and quality.
When we shall, in the fulness of our fate,—
Whose minister, necessity, will perfect,—
Sit on our own throne; then our arms, laid open
To gratitude, in sacred memory
Of these large benefits, shall twine them close,
Even to our thoughts and heart, without distinction.
Then James and Richard, being in effect
One person, shall unite and rule one people,
Divisible in titles only.
   King James.   Seat ye.—
Are the presenters ready?
   Crawford.   All are entering.
   Huntley. Dainty sport toward, Dalyell! sit; come, sit,
Sit and be quiet; here are kingly bug's-words! [23]

Enter at one door Four Scotch Antics, *accordingly habited;
at another,* WARBECK'S *followers, disguised as* Four Wild
Irish *in trowses,*[24] *long-haired, and accordingly habited.
Music. A dance by the* Masquers.

[23] Alarming words; "bug" means a hobgoblin.
[24] Tight-fitting drawers.

King James. To all a general thanks!

Warbeck.   In the next room
Take your own shapes again; you shall receive
Particular acknowledgment.   [*Exeunt the* Masquers.

King James.   Enough
Of merriments.—Crawford, how far's our army
Upon the march?

Crawford.   At Hedon-hall, great king;
Twelve thousand, well-prepared.

King James.   Crawford, to-night
Post thither. We in person, with the prince,
By four o'clock to-morrow after dinner
Will be wi' ye; speed away!

Crawford.   I fly, my lord.   [*Exit.*

King James. Our business grows to head now: where's
          your secretary,
That he attends ye not to serve?

Warbeck.   With Marchmont,
Your herald.

King James. Good: the proclamation's ready;
By that it will appear how the English stand
Affected to your title.—Huntley, comfort
Your daughter in her husband's absence; fight
With prayers at home for us, who for your honours
Must toil in fight abroad.

Huntley.   Prayers are the weapons
Which men so near their graves as I do use;
I've little else to do.

King James.   To rest, young beauties!—
We must be early stirring; quickly part:
A kingdom's rescue craves both speed and art.—
Cousins, good-night.   [*A flourish.*

Warbeck.   Rest to our cousin-king.

Katherine. Your blessing, sir.

Huntley. Fair blessings on your highness! sure, you need
          'em.
          [*Exeunt all but* WARBECK, *Lady* KATHERINE, *and*
                    JANE.

Warbeck. Jane, set the lights down, and from us return
To those in the next room this little purse;

Say we'll deserve their loves.

Jane.   It shall be done, sir.   [*Exit.*

Warbeck. Now, dearest, ere sweet sleep shall seal those
      eyes,
Love's precious tapers, give me leave to use
A parting ceremony; for to-morrow
It would be sacrilege t' intrude upon
The temple of thy peace: swift as the morning
Must I break from the down of thy embraces,
To put on steel, and trace the paths which lead
Through various hazards to a careful throne.

  Katherine. My lord, I'd fain go wi' ye; there's small for-
      tune
In staying here behind.

  Warbeck.   The churlish brow
Of war, fair dearest, is a sight of horror
For ladies' entertainment: if thou hear'st
A truth of my sad ending by the hand
Of some unnatural subject, thou withal
Shalt hear how I died worthy of my right,
By falling like a king; and in the close,
Which my last breath shall sound, thy name, thou fairest,
Shall sing a requiem to my soul, unwilling
Only of greater glory, 'cause divided
From such a Heaven on earth as life with thee.
But these are chimes for funerals: my business
Attends on fortune of a sprightlier triumph;
For love and majesty are reconciled,
And vow to crown thee empress of the west.

  Katherine. You have a noble language, sir; your right
In me is without question, and however
Events of time may shorten my deserts
In others' pity, yet it shall not stagger
Or constancy or duty in a wife.
You must be king of me; and my poor heart
Is all I can call mine.

  Warbeck.   But we will live,
Live, beauteous virtue, by the lively test
Of our own blood, to let the counterfeit

Be known the world's contempt.

Katherine.   Pray, do not use
That word; it carries fate in't. The first suit
I ever made, I trust your love will grant.

Warbeck. Without denial, dearest.

Katherine.   That hereafter,
If you return with safety, no adventure
May sever us in tasting any fortune:
I ne'er can stay behind again.

Warbeck.   You're lady
Of your desires, and shall command your will;
Yet 'tis too hard to promise.

Katherine.   What our destinies
Have ruled-out in their books we must not search,
But kneel to.

Warbeck. Then to fear when hope is fruitless,
Were to be desperately miserable;
Which poverty our greatness dares not dream of,
And much more scorns to stoop to: some few minutes
Remain yet; let's be thrifty in our hopes.   [*Exeunt.*

SCENE III—*The Palace at Westminster*

Enter King HENRY, HIALAS, *and* URSWICK.

King Henry. Your name is Pedro Hialas,[25] a Spaniard?

Hialas. Sir, a Castilian born.

King Henry.   King Ferdinand,
With wise Queen Isabel his royal consort,
Write ye a man of worthy trust and candour.
Princes are dear to heaven who meet with subjects
Sincere in their employments; such I find
Your commendation, sir. Let me deliver

[25] "Amongst these troubles came into England from Spain Peter Hialas, some call him Elias (surely he was the forerunner of the good hap that we enjoy at this day; for his ambassage set the truce between England and Scotland; the truce drew on the peace; the peace the marriage; and the marriage the union of the kingdoms); a man of great wisdom, and, as those times were, not unlearned."— *Bacon.*

How joyful I repute the amity
With your most fortunate master, who almost
Comes near a miracle in his success
Against the Moors, who had devoured his country,
Entire now to his sceptre. We, for our part,
Will imitate his providence, in hope
Of partage in the use on't: we repute
The privacy of his advisement to us
By you, intended an ambassador
To Scotland, for a peace between our kingdoms,
A policy of love, which well becomes
His wisdom and our care.

Hialas.   Your majesty
Doth understand him rightly.

    King Henry.   Else
Your knowledge can instruct me; wherein, sir,
To fall on ceremony would seem useless,
Which shall not need; for I will be as studious
Of your concealment in our conference
As any council shall advise.

Hialas.   Then, sir,
My chief request is, that on notice given
At my dispatch in Scotland, you will send
Some learnèd man of power and experience
To join entreaty with me.

    King Henry.   I shall do it,
Being that way well provided by a servant
Which may attend ye ever.

Hialas.   If King James,
By any indirection, should perceive
My coming near your court, I doubt the issue
Of my employment.

    King Henry.   Be not your own herald:
I learn sometimes without a teacher.

Hialas.   Good days
Guard all your princely thoughts!

    King Henry.   Urswick, no further
Than the next open gallery attend him.—
A hearty love go with you!

Hialas.   Your vowed beadsman.[26]

                 [Exeunt URSWICK *and* HIALAS.

   King Henry. King Ferdinand is not so much a fox,
But that a cunning huntsman may in time
Fall on the scent: in honourable actions
Safe imitation best deserves a praise.

Re-enter URSWICK.

What, the Castilian's passed away?
   Urswick.   He is,
And undiscovered; the two hundred marks
Your majesty conveyed, he gently pursed
With a right modest gravity.
   King Henry.   What was't
He muttered in the earnest of his wisdom?
He spoke not to be heard; 'twas about—
   Urswick.   Warbeck:
How if King Henry were but sure of subjects,
Such a wild runagate might soon be caged,
No great ado withstanding.
   King Henry.   Nay, nay; something
About my son Prince Arthur's match.
   Urswick.   Right, right, sir:
He hummed it out, how that King Ferdinand
Swore that the marriage 'twixt the Lady Katherine
His daughter and the Prince of Wales your son
Should never be consummated as long
As any Earl of Warwick lived in England,
Except by new creation.
   King Henry.   I remember
'Twas so, indeed: the king his master swore it?
   Urswick. Directly, as he said.
   King Henry.   An Earl of Warwick!—
Provide a messenger for letters instantly
To Bishop Fox. Our news from Scotland creeps;
It comes so slow, we must have airy spirits;
Our time requires dispatch.—*[Aside]* The Earl of War-
      wick!

---

[26] Servant; literally one bound to pray for his benefactor.

Let him be son to Clarence, younger brother
To Edward! Edward's daughter is, I think,
Mother to our Prince Arthur.—Get a messenger.   [*Exeunt.*

SCENE IV—*Before the Castle of Norham*

Enter King JAMES, PERKIN WARBECK, Earl of CRAWFORD,
Lord DALYELL, HERON, ASTLEY, JOHN a-WATER, SKELTON,
and Soldiers.

King James. We trifle time against these castle-walls;
The English prelate will not yield: once more
Give him a summons.   [*A parley is sounded.*

Enter on the walls the Bishop of DURHAM, *armed, a truncheon in his hand, with* Soldiers.

Warbeck.   See, the jolly clerk
Appears, trimmed like a ruffian!
  King James.   Bishop, yet
Set ope the ports, and to your lawful sovereign,
Richard of York, surrender up this castle,
And he will take thee to his grace; else Tweed
Shall overflow his banks with English blood,
And wash the sand that cements those hard stones
From their foundation.
  Durham.   Warlike King of Scotland,
Vouchsafe a few words from a man enforced
To lay his book aside, and clap on arms
Unsuitable to my age or my profession.
Courageous prince, consider on what grounds
You rend the face of peace, and break a league
With a confederate king that courts your amity,
For whom too? for a vagabond, a straggler,
Not noted in the world by birth or name,
An obscure peasant, by the rage of hell
Loosed from his chains to set great kings at strife.
What nobleman, what common man of note,
What ordinary subject hath come in,
Since first you footed on our territories,

To only feign a welcome? Children laugh at
Your proclamations, and the wiser pity
So great a potentate's abuse by one
Who juggles merely with the fawns and youth
Of an instructed compliment: such spoils,
Such slaughters as the rapine of your soldiers
Already have committed, is enough
To show your zeal in a conceited justice.
Yet, great king, wake not yet my master's vengeanc
But shake that viper off which gnaws your entrails.
I and my fellow-subjects are resolved,
If you persist, to stand your utmost fury,
Till our last blood drop from us.

   Warbeck.　　　　　　　　　O, sir, lend
No ear to this traducer of my honour!—
What shall I call thee, thou gray-bearded scandal,
That kick'st against the sovereignty to which
Thou ow'st allegiance?—Treason is bold-faced
And eloquent in mischief: sacred king,
Be deaf to his known malice.

   Durham.　　　　　　　　Rather yield
Unto those holy motions which inspire
The sacred heart of an anointed body.
It is the surest policy in princes
To govern well their own than seek encroachment
Upon another's right.

   Crawford.　　　　　The king is serious,
Deep in his meditations.

   Dalyell.　　　　　　Lift them up
To Heaven, his better genius!

   Warbeck.　　　　　　Can you study
While such a devil raves? O, sir!

   King James.　　　　　Well, bishop,
You'll not be drawn to mercy?

   Durham.　　　　　　　Construe me
In like case by a subject of your own:
My resolution's fixed: King James, be counselled,
A greater fate waits on thee.

           [*Exeunt* Bishop of DURHAM *and* Soldiers *from
            the walls.*

King James.   Forage through
The country; spare no prey of life or goods.
    Warbeck. O, sir, then give me leave to yield to nature;
I am most miserable: had I been
Born what this clergyman would by defame
Baffle belief with, I had never sought
The truth of mine inheritance with rapes
Of women or of infants murdered, virgins
Deflowered, old men butchered, dwellings fired,
My land depopulated, and my people
Afflicted with a kingdom's devastation:
Show more remorse, great king, or I shall never
Endure to see such havoc with dry eyes;
Spare, spare, my dear, dear England!
    King James.   You fool your piety
Ridiculously careful of an interest
Another man possesseth. Where's your faction?
Shrewdly the bishop guessed of your adherents,
When not a petty burgess of some town,
No, not a villager hath yet appeared
In your assistance: that should make ye whine,
And not your country's sufferance, as you term it.
    Dalyell. The king is angry.
    Crawford.   And the passionate duke
Effeminately dolent.
    Warbeck.   The experience
In former trials, sir, both of mine own
Or other princes cast out of their thrones,
Have so acquainted me how misery
Is destitute of friends or of relief,
That I can easily submit to taste
Lowest reproof without contempt or words.
    King James. An humble-minded man!

                    Enter FRION.

                                Now, what intelligence
Speaks Master Secretary Frion?
    Frion.   Henry
Of England hath in open field o'erthrown

The armies who opposed him in the right
Of this young prince.

    King James.   His subsidies, you mean:—
More, if you have it?

    Frion.   Howard, Earl of Surrey,
Backed by twelve earls and barons of the north,
An hundred knights and gentlemen of name,
And twenty thousand soldiers, is at hand
To raise your siege. Brooke, with a goodly navy,
Is admiral at sea; and Dawbeney follows
With an unbroken army for a second.

    Warbeck. 'Tis false! they come to side with us.

    King James.   *Retreat*
We shall not find them stones and walls to cope with.—
Yet, Duke of York, for such thou sayst thou art,
I'll try thy fortune to the height: to Surrey,
By Marchmont, I will send a brave defiance
For single combat; once a king will venture
His person to an earl, with condition
Of spilling lesser blood: Surrey is bold,
And James resolved.

    Warbeck.   O, rather, gracious sir,
Create me to this glory, since my cause
Doth interest this fair quarrel; valued least,
I am his equal.

    King James. I will be the man.—
March softly off: where victory can reap
A harvest crowned with triumph, toil is cheap. [*Exeunt.*

ACT THE FOURTH

SCENE I—*The English Camp near Ayton, on the Borders*

Enter Earl of SURREY, Bishop of DURHAM, Soldiers, *with drums and colours.*

SURREY. Are all our braving enemies shrunk back,
Hid in the fogs of their distempered climate,

Not daring to behold our colours wave
In spite of this infected air? Can they
Look on the strength of Cundrestine defaced?
The glory of Hedon-hall devasted? that
Of Edington cast down? the pile of Fulden
O'erthrown? and this the strongest of their forts,
Old Ayton-castle,[27] yielded and demolished?
And yet not peep abroad? The Scots are bold,
Hardy in battle; but it seems the cause
They undertake, considerèd, appears
Unjointed in the frame on't.
    Durham.   Noble Surrey,
Our royal master's wisdom is at all times
His fortune's harbinger; for when he draws
His sword to threaten war, his providence
Settles on peace, the crowning of an empire.

                              [A trumpet within.

    Surrey. Rank all in order: 'tis a herald's sound;
Some message from King James: keep a fixed station.

    Enter MARCHMONT *and another in* Heralds' *coats.*

    Marchmont. From Scotland's awful majesty we come
Unto the English general.
    Surrey.   To me?
Say on.
    Marchmont. Thus, then; the waste and prodigal
Effusion of so much guiltless blood
As in two potent armies of necessity
Must glut the earth's dry womb, his sweet compassion
Hath studied to prevent; for which to thee,
Great Earl of Surrey, in a single fight
He offers his own royal person; fairly
Proposing these conditions only, that
If victory conclude our master's right,
The earl shall deliver for his ransom
The town of Berwick to him, with the fishgarths;
If Surrey shall prevail, the king will pay
A thousand pounds down present for his freedom,

---

[27] At that time considered one of the strongest places between Berwick and Edinburgh.

And silence further arms: so speaks King James.

 Surrey. So speaks King James! so like a king he speaks.
Heralds, the English general returns
A sensible devotion from his heart,
His very soul, to this unfellowed grace:
For let the king know, gentle heralds, truly,
How his descent from his great throne, to honour
A stranger subject with so high a title
As his compeer in arms, hath conquered more
Than any sword could do; for which—my loyalty
Respected—I will serve his virtues ever
In all humility: but Berwick, say,
Is none of mine to part with; in affairs
Of princes subjects cannot traffic rights
Inherent to the crown. My life is mine,
That I dare freely hazard; and—with pardon
To some unbribed vainglory—if his majesty
Shall taste a change of fate, his liberty
Shall meet no articles. If I fall, falling
So bravely, I refer me to his pleasure
Without condition; and for this dear favour,
Say, if not countermanded, I will cease
Hostility, unless provoked.

 Marchmont.   This answer
We shall relate unpartially.

 Durham.   With favour,
Pray have a little patience.—[*Aside to* SURREY] Sir, you find
By these gay flourishes how wearied travail
Inclines a willing rest; here's but a prologue,
However confidently uttered, meant
For some ensuing acts of peace: consider
The time of year, unseasonableness of weather,
Charge, barrenness of profit; and occasion
Presents itself for honourable treaty,
Which we may make good use of. I will back,
As sent from you, in point of noble gratitude
Unto King James, with these his heralds: you
Shall shortly hear from me, my lord, for order
Of breathing or proceeding; and King Henry,
Doubt not, will thank the service.

Surrey. [*Aside to* Durham]   To your wisdom,
Lord Bishop, I refer it.

Durham. [*Aside to* Surrey] Be it so, then.

Surrey. Heralds, accept this chain and these few crowns.

Marchmont. Our duty, noble general.

Durham.   In part
Of retribution for such princely love,
My lord the general is pleased to show
The king your master his sincerest zeal,
By further treaty, by no common man:
I will myself return with you.

Surrey.   Y' oblige
My faithfullest affections t'ye, Lord Bishop.

Marchmont. All happiness attend your lordship!
                                        [*Exit with* Herald.

Surrey.   Come, friends
And fellow-soldiers; we, I doubt, shall meet
No enemies but woods and hills to fight with;
Then 'twere as good to feed and sleep at home:
We may be free from danger, not secure.   [*Exeunt.*

SCENE II—*The Scottish Camp*

Enter Perkin Warbeck *and* Frion.

Warbeck. Frion, O, Frion, all my hopes of glory
Are at a stand! the Scottish king grows dull,
Frosty, and wayward, since this Spanish agent
Hath mixed discourses with him; they are private,
I am not called to council now:—confusion
On all his crafty shrugs! I feel the fabric
Of my designs are tottering.

Frion.   Henry's policies
Stir with too many engines.

Warbeck.   Let his mines,
Shaped in the bowels of the earth, blow up
Works raised for my defence, yet can they never
Toss into air the freedom of my birth,
Or disavow my blood Plantagenet's:
I am my father's son still. But, O, Frion,

When I bring into count with my disasters
My wife's compartnership, my Kate's my life's,
Then, then my frailty feels an earthquake. Mischief
Damn Henry's plots! I will be England's king,
Or let my aunt of Burgundy report
My fall in the attempt deserved our ancestors!

   Frion. You grow too wild in passion: if you will
Appear a prince indeed, confine your will
To moderation.

   Warbeck.   What a saucy rudeness
Prompts this distrust! If? If I will appear!
Appear a prince! death throttle such deceits
Even in their birth of utterance! cursèd cozenage
Of trust! Ye make me mad: 'twere best, it seems,
That I should turn impostor to myself,
Be mine own counterfeit, belie the truth
Of my dear mother's womb, the sacred bed
Of a prince murdered and a living baffled!

   Frion. Nay, if you have no ears to hear, I have
No breath to spend in vain.

   Warbeck.   Sir, sir, take heed!
Gold and the promise of promotion rarely
Fail in temptation.

   Frion.   Why to me this?

   Warbeck.   Nothing.
Speak what you will; we are not sunk so low
But your advice may piece again the heart
Which many cares have broken: you were wont
In all extremities to talk of comfort;
Have ye none left now? I'll not interrupt ye.
Good, bear with my distractions! If King James
Deny us dwelling here, next whither must I?
I prithee, be not angry.

   Frion.   Sir, I told ye
Of letters come from Ireland; how the Cornish
Stomach their last defeat, and humbly sue
That with such forces as you could partake
You would in person land in Cornwall, where
Thousands will entertain your title gladly.

   Warbeck. Let me embrace thee, hug thee; thou'st revived

My comforts; if my cousin-king will fail,
Our cause will never.

> *Enter* JOHN A-WATER, HERON, ASTLEY, *and* SKELTON.

                Welcome, my tried friends!
You keep your brains awake in our defence.—
Frion, advise with them of these affairs,
In which be wondrous secret; I will listen
What else concerns us here: be quick and wary.   [*Exit.*

    Astley. Ah, sweet young prince!—Secretary, my fellow-counsellors and I have consulted, and jump all in one opinion directly; an if these Scotch garboils[28] do not fadge to our minds, we will pell-mell run amongst the Cornish choughs presently and in a trice.

    Skelton. 'Tis but going to sea and leaping ashore, cut ten or twelve thousand unnecessary throats, fire seven or eight towns, take half a dozen cities, get into the market-place, crown him Richard the Fourth, and the business is finished.

    John a-Water. I grant ye, quoth I, so far forth as men may do, no more than men may do; for it is good to consider when consideration may be to the purpose, otherwise—still you shall pardon me—little said is soon amended.

    Frion. Then you conclude the Cornish action surest?

    Heron. We do so, and doubt not but to thrive abundantly. Ho, my masters, had we known of the commotion when we set sail out of Ireland, the land had been ours ere this time.

    Skelton. Pish, pish! 'tis but forbearing being an earl or a duke a month or two longer. I say, and say it again, if the work go not on apace, let me never see new fashion more. I warrant ye, I warrant ye; we will have it so, and so it shall be.

    Astley. This is but a cold phlegmatic country, not stirring enough for men of spirit. Give me the heart of England for my money!

    Skelton. A man may batten there in a week only, with hot loaves and butter, and a lusty cup of muscadine and sugar at breakfast, though he make never a meal all the month after.

---

[28] Tumults.

John a-Water. Surely, when I bore office I found by experience that to be much troublesome was to be much wise and busy: I have observed how filching and bragging has been the best service in these last wars; and therefore conclude peremptorily on the design in England. If things and things may fall out, as who can tell what or how—but the end will show it.

Frion. Resolved like men of judgment! Here to linger
More time is but to lose it: cheer the prince
And haste him on to this; on this depends
Fame in success, or glory in our ends.   [*Exeunt.*

SCENE III—*Another part of the same*

Enter King JAMES, *the* Bishop of DURHAM, *and* HIALAS.

Hialas. France, Spain, and Germany combine a league
Of amity with England: nothing wants
For settling peace through Christendom, but love
Between the British monarchs, James and Henry.

Durham. The English merchants, sir, have been received
With general procession into Antwerp;
The emperor confirms the combination.

Hialas. The king of Spain resolves a marriage
For Katherine his daughter with Prince Arthur.

Durham. France courts this early contract.

Hialas.   What can hinder
A quietness in England?—

Durham.   But your suffrage
To such a silly creature, mighty sir,
As is but in effect an apparition,
A shadow, a mere trifle?

Hialas.   To this union
The good of both the church and commonwealth
Invite ye.

Durham. To this unity, a mystery
Of providence points out a greater blessing
For both these nations than our human reason
Can search into. King Henry hath a daughter,
The Princess Margaret; I need not urge

What honour, what felicity can follow
On such affinity 'twixt two Christian kings
Inleagued by ties of blood; but sure I am,
If you, sir, ratify the peace proposed,
I dare both motion and effect this marriage
For weal of both the kingdoms.

    King James.   Dar'st thou, lord bishop?

    Durham. Put it to trial, royal James, by sending
Some noble personage to the English court
By way of embassy.

    Hialas.   Part of the business
Shall suit my mediation.

    King James.   Well; what Heaven
Hath pointed out to be, must be: you two
Are ministers, I hope, of blessèd fate.
But herein only I will stand acquitted,
No blood of innocents shall buy my peace:
For Warbeck, as you nick him, came to me,
Commended by the states of Christendom,
A prince, though in distress; his fair demeanour,
Lovely behaviour, unappallèd spirit,
Spoke him not base in blood, however clouded.
The brute beasts have both rocks and caves to fly to,
And men the altars of the church; to us
He came for refuge: kings come near in nature
Unto the gods in being touched with pity.
Yet, noble friends, his mixture with our blood,
Even with our own, shall no way interrupt
A general peace; only I will dismiss him
From my protection, throughout my dominions,
In safety; but not ever to return.

    Hialas. You are a just king.

    Durham.   Wise, and herein happy

    King James. Nor will we dally in affairs of weight:
Huntley, lord bishop, shall with you to England
Ambassador from us: we will throw down
Our weapons; peace on all sides! Now repair
Unto our council; we will soon be with you.

    Hialas. Delay shall question no dispatch; Heaven crown
      it.   [*Exeunt* Bishop of DURHAM *and* HIALAS.

King James. A league with Ferdinand! a marriage
With English Margaret! a free release
From restitution for the late affronts!
Cessation from hostility! and all
For Warbeck, not delivered, but dismissed!
We could not wish it better.—Dalyell!

Enter Lord DALYELL.

Dalyell.   Here sir.
King James. Are Huntley and his daughter sent for?
Dalyell.   Sent for
And come, my lord.
King James.   Say to the English prince,
We want his company.
Dalyell.   He is at hand, sir.

Enter PERKIN WARBECK, Lady KATHERINE, JANE, FRION,
    HERON, SKELTON, JOHN A-WATER, *and* ASTLEY.

King James. Cousin, our bounty, favours, gentleness,
Our benefits, the hazard of our person,
Our people's lives, our land, hath evidenced
How much we have engaged on your behalf:
How trivial and how dangerous our hopes
Appear, how fruitless our attempts in war,
How windy, rather smoky, your assurance
Of party shows, we might in vain repeat:
But now obedience to the mother church,
A father's care upon his country's weal,
The dignity of state, direct our wisdom
To seal an oath of peace through Christendom;
To which we're sworn already: it is you
Must only seek new fortunes in the world,
And find an harbour elsewhere. As I promised
On your arrival, you have met no usage
Deserves repentance in your being here;
But yet I must live master of mine own:
However, what is necessary for you
At your departure, I am well content
You be accommodated with, provided
Delay prove not my enemy.

Warbeck.   It shall not
Most glorious prince. The fame of my designs
Soars higher than report of ease and sloth
Can aim at: I acknowledge all your favours
Boundless and singular; am only wretched
In words as well as means to thank the grace
That flowed so liberally. Two empires firmly
You're lord of,—Scotland and Duke Richard's heart:
My claim to mine inheritance shall sooner
Fail than my life to serve you, best of kings;
And, witness Edward's blood in me! I am
More loth to part with such a great example
Of virtue than all other mere respects.
But, sir, my last suit is, you will not force
From me what you have given,—this chaste lady,
Resolved on all extremes.
    Katherine.   I am your wife;
No human power can or shall divorce
My faith from duty.
    Warbeck.   Such another treasure
The earth is bankrupt of.
    King James.   I gave her, cousin,
And must avow the gift; will add withal
A furniture becoming her high birth
And unsuspected constancy; provide
For your attendance: we will part good friends.
                              [*Exit with* Lord DALYELL

    Warbeck. The Tudor hath been cunning in his plots:
His Fox of Durham would not fail at last.
But what? our cause and courage are our own:
Be men, my friends, and let our cousin-king
See how we follow fate as willingly
As malice follows us. Ye're all resolved
For the west parts of England?
    All.   Cornwall, Cornwall!
    Frion. The inhabitants expect you daily.
    Warbeck.   Cheerfully
Draw all our ships out of the harbour, friends;
Our time of stay doth seem too long, we must
Prevent intelligence; about it suddenly.

All. A prince, a prince, a prince!

      [*Exeunt* Heron, Skelton, Astley, *and* John
        a-Water.

Warbeck. Dearest, admit not into thy pure thoughts
The least of scruples, which may charge their softness
With burden of distrust. Should I prove wanting
To noblest courage now, here were the trial:
But I am perfect, sweet; I fear no change,
More than thy being partner in my sufferance.

    Katherine. My fortunes, sir, have armed me to encounter
What chance soe'er they meet with.—Jane, 'tis fit
Thou stay behind, for whither wilt thou wander?

    Jane. Never till death will I forsake my mistress,
Nor then in wishing to die with ye gladly.

    Katherine. Alas, good soul!

    Frion.   Sir, to your aunt of Burgundy
I will relate your present undertakings:
From her expect on all occasions welcome.
You cannot find me idle in your services.

    Warbeck. Go, Frion, go: wise men know how to soothe
Adversity, not serve it: thou hast waited
Too long on expectation; never yet
Was any nation read of so besotted
In reason as t' adore the setting sun.
Fly to the archduke's court; say to the duchess,
Her nephew, with fair Katherine his wife,
Are on their expectation to begin
The raising of an empire: if they fail,
Yet the report will never. Farewell, Frion!   [*Exit* Frion.
This man, Kate, has been true, though now of late
I fear too much familiar with the Fox.

    Re-enter Lord Dalyell *with the* Earl of Huntley.

    Huntley. I come to take my leave: you need not doubt
My interest in this sometime child of mine;
She's all yours now, good sir.—O, poor lost creature,
Heaven guard thee with much patience! if thou canst
Forget thy title to old Huntley's family,
As much of peace will settle in thy mind
As thou canst wish to taste but in thy grave.

Accept my tears yet, prithee; they are tokens
Of charity as true as of affection.

    Katherine. This is the cruell'st farewell!

    Huntley.   Love, young gentleman,
This model of my griefs; she calls you husband;
Then be not jealous of a parting kiss,—
It is a father's, not a lover's offering;
Take it, my last [*Kisses her*].—I am too much a child.
Exchange of passion is to little use,
So I should grow too foolish: goodness guide thee! [*Exit.*

    Katherine. Most miserable daughter!—Have you aught
To add, sir, to our sorrows?

    Dalyell.   I resolve,
Fair lady, with your leave, to wait on all
Your fortunes in my person, if your lord
Vouchsafe me entertainment.

    Warbeck. We will be bosom-friends, most noble Dalyell;
For I accept this tender of your love
Beyond ability of thanks to speak it.—
Clear thy drowned eyes, my fairest: time and industry
Will show us better days, or end the worst.   [*Exeunt.*

SCENE IV—*The Palace at Westminster*

Enter Earl of OXFORD *and* Lord DAWBENEY.

    Oxford. No news from Scotland yet, my lord?

    Dawbeney.   Not any
But what King Henry knows himself: I thought
Our armies should have marched that way; his mind,
It seems, is altered.

    Oxford.   Victory attends
His standard everywhere.

    Dawbeney.   Wise princes, Oxford,
Fight not alone with forces. Providence
Directs and tutors strength; else elephants
And barbèd horses might as well prevail
As the most subtle stratagems of war.

    Oxford. The Scottish king showed more than common
        bravery

In proffer of a combat hand to hand
With Surrey.

    Dawbeney. And but showed it: northern bloods
Are gallant being fired; but the cold climate,
Without good store of fuel, quickly freezeth
The glowing flames.

    Oxford.   Surrey, upon my life,
Would not have shrunk an hair's-breadth.

    Dawbeney.   May he forfeit
The honour of an English name and nature,
Who would not have embraced it with a greediness
As violent as hunger runs to food!
'Twas an addition any worthy spirit
Would covet, next to immortality,
Above all joys of life: we all missed shares
In that great opportunity.

Enter King Henry, *in close conversation with* Urswick.

    Oxford.   The king!
See, he comes smiling.

    Dawbeney.   O, the game runs smooth
On his side, then, believe it: cards well shuffled
And dealt with cunning bring some gamester thrift,
But others must rise losers.

    King Henry.   The train takes?

    Urswick. Most prosperously.

    King Henry.   I knew it should not miss.
He fondly angles who will hurl his bait
Into the water 'cause the fish at first
Plays round about the line and dares not bite.—
Lords, we may reign your king yet: Dawbeney, Oxford,
Urswick, must Perkin wear the crown?

    Dawbeney.   A slave!

    Oxford. A vagabond!

    Urswick.   A glow-worm!

    King Henry.   Now, if Frion,
His practised politician, wear a brain
Of proof, King Perkin will in progress ride
Through all his large dominions; let us meet him,

And tender homage: ha, sirs! liegemen ought
To pay their fealty.
    Dawbeney.   Would the rascal were,
With all his rabble, within twenty miles
Of London!
    King Henry. Farther off is near enough
To lodge him in his home: I'll wager odds,
Surrey and all his men are either idle
Or hasting back; they have not work, I doubt,
To keep them busy.
    Dawbeney.   'Tis a strange conceit, sir.
    King Henry. Such voluntary favours as our people
In duty aid us with, we never scattered
On cobweb parasites, or lavished out
In riot or a needless hospitality:
No undeserving favourite doth boast
His issues from our treasury; our charge
Flows through all Europe, proving us but steward
Of every contribution which provides
Against the creeping canker of disturbance.
Is it not rare, then, in this toil of state
Wherein we are embarked, with breach of sleep,
Cares, and the noise of trouble, that our mercy
Returns nor thanks nor comfort? Still the West
Murmur and threaten innovation,
Whisper our government tyrannical,
Deny us what is ours, nay, spurn their lives,
Of which they are but owners by our gift:
It must not be.
    Oxford.   It must not, should not.

           Enter Messenger *with a packet.*

    King Henry.   So then—
To whom?
    Messenger. This packet to your sacred majesty.
    King Henry. Sirrah, attend without.   [*Exit* Messenger.
    Oxford. News from the North, upon my life.
    Dawbeney.   Wise Henry
Divines aforehand of events; with him
Attempts and executions are one act.

King Henry. Urswick, thine ear: Frion is caught; the man
Of cunning is outreached; we must be safe.
Should reverend Morton, our archbishop, move
To a translation higher yet, I tell thee
My Durham owns a brain deserves that see;
He's nimble in his industry, and mounting—
Thou hear'st me?

Urswick.   And conceive your highness fitly.

King Henry. Dawbeney and Oxford, since our army stands
Entire, it were a weakness to admit
The rust of laziness to eat amongst them:
Set forward toward Salisbury; the plains
Are most commodious for their exercise.
Ourself will take a muster of them there;
And or disband them with reward, or else
Dispose as best concerns us.

Dawbeney.   Salisbury!
Sir, all is peace at Salisbury.

King Henry.   Dear friend,
The charge must be our own; we would a little
Partake the pleasure with our subjects' ease.—
Shall I entreat your loves?

Oxford.   Command our lives.

King Henry. Ye're men know how to do, not to forethink.
My bishop is a jewel tried and perfect;
A jewel, lords. The post who brought these letters
Must speed another to the Mayor of Exeter;
Urswick, dismiss him not.

Urswick.   He waits your pleasure.

King Henry. Perkin a king? a king!

Urswick.   My gracious lord,—

King Henry. Thoughts busied in the sphere of royalty
Fix not on creeping worms without their stings,
Mere excrements of earth. The use of time
Is thriving safety, and a wise prevention
Of ills expected. We're resolved for Salisbury.   [*Exeunt.*

SCENE V—*The Coast of Cornwall*

A general shout within. Enter PERKIN WARBECK, *Lord*
DALYELL, *Lady* KATHERINE, *and* JANE.

Warbeck. After so many storms as wind and seas
Have threatened to our weather-beaten ships,
At last, sweet fairest, we are safe arrived
On our dear mother earth, ingrateful only
To heaven and us in yielding sustenance
To sly usurpers of our throne and right.
These general acclamations are an omen
Of happy process to their welcome lord:
They flock in troops, and from all parts with wings
Of duty fly to lay their hearts before us.—
Unequalled pattern of a matchless wife,
How fares my dearest yet?
    Katherine.   Confirmed in health,
By which I may the better undergo
The roughest face of change; but I shall learn
Patience to hope, since silence courts affliction,
For comforts, to this truly noble gentleman,—
Rare unexampled pattern of a friend!—
And my belovèd Jane, the willing follower
Of all misfortunes.
    Dalyell.   Lady, I return
But barren crops of early protestations,
Frost-bitten in the spring of fruitless hopes.
    Jane. I wait but as the shadow to the body;
For madam, without you let me be nothing.
    Warbeck. None talk of sadness; we are on the way
Which leads to victory: keep cowards thoughts
With desperate sullenness! The lion faints not
Locked in a grate, but loose disdains all force
Which bars his prey,—and we are lion-hearted,—
Or else no king of beasts. [*Another general shout within.*]
    —Hark, how they shout,
Triumphant in our cause! bold confidence
Marches on bravely, cannot quake at danger.

Enter SKELTON.

Skelton. Save King Richard the Fourth! save thee, king of hearts! The Cornish blades are men of mettle; have proclaimed, through Bodmin and the whole county, my sweet prince Monarch of England: four thousand tall yeomen, with bow and sword, already vow to live and die at the foot of King Richard.

Enter ASTLEY.

Astley. The mayor, our fellow-counsellor, is servant for an emperor. Exeter is appointed for the rendezvous, and nothing wants to victory but courage and resolution. *Sigillatum et datum decimo Septembris, anno regni regis primo, et cætera; confirmatum est.* All's cock-sure.

Warbeck. To Exeter! to Exeter, march on!
Commend us to our people: we in person
Will lend them double spirits; tell them so.

 Skelton and Astley. King Richard, King Richard!

        [*Exeunt* SKELTON *and* ASTLEY.

Warbeck. A thousand blessings guard our lawful arms!
A thousand horrors pierce our enemies' souls!
Pale fear unedge their weapons' sharpest points!
And when they draw their arrows to the head,
Numbness shall strike their sinews! Such advantage
Hath Majesty in its pursuit of justice,
That on the proppers-up of Truth's old throne
It both enlightens counsel and gives heart
To execution; whiles the throats of traitors
Lie bare before our mercy. O, divinity
Of royal birth! how it strikes dumb the tongues
Whose prodigality of breath is bribed
By trains to greatness! Princes are but men
Distinguished in the fineness of their frailty,
Yet not so gross in beauty of the mind;
For there's a fire more sacred purifies
The dross of mixture. Herein stand the odds,
Subjects are men on earth, kings men and gods. [*Exeunt.*

ACT THE FIFTH

SCENE I—*St. Michael's Mount, Cornwall*

Enter Lady KATHERINE *and* JANE *in riding-suits, with one* Servant.

LADY KATHERINE. It is decreed; and we must yield to fate,
Whose angry justice, though it threaten ruin,
Contempt, and poverty, is all but trial
Of a weak woman's constancy in suffering.
Here, in a stranger's and an enemy's land,
Forsaken and unfurnished of all hopes
But such as wait on misery, I range,
To meet affliction wheresoe'er I tread.
My train and pomp of servants is reduced
To one kind gentlewoman and this groom.—
Sweet Jane, now whither must we?

   Jane.   To your ships,
Dear lady, and turn home.

   Katherine.   Home! I have none.
Fly thou to Scotland; thou hast friends will weep
For joy to bid thee welcome; but, O, Jane,
My Jane! my friends are desperate of comfort,
As I must be of them: the common charity,
Good people's alms and prayers of the gentle,
Is the revenue must support my state.
As for my native country, since it once
Saw me a princess in the height of greatness
My birth allowed me, here I make a vow
Scotland shall never see me being fall'n
Or lessened in my fortunes. Never, Jane,
Never to Scotland more will I return.
Could I be England's queen,—a glory, Jane,
I never fawned on,—yet the king who gave me
Hath sent me with my husband from his presence,
Delivered us suspected to his nation,
Rendered us spectacles to time and pity;

And is it fit I should return to such
As only listen after our descent
From happiness enjoyed to misery
Expected, though uncertain? Never, never!
Alas, why dost thou weep? and that poor creature
Wipe his wet cheeks too? let me feel alone
Extremities, who know to give them harbour;
Nor thou nor he has cause: you may live safely.

Jane. There is no safety whiles your dangers, madam,
Are every way apparent.

   Servant.   Pardon, lady,
I cannot choose but show my honest heart;
You were ever my good lady.

   Katherine.   O, dear souls,
Your shares in grief are too-too much!

          Enter Lord DALYELL.

Dalyell.   I bring,
Fair princess, news of further sadness yet
Than your sweet youth hath been acquainted with.

   Katherine. Not more, my lord, than I can welcome: speak
      it;
The worst, the worst I look for.

   Dalyell.   All the Cornish
At Exeter were by the citizens
Repulsed, encountered by the Earl of Devonshire
And other worthy gentlemen of the country.
Your husband marched to Taunton, and was there
Affronted [29] by King Henry's chamberlain;
The king himself in person with his army
Advancing nearer, to renew the fight
On all occasions: but the night before
The battles were to join, your husband privately,
Accompanied with some few horse, departed
From out the camp, and posted none knows whither.

   Katherine. Fled without battle given?

   Dalyell.   Fled, but followed
By Dawbeney; all his parties left to taste

---

[29] Confronted.

King Henry's mercy,—for to that they yielded,—
Victorious without bloodshed.

    Katherine.   O, my sorrows!
If both our lives had proved the sacrifice
To Henry's tyranny, we had fall'n like princes,
And robbed him of the glory of his pride.

    Dalyell. Impute it not to faintness or to weakness
Of noble courage, lady, but to foresight;
For by some secret friend he had intelligence
Of being bought and sold by his base followers.
Worse yet remains untold.

    Katherine.   No, no, it cannot.

    Dalyell. I fear you are betrayed: the Earl of Oxford
Runs hot in your pursuit.[30]

    Katherine.   He shall not need;
We'll run as hot in resolution gladly
To make the earl our jailer.

    Jane.   Madam, madam,
They come, they come!

    Enter Earl of OXFORD *with his* Followers.

    Dalyell.   Keep back! or he who dares
Rudely to violate the law of honour
Runs on my sword.

    Katherine.   Most noble sir, forbear.—
What reason draws you hither, gentlemen?
Whom seek ye?

    Oxford.   All stand off!—With favour, lady,
From Henry, England's king, I would present
Unto the beauteous princess, Katherine Gordon,
The tender of a gracious entertainment.

    Katherine. We are that princess, whom your master-king
Pursues with reaching arms to draw into
His power: let him use his tyranny,
We shall not be his subject.

    Oxford.   My commission
Extends no further, excellentest lady,

---

[30] "There were also sent with all speed some horse to St. Michael's Mount in Cornwall, where the Lady Katherine Gordon was left by her husband, whom in all fortunes she entirely loved, adding the virtues of a wife to the virtues of her sex."—*Bacon.*

Than to a service; 'tis King Henry's pleasure
That you, and all that have relation t'ye,
Be guarded as becomes your birth and greatness;
For, rest assured, sweet princess, that not aught
Of what you do call yours shall find disturbance,
Or any welcome other than what suits
Your high condition.

   Katherine.   By what title, sir,
May I acknowledge you?

   Oxford.   Your servant, lady,
Descended from the line of Oxford's earls,
Inherits what his ancestors before him
Were owners of.

   Katherine.   Your king is herein royal,
That by a peer so ancient in desert
As well as blood commands us to his presence.

   Oxford. Invites ye, princess, not commands.

   Katherine.   Pray use
Your own phrase as you list: to your protection
Both I and mine submit.

   Oxford.   There's in your number
A nobleman whom fame hath bravely spoken.
To him the king my master bade me say
How willingly he courts his friendship; far
From an enforcement, more than what in terms
Of courtesy so great a prince may hope for.

   Dalyell. My name is Dalyell.

   Oxford.   'Tis a name hath won
Both thanks and wonder from report, my lord:
The court of England emulates your merit,
And covets to embrace you.

   Dalyell.   I must wait on
The princess in her fortunes.

   Oxford.   Will you please,
Great lady, to set forward?

   Katherine.   Being driven
By fate, it were in vain to strive with Heaven.   [*Exeunt.*

SCENE II—*Salisbury*

Enter King HENRY, Earl of SURREY, URSWICK, and a
guard of Soldiers.

King Henry. The counterfeit, King Perkin, is escaped:—
Escaped! so let him; he is hedged too fast
Within the circuit of our English pale
To steal out of our ports, or leap the walls
Which guard our land; the seas are rough and wider
Than his weak arms can tug with. Surrey, henceforth
Your king may reign in quiet; turmoils past,
Like some unquiet dream, have rather busied
Our fancy than affrighted rest of state.
But, Surrey, why, in articling a peace
With James of Scotland, was not restitution
Of losses which our subjects did sustain
By the Scotch inroads questioned?

Surrey.   Both demanded
And urged, my lord; to which the king replied,
In modest merriment, but smiling earnest,
How that our master Henry was much abler
To bear the detriments than he repay them.

King Henry. The young man, I believe, spake honest
      truth;
He studies to be wise betimes.—Has, Urswick,
Sir Rice ap Thomas, and Lord Brook our steward,
Returned the Western gentlemen full thanks
From us for their tried loyalties?

Urswick.   They have;
Which, as if health and life had reigned amongst 'em,
With open hearts they joyfully received.

King Henry. Young Buckingham is a fair-natured prince,
Lovely in hopes, and worthy of his father;
Attended by an hundred knights and squires
Of special name he tendered humble service,
Which we must ne'er forget: and Devonshire's wounds,
Though slight, shall find sound cure in our respect.

Enter Lord DAWBENEY *with a* Guard, *leading in* PERKIN
   WARBECK, HERON, JOHN A-WATER, ASTLEY, *and* SKELTON,
   chained.

Dawbeney. Life to the king, and safety fix his throne!
I here present you, royal sir, a shadow
Of majesty, but in effect a substance
Of pity; a young man, in nothing grown
To ripeness but the ambition of your mercy,—
Perkin, the Christian world's strange wonder.
   King Henry.   Dawbeney,
We observe no wonder: I behold, 'tis true,
An ornament of nature, fine and polished,
A handsome youth indeed, but not admire him.
How came he to thy hands?
   Dawbeney.   From sanctuary
At Bewley, near Southampton; registered,
With these few followers, for persons privileged.
   King Henry. I must not thank you, sir; you were to blame
T' infringe the liberty of houses sacred:
Dare we be irreligious?
   Dawbeney.   Gracious lord,
They voluntarily resigned themselves
Without compulsion.
   King Henry.   So? 'twas very well;
'Twas very, very well.—Turn now thine eyes,
Young man, upon thyself and thy past actions;
What revels in combustion through our kingdom
A frenzy of aspiring youth hath danced,
Till, wanting breath, thy feet of pride have slipt
To break thy neck!
   Warbeck.   But not my heart; my heart
Will mount till every drop of blood be frozen
By death's perpetual winter: if the sun
Of majesty be darkened, let the sun
Of life be hid from me in an eclipse
Lasting and universal. Sir, remember
There was a shooting-in of light when Richmond,
Not aiming at a crown, retired, and gladly,
For comfort to the Duke of Bretaine's court.

Richard, who swayed the sceptre, was reputed
A tyrant then; yet then a dawning glimmered
To some few wandering remnants, promising day
When first they ventured on a frightful shore
At Milford Haven;—

Dawbeney.　　　　　Whither speeds his boldness?
Check his rude tongue, great sir.

King Henry.　　　　　　　O, let him range:
The player's on the stage still, 'tis his part;
He does but act.—What followed?

Warbeck.　　　　　　　　Bosworth Field;
Where, at an instant, to the world's amazement,
A morn to Richmond, and a night to Richard,
Appeared at once: the tale is soon applied;
Fate, which crowned these attempts when least assured,
Might have befriended others like resolved.

King Henry. A pretty gallant! Thus your aunt of Bur-
　　　　　gundy,
Your duchess-aunt, informed her nephew; so,
The lesson prompted and well conned, was moulded
Into familiar dialogue, oft rehearsed,
Till, learnt by heart, 'tis now received for truth.

Warbeck. Truth, in her pure simplicity, wants art
To put a feignèd blush on: scorn wears only
Such fashion as commends to gazers' eyes
Sad ulcerated novelty, far beneath
The sphere of majesty: in such a court
Wisdom and gravity are proper robes,
By which the sovereign is best distinguished
From zanies to his greatness.

King Henry.　　　　　　Sirrah, shift
Your antic pageantry, and now appear
In your own nature, or you'll taste the danger
Of fooling out of season.

Warbeck.　　　　　　I expect
No less than what severity calls justice,
And politicians safety; let such beg
As feed on alms: but if there can be mercy
In a protested enemy, then may it
Descend to these poor creatures, whose engagements,

To the bettering of their fortunes, have incurred
A loss of all; to them if any charity
Flow from some noble orator, in death
I owe the fee of thankfulness.
 King Henry.   So brave!
What a bold knave is this!—Which of these rebels
Has been the Mayor of Cork?
 Dawbeney.   This wise formality.—
Kneel to the king, ye rascals!   [*They kneel.*
 King Henry.   Canst thou hope
A pardon, where thy guilt is so apparent?
 John a-Water. Under your good favours, as men are men,
they may err; for I confess, respectively, in taking great
parts, the one side prevailing, the other side must go down:
herein the point is clear, if the proverb hold, that hanging
goes by destiny, that it is to little purpose to say, this thing
or that shall be thus or thus; for, as the Fates will have it,
so it must be; and who can help it?
 Dawbeney. O, blockhead! thou a privy-counsellor?
Beg life, and cry aloud, "Heaven save King Henry!"
 John a-Water. Every man knows what is best, as it hap-
pens; for my own part, I believe it is true, if I be not deceived, that kings must be kings and subjects subjects; but
which is which, you shall pardon me for that: whether we
speak or hold our peace, all are mortal; no man knows his
end.
 King Henry. We trifle time with follies.
 Heron. John a-Water. Astley. Skelton. Mercy, mercy!
 King Henry. Urswick, command the dukeling and these
   fellows   [*They rise.*
To Digby, the lieutenant of the Tower:
With safety let them be conveyed to London.
It is our pleasure no uncivil outrage,
Taunts or abuse be suffered to their persons;
They shall meet fairer law than they deserve.
Time may restore their wits, whom vain ambition
Hath many years distracted.
 Warbeck.   Noble thoughts
Meet freedom in captivity: the Tower,—
Our childhood's dreadful nursery!

King Henry.   No more!

Urswick. Come, come, you shall have leisure to bethink
 ye. [*Exit* URSWICK *with* PERKIN WARBECK *and*
    his Followers, *guarded.*

King Henry. Was ever so much impudence in forgery?
The custom, sure, of being styled a king
Hath fastened in his thought that he is such;
But we shall teach the lad another language:
'Tis good we have him fast.

Dawbeney.   The hangman's physic
Will purge this saucy humour.

King Henry.   Very likely;
Yet we could temper mercy with extremity,
Being not too far provoked.

Enter Earl of OXFORD, Lady KATHERINE *in her richest attire,*
  Lord DALYELL, JANE, *and* Attendants.

Oxford.   Great sir, be pleased,
With your accustomed grace to entertain
The Princess Katherine Gordon.

King Henry.   Oxford, herein
We must beshrew thy knowledge of our nature.
A lady of her birth and virtues could not
Have found us so unfurnished of good manners
As not, on notice given, to have met her
Half way in point of love.—Excuse, fair cousin,
The oversight: O, fie! you may not kneel;
'Tis most unfitting: first, vouchsafe this welcome,
A welcome to your own; for you shall find us
But guardian to your fortune and your honours.

Katherine. My fortunes and mine honours are weak
 champions,
As both are now befriended, sir: however,
Both bow before your clemency.

King Henry.   Our arms
Shall circle them from malice.—A sweet lady!
Beauty incomparable!—here lives majesty
At league with love.

Katherine.   O, sir, I have a husband.

King Henry. We'll prove your father, husband, friend,
    and servant,
Prove what you wish to grant us.—Lords, be careful
A patent presently be drawn for issuing
A thousand pounds from our exchequer yearly
During our cousin's life.—Our queen shall be
Your chief companion, our own court your home,
Our subjects all your servants.

Katherine.   But my husband?

King Henry. By all descriptions, you are noble Dalyell,
Whose generous truth hath famed a rare observance.
We thank ye; 'tis a goodness gives addition
To every title boasted from your ancestry,
In all most worthy.

Dalyell.   Worthier than your praises,
Right princely sir, I need not glory in.

King Henry. Embrace him, lords.—Whoever calls you
    mistress
Is lifted in our charge.—A goodlier beauty
Mine eyes yet ne'er encountered.

Katherine.   Cruel misery
Of fate! what rests to hope for?

King Henry.   Forward, lords,
To London.—Fair, ere long I shall present ye
With a glad object, peace, and Huntley's blessing. [*Exeunt.*

SCENE III—*London: The Tower-hill*

Enter Constable *and* Officers, PERKIN WARBECK, URSWICK,
and LAMBERT SIMNEL *as a* Falconer, *followed by the
rabble.*

Constable. Make room there! keep off, I require ye; and
none come within twelve foot of his majesty's new stocks,
upon pain of displeasure.—Bring forward the malefactors.
—Friend, you must to this gear, no remedy.—Open the
hole, and in with his legs, just in the middle hole; there,
that hole. [WARBECK *is put in the stocks.*]—Keep off, or
I'll commit you all: shall not a man in authority be obeyed!

—So, so, there; 'tis as it should be: put on the padlock, and
give me the key.—Off, I say, keep off!

Urswick. Yet, Warbeck, clear thy conscience: thou hast
tasted
King Henry's mercy liberally; the law
Has forfeited thy life; an equal jury
Have doomed thee to the gallows; twice most wickedly,
Most desperately, hast thou escaped the Tower,
Inveigling to thy party with thy witchcraft
Young Edward Earl of Warwick, son to Clarence,
Whose head must pay the price of that attempt;
Poor gentleman, unhappy in his fate,
And ruined by thy cunning! so a mongrel
May pluck the true stag down. Yet, yet, confess
Thy parentage; for yet the king has mercy.

Simnel. You would be Dick the Fourth; very likely!
Your pedigree is published;[31] you are known
For Osbeck's son of Tournay, a loose runagate,
A landloper;[32] your father was a Jew,
Turned Christian merely to repair his miseries:
Where's now your kingship?

Warbeck.   Baited to my death?
Intolerable cruelty! I laugh at
The Duke of Richmond's practice on my fortunes:
Possession of a crown ne'er wanted heralds.

Simnel. You will not know who I am?

Urswick.   Lambert Simnel,
Your predecessor in a dangerous uproar;
But, on submission, not alone received
To grace, but by the king vouchsafed his service.

Simnel. I would be Earl of Warwick, toiled and ruffled
Against my master, leaped to catch the moon,

---

[31] "Thus therefore it came to pass. There was a townsman of Tournay . . .
whose name was John Osbeck, a converted Jew, married to Katherine de Faro,
whose business drew him to live for a time with his wife at London, in King
Edward the IVth's days. During which time he had a son by her; and being
known in court, the king . . . did him the honour as to be godfather to his
child, and named him Peter. But afterwards proving a dainty and effeminate youth,
he was commonly called by the diminutive of his name, *Peter-kin* or *Perkin.*"—
Bacon.

[32] "He (Perkin) had been from his childhood such a *wanderer,* or, as the king
called it, such a *landloper,* as it was extreme hard to hunt out his nest."—
Bacon.

Vaunted my name Plantagenet, as you do;
An earl, forsooth! whenas in truth I was,
As you are, a mere rascal: yet his majesty,
A prince composed of sweetness,—Heaven protect him!—
Forgave me all my villainies, reprieved
The sentence of a shameful end, admitted
My surety of obedience to his service,
And I am now his falconer; live plenteously,
Eat from the king's purse, and enjoy the sweetness
Of liberty and favour; sleep securely:
And is not this, now, better than to buffet
The hangman's clutches, or to brave the cordage
Of a tough halter which will break your neck?
So, then, the gallant totters!—prithee, Perkin,
Let my example lead thee; be no longer
A counterfeit; confess, and hope for pardon.

 Warbeck. For pardon! hold, my heart-strings, whiles con-
   tempt
Of injuries, in scorn, may bid defiance
To this base man's foul language!—Thou poor vermin,
How dar'st thou creep so near me? thou an earl!
Why, thou enjoy'st as much of happiness
As all the swing of slight ambition flew at.
A dunghill was thy cradle. So a puddle,
By virtue of the sunbeams, breathes a vapour
T' infect the purer air, which drops again
Into the muddy womb that first exhaled it.
Bread and a slavish ease, with some assurance
From the base beadle's whip, crowned all thy hopes:
But, sirrah, ran there in thy veins one drop
Of such a royal blood as flows in mine,
Thou wouldst not change condition, to be second
In England's state, without the crown itself.
Coarse creatures are incapable of excellence:
But let the world, as all to whom I am
This day a spectacle, to time deliver,
And by tradition fix posterity
Without another chronicle than truth,
How constantly my resolution suffered
A martyrdom of majesty.

Simnel.   He's past
Recovery; a Bedlam cannot cure him.

   Urswick. Away, inform the king of his behaviour.

   Simnel. Perkin, beware the rope! the hangman's coming.
                                             [*Exit*.

   Urswick. If yet thou hast no pity of thy body,
Pity thy soul!

        Enter Lady KATHERINE, JANE, Lord DALYELL, *and*
                       Earl of OXFORD.

Jane.   Dear lady!
Oxford.   Whither will ye,
Without respect of shame?

   Katherine.   Forbear me, sir,
And trouble not the current of my duty.—
O, my loved lord! can any scorn be yours
In which I have no interest.—Some kind hand
Lend me assistance, that I may partake
The infliction of this penance.—My life's dearest,
Forgive me; I have stayed too long from tendering
Attendance on reproach; yet bid me welcome.

   Warbeck. Great miracle of constancy! my miseries
Were never bankrupt of their confidence
In worst afflictions, till this; now I feel them.
Report and thy deserts, thou best of creatures,
Might to eternity have stood a pattern
For every virtuous wife without this conquest.
Thou hast outdone belief; yet may their ruin
In after-marriages be never pitied,
To whom thy story shall appear a fable!
Why wouldst thou prove so much unkind to greatness
To glorify thy vows by such a servitude?
I cannot weep; but trust me, dear, my heart
Is liberal of passion.—Harry Richmond,
A woman's faith hath robbed thy fame of triumph.

   Oxford. Sirrah, leave-off your juggling, and tie up
The devil that ranges in your tongue.

   Urswick.   Thus witches,
Possessed, even to their deaths deluded, say

They have been wolves and dogs, and sailed in egg-shells
Over the sea, and rid on fiery dragons,
Passed in the air more than a thousand miles,
All in a night:—the enemy of mankind
Is powerful, but false, and falsehood confident.

   Oxford. Remember, lady, who you are; come from
That impudent impostor.

   Katherine.   You abuse us:
For when the holy churchman joined our hands,
Our vows were real then; the ceremony
Was not in apparition, but in act.—
Be what these people term thee, I am certain
Thou art my husband, no divorce in Heaven
Has been sued-out between us; 'tis injustice
For any earthly power to divide us:
Or we will live or let us die together.
There is a cruel mercy.

   Warbeck.   Spite of tyranny
We reign in our affections, blessèd woman!
Read in my destiny the wreck of honour;
Point out, in my contempt of death, to memory
Some miserable happiness; since herein,
Even when I fell, I stood enthroned a monarch
Of one chaste wife's troth pure and uncorrupted.
Fair angel of perfection, immortality
Shall raise thy name up to an adoration,
Court every rich opinion of true merit,
And saint it in the calendar of Virtue,
When I am turned into the self-same dust
Of which I was first formed.

   Oxford.   The lord ambassador,
Huntley, your father, madam, should he look on
Your strange subjection in a gaze so public,
Would blush on your behalf, and wish his country
Unleft for entertainment to such sorrow.

   Katherine. Why art thou angry, Oxford? I must be
More peremptory in my duty.—Sir,
Impute it not unto immodesty
That I presume to press you to a legacy
Before we part for ever.

Warbeck.   Let it be, then,
My heart, the rich remains of all my fortunes.
   Katherine. Confirm it with a kiss, pray.
   Warbeck.   O, with that
I wish to breathe my last! upon thy lips,
Those equal twins of comeliness, I seal
The testament of honourable vows: [*Kisses her.*
Whoever be that man that shall unkiss
This sacred print next, may he prove more thrifty
In this world's just applause, not more desertful!
   Katherine. By this sweet pledge of both our souls, I swear
To die a faithful widow to thy bed;
Not to be forced or won: O, never, never!

   Enter Earls of SURREY, HUNTLEY, *and* CRAWFORD, *and*
                Lord DAWBENEY.

   Dawbeney. Free the condemnèd person; quickly free him!
What has he yet confessed?
          [PERKIN WARBECK *is taken out of the stocks.*
   Urswick.   Nothing to purpose;
But still he will be king.
   Surrey.   Prepare your journey
To a new kingdom, then, unhappy madman,
Wilfully foolish!—See, my lord ambassador,
Your lady daughter will not leave the counterfeit
In this disgrace of fate.
   Huntley.   I never pointed
Thy marriage, girl; but yet, being married,
Enjoy thy duty to a husband freely.
The griefs are mine. I glory in thy constancy;
And must not say I wished that I had missed
Some partage in these trials of a patience.
   Katherine. You will forgive me, noble sir?
   Huntley.   Yes, yes;
In every duty of a wife and daughter
I dare not disavow thee. To your husband,—
For such you are, sir,—I impart a farewell
Of manly pity; what your life has passed through,
The dangers of your end will make apparent;
And I can add, for comfort to your sufferance,

No cordial, but the wonder of your frailty,
Which keeps so firm a station. We are parted.
  Warbeck. We are. A crown of peace renew thy age,
Most honourable Huntley!—Worthy Crawford!
We may embrace; I never thought thee injury.
  Crawford. Nor was I ever guilty of neglect
Which might procure such thought. I take my leave, sir.
  Warbeck. To you, Lord Dalyell,—what? accept a sigh,
'Tis hearty and in earnest.
  Dalyell.   I want utterance;
My silence is my farewell.
  Katherine.   O, O!
  Jane.   Sweet madam,
What do you mean?—My lord, your hand. [*To* DALYELL.
  Dalyell.   Dear lady,
Be pleased that I may wait ye to your lodging.[33]

                    [*Exeunt* Lord DALYELL *and* JANE, *supporting*
                        Lady KATHERINE.

Enter Sheriff *and* Officers *with* SKELTON, ASTLEY, HERON,
    and JOHN A-WATER, *with halters about their necks.*

  Oxford. Look ye; behold your followers, appointed
To wait on ye in death!
  Warbeck.   Why, peers of England,
We'll lead 'em on courageously: I read
A triumph over tyranny upon
Their several foreheads.—Faint not in the moment
Of victory! our ends, and Warwick's head,
Innocent Warwick's head,—for we are prologue
But to his tragedy,—conclude the wonder

---

[33] Gifford quotes the following passage concerning her subsequent history from
Sir R. Gordon: "Shoe wes brought from St. Michael's Mount in Cornuall, ane
delyvered to King Henrie the Seaventh, who intertayned her honorablie, and
for her better mantenance, according to her birth and vertu, did a signe vnto her
good lands and rents for all the dayes of her lyff. After the death of her husband
Richard, shoe mareid Sir Mathie Cradock (a man of great power at that tyme in
Clamorganshyre in Wales), of the which mariage is descended this William Earle
of Pembroke, by his grandmother, and had some lands by inheritance from the
Cradockes. Lady Katheren Gordon died in Wales, and was buried in a chappell at
one of the Earle of Pembrok his dwelling-places in that cuntrey. The Englesh
histories doe much commend her for her beauty, comliness, and chastetie." And
Bacon ends her story thus: "The name of the White Rose, which had been given
to her husband's false title, was continued in common speech to her true beauty."

Of Henry's fears; and then the glorious race
Of fourteen kings, Plantagenets, determines
In this last issue male; Heaven be obeyed!
Impoverish time of its amazement, friends,
And we will prove as trusty in our payments
As prodigal to nature in our debts.
Death? pish! 'tis but a sound; a name of air;
A minute's storm, or not so much: to tumble
From bed to bed, be massacred alive
By some physicians, for a month or two,
In hope of freedom from a fever's torments,
Might stagger manhood; here the pain is past
Ere sensibly 'tis felt. Be men of spirit!
Spurn coward passion! so illustrious mention
Shall blaze our names, and style us kings o'er Death.

    Dawbeney. Away, impostor beyond precedent!

    [*Exeunt* Sheriff *and* Officers *with the* Prisoners.
No chronicle records his fellow.

    Huntley.   I have
Not thoughts left: 'tis sufficient in such cases
Just laws ought to proceed.

       Enter King HENRY, *the* Bishop *of* DURHAM, *and*
                    HIALAS.

    King Henry.   We are resolved.
Your business, noble lords, shall find success
Such as your king impórtunes.

    Huntley.   You are gracious.

    King Henry. Perkin, we are informed, is armed to die;
In that we'll honour him. Our lords shall follow
To see the execution; and from hence
We gather this fit use,[34]—that public states,
As our particular bodies, taste most good
In health when purgèd of corrupted blood.   [*Exeunt.*

[34] The poet seems to apply this word in the puritanical sense (then sufficiently
familiar) of doctrinal or practical deduction.—*Gifford.*

EPILOGUE

Here has appeared, though in a several fashion,
The threats of majesty, the strength of passion,
Hopes of an empire, change of fortunes; all
What can to theatres of greatness fall,
Proving their weak foundations. Who will please,
Amongst such several sights, to censure these
No births abortive, nor a bastard brood,—
Shame to a parentage or fosterhood,—
May warrant by their loves all just excuses,
And often find a welcome to the Muses.

DRAMABOOKS
(Plays)

WHEN ORDERING, please use the Standard Book Number consisting of the publisher's prefix, 8090-, plus the five digits following each title. (Note that the numbers given in this list are for paperback editions only. Many of the books are also available in cloth.)

MERMAID DRAMABOOKS

Christopher Marlowe (Tamburlaine the Great, Parts I & II, Doctor Faustus, The Jew of Malta, Edward the Second) (0701-0)

William Congreve (Complete Plays) (0702-9)

Webster and Tourneur (The White Devil, The Duchess of Malfi, The Atheist's Tragedy, The Revenger's Tragedy) (0703-7)

John Ford (The Lover's Melancholy, 'Tis Pity She's a Whore, The Broken Heart, Love's Sacrifice, Perkin Warbeck) (0704-5)

Richard Brinsley Sheridan (The Rivals, St. Patrick's Day, The Duenna, A Trip to Scarborough, The School for Scandal, The Critic) (0705-3)

Camille and Other Plays (Scribe: A Peculiar Position, The Glass of Water; Sardou: A Scrap of Paper; Dumas: Camille; Augier: Olympe's Marriage) (0706-1)

John Dryden (The Conquest of Granada, Parts I & II, Marriage à la Mode, Aureng-Zebe) (0707-X)

Ben Jonson Vol. 1 (Volpone, Epicoene, The Alchemist) (0708-8)

Oliver Goldsmith (The Good Natur'd Man, She Stoops to Conquer, An Essay on the Theatre, A Register of Scotch Marriages) (0709-6)

Jean Anouilh Vol. 1 (Antigone, Eurydice, The Rehearsal, Romeo and Jeannette, The Ermine) (0710-X)

Let's Get a Divorce! and Other Plays (Labiche: A Trip Abroad, and Célimare; Sardou: Let's Get a Divorce!; Courteline: These Cornfields; Feydeau: Keep an Eye on Amélie; Prévert: A United Family; Achard: Essays on Feydeau) (0711-8)

Jean Giraudoux Vol. 1 (Ondine, The Enchanted, The Madwoman of Chaillot, The Apollo of Bellac) (0712-6)

Jean Anouilh Vol. 2 (Restless Heart, Time Remembered, Ardèle, Mademoiselle Colombe, The Lark) (0713-4)

Henrik Ibsen: The Last Plays (Little Eyolf, John Gabriel Borkman, When We Dead Awaken) (0714-2)

Ivan Turgenev (A Month in the Country, A Provincial Lady, A Poor Gentleman) (0715-0)

Jean Racine (Andromache, Britannicus, Berenice, Phaedra, Athaliah) (0717-7)

The Storm and Other Russian Plays (The Storm, The Government Inspector, The Power of Darkness, Uncle Vanya, The Lower Depths) (0718-5)

Michel de Ghelderode: Seven Plays Vol. 1 (The Ostend Interviews, Chronicles of Hell, Barabbas, The Women at the Tomb, Pantagleize, The Blind Men, Three Players and a Play, Lord Halewyn) (0719-3)

Lope de Vega: Five Plays (Peribáñez, Fuenteovejuna, The Dog in the Manger, The Knight from Olmedo, Justice Without Revenge) (0720-7)

Calderón: Four Plays (Secret Vengeance for Secret Insult, Devotion to the Cross, The Mayor of Zalamea, The Phantom Lady) (0721-5)

Jean Cocteau: Five Plays (Orphée, Antigone, Intimate Relations, The Holy Terrors, The Eagle with Two Heads) (0722-3)

Ben Jonson Vol. 2 (Every Man in His Humour, Sejanus, Bartholomew Fair) (0723-1)

Port-Royal and Other Plays (Claudel: Tobias and Sara; Mauriac: Asmodée; Copeau: The Poor Little Man; Montherlant: Port-Royal) (0724-X)

Edwardian Plays (Maugham: Loaves and Fishes; Hankin: The Return of the Prodigal; Shaw: Getting Married; Pinero: Mid-Channel; Granville-Barker: The Madras House) (0725-8)

Georg Büchner: Complete Plays and Prose (0727-4)

Paul Green: Five Plays (Johnny Johnson, In Abraham's Bosom, Hymn to the Rising Sun, The House of Connelly, White Dresses) (0728-2)

François Billetdoux: Two Plays (Tchin-Tchin, Chez Torpe) (0729-0)

Michel de Ghelderode: Seven Plays Vol. 2 (Red Magic, Hop, Signor!, The Death of Doctor Faust, Christopher Columbus, A Night of Pity, Piet Bouteille, Miss Jairus) (0730-4)

Jean Giraudoux Vol. 2 (Siegfried, Amphitryon 38, Electra) (0731-2)

Kelly's Eye and Other Plays by Henry Livings (Kelly's Eye, Big Soft Nellie, There's No Room for You Here for a Start) (0732-0)

Gabriel Marcel: Three Plays (Man of God, Ariadne, Votive Candle) (0733-9)

New American Plays Vol. 1 ed. by Robert W. Corrigan (0734-7)

Elmer Rice: Three Plays (Adding Machine, Street Scene, Dream Girl) (0735-5)
The Day the Whores Came Out to Play Tennis . . . by Arthur Kopit (0736-3)
Platonov by Anton Chekhov (0737-1)
Ugo Betti: Three Plays (The Inquiry, Goat Island, The Gambler) (0738-X)
Jean Anouilh Vol. 3 (Thieves' Carnival, Medea, Cécile, Traveler Without Luggage, Orchestra, Episode in the Life of an Author, Catch As Catch Can) (0739-8)
Max Frisch: Three Plays (Don Juan, The Great Rage of Philip Hotz, When the War Was Over) (0740-1)
New American Plays Vol. 2 ed. by William M. Hoffman (0741-X)
Plays from Black Africa ed. by Fredric M. Litto (0742-8)
Anton Chekhov: Four Plays (The Seagull, Uncle Vanya, The Cherry Orchard, The Three Sisters) (0743-6)
The Silver Foxes Are Dead and Other Plays by Jakov Lind (The Silver Foxes Are Dead, Anna Laub, Hunger, Fear) (0744-4)
New American Plays Vol. 3 ed. by William M. Hoffman (0745-2)
The Modern Spanish Stage: Four Plays, ed. by Marion Holt (The Concert at Saint Ovide, Condemned Squad, The Blindfold, The Boat Without a Fisherman) (0746-0)
Life Is a Dream by Calderón (0747-9)
New American Plays Vol. 4 ed. by William M. Hoffman (0748-7)

THE NEW MERMAIDS

Bussy D'Ambois by George Chapman (1101-8)
The Broken Heart by John Ford (1102-6)
The Duchess of Malfi by John Webster (1103-4)
Doctor Faustus by Christopher Marlowe (1104-2)
The Alchemist by Ben Jonson (1105-0)
The Jew of Malta by Christopher Marlowe (1106-9)
The Revenger's Tragedy by Cyril Tourneur (1107-7)
A Game at Chess by Thomas Middleton (1108-5)
Every Man in His Humour by Ben Jonson (1109-3)
The White Devil by John Webster (1110-7)
Edward the Second by Christopher Marlowe (1111-5)
The Malcontent by John Marston (1112-3)
'Tis Pity She's a Whore by John Ford (1113-1)
Sejanus His Fall by Ben Jonson (1114-X)
Volpone by Ben Jonson (1115-8)
Women Beware Women by Thomas Middleton (1116-6)
Love for Love by William Congreve (1117-4)
The Spanish Tragedy by Thomas Kyd (1118-2)

SPOTLIGHT DRAMABOOKS

The Last Days of Lincoln by Mark Van Doren (1201-4)
Oh Dad, Poor Dad . . . by Arthur Kopit (1202-0)
The Chinese Wall by Max Frisch (1203-0)
Billy Budd by Louis O. Coxe and Robert Chapman (1204-9)
The Firebugs by Max Frisch (1206-5)
Andorra by Max Frisch (1207-3)
Balm in Gilead and Other Plays by Lanford Wilson (1208-1)
Matty and the Moron and Madonna by Herbert Lieberman (1209-X)
The Brig by Kenneth H. Brown (1210-3)
The Cavern by Jean Anouilh (1211-1)
Saved by Edward Bond (1212-X)
Eh? by Henry Livings (1213-8)
The Rimers of Eldritch and Other Plays by Lanford Wilson (1214-6)
In the Matter of J. Robert Oppenheimer by Heinar Kipphardt (1215-4)
Ergo by Jakov Lind (1216-2)
Biography: A Game by Max Frisch (1217-0)
Indians by Arthur Kopit (1218-9)
Narrow Road to the Deep North by Edward Bond (1219-7)
Ornifle by Jean Anouilh (1220-0)
Inquest by Donald Freed (1221-9)
Lemon Sky by Lanford Wilson (1222-7)
The Night Thoreau Spent in Jail by Jerome Laurence and Robert E. Lee (1223-5)

For a complete list of books of criticism and history of the drama, please write to Hill and Wang, 72 Fifth Avenue, New York, New York 10011.